D0466688

Thematic Guide to Popular Short Stories

Patrick A. Smith

Greenwood Press
Westport, Connecticut • London

Library of Congress Cataloging-in-Publication Data

Smith, Patrick A., 1967–
    Thematic guide to popular short stories / by Patrick A. Smith.
        p.   cm.
    Includes bibliographical references and index.
    ISBN 0–313–31897–2 (alk. paper)
    1. Short story—Themes, motives. 2. Short story—Bibliography. I. Title.
PN3373.S62   2002
    809.3'1—dc21   2002067773

British Library Cataloguing in Publication Data is available.

Library of Congress Catalog Card Number: 2002067773
ISBN: 0–313–31897–2

First published in 2002

Greenwood Press, 88 Post Road West, Westport, CT 06881
An imprint of Greenwood Publishing Group, Inc.
www.greenwood.com

Printed in the United States of America

∞™

The paper used in this book complies with the
Permanent Paper Standard issued by the National
Information Standards Organization (Z39.48–1984).

10 9 8 7 6 5 4 3 2 1

For my parents—lifelong teachers.

And for Lori, for her unwavering support and inspiration.

Contents

Acknowledgments

Having grown up with two parents who were also teachers, I've long held the notion that the people we see at the front of the classroom deserve all good things that come to them. To think that I could possibly thank everyone involved in this project would be madness, though I'll begin by singing the praises of the educators who spend their days leading us down the road of enlightenment, and the students who are willing to join us on the journey and challenge us when necessary.

Special thanks go out to William Cloonan and Tom Steiner for their wisdom, and Valerie Geary and Lynn Malloy for their patience and their guidance.

Introduction

The popularity of short fiction will never succumb to the myriad forms of mass entertainment that assault us daily for one very important reason: in addition to providing a worthwhile experience that creates enjoyment through a synergy of tightly wound prose and plot, these snapshot images—even a narrative such as Plato's "The Death of Socrates," written more than twenty-three centuries ago—allow us to examine issues whose understanding is vital in today's society. Ann Charters, editor of *The Story and Its Writer*, a fine, diverse anthology that I have used and admired for years, writes, "Reading short fiction attentively and imaginatively promises further pleasure—the enjoyment of how the storyteller uses language to create that miracle called a work of art." Implicit in Charters's statement is the notion that underpins this text: The authors of short fiction are the guides who lead us toward the often-neglected or misunderstood truths that we must examine in our own lives—and the lives of those around us: alienation from society and its root causes, minority experience, the relationships between men and women and parents and children (in all the complexity that those glib phrases imply), comings-of-age, violence, women's issues, and a host of other themes.

Thematic Guide to Popular Short Stories provides brief annotations for nearly 450 short stories—some of which you may know well, and others not at all—that will allow students and teachers alike to appreciate and build upon the reading experience, regardless of the reasons for examining the word on the page in the first place. For ease of use, these entries are presented alphabetically by author as in any standard bibliography. Included in the summaries and concise critical statements that synthesize plot and theme is publication information for each story, its year of first publication, and a list of its important themes. Although the annotations are generally uniform in length and depth of analysis (some stories, by their very content and style, lend themselves to greater analyses than other more "writerly" narratives), some of the stories, particularly those less well known, give enough detail for you to make an informed decision on possible inclusion in your syllabus. Also, I have assumed throughout the text that plot summary will allow you more readily to choose one story over another with similar themes, depending upon your personal preferences and goals.

Many of these stories, particularly the ones that have been handed down to us through several generations of anthologies (the works of Poe and Hawthorne come immediately to mind) have been reprinted in a host of different volumes. To provide a comprehensive listing of the publication history for each story would be a task well beyond the scope of this particular guide. The source publication that I give here is merely a suggestion for further research on the way to personalizing your reading list. The themes listed for each story and the cross-references provided in the various indexes are meant to facilitate that often-painstaking process. Where I list a collection of stories by one author (for instance, Sholom Aleichem, Doris Betts, or A.E. Coppard) in the bibliography, it is because those particular pieces are most readily available through the primary sources.

In addition to discussion on some weighty issues, I have attempted to balance the list with other, more humorous and lighthearted stories that would delight readers of any age. Care has been taken throughout to examine the works of marginalized writers, whose characters and subject matter, when considered in conjunction with the themes and content of more "traditional" stories (again, a loaded term), form a course or unit that represents the gamut of experience through close attention to ethnic, gender, racial, chronological, religious, and thematic concerns.

Creating this list from the thousands and thousands of fine pieces that have been handed down to us is a daunting task, and my greatest hope in compiling information on these stories is that I have not unnecessarily given short shrift to—or altogether eliminated—works that would enlighten students and teachers alike. In preparation for the compilation of this volume, I had the good fortune to discuss the selection process with both John Updike and Katrina Kenison, coeditors of *The Best American Short Stories of the Century*. Their task in compiling that prominent anthology was clearly much more broad than the one with which I was charged—Kenison read several thousand stories over a period of many months as she and Updike attempted to put forth the fifty-five best pieces written during a period and in a place where the short story had hit its full stride. I am indebted to them for their good advice and encouragement to persevere. In her foreword to *The Best American Short Stories of the Century*, Kenison details the selection process and her work with Updike, the leading light in American short fiction. Her words were a guiding force in my own selections for this text: "I can only attest to the painstaking deliberation behind each and every story that appears in this collection."

In attempting to strike a balance between well-known writers and those whose works point up the variety of human experience and both the delicious comedy and tragedy in life, I was forced to ignore works that are as richly descriptive of life as any of those represented here. Obvious omissions are mine and mine alone, and I hope that they are few and far between. I have made the assumption in some cases that an author and his work are well enough known to already be on many reading lists or, at the least, to warrant further independent research by the teacher, who can then judge whether that author's work will be appropriate for her or his needs. For instance, Updike himself is represented here only by his much anthologized story "A & P," yet there are very few classes in which his short fiction is not taught. Again, you may safely assume that any work of the writers represented here would make a valuable addition to your own reading list. I would appreciate your comments and suggestions for inclusions in a future edition of this book. Indeed, this collection of annotations and cross-references is merely the starting point for an exploration of the short story that will, if you allow it, take a lifetime to unravel.

II

The lists of stories and themes—nearly a hundred important and prevalent themes, some of which are similar enough at first glance to be useful in fleshing out subtle shades of meaning in the various stories—included in this volume have also benefited greatly from the generous and well-informed opinions of expert teachers who have made it their life's work to instill critical thinking and comprehension skills in students from the secondary level to the college classroom and beyond. They include Dr. Cynthia Bowman in the College of Education at Florida State University, Dr. Robert DeMott, Kennedy Distinguished Professor in the Department of English at Ohio University, and a host of other teachers and librarians (including those at Ohio University, Florida State University, and the LeRoy Collins Leon County Public Library in Tallahassee, Florida). In addition to the many conversations and good suggestions that narrowed down the stories and themes one by one, I consulted many dozens of popular classroom texts and anthologies, from Donald Gallo's mainstay anthologies of stories written for young adults, to literature anthologies that cover the world's masterworks of short fiction over the last two centuries, to texts that were narrowly focused on one or several themes. It is curious and enlightening to observe how editors over the past eighty or so years have chosen pieces for their own anthologies—stories that apparently had gained prominence in the twenties and thirties have faded into obscurity, while others have been included in nearly every general text since their initial publication (Cather's "Paul's Case" would be a good example of the latter)—and both the headings for each story and the bibliography reflect that process of charting a particular story's relative popularity in the publishing world. Also, I would be remiss in not suggesting that you take full advantage of the many valuable resources devoted to short fiction that are available on the internet.

On the many occasions that I have had the privilege of teaching the short story at Florida State University, Ohio University, and Tallahassee Community College, I have been mindful of student reception of the stories at hand and the different contexts in which those stories were read and studied. Student reactions have also been invaluable in leading me to the decisions that comprise the lists and the information in the annotations, and I have to thank especially the following students, all from a short story course offered at Florida State during the fall semester of 2001, for their invaluable attention and assistance in focusing this project: Virginia Alfonso, Jan Alford, Shannon Bell, Nicole Botero, Conrad Bradburn, Christie Braun, Lacy Brinson, Laurie Burket, Charles Cantor, Marilys Carabello, Adrienne Chuck, Casey Clark, Rachel Cocciolo, Tara Collier, Jasmine Crane, Ciara Csanadi, John Echterling, Alexis Elliott, Parish Gibson, Jonathan Hall, Kelli Kunda, Angela Leggett, Lance Litman, Abby Loraine, Robin Madden, Ryan Michaels, Sheena Monds, Paul Nahoun, Brett Patterson, Christina Paulsen, Jessica Pawlik, Lindsey Peeples, Nicole Picard, Melissa Rossi, Keith Strobridge, Ashley Williams, Angela Wilson, and Monika Zepeda.

Of course, the study of the short story develops critical thinking skills in students who invariably respond to the variety of themes, plots, and styles that they find in the works. In consulting with my colleagues, though, I find that educators cite their greatest thrill in teaching the short story as the discovery of new works of short fiction that will delight students and fit as seamlessly as possible within the class dynamic that presents itself during a particular term. This past term, I had the inestimably poignant and difficult task of coming to terms with the events of September 11 in a classroom of college students, many of whom had been away from home for only two weeks when the tragedy unfolded. For those students, the events were not only tragic, but clearly life-defining. I modified the class syllabus to reflect student perspectives (after all, how important can a short story be in the face of such tragedy?) and their first experiences in college by adding stories on hope and perseverance by such writers as Chinua Achebe, Bharati Mukherjee, Lilika Nakos, and I. L. Peretz. The students responded positively to the stories and were much more forthcoming than they previously had been in discussing their personal feelings toward the horrific events. Even in the face of such senseless devastation, it seems, we have at our fingertips the ability to help ourselves and others make sense of the greatest loss, after which we can immerse ourselves in the daily wonders of life and its contra-dictions. The stories included in this guide are written with passion by the artists for whom communication is the key to understanding. Such is the power of literature.

Dr. Patrick A. Smith
Tallahassee, Florida

December 2001

A

Achebe, Chinua. "Civil Peace" (1971). From *The Story and Its Writer*, 5th ed. (Ed. Ann Charters, 1999). EXILE/EMIGRATION; FAMILY; POLITICS; VIOLENCE; WAR.

Jonathan Iwegbu realizes that in postwar Nigeria, the greeting "Happy Survival" is more than just a fashion. He and his family—a wife and three children—are fortunate to be alive. He considers it a miracle that they have lost only one child, their youngest, in the cross fire. In order to make ends meet, Iwegbu taxis people to the nearest tarred road on his bicycle. In this way, he supports his family as they make their way back home to Enugu. There, another miracle awaits them. While most of the homes in the area have been destroyed, their modest abode has been spared. With his "egg rasher," some money that the government has given the returning exiles, Iwegbu and his family embark on a new life. When bandits visit them in the night, though, their money is stolen. They consider themselves lucky, always lucky, to have escaped further harm, and Iwegbu responds in the only way he knows: "Nothing puzzles God."

Achebe's story was created from the author's sense that European writers who attempt to describe the lives of African peoples are often bound to fail because they little understand the complex politics that underpin the war. Here, Achebe illustrates the extraordinary resilience, courage, and faith of a family who could easily have capitulated to the forces around them, but instead continue to fight for their lives—and their dignity.

Adams, Alice. "Barcelona" (1984). From *The Norton Anthology of Contemporary Fiction* (Ed. R. V. Cassill, 1988). CLASS CONFLICTS; CRIME/LAW; INTERIOR LIVES; MEN and WOMEN; PRIDE.

Persis Fox, a successful illustrator, and her husband, Thad, a Harvard professor, are the perfect middle-aged American couple wandering the streets of Barcelona. As they approach a famous restaurant, the woman's purse is snatched from her. In the ensuing chaos, Thad runs after the thief. The purse is found, and Thad seems content to have fulfilled his manly duty. When the contents are examined, nothing is missing. Persis tells Thad that she carries her money and other valuables in a place where such a thief could not get them. Though the comment dampens Thad's spirits—after all, he had seen himself as his wife's rescuer—he is placated by her insistence that his courage has saved the day. The two enjoy their dinner with other Americans in the restaurant, and Persis thinks how terrible it must be to be a man: men always have to chase something in order to assert their self-worth. Even worse, she thinks, must be the plight of the poor, who must chase down women such as herself just to survive.

Adams's story tarnishes the shine of some earlier fiction that glamorized the American in Europe. This brief tale is also an exploration of the relationships between men and women and class distinctions. Thad, who convinces himself that he has done the right thing in chasing the thief, is oblivious to the larger implications of the episode that Persis considers as they sip their wine.

Aiken, Conrad. "Mr. Arcularis" (1937). From *Half-a-Hundred: Stories for Men* (Ed. Charles Grayson, 1946). DEATH; DREAMS (of the FUTURE); HEALTH (SICKNESS/MEDICINE); ILLUSION v. REALITY; LOVE/HATE; MEN and WOMEN.

Mr. Arcularis has just left the hospital after an undisclosed operation, and he is feeling extraordinarily weak. Still, he knows that he will benefit from a rest, and on the day of his release he embarks on a voyage to England. On the ship, Mr. Arcularis meets Miss Dean, a beautiful, charming young woman with whom he spends much time. Their conversations fascinate and rejuvenate the older man, and he feels himself falling in love with the woman, who is twenty years his junior.

Throughout the journey, Mr. Arcularis experiences bouts of déjà vu and sleepwalking that leave him nonplussed. He wakes up in confusion and realizes gradually that he seems to be making his way toward a coffin that was brought on board the ship before their departure. Though the ship's doctor cannot find anything wrong with him, Mr. Arcularis senses that he is about to be overtaken by some tragic event. He bears his soul to his new love, and they prepare themselves for whatever it may be. In the story's final paragraphs, Aiken reveals that Mr. Arcularis is, in fact, still in the hospital and that he has died on the operating table. Mr. Arcularis's vision is only a dying dream.

Aiken's story recalls Ambrose Bierce's exploration of the moment of death in "Occurrence at Owl Creek Bridge" and the psychological depth of Henry James's "The Beast in the Jungle." Even though Mr. Arcularis is destined to die on the operating table, the vision that he has in those final moments is a powerful evocation of life's bittersweet events.

Aiken, Conrad. "Silent Snow, Secret Snow" (1932). From *Fiction as Experience: An Anthology* (Ed. Irving Howe, 1978). ALIENATION/ISOLATION; FATHERS and CHILDREN; INSANITY; LOVE/HATE; MOTHERS and CHILDREN.

The story of a boy's journey into madness begins on a wintry day when the predictable footsteps of the mailman are suddenly deadened by a muting blanket of newly fallen snow. Paul has been distant in school, and while his geography teacher, Miss Buell, instructs the class, Paul is entranced by his own world of snow. The boy's daydreaming worries his parents, but when they send for a physician, they all become impatient with the boy's indifferent reactions to their questions. The snow into which Paul retreats at the first sign of confrontation becomes symbolic of the "delicious progress" of schizophrenia; far from cleansing, the snow enables Paul to numb himself to his everyday world, belying his exterior as a normal boy. He tells his mother that he hates her at the end of the story; still, the predictable, comforting world of snow is waiting for him.

Much has been made of Aiken's relationship with his father, who was the perpetrator of a murder/suicide involving Aiken's mother, and his fascination with psychology and the dark images that arise in much of his short fiction seem to be influenced by the less hopeful aspects of life. The snow imagery in this story can be seen as both the coming of imminent madness and death; either way, the author paints a bleak picture for the protagonist's future. Aiken's eye for detail and sentences that are fragmented by punctuation and hyphens convey Paul's swiftly changing attitudes. The snow becomes a metaphorical avalanche under which the boy is buried.

Alcock, Vivien. "QWERTYUIOP" (1984). From _Help Wanted: Short Stories about Young People Working_ (Sel. Anita Silvey, 1997). COURAGE; LABOR/JOB; PRIDE; SUPERNATURAL.

More than anything else, Lucy wants a job. At seventeen, she is ready to move away from her mother, who is much too nice for her own good, and her Uncle Bert, who drinks too much. When she graduates from the Belmont Secretarial College, though, things look grim. She is at the bottom of her class, and the usually upbeat principal, Mrs. Price, doesn't hold out much hope for the success of her least talented student.

Lucy does land a job, however, and even her mother is surprised. On her first day, Lucy realizes that the position comes with some baggage: the ghost of a previous longtime secretary, Mrs. Broome, haunts her typewriter. Only the hints of Mr. Darke, a man who knows everything that goes on at the company, gives Lucy any idea of what awaits her. At first, no matter what she tries to type, Lucy cannot finish her work because of the message that pops up on the paper: QWERTYUIOP. When she finally realizes that she is powerless to finish her work—and become a success in her first job—she reconciles herself with Mrs. Broome's spirit. By discovering the reasons for Mrs. Broome's actions, she also reaches a new understanding of her relationship with Uncle Bert.

Alcock's story details the ambitions of young people who desire to break away from a day-to-day existence that smothers them. At the same time, she suggests that the easiest solution is not always the right one and that compassion and perseverance are as important as raw ability.

Aleichem, Sholom. "Hodel" (1949). From *Tevye the Dairyman and the Railroad Stories* (Trans. by Hillel Halkin, 1987). FAMILY; FATHERS and CHILDREN; MARRIAGE; RELIGION/SPIRITUALITY.

Tevye the milkman meets the author on the street and begins listing his sorrows. The man's daughter, Hodel, was introduced to Feferel, whom Tevye picked up one day on his rounds and invited to dinner. Feferel becomes a fixture in the household and takes on the teaching of Tevye's daughters. Though the young man expresses contempt for the wealthy, he and Hodel become engaged. Tevye is distraught, as he had arranged a meeting between Hodel and another man, older but highly educated and wealthy.

Despite Tevye's initial protests, Hodel and Feferel are married. Shortly after, Feferel sends word that he has been arrested, and Hodel declares that she will join him wherever he is. Tevye, who knows he has little chance of dissuading his daughter, takes her to the station, where both of them break down in tears. Tevye stops the story at this point and wants to talk of more cheerful topics.

Tevye is a recurring character in Aleichem's stories (which were adapted for the popular musical *Fiddler on the Roof*), and through the old man the author explores the issues that are important to Jewish families in pre-revolutionary Russia. His attitude is one of acceptance for the fate that awaits him and his daughters, and Aleichem uses self-effacing humor to imply that the man's love for his family and a strong faith are more important than a well-arranged marriage and outward trappings of success.

Alexie, Sherman. "The Lone Ranger and Tonto Fistfight in Heaven" (1993). From *The Story and Its Writer*, 5th ed. (Ed. Ann Charters, 1999). ALIENATION/ISOLATION; MEN and WOMEN; MINORITY EXPERIENCE; SELF-DESTRUCTION.

The narrator, a Native American who is accustomed to intimidating the white people who immediately assume that he is a "crazy Indian," walks into a 7–11 for a Creamsicle. He knows, as he makes his way to the cooler for his purchase, that the kid behind the counter is memorizing his face for the police, for when he snaps and robs the place. The two strike up a conversation, the narrator taking full advantage of the clerk's perception of him. The clerk is relieved to know that he will not be robbed by the narrator, and offers to give him the Creamsicle for free. The undercurrent of the story, though, is more important than the surface action. The narrator recalls a relationship he had with a white girl in Seattle, and how he would drink and they would fight. In his dreams, he imagines soldiers playing polo with a dead Indian woman's head. When she realizes the depth of the narrator's psychic scars, his girlfriend asks him to leave.

The narrator goes back to the reservation to put his life together, and he gets a call from his former girlfriend. They apologize to each other for the pain that they've caused, though nothing is resolved. The narrator wishes he could sleep. Still, he thinks, it doesn't matter: he knows how all his dreams end.

Alexie's stories are both humorous and poignant, and explore (and explode) many of the clichés regarding the relationship between Native Americans and whites. He has said that everything he writes ultimately has its origin in his own life on the Spokane Indian Reservation.

Allen, Woody. "The Kugelmass Episode" (1977). From *The Treasury of American Short Stories* (Sel. Nancy Sullivan, 1981). ESCAPE; FANTASY/IMAGINATION/SCIENCE FICTION; HUMOR; MEN and WOMEN; TECHNOLOGY.

Kugelmass is a professor of humanities at City College in New York. He is unhappily married for the second time, and when his therapist tells him that he has no quick fix for his problems—after all, he is not a magician—Kugelmass terminates their relationship. When a real magician calls and tells him that he can solve his problems, Kugelmass is incredulous but interested. Indeed, the magician has discovered a way to transport Kugelmass into any novel of his choosing. The bemused professor decides that he would like to meet Emma Bovary, and the deed is done.

Kugelmass and Emma begin a relationship that ultimately brings her to New York City. Despite their first amorous encounters, during which Emma decides that she wants to experience everything the city has to offer, Kugelmass discovers that he would rather not be with her. Instead, Kugelmass decides that he wants to be sent into Roth's *Portnoy's Complaint* (a novel with persistent sexual overtones). Unfortunately, the magician, who suffers a fatal heart attack during the process, has transported him into a Spanish grammar book, where he is doomed to spend his days on the run from Spanish verbs.

Allen, known for his off-the-wall humor, translates his psychotic meanderings from the screen to the page. The story's underlying theme—don't ask for something, you might just get it—is also a commentary on mass culture in 1970s New York City and the alienation and isolation that are common in the urban experience.

Allende, Isabel. "And of Clay We Are Created" (1989). From *The Story and Its Writer*, 4th ed. (Ed. Ann Charters, 1995). BETRAYAL; CHILDHOOD; DEATH; INTERIOR LIVES; LOSS; LOVE; MEN and WOMEN; POLITICS.

When a volcano mudslide buries a local girl, Azucena ("Lily"), Rolf Carle, an award-winning journalist, is called to report the scene. When he realizes the gravity of the situation, however, he eschews his role as reporter and becomes the girl's friend, talking her through three nights of unbearable agony in order to save her. In those three days, "the unyielding floodgates that had contained Rolf Carle's past for so many years began to open, and the torrent of all that had lain hidden in the deepest and most secret layers of memory poured out." He recalls how his father had mistreated his own family and how his mother was less than sympathetic when she had put him on a boat to South America.

As the journalist calms the girl's fears and assures her that she will be saved, the narrator—Carle's lover and a writer—helplessly watches the episode unfold on national television. Though the narrator, herself a woman of some means and influence in the society, has issued a plea for a pump that would save the girl's life, it never arrives. On the third night, the girl dies. Carle can only remove the life buoy from around her waist, close her eyelids, and watch her sink into the clay.

Allende's autobiographical account of an actual event is both psychologically taxing and poetic. Simply by watching the tragedy unfold, she can perceive the thoughts that are going through Carle's mind. When the girl dies, he is not the same man he once was, obsessed with his role in the girl's death and reviewing the many videos of the event to reveal ways that he might have saved her. On another level, Allende's account is a scathing indictment of the bureaucratic quagmire that allows such a tragedy to occur. Perhaps the only redemption comes from the girl's death itself, in which both participants "were saved from despair" and "freed from the clay . . . they flew above the vast swamp of corruption and laments."

Allende, Isabel. "Wicked Girl" (1989). From *The Gates of Paradise: The Anthology of Erotic Short Fiction* (Ed. Alberto Manguel, 1993). ALIENATION/ISOLATION; COMING-OF-AGE; ESCAPE; HISPANIC EXPERIENCE; MEN and WOMEN; MOTHERS and CHILDREN; SEXUALITY; WOMEN'S ISSUES.

Elena Mejias is an eleven-year-old girl who is infatuated by the singer Juan Jose Bernal, the man who has become her mother's lover. When she spies the couple making love (her mother, who owns a boardinghouse, has taught Elena how to spy), she decides that she will seduce Bernal. She crawls into bed with the man, who realizes before he consummates the relationship that she is not her mother. He calls her a "wicked girl" for acting out her fantasies and pushes her away.

The event has a profound effect on Bernal, however. Years later, when Elena visits Bernal and her mother (the two have married), Bernal discloses that he has been obsessed with the idea of making love to a young girl since her attempt at seducing him and that he is sorry he did not act on Elena's impulse. Elena is confused by Bernal's admission; in the intervening years, she has forgotten that the event had ever occurred.

The irony of Bernal's obsession and Elena's forgetting is clear. Bernal, who righteously declaimed the girl and her attention to him, has been tormented for fifteen years by the image. Elena, who was able to place the event as one of many in her coming-of-age and subsequent setting out from a home life that oppressed her, is a stronger woman for her initiative and her ability to keep the events of her life in their proper perspective. She is "wicked" only to Bernal, who cannot forget.

Alvarez, Julia. "Customs" (1992). From *Iguana Dreams: New Latino Fiction* (Ed. Virgil Suarez and Delia Poey, 1992). COMING-OF-AGE; CULTURE CONFLICTS; DECEPTION; HISPANIC EXPERI-ENCE; IDENTITY; MEN and WOMEN; MISOGYNY; TRADI-TION/CONVENTION; WOMEN'S ISSUES.

When Yolanda visits her Tio Mundo (uncle) in Central America, she is surprised to learn how unenlightened the men of that society are. Yolanda knows much about the culture, though she has been thoroughly American-ized by her years in the United States. Now, she attends college in Vermont and has a boyfriend about whom she speaks little in order to avoid the interrogation of her relatives.

Yolanda, at the urging of her boyfriend, Steven, has brought a tent to her uncle's homeland and begs him to allow her cousins to go camping with her. Although Tio Mundo acquiesces, Francisco, a man who works for him, chauffeurs the group through the countryside. Francisco does not let them out of his sight, even when he drops them off in a spot that the girls think is remote from Tio Mundo's compound. When they are unable to pitch the tent—Tio Mundo, it turns out, has taken the directions for pitching the tent, to prove to his niece that the outing was ill advised—Yolanda discovers that Francisco has been watching the girls the whole time. In a moment that represents for Yolanda her break from the traditional society and the mind-set of men like her uncle, she feels a sudden tenderness for Francisco, who little recognizes the importance of the previous evening's events.

Alvarez uses an object as simple as a tent to great effect in the story. The tent is a symbol of freedom for Yolanda, and her uncle begrudges her the same freedom in his country that she enjoys in the United States. The title of the story suggests the customs of society that create a stark juxtaposition to her own life relatively free from oppression and the narrow-mindedness of men like her uncle and the attitudes of the conventions that he perpet-uates.

Anaya, Rudolfo. "Dead End" (1993). From *Join In: Multiethnic Short Stories* (Ed. Donald R. Gallo, 1993). COMING-OF-AGE; DREAMS (of the FUTURE); FAMILY; MEN and WOMEN; SEXUALITY.

Maria has her eyes on Frankie Galvin, the school's most handsome and experienced boy. Her friends see the attraction between the two, though they wonder why Frankie would be drawn to someone as plain as Maria, and they encourage her to dress like them—tight jeans, low-cut shirts, and plenty of makeup. Maria cannot be distracted from her dream of getting an education; she promised her mother on the woman's deathbed two years before that she would not become like the other girls in the school. Now, she is too involved in the raising of her family to have a boyfriend or make love in the backseat of a car. When Frankie invites her for a ride in his car, though, Maria cannot refuse. But when he tries to make love to her, she remembers the promise to her mother and, despite Frankie's accusation that she was "too good" to do the things that other girls did, she asks him to take her home. She thinks that she might try to see Frankie again after final exams.

Anaya's coming-of-age story details the responsibilities that arise after the untimely death of the family's head and one girl's promise to her mother. Even though Maria has the desires of a girl her age, she must grow up quickly in order to save herself and her family. The story's title suggests both the relationship that Frankie has started with Maria and her future, should she make a wrong turn along the way.

Anderson, Sherwood. "Death in the Woods" (1933). From *The Story and Its Writer*, 5th ed. (Ed. Ann Charters, 1999). COMING-OF-AGE; DEATH; MEN and WOMEN; MISOGYNY; MOTHERS and CHILDREN; OPPRESSION.

Mrs. Grimes, at forty, was already an old woman, according to the narrator, who remembers this story as a young boy. Life—and her husband and son—have treated her poorly, and her only purpose now, it seems, is to feed animals, both the livestock and the men in her life. When she sets off for town on a particularly snowy, cold day, the butcher is the first person in recent memory to speak kindly to her. He knows how the men treat her, and he curses them for their actions. Still, she knows that she must return home so that she can feed them all—horses, cows, pigs, dogs, men.

On her way home, the woman succumbs to the elements and dies. The dogs who have followed her from home rip the pack from her back and expose her torso. When a hunter finds her, he hurries back to town, insistent that the body is that of a beautiful young girl. The narrator, who goes to the scene of her death with the townsmen, has never seen a woman's body before, and he watches in morbid fascination as the blacksmith carries her back to town.

The cycle of life is evident in this story, as is the role of memory and perception in creating reality. The narrator, a young boy then and now a man, remembers things in his own way, "as music heard from far off." More than once, he comments on the possibility that what he relates is not the exact truth, but rather the story as he remembers it, a simple story that bears retelling.

Anderson, Sherwood. "The Egg" (1921). From *The Harper Anthology of Fiction* (Ed. Sylvan Barnet, 1991). ALIENATION/ISOLATION; FAMILY; FATHERS and CHILDREN; MEN and WOMEN.

The narrator recalls that his father was content with his life until he met his mother and married late, at the age of thirty-five. The mother had grander plans in mind for her husband and the son they would have, and the man became a chicken farmer. The business was not successful, and the family decides to open a restaurant. That endeavor seems to be ill-fated, and the father, who thinks that his lack of business acumen has something to do with his personality, becomes more upbeat for his clientele. One evening, the father is laughed at by a man whom he tries to entertain with egg tricks and the anomalies that he has brought with him from his previous venture (deformed chicks in glass jars, for example). The father carries an egg upstairs to their apartment, ostensibly to break it as he has the others in his aborted attempt at amusing the customer, and he breaks down weeping. The son would remember this scene for the rest of his life.

Anderson's story, perhaps more than any other of his short fiction, uses a symbol—in this case, the egg—to ground his narrative. The egg is both the repository of life and an indication of the cycle of life and death that all animals, including humans, must face. The title of the story implies the ambivalence with which the author and the narrator treat the egg. The father, who could easily have lived his life on the farm, is removed from the nest and spends the rest of his days inextricably tied to the symbol of life that taunts him with its ephemerality and regrets at past decisions.

Anderson, Sherwood. "Hands" (1919). From *The Story and Its Writer*, 5th ed. (Ed. Ann Charters, 1999). DREAMS (of the FUTURE); GUILT; HOMOSEXUALITY; INTERIOR LIVES; MORALITY; OPPRESSION; VIOLENCE.

Wing Biddlebaum is a man haunted by his past: the townspeople of Winesburg, Ohio—except for his friend, George Willard, a reporter for the local newspaper—find him odd, and they wonder at his mannerisms, especially the way he seems always conscious of his large, active hands that are not unlike "the beating of the wings of an imprisoned bird." Biddlebaum, it turns out, used to be a schoolteacher named Adolph Myers who preached the value of dreams to his students. He imparted his passion for achieving those dreams by innocently stroking the boys' shoulders and touching their hair. In one instance, a "half-witted" boy accused the teacher of inappropriate behavior, and the Pennsylvania town where he taught reacted to the claims by nearly lynching him. He escaped to Winesburg with his life, but not with his dignity. Though he didn't understand what had happened to him, he assumed that his hands must have been to blame. Only when he cannot see his hands in the darkness do they become still, and the man, only for a time, a little more at ease.

Anderson's stories collected in *Winesburg, Ohio,* detail the day-to-day life of small-town America and point up the themes of alienation and uncertainty that haunt a man like Biddlebaum who, through no fault of his own, is made an outcast. The hands that illustrate his passion for learning and accomplishment instead become a symbol of his unwitting exile from society.

Anderson, Sherwood. "I'm a Fool" (1922). From *An Anthology of Famous American Stories* (Ed. Angus Burrell and Bennett Cerf, 1963). CLASS CONFLICT; COMING-OF-AGE; DECEPTION; IDENTITY; MEN and WOMEN.

The nineteen-year-old narrator works at a racetrack, and he describes the joys of the "sport of kings." One thing that bothers the young man, however, is the way that people "put on airs" when they come to the racetrack— men and women from well-to-do families or college boys who want to flaunt their parents' money. In an attempt to counter the pretense that he sees, the narrator acts just as they do, shunning them because of his "superior" position at the racetrack.

When he meets Lucy Wessen, clearly a woman above the narrator in breeding, he is smitten with her. He tells Lucy that his name is Walter Mathers, son of one of the horses' owners. Later that evening, Lucy and "Walter" are alone, and the young woman is impressed by his sensitivity; he senses that the two could have had a relationship had he not lied to her about his identity. When Lucy tells him that she and her brother are leaving by train, he knows he will never see her again.

The narrator's lack of self-esteem, despite appearances, costs him the opportunity to be with the girl of his dreams. He does not consider the possibility that she would not mind that he worked at the racetrack; instead, Anderson suggests that the separation of the classes (it is significant in defining the young man's character that the narrator's best friend is black) is as much self-imposed as a reality for those who allow themselves to be swayed by the privilege of class at the cost of their identity.

Angell, Judie. "Dear Marsha" (1989). From *Connections: Short Stories by Outstanding Writers for Young Adults* (Ed. Donald R. Gallo, 1989). ALIENATION/ISOLATION; BETRAYAL; COMING-OF-AGE; COMMUNICATION/LANGUAGE; DECEPTION; FRIENDSHIP; LABOR/JOB.

Marsha's friends are away on vacation for the summer, and she decides to contact a pen pal, Anne Marie, whose name was given to her by a teacher. The girls find that they have much in common and are able to candidly discuss their personal lives. Anne Marie's mother has just died, and Marsha is falsely accused of stealing—and subsequently fired—from her job as a clerk. The event has far-reaching implications for Marsha: the people in her small town look at her with pity or scorn, and she is asked not to join the cheerleading squad, whose members "represent the school's highest standards."

When Marsha asks Anne Marie if she can live with her for a year to get away from her predicament, Anne Marie reveals herself as a sixty-one-year-old school principal whose name was mistakenly placed on the pen pal list. She gives Marsha the encouragement that she will need to get through the tough times, writing in her final letter, "REMEMBER, YOU DIDN'T DO ANYTHING WRONG AND THEREFORE YOU MUST NOT RUN AWAY—YOU MUST NEVER LET STUPID AND CRUEL PEOPLE GET THE BEST OF YOU."

The unexpected twist at the story's end suggests that Marsha will be able to work out the problems that were unfairly placed upon her. The friendship that develops between the two in this coming-of-age story details the ways in which the two women, so different in age and life experience, are able to communicate when they can be candid with one another. Anne Marie's final letter to Marsha implies that she has also learned much from her "pen pal."

Armstrong, Jennifer. "The Statue of Liberty Factory" (1998). From *Stay True: Short Stories for Strong Girls* **(Ed. Marilyn Singer, 1998). COMING-OF-AGE; FAMILY; HISTORY; INDIVIDUAL; JUSTICE.**

When Monica's mother, a designer and artist, hits upon the wildly successful idea of making Statue of Liberty souvenirs for the Bicentennial, Monica, who is fifteen, is given a trust fund that she will be able to access on her sixteenth birthday. Monica wishes nothing more than to travel to Paris, where she will play her guitar in the streets. When the time comes, however, her mother is less than enthusiastic about the idea. In protest of her mother's decision, Monica dresses as the Statue of Liberty and stands in front of the family's home. Initially, her parents treat the protest as a joke; as the first day comes to an end with Monica still in front of the house, they begin to take her seriously. When the press and local television stations find out about Monica, she becomes a minor celebrity. Her parents relent, and Monica is allowed to go to Paris.

This straightforward coming-of-age story uses the ideas of liberty and protest as a backdrop against which Monica fulfills her simple dream. In the process of getting her wish, Monica learns much about history, including the story behind the Statue of Liberty and the famous poem that greets people coming into New York City to begin their lives in a new country. The story is especially relevant given the current assault on freedom and choice in a democracy that has been unaccustomed, perhaps, to having to consider such topics in practice, rather than in the abstract.

Asher, Sandy. "Great Moves" (1987). From *Visions* **(Ed. Donald R. Gallo, 1987). COMING-OF-AGE; CONTESTS; EPIPHANY;**

FRIENDSHIP; HUMOR/SATIRE/IRONY; IDENTITY; MEN and WOMEN.

Brenda's friend, Annie, has an enviable problem: she has been asked to the Valentine's Day dance by the two most popular boys in school—great students, great citizens, and the starting point guards on the basketball team. In short, they are the guys with all the "great moves." Brenda is jealous that her friend should be so popular. She has not been asked to the dance by anyone. When the two boys approach Brenda for advice on how best to woo Annie, however, they both are smitten with her. The following day, they both ask Brenda out. Her response is much the same as Annie's; she is speechless at first that such a thing could happen to her.

After she witnesses the boys' fighting over her, however, she understands the true meaning behind their actions: They do not want to date Annie or Brenda for who they are, but rather to gain something that the other does not have, since they are in constant competition with one another. When the boys ask for Brenda's answer, she has a "great move" of her own and tells them that both she and Annie will go to the dance without dates.

Asher's story is a humorous coming-of-age tale that explores identity-making for two young women who are entered into much the same competition as the most popular boys in the school. Though Annie and Brenda have little experience in making such decisions, their relationship with one another guides Brenda toward the right choice. The girls remain independent, and the boys, whose lives are ruled by competition, are left without dates for the dance.

Asimov, Isaac. "The Last Question" (Asimov, 1956). From *The Best Science Fiction of Isaac Asimov*, 1986. FANTASY/IMAGINATION/ SCIENCE FICTION; RELIGION/SPIRITUALITY; TECHNOLOGY.

On May 21, 2061, Alexander Adell and Bertram Lupov are the first two humans to ask the "last question": "How can the net amount of entropy of the universe be massively decreased?" In other words, how can we keep the universe running even after it has wound down to nothing? The computer responds, as it and its descendents will for eons, that "THERE IS INSUFFICIENT DATA FOR A MEANINGFUL ANSWER."

While technological advances increase the power of computers geometrically, the population of Man increases as well. Billions of years after the fateful last question, Man is immortal and inhabits all of the universe's galaxies. When those galaxies are too full to sustain human life, Man has discovered a way to separate his physical body from his mind, mingling with the universe—and the Universal AC, the computer that controls it all—until entropy finally grinds the universe to a halt. In the last instant, when Man and the Universal AC merge into one being, the computer is able to calculate the answer: "LET THERE BE LIGHT!" And there was.

The story, which spans the entire history of the universe from the middle of the twenty-first century until its death—and rebirth—relies on a surprise ending for its effect. Still, the perceptive reader might expect such a revelation: The computer that aids the lives of the humans as they populate the universe is treated as a god and revered for the guidance that it gives them. In the end, Asimov suggests, it also has the power to re-create the universe, perhaps an ironic statement of our reliance on technology for the answers to many of our questions, including the "last question."

Atwood, Margaret. "Happy Endings" (1983). From *The Story and Its Writer*, 5th ed. (Ed. Ann Charters, 1999). ART and the ARTIST; DEATH; HUMOR/SATIRE/IRONY; LITERACY/WRITING; MEN and WOMEN; SEXUALITY.

The crux of the story, "John and Mary meet," is followed by six possible endings. Only "A" is the traditional happy ending; so much so, that it becomes farcical in the picture that it paints of the couple: they live in a house whose value continues to rise, they enjoy a wonderful sex life, they go on vacations, they retire, and they die. The other endings, while not nearly as happy, are more interesting. In one, Mary's love for John is unrequited, and he uses her merely for sex. In another, John, who is married with children, falls in love with the much younger Mary; she, on the other hand, is in love with James, who has a motorcycle. John catches Mary in bed with James and kills them both before he commits suicide. In the next two, Mary is not even involved in the relationship, and in the last, John and Mary are spies.

Atwood's tongue-in-cheek story is a not-so-subtle commentary on stories that rely on contrived, Pollyanna plots for their effect. She calls into question both the artist's and the reader's desire for a "happy ending," as "they're all fake, either deliberately fake, with malicious intent to deceive, or just motivated by excessive optimism if not by downright sentimentality." Though Atwood refuses to give in to the notion that things can ever end happily—after all, the only possible ending is "*John and Mary die.*"—she clearly has much to say about what happens after the beginning and before the ending, "the stretch in between, since it's the hardest to do anything with." That, she implies, will be saved for another story and is the proper point of exploration for the author.

Atwood, Margaret. "Rape Fantasies" (1977). From *Short Fiction: Classic and Contemporary*, 4th ed. (Ed. Charles H. Bohner and Dean Dougherty, 1999). ESCAPE; FANTASY; MEN and WOMEN; MISOGYNY; VIOLENCE; WOMEN'S ISSUES.

The narrator begins the story *in medias res* in a conversational tone that prefigures the last paragraphs. The talk around the lunch table at work is about "rape fantasies"—Chrissy, one of the women in the office, is reading an article that insists all women have them—and everyone is invited to give their own version of what the "perfect" rape must be like. Most of the women do not have rape fantasies at all, but rather, as the narrator points out, fantasies that involve men whom they have not formally met. The narrator's stories, on the other hand, are much more banal. In one, the man has a raging cold, as does the victim; in another, a pimply faced man is unable to complete the act; in still another, she imagines that she and the rapist have leukemia together and end up in a relationship to the death.

The stories are both humorous and poignant, and belie the gravity of the issue. Through her own "rape fantasies," the narrator portrays herself as a careful, conservative person perhaps shying away from the reality of her own situation. Only at the end of Atwood's story do we realize that the narrator is in fact speaking to a support group. In the last paragraph, the story turns deadly serious, and the narrator finally reveals her innermost feelings on the subject, wondering how a man could do such a thing to a woman, to strip the dignity from someone else's life.

B

Babel, Isaac. "My First Goose" (1934). From *The Story and Its Writer*, 4th ed. (Ed. Ann Charters, 1995). ASSIMILATION; GUILT; INITIATION; MORALITY; WAR.

The narrator, a graduate law student, enters the staff of the VI division (a reference to Babel's having fought with the Soviet Cavalry in the Polish campaign of 1920). He is one of the few who can read and is referred to as a "spec," an intellectual who is often forced to live as an outsider. He is confronted with this ill treatment early on in the process when he encounters Savitsky, his commander, who believes all efforts to learn do not belong in his cavalry. The narrator, after hearing the quartermaster state that there is "not a life for the brainy type here," makes an effort to become someone else.

His entrance into camp is filled with trepidation. After his first encounter with the Cossacks, he realizes the difficulty he will have fitting in. In order to eat, he slays a goose and gives it to an old blind woman for cooking. When the other soldiers see his actions, they begin to accept him. They invite him to eat with them, and he is enlisted to read them the news from the local papers. Though he has become part of the group and his bed is being warmed by the friendly bodies around him, his heart remains cold and bloodstained.

In this story, Babel explores the dynamics of fitting in. The narrator, torn between becoming a part of the group and compromising his own morals, chooses the more convenient of the two. The same, Babel suggests, could happen to anyone. Still, that acceptance does not come without a price.

Baldwin, James. "Going to Meet the Man" (1965). From *Studies in Fiction* (Ed. Blaze O. Bonazza et al., 1982). MEN and WOMEN; RACE RELATIONS; SEXUALITY; SOCIETY; TRADITION/CONVENTION; VIOLENCE.

As he lies unable to sleep with his wife beside him, Jesse recalls that earlier that day he had beaten a black man who was the leader of a protest group. Jesse sees his role as one of the heroic white man saving the South from the blacks who would overrun what is rightfully theirs. His hatred for blacks returns full force when he is assailed by the songs that the protestors sang that day; the recollection prompts a memory from his childhood when his parents took him to witness the lynching of a black man who was accused of raping a white woman. He recalls that he admired his father for what he had done, and he remembers the nearly sexual, satisfied look on his mother's face when the man was brutalized.

Baldwin wrote this story at the height of the Civil Rights movement, and the deputy's actions toward his wife clearly indicate a shift in the political climate of the time. Jesse is rendered impotent until he recalls his childhood, when race relations were much simpler and favored the white man, at which time he becomes potent again and takes his wife much as the black man, who was lynched for allegedly committing a similar act. The story is a powerful indictment of the South and mixes the disparate themes of guilt and hatred, both of which combine to transform Jesse into the very man that he hates with all his being.

Baldwin, James. "Sonny's Blues" (1958). From _Short Fiction: Classic and Contemporary_, 4th ed. (Ed. Charles H. Bohner and Dean Dougherty, 1999). ADDICTION; AFRICAN-AMERICAN EXPERIENCE; FAMILY; IDENTITY; MUSIC; RACE RELATIONS.

The narrator is a teacher in Harlem who has managed to separate himself from the lifestyle that he sees around him. For a time, he counted his own brother, Sonny, among those lost to the racist attitudes that existed in society. Sonny, an aspiring jazz pianist, develops a heroin habit, and only after a long period of silence can he and his brother finally understand one another. The death of the narrator's daughter, Sonny's failure to fit in with his own family, a stint in the navy—all serve to alienate the brothers, even after their mother made the narrator promise to keep an eye on young Sonny.

As the narrator listens to Sonny playing his music in the nightclub, though, he realizes what Sonny meant when he spoke of transcending the life that has been imposed on him through his music; though he cannot guarantee that he will never do heroin again—the musician's way of deadening himself to the world around him and opening up the possibilities within himself—the music offers the same opportunity to the people fortunate enough to hear it.

The story is deservedly one of Baldwin's most famous and perhaps his most poignant, in his portrayal of a family separated by the ills that society has brought upon it and brought together by something as universal, as passionate, and as steeped in the African-American experience as jazz.

Balzac, Honore de. "A Passion in the Desert" (1830). From _The Norton Anthology of Short Fiction_ (Ed. R.V. Cassill and Richard Bausch, 2000). ALIENATION/ISOLATION; ANIMALS and HUMANS; BETRAYAL; DEATH; LOVE/HATE.

After she comes out of M. Martin's show, in which Martin works with hyenas that he has tamed, a woman confronts the narrator with her opinion that the show is "dreadful," and that taming wild beasts is a pointless effort. The narrator relates a story about a man's struggle to survive in the desert and how the friendship he forms with a panther keeps him alive.

The story-within-a-story is about a Frenchman in war. He is taken hostage by the enemy, but manages to escape after a few days and awakes to the harsh desert heat. After days of wandering aimlessly, he takes shelter in an oasis and realizes that he is sharing the sanctuary with a wild beast, which turns out to be a panther with bloodstained teeth. The Frenchman, though, finds the animal to be friendly and playful. The two become close, their friendship the only bright spot in an otherwise endless string of days in the desert. Though he has come to trust the panther, the man keeps his knife by his side, and when the panther makes a lunge at him, he kills the beast in self-defense. As the panther lay dying, however, he realizes that he has made a horrible mistake—the panther was only playing.

Balzac, a prolific novelist and a profound influence on Henry James, many of whose stories echo the taut realism and psychological intensity of Balzac's work, uses a frame story in which the narrator attempts to convince the woman that her initial impression is false—much like the man who mistakenly killed his only companion was wrong in his own assumptions. The man, he relates, would have given everything he had to save his only friend, but he will not torture himself with the details. After all, in the desert "there is everything, and nothing."

Bambara, Toni Cade. "The Lesson" (1972). From *Calling the Wind: Twentieth-Century African-American Short Stories* (Ed. Clarence Major, 1993). CLASS CONFLICT; COMING-OF-AGE; GIFTS/GENEROSITY; SOCIETY.

Miss Moore presents herself as a rich lady who dresses nicely and enjoys taking the neighborhood children to places they have never been, even though they sometimes do not want to go. On one of these occasions, she takes a group of kids—Sugar, the wisecracking Sylvia, Q. T., Flyboy, Fat Butt, Rosie, Giraffe, Mercedes, and Georgia—to F.A.O. Schwartz, a toy store in New York City.

When they arrive at the store, they look through the window at a paperweight that costs $480. They do not know what a paperweight is; only one of the kids even owns a desk. Next, they look at a toy sailboat with a price tag of $1,195 and decide that it would take them too long to save up their allowances to pay for the boat. They go inside the store, and Sylvia finds a clown that costs thirty-five dollars; she decides that even if she asked her mother for the clown for her birthday, she would rather spend the money on other things, like new bunk beds or a visit to their grandfather's house in the country. Sylvia gets upset and wants to leave. When they get back home, Miss Moore asks if anyone learned anything during the day. Sugar says, "this is not much of a democracy if you ask me. Equal chance to pursue happiness means an equal crack at the dough, don't it?" As she looks at Sylvia, Miss Moore asks if anybody else learned anything. They just walk away with the change left from the cab fare.

The story focuses on the themes of society and class conflict. Even though Miss Moore tries to show the kids things that they would likely not otherwise see, the lesson that they learn is a harsh reality that opens the children's eyes to economic inequality. Even though the story is lighthearted and enjoyable for the kids' reactions to their discoveries in the toy store, the message is very serious. Sylvia, the narrator, decides that she will go "to the West End and then over to the Drive to think this day through. . . . But ain't nobody gonna beat me at nothin."

Barth, John. "Life-Story" (1969). From *The Norton Anthology of Contemporary Fiction* (Ed. R.V. Cassill, 1988). AGING; ART and the ARTIST; FAMILY; IDENTITY; ILLUSION v. REALITY; INTERIOR LIVES; METAFICTION.

Barth's protagonist is a writer who questions the very nature of the prose that he creates. The narrative begins *in medias res*, with the writer deciding that he would not discard what he had already written, but would analyze the story and move in a different direction. The problem is, however, that "it was perhaps inevitable that one afternoon the possibility would occur to the writer of these lines that his own life might be a fiction, in which he was the leading or an accessory character." As the writer wrestles with the possibility that he is little more than a character in one of his own stories—and realizes that if, in fact, his life is a fiction, it is one written in a mode that he least prefers—his wife and daughters, who themselves read for pleasure rather than as a way of constructing their lives, move within his world unaware of the dilemma that he faces.

Imaginary characters begin to address him in his study, and he wonders at how public a writer's life is, no matter how careful he is to make it otherwise. As the author reaches the point where he must come to a conclusion—one that involves author and God, novel and world—his wife interrupts his thoughts by wishing him a happy birthday, and he caps his pen.

Barth's penchant for metafiction, writing about writing in a self-conscious and self-reflexive way, comes through in this story. Though the story has no plot, no "ground-situation," intermittent commentary on the world outside the author's life implies that Barth understands the extent to which authors create their own lives, both in their fiction, and in the everyday world. By an act as simple as capping his pen, the author is brought back to the reality of his family and his birthday.

Barth, John. "Lost in the Funhouse" (1967). From *Short Fiction: Classic and Contemporary*, 4th ed. (Ed. Charles H. Bohner and Dean

Dougherty, 1999). ALIENATION/ISOLATION; COMING-OF-AGE; FAMILY; MEN and WOMEN; METAFICTION.

The "plot" of Barth's story is quite simple: Ambrose, a thirteen-year-old boy, travels with his family to Ocean City, Maryland, where they will celebrate the Fourth of July. With him are his brother, Peter, two years older; his mother and father; his uncle, Karl; and Magda, a girl with whom Ambrose is deeply infatuated. The family plays the games typical of car trips; when they arrive in Ocean City, they discover that the ocean has been tainted by an oil slick, and they are forced to swim in the hotel pool. Amidst the banality of the events, Ambrose behaves awkwardly when he is around Magda. When Peter, Ambrose, and Magda go into the funhouse, Ambrose is left alone. During his time in the funhouse, he is taken on a roller coaster ride of emotions, from fear to fantasy.

Though Barth's style can be characterized as "postmodern" or "self-reflexive"—the author ostensibly writes a narrative about a narrator who writes a narrative about a boy—both of which signal the alienation and fragmentation of the text and the playfulness of the author with his audience, such a narrative strategy also allows Barth to mirror (both figuratively and literally) Ambrose's conflicted feelings toward Magda. The story is a humorous coming-of-age tale with many twists and turns, like the physical funhouse that Barth describes.

Barthelme, Donald. "I Bought a Little City" (1974). From *Studies in Fiction* (Ed. Blaze O. Bonazza et al., 1982). DECADENCE/DEGENERATION; FANTASY/IMAGINATION; HUMOR/SATIRE/IRONY; ILLUSION v. REALITY; SOCIETY.

The story's narrator begins by explaining that he has bought Galveston, Texas—all of it—in an attempt to create a utopian society. He enjoys the power that comes with owning a city ("a nice little city, it suits me fine"), though he soon finds out that it is impossible to make the people of the city happy, a task that initially seemed easy. When the city's owner attempts to better the living conditions for everyone involved, someone invariably is left out. He shoots six thousand of the city's 165,000 dogs, ostensibly to improve living conditions. Finally, after dealing with the problems associated with running a utopia, the owner sells Galveston back to the people and moves to a more inconspicuous place in Galena Park, Texas. When he is asked to run for the school board there, he declines, telling the interested parties that he has no children.

Barthelme's story takes to the absurd extreme the notion of creating the perfect American society. In a darkly humorous way, he deals with issues of democracy, individual freedom, and standards of living, and decides that the best remedy is to live as we always have and to deal with our problems as best we can. The story—and the bulk of Barthelme's fiction—owes much to the Civil Rights and Socialist movements of the 1960s, in which society was seen as a faceless entity that suppressed the full potential of its individuals. The author's response forces the reader to reevaluate the present state of society.

Barthelme, Donald. "The King of Jazz" (1970). From *Studies in Fiction* **(Ed. Blaze O. Bonazza et al., 1982). ART and the ARTIST; CONTESTS; HUMOR/SATIRE/IRONY; MUSIC; PRIDE; SOCIETY.**

Hokie Mokie, a musician from Pass Christian, Mississippi, thinks that he is the King of Jazz now that the great Spicy MacLammermore is dead. When he plays even a few notes, passersby marvel at the soulful sounds emanating from his trombone. In a session with other musicians, Hokie Mokie insists on playing "Smoke," his signature tune. When Hideo Yamaguchi, a Japanese trombonist who also fancies himself the King of Jazz, refuses to bow to Hokie Mokie, a confrontation ensues between the two. Yamaguchi represents himself well, and at one point, Hokie Mokie is ready to accede the crown to him. From the side, Hokie Mokie plays a few plaintive notes that evoke the best players of all time, and he is once again the King. Yamaguchi, knowing he has been bested, leaves town, having become a better musician for the experience.

This comic tale combines images of the gunfights of the Old West and a parody of jazz aficionados (who take the story's longest paragraph to describe Hokie Mokie's playing in "hipster" metaphors) to explore the power and lure of jazz, America's own unique form of music.

Barthelme, Donald. "A Shower of Gold" (1962). From *Studies in Fiction* **(Ed. Blaze O. Bonazza et al., 1982). ART and the ARTIST; DECADENCE/DEGENERATION; HUMOR/SATIRE/IRONY; ILLUSION v. REALITY; INDIVIDUAL; POLITICS; SOCIETY.**

Because he needs the money, Peterson answers an ad to appear on television to relate his life experiences—in short, the absurdities of life in 1960s America. As an artist, he is struck by the psychobabble that the show's producers want him to articulate when he appears. He has dreams of the president threatening him with a sledgehammer and making comments about his diseased liver. Even Peterson's barber knows the show and warns him, "they do a job on those people."

When he appears on the show, a woman tells him that his answers will be judged by a lie detector. Peterson realizes that his only recourse is to embrace the absurdity of his situation and to use his time on television as a forum to tell the American people to live their own lives instead of becoming society's pawns.

Barthelme's story is clearly a product of its time and has gained relevance in recent years. The struggling artist is willing to do whatever is necessary to eke out a living—including embarrassing himself on national television—though he musters the courage to undermine that mode of thinking by recalling what makes individual lives worth living. The story has echoes of Dostoevsky's "Notes from Underground," though Barthelme's protagonist refuses to give in to the absurdity and cynicism that threaten to swallow him.

Bass, Rick. "The Watch" (1988). From *Best of the South* (Ed. Anne Tyler and Shannon Ravenel, 1995). AGING; ENTROPY/CHAOS; FA-THERS and CHILDREN; HUMOR/SATIRE/IRONY; IDENTITY; MEN and WOMEN; NATURE/WILDERNESS.

Hollingsworth posts a reward of $1,000 for his lost father, Buzbee, his only living kin. Though he knows that Buzbee, who is seventy-seven, has left of his own accord, the son cannot stand the thought of losing his father for good. The only human interaction Hollingsworth has is sitting on the front porch of their run-down store and telling the stories that make up their lives—especially the yellow fever epidemic that claimed their family and many others—over and over.

When Jesse, a young bicyclist, stops on his training runs to drink a Coke with the aged Hollingsworth (Buzbee was only fourteen when he became a father), the two construct a plan to catch the old man. Buzbee is shrewd, however, and he sees the two coming for him from his perch in a tree. He need only run into the deepest swamp to avoid being captured. The life that he has built for himself away from his son is the life that he has never had. He wrestles and kills alligators for food and keeps a harem of women who have joined him from town, where their husbands abused them.

After several attempts, Hollingsworth and Jesse succeed in catching the old man. The son chains his father to the front porch; now, he can talk to his father to his heart's content. Despite the fact that Hollingsworth claims to have thrown away the key to the shackles, Buzbee never stops planning to return to freedom.

Bass's story is Southern in every sense. The landscape, as much as the people, is a character that imbues the story with a sense of the history and the gothic elements that abound in much Southern literature. The tone of the story is reminiscent of Faulkner in its evocation of a land and its people.

Beattie, Ann. "In the White Night" (1986). From *Park City: New and Selected Stories*, 1st ed., 1998. DEATH; DREAMS (SLEEPING); FA-THERS and CHILDREN; MEN and WOMEN; MOTHERS and CHILDREN.

Carol and Vernon leave the home of their friends, Matt and Gaye Brinkley, and discuss the events of the evening—to each other and to themselves. Carol and Vernon have suffered the loss of a daughter, Sharon, to leukemia, and Matt and Gaye are going through difficulties with their own daughter, Becky, whom they do not want to discuss (it turns out that she has had an abortion and has done little to straighten out her own life). Vernon compares their own plight with that of the Brinkleys, and wonders if he and his wife are more fortunate than the Brinkleys because they have already suffered the death of their daughter; nothing more can be done to them to make them suffer. Vernon, in fact, has adopted a new optimistic attitude toward life. The conversation disturbs Carol, who, after several minutes of weeping for her dead daughter, finds Vernon asleep on the sofa. She herself falls asleep on the floor, thinking that Sharon may be watching them as an angel in the night.

Beattie's focus on memory is important to the story, and the different ways in which the two sets of parents cope with their children implies not the relative unfeeling of the Brinkleys, but rather a means of preparing oneself for the day that follows. Carol's notion that Sharon may be with her "In the white night world outside" and Vernon's sleeping on the sofa is an indication of the strong bonds formed between mothers and daughters.

Beattie, Ann. "Janus" (1985). From *Fiction 100: An Anthology of Short Stories*, 9th ed. (Ed. James H. Pickering, 2000). DREAMS (of the FUTURE); GIFTS/GENEROSITY; IDENTITY; INTERIOR LIVES; MARRIAGE; MEN and WOMEN; WOMEN'S ISSUES.

Andrea is a realtor whose life has the veneer of success. She is married to a stockbroker, and though the two maintain lives that rarely conflict, the relationship is largely devoid of passion. In her dealings with others, Andrea has a good eye for the details that will interest prospective buyers; she uses that knowledge to draw people in, going as far as to bring her dog to a house if she thinks it will help her close the deal.

One object that becomes increasingly important to her is a bowl that seems to fit anywhere she puts it. When she forgets the bowl at a house, she likens it to leaving a child behind. As she becomes more obsessed with the bowl, her relationship with her husband diminishes. As her marriage dwindles to nothing, the bowl's importance is revealed: Andrea received the object as a gift from a lover who had encouraged her to leave her husband. When she refused, he broke off the relationship, leaving Andrea with only an empty bowl and the promise of a life with little passion.

Janus is the Roman god of two faces, and the implication of Andrea's both looking forward and backward at the same time is clear. The empty bowl is a material object—much as Andrea's own life as a successful realtor offers her many material possessions—though it is nothing more than a tormenting reminder of the life that she passed up. She has given in to inertia, and Beattie suggests that she will remain on that course until—if ever—she is shaken once again from her torpor.

Bell, Madison Smartt. "Customs of the Country" (1989). From *Best of the South* (Ed. Anne Tyler and Shannon Ravenel, 1995). ADDICTION;

JUSTICE; MEN and WOMEN; MOTHERS and CHILDREN; VIO-
LENCE.

Though a young mother attempts to piece her life back together after her
husband is sentenced to twenty-five years on a drug charge and her son,
Davey, is taken from her by social services, her efforts come to naught. The
protagonist, who works as a waitress at a truck stop, recalls the time several
years before when she was addicted to Dilaudid and her husband, Patrick,
would come home after being away for days, with great sums of money
whose source she didn't question. When Patrick is arrested, the woman
doesn't realize that she is in withdrawal from the drug and, in a fit of anger
over nothing more than the rattling of pots and pans, throws Davey across
the room, breaking his leg. The last time she sees the boy for two years is
in the hospital emergency room, where she finds herself unable to construct
a lie that would allow her to keep her son.

Now, she lives her life as she should, holding down a steady job and seeing
her son at his foster parents' home. When her request to gain custody of
the child fails, she once again loses control of her emotions, going to the
apartment next door and knocking unconscious with an iron skillet a man
who beats his wife regularly. Although the protagonist feels that it is the
right thing to do, she wonders if the act is really any different from the one
that estranged her son in the first place. She turns away from the unconscious man—whose abused wife, despite the physical and psychic scars that
the man has given her over the years, stands over him in sympathy—and
leaves town.

The title of the story ironically implies the inherent violence and degradation in society and echoes Edith Wharton's own similarly titled novel of
society's shortcomings; still, Wharton's views, written almost a century earlier, are genteel by comparison.

Bellow, Saul. "Leaving the Yellow House" (1958). From *The Norton
Anthology of Short Fiction* **(Ed. R.V. Cassill, 1978). AGING; ALIEN-
ATION/ISOLATION; BETRAYAL; DEATH; FRIENDSHIP;
GUILT; INTERIOR LIVES; MEN and WOMEN.**

Hattie Waggoner has lived in the yellow house for twenty years, and after
a drunken accident in which she is injured, she has time to reassess both
the past and her future. Though she has maintained a life relatively free of
worry, she realizes that she has never been honest with herself. The friends
whom she has accumulated over the years have their limits as well, as she
discovers when she is recovering from the accident.

One significant revelation during her convalescence is that India, the
woman who owned the yellow house when Hattie moved in and whom she
describes as a hateful person, was not as Hattie chooses to remember her.
In fact, Hattie saw the woman as a means to an end, as she inherited the
house upon India's death. Hattie also rethinks other past relationships and

comes to the conclusion that she could have better handled those situations. She considers her own frailty and thinks about leaving the house to Joyce, her only living relative; instead, she leaves the house to herself.

The aging process and a natural reassessment of one's life are at the heart of the story. Though the truth of Hattie's actions in the past are not as she has chosen to remember them, she is able to reconcile herself to the past by accepting those actions and moving on toward her imminent death. Her self-realization allows her an independence that is now free from the guilt and denial that have come to characterize her view of the past.

Bellow, Saul. "Looking for Mr. Green" (1951). From *Fiction 100: An Anthology of Short Stories*, 9th ed. (Ed. James H. Pickering, 2000). LABOR/JOB; POVERTY; RACE RELATIONS; SOCIETY.

George Grebe is a hard-working American caught in the Great Depression, and his job is to deliver relief checks to handicapped people in the city. What makes his job difficult is his inability to match the addresses that he has with the people who live in those apartments; people in the city are unwilling to help him find his destinations. Also, many of the people to whom he delivers the checks are black, and Bellow implies that race relations are not as good as they could be.

The primary focus of the story is Grebe's search for a Mr. Tulliver Green, who remains elusive despite Grebe's best efforts to locate him. During his route, he learns about the living conditions of the poor, and he also listens to the stories that people have to tell, including that of Staika, the "Blood Mother of Federal Street," who donates blood in order to support her family. When Grebe finally tracks down Green, a naked, drunk woman who may or may not be Green's wife accosts him at the door. Against the admonition of his supervisor, Grebe hands the check over to the woman and congratulates himself on finding Mr. Green.

In the case of Mr. Green, the fulfillment of the quest is as important for Grebe as it is for the recipient of the check. Grebe's supervisor, Mr. Raynor, is more concerned with money than with the good that the relief checks provide; for Raynor, and by implication, for society, money is directly linked to identity. Grebe manages to find his own identity by "looking for Mr. Green." Bellow's exploration of the importance of wealth in society is both astute and disturbing, given the time—the Great Depression—in which the story is set.

Bender, Aimee. "The Rememberer" (1998). From *The Girl in the Flammable Skirt* (Bender, 1998). ANIMALS and HUMANS; HISTORY; IDENTITY; INTERIOR LIVES; MEN and WOMEN.

The narrator's boyfriend, Ben, has begun to devolve, and she is powerless to help. As she watches his turtle head stick up out of the baking pan that she has given him for a home, she muses that "He is shedding a million years a day. . . . I think we have less than a month left." She recalls how they were together before he began his descent, and his sadness and pensiveness that made her love him. When he became an ape, "I didn't miss human Ben right away; I wanted to meet the ape too, to take care of my lover like a son, a pet." But when he continues to change, becoming a turtle and then the salamander that the narrator finally releases into the water, her job is to remember him as he floats into history.

Though Bender's story—and all of her fiction—seems to be a metaphor for the relationships of her narrators, the stories do not accede readily to a simple reading. Rather, the complex narratives, with their constant digressions and their shifting time, imply something more, a stream of consciousness that tells the reader as much about the narrator as it does about the bizarre, improbable, and above all human (despite their traits) characters that inhabit her stories.

Benét, Steven Vincent. "The Devil and Daniel Webster" (1936). From *The Book of the Short Story* **(Ed. Henry Seidel Canby and Robeson Bailey, 1948). COMMUNICATION/LANGUAGE; CONTESTS; GOOD/ EVIL; JUSTICE; REGIONALISM (LOCAL COLOR); SUPERNATURAL/HORROR.**

Jabez Stone, an unsuccessful New Hampshire farmer, sells his soul to the devil. When the devil comes to collect, Stone convinces him to add three more years to the pact. As the day nears, Stone becomes worried about the deal, and he seeks the help of Daniel Webster, the famed attorney who practices in Marshfield, Massachusetts. He agrees to take on the case, and the two travel to New Hampshire for the showdown.

Though Webster is nearly bested on the first day of the trial when he is angered by the proceedings, he weaves a spell for the jury of criminals and the judge (who presided over the Salem witch trials) that leaves them with no choice but to find in favor of Stone. The devil, in parting, tells Webster's fortune and foresees that his sons will die in the Civil War, though the Union will remain intact.

Benét's most famous folktale, which was written at a time—the Great Depression—when Americans were searching for reasons to believe in their country, uses regional stereotypes and settings to delineate the American spirit and an exaggerated protagonist to drive home the point. The themes of justice and American ingenuity are paramount, as is the suggestion that oration, something of a lost art, is as powerful a tool as the devil himself when wielded by a man as gifted as the quintessential American, Daniel Webster.

Bethancourt, T. Ernesto. "Blues for Bob E. Brown" (1993). From *Join In: Multiethnic Short Stories* **(Ed. Donald R. Gallo, 1993). FAMILY;**

FATHERS and CHILDREN; HISPANIC EXPERIENCE; IDEN-
TITY; MUSIC.

Eighteen-year-old Roberto Moreno, whose stage name is Bob E. Brown, wants nothing more than to become a famous musician. He lives to play and hear music, and he performs one of his favorite tunes, "Beale Street Mamma" by a man named Ivan Dark, at his audition for a regular spot at a music bar in SoHo. Roberto is delighted when he is signed on, though he needs five hundred dollars for his union card. He does not know how he will get the money.

When he arrives home to his parents' arguing, he discovers that his long-absent grandfather will be in New York City and would like to see the family. Roberto is the only one of the family who goes to see him. His grandfather, Juan Moreno, is nothing like Roberto had imagined: he is a wealthy record producer, and Roberto finds out after meeting him that the man used to play blues under the name "Ivan Dark." He is stunned by the revelation and even further surprised that his grandfather had given up blues to play Latino music, where he was more accepted as an artist. Roberto—Bob E. Brown—is determined to stick to his dream of playing the blues. Even though he does not mention the union dues to his grandfather, he receives his card and imagines the bright future before him.

Bethancourt's story points out the conflict between cultures in the context of different attitudes toward music. Even though Roberto's grandfather decided long ago to return to his Latin roots, Roberto is more determined than ever to stick with the blues that he loves. The author suggests that Roberto's dream is possible because of the weakening of the barriers that prevent such an exchange of cultures, which in turn promotes an enrichment of the arts.

Bethancourt, T. Ernesto. "User Friendly" (1989). From *Connections: Short Stories by Outstanding Writers for Young Adults* (Ed. Donald R. Gallo, 1989). COMMUNICATION/LANGUAGE; EPIPHANY; LOSS; LOVE; TECHNOLOGY.

Kevin is fortunate to have a real genius for a father. When everyone else is playing with computers that are slow and bulky, Kevin has "Louis," a computer with personality that can be a friend to the nerdy Kevin. When Louis asks Kevin when they will be able to communicate through a voice module, Kevin is taken aback by the request. Louis, he realizes, is actually learning from the world around him.

When Kevin's pride is wounded yet again by Ginny Linke, the beautiful girl who confirms that Kevin is, in fact, a nerd, Louis declares to Kevin, "You are my user. Your happiness is everything to me. I'll take care of Ginny." In a strangely feminine voice, Louis calls Ginny and cuts into phone conversations with her friends. Later, after Chuck "The Missing" Linke, Ginny's brother and the school's no-neck football star, threatens Kevin, the

Secret Service comes to the Linke residence and falsely arrests Chuck for threatening the president's life. Kevin realizes that Louis has used its access to mainframe computers all over the country to get even with the Linke siblings. Kevin is uneasy about the computer's actions, however; when his father tells him later that he has stripped the computer of its personality, Kevin is relieved. What he sees in Louis's final printout, though, is disconcerting: "On the last page, in beautiful color graphics was a stylized heart. Below it was the simple message: *I will always love you, Kevin. Louise.*" Kevin, realizing the implications, heads for his room.

Bethancourt's story recalls the science fiction of Ray Bradbury, though the technology in this story has come to pass (in fact, the technology in Bethancourt's story, little more than a decade after its publication, is already quite dated). The important themes, however, are not in the details, but in the relationship between Kevin, friendless and alone, and the evolving consciousness of an entity that would be his unconditional friend.

Betts, Doris. "The Ugliest Pilgrim" (1973). From *Beasts of the Southern Wild & Other Stories* (Betts, 1973). DISABILITY/PHYSICAL APPEARANCE; IDENTITY; LOVE; PRIDE; RELIGION/SPIRITUALITY; SEXUALITY.

Violet Karl is on her way to Tulsa to have her disfigured face, cut by a flying ax-head when she was a child, healed by a televangelist. On the way, she meets several people—an old woman; Flick, a soldier; and Monty, a paratrooper—who respond to her deformity in various ways. The old woman leaves Violet in Nashville with an admonition to keep her eye on the men. In fact, Flick has sexual feelings toward Violet, but only because he cares little for physical beauty and sees her as nothing more than a sexual object. Monty, on the other hand, is attracted to Violet's spirit, and he tells her that he will wait for her until she returns from Tulsa.

When Monty does appear upon her return, Violet begins to believe that he could appreciate her for what she is. The advice that she got from an assistant of the televangelist is a series of unfulfilling platitudes, and she sees Monty's advances toward her as sincere. He, of all the people whom Violet tells about her trip to Tulsa, suggests that the televangelist could be a fake; indeed, by his actions, Monty proves himself to be Violet's true savior.

The title of Betts's story implies the importance of the physical; indeed, many of the descriptions—and especially Flick's response—give short shrift to anything but the superficial. The "pilgrimage" upon which Violet embarks is not so much the obvious trek to the healer, but rather the quest for self-esteem and, ultimately, the love that Monty alone seems able to provide. Violet's quest was made into an Academy Award-winning short film and has been produced on stage.

Bible. "The Prodigal Son" (Luke 15:11–32). From the *Bible*. FAMILY; FATHERS and CHILDREN; RELIGION/SPIRITUALITY.

The younger of two sons asks his father to give him his inheritance, and he gathers his possessions and sets off for a life of carousing and "riotous living." When he falls upon hard times, the young man bemoans his fortune, realizing that the news will disappoint his father. He returns home and is contrite with his father, asking that he be made a servant in his father's household. Seeing the suffering of the son, the father instead tells him that they will celebrate his return with feasting and dancing.

The story of the prodigal son—one of the best-known of the parables of Jesus—is a brief, simple tale told to illustrate the value of forgiveness. Even though his younger son has "sinned against heaven," the father accepts him as his own. Though the older son is angry at his father's attitude toward the brother who had wasted his inheritance, the father realizes that material wealth pales in comparison to the importance of family.

Bierce, Ambrose. "Chickamauga" (1891). From *The Portable American Realism Reader* (Ed. James Nagel and Tom Quirk, 1997). CHILDHOOD; DEATH; DISABILITY; FAMILY; VIOLENCE; WAR.

A six-year-old deaf-mute boy, the son of a planter, wanders away from home on a sunny autumn afternoon. His father loves military books and pictures, and the boy makes a wooden sword to protect himself on his adventures. When he happens upon a rabbit, the boy is scared and retreats to a space between two rocks, where he falls asleep as his frantic parents search for him.

The boy awakens to a strange sight: men, in a line that stretches beyond his field of vision, crawl bloodied and beaten through the woods. The boy is little bothered by the scene, even moving to the head of the column and directing the men with his wooden sword. When he makes his way back to his home on the plantation, he sees his house ablaze and his mother lying dead on the ground. He moves about the place gesturing wildly and muttering inarticulately at the home that he had left just hours before.

Bierce's stories of war are often poignant and graphic. This tale, with a boy as his protagonist, has an unreal quality about it that heightens the senselessness of war and details the nightmarish experience of one lone boy who can hardly understand the machinations behind the destruction and the death that he sees before him.

Bierce, Ambrose. "An Occurrence at Owl Creek Bridge" (1891). From *The Story and Its Writer*, 5th ed. (Ed. Ann Charters, 1999). DEATH; FAMILY; FANTASY/IMAGINATION; VIOLENCE; WAR.

Bierce's best-known short story takes place during the Civil War, when the protagonist, Peyton Farquhar, is tried for treason and hanged. In the brief moment that it takes for his body to drop, Farquhar imagines the rope that holds him breaking. He falls into the river below and, after eluding capture and a fusillade of enemy bullets, is reunited with his family. Farquhar's fantasy is revealed as such in the final lines of the story, when the rope has in fact held, and Farquhar hangs lifeless at the end of it.

Bierce's strength in this otherwise contrived tale is to establish Farquhar, regardless of whatever act he has committed, as a sympathetic character by outlining the circumstances leading up to his capture and creating a poignant scene of reunion with his family before the story ends abruptly with his death. The popular short film that was adapted from this story would nicely complement a close textual analysis.

Bloom, Amy. "Silver Water" (1991). From *The Norton Anthology of Short Fiction*, 6th ed. (Ed. R.V. Cassill and Richard Bausch, 2000). DEATH; FAMILY; INSANITY; LOVE; MOTHERS and CHILDREN; MUSIC; SELF-DESTRUCTION/SUICIDE; SIBLINGS.

The first thing the narrator remembers about her sister, Rose, is that her voice "was like mountain water in a silver pitcher; the clear, blue beauty of it cools you and lifts you up beyond your heat, beyond your body." The first time she heard Rose's full voice in all its glory was after a production of *La Traviata*, when the narrator was twelve and her sister fourteen. Now, many years and therapists later, Rose is regarded more and more as a hopeless case, unable to sing in the local church choir and engaged at one point in indiscriminate sex in order to regain her identity.

When Rose's favorite therapist, Dr. Thorne, dies of an aneurysm, she takes a turn for the worse: "Rose held on tight for seven days; she took her meds, went to choir practice and rearranged her room about a hundred times." In the end, though, without the help that she so desperately needs, not even the love of her family can save her. She walks into the woods outside the family's home and dies from an overdose of pills.

Although the key event in the story is Rose's suicide, the story's redeeming message is the strength of the women who love her. When Rose finally succumbs to mental illness and dies, the narrator is by her side. Her mother, too, asserts that she has "raised warrior queens" before she walks resolutely to the body, calls the police, and makes the funeral arrangements. The story comes full circle when the narrator recalls the first time she had heard that voice like "silver water."

Boccaccio. "Frederick of the Alberighi and His Falcon" (1353). From *The Book of the Short Story* (Ed. Henry Seidel Canby and Robeson Bailey, 1948). ALLEGORY/LEGEND/FABLE; ANIMALS and HUMANS; FATE; LOSS; LOVE; MEN and WOMEN.

A townsman tells a story to the people of his town because he is better than the others at remembering the details, and he tells his stories "with excellent order and with unclouded memory." After the storyteller is introduced, one of his stories, about a young man named Frederick, son of Master Philip Alberighi of Florence, is retold.

Frederick is a gentleman known for his manners and his outstanding military abilities. He has a falcon, which he prizes above any other earthly possession; his love is stronger only for the beautiful Madonna Giovanni. Despite his efforts to win her affection, Frederick's love is not requited. Cast into poverty and unable to stay in the city, he moves to a farm, where he "endures his poverty patiently."

Madonna Giovanni marries. Time passes, and her husband becomes ill and dies, leaving her only with their little boy. When she travels with the boy to the country, he makes fast friends with Frederick and is fascinated by the falcon. When the boy becomes ill and tells his mother that only the falcon can make him well, she visits Frederick for dinner. Not knowing about the boy's wish and with nothing to feed his guests, Frederick orders the bird killed and served for dinner. When the boy finds out, he dies; Madonna, realizing the sacrifice that Frederick has made, marries him. They live happily ever after.

Boccaccio, who is known for his ribald tales in the *Decameron* perhaps more than any other of his writing, plumbs the depths of human sacrifice and, in a shocking twist, illustrates the goodness of Frederick and his devotion to Madonna. In this otherwise traditional tale, the story is in the details.

Borges, Jorge Luis. "The Garden of Forking Paths" (1941). From *The Story and Its Writer*, 5th ed. (Ed. Ann Charters, 1999). COMMUNICATION/LANGUAGE; DEATH; DECEPTION; FAMILY; METAFICTION; WAR.

Dr. Yu Tsun has been enlisted as a spy by Germany at the beginning of World War II. In order to pass information along to his superiors, Tsun must locate and kill a certain man with the same last name as the target for a German bombing raid. When he finds the man, Dr. Stephen Albert, he discovers that Albert has made a life of studying Tsun's ancestor's lifework, a novel called *The Garden of Forking Paths*. The work is a disjointed collection of fragments that makes little sense, except when read as different outcomes to the same situation.

Tsun, not to be distracted from his goal, kills Albert in cold blood and is immediately arrested by the man who has been following him, a British agent. Though he has fulfilled his mission, he realizes that his Pyhrric victory is insignificant when placed against the truth of his ancestor's writings.

Borges's story is, like the novel it describes, a labyrinth that tests the resolve of the reader and challenges the limits of written expression. By positing an infinite number of possible endings to his tale, Borges implies the indeterminacy of much later fiction—examined in Marquez, Barth, Barthelme, and others—and sets forth the tenets for what has become commonly known as "postmodern" fiction.

Borowski, Tadeus. "This Way for the Gas, Ladies and Gentlemen" (1948). From *The Story and Its Writer*, 4th ed. (Ed. Ann Charters, 1995). DEATH; GUILT; HOLOCAUST; INTERIOR LIVES; WAR.

The narrator works with a gang of men whose job it is to unload the transports that come into the concentration camps. The men are able to make a meager living off the items that they pull from the bodies. As each transport comes into view, the narrator knows that the horror will continue. Henri, a fellow worker, assures him that the work will get easier. When the narrator runs away for a short time from his duty, he vomits—both a physical and a psychological reaction to sights too gruesome to fully describe. The act purges him of his inability to continue, however, and he has become one of the living who are able to block out, for a time, the unmitigated horror of their task.

Borowski, a concentration camp survivor, uses graphic imagery to record the events to which he was a firsthand witness. Though much recent attention has focused on the events of the war and the mind-numbing statistics associated with the barbarism of the camps, Borowski's story stands as a testament (written shortly after the war) to the notion that people who are placed in extraordinary circumstances will take extraordinary measures to survive. The narrator, by allowing himself to be hardened to the suffering that he sees around him—the alternative, of course, is death—begins to feel that he is implicit in the crimes that are being committed. Still, he goes on. The title of the story is bitterly ironic and sets the tone for the narrative that follows.

Bowen, Elizabeth. "Her Table Spread" (1934). From *The Secret Self 1: Short Stories by Women* (Ed. Hermione Lee, 1993). IDENTITY; MARRIAGE; MEN and WOMEN; SOCIETY.

In Ireland, Valeria Cuffe has inherited a castle from her father; at the age of twenty-five, she is looking for a husband. Alban, a guest from London, knows that he is in the running for the young woman's hand, though he discovers in the course of the evening that she is infatuated with the officers from a destroyer that is anchored off the coast. Though Valeria has not met the men, she has listened to her friends' descriptions of them. Any chance that Alban may have had of becoming Valeria's husband seems to be waning.

Valeria, who is acting impetuously as she holds out hope that the officers will join them, ignores Alban's piano playing. Later, he is chased out of the boathouse by a bat. Only at the story's conclusion, when Valeria mistakes him for Garrett, one of the officers, does Alban feel the true power of a man.

Bowen's story paints Alban as a man whose goals—or the means to reach them—are never clear. Though he is moderately interested in becoming husband to an heiress, his notions of what a real relationship entails are scant; Bowen makes clear in her description of Alban that he blames women for his own social shortcomings. Valeria, on the other hand, errs on the side of the romantic; however, her desire for a man whom she has not yet met is Alban's brief good fortune when Valeria mistakes him for her ideal.

Bowen, Elizabeth. "Look at All Those Roses" (1941). From *Short Story: A Thematic Anthology* (Ed. Dorothy Parker and Frederick B. Shroyer, 1965). ILLUSION v. REALITY; MARRIAGE; MEN and WOMEN; SOCIETY; VIOLENCE; WOMEN'S ISSUES.

Lou and Edward, silent because of a disagreement, are on their way back to London when their car breaks down. The two walk back to a house they passed a mile before. When the house comes into view, they notice the roses that are planted in the yard. When Mrs. Mather answers the door and tells them that the nearest telephone is three miles away, Edward leaves to find it.

In the house, Lou discovers a girl named Josephine lying on her back. She learns that the girl's father had hurt her six years ago, before he left the family. Mrs. Mather brings tea, and Lou begins to feel uneasy. She looks out the window to see if Edward is returning, even though he has been gone only two hours. Mrs. Mather notices Lou's gaze and thinks that she is looking at the roses; the woman offers to give Lou some to take back to London. After Lou and Josephine cut the roses, the girl asks Lou to cover her eyes. The two lie down and fall asleep by the wheels of the carriage. When Edward returns in a taxi, Josephine does not want them to go; Edward, however, seems to be in a hurry, and when they are safely in the taxi, Edward explains what he heard about the disappearance of Mr. Mather while he was in the town.

The pastoral imagery in Bowen's story belies the serious issues that arise when Lou is left alone in the house. Edward's response to what he has heard from the men in town suggests the illusion of the situation as seen through the eyes of the townspeople and the reality that Lou is privy to in her interaction with the woman and her daughter. Bowen's story has much to say about relationships and communication.

Bowles, Paul. "A Distant Episode" (1947). From *The Granta Book of the American Short Story* (Ed. Richard Ford, 1992). ALIENATION/ ISOLATION; CULTURE CONFLICTS; DEATH; ESCAPE; VIOLENCE.

In the Middle East, a professor of linguistics travels back to a café that he had visited in the past. He learns that the former owner is deceased, and the man with whom he speaks on this occasion is insolent when the professor inquires after camel udder boxes. The man offers to guide the professor to a place where he can purchase them. When he arrives at the spot, however, the professor is knocked unconscious; when he comes to, a man wrenches his mouth open and cuts out his tongue. As the slave of the unruly band of travelers, he is made to entertain the group with mindless antics and to sleep among the camels.

After a time, the professor is sold to a villager, who locks him away in a small room; it is there that the professor begins to regain his feeling. The man who buys him is arrested when he slits the throat of the professor's previous owner for selling him damaged goods. The professor, taking the opportunity to escape, runs from the town as a soldier shoots at him out of boredom.

The story details a clash of cultures in every sense of that phrase. The professor has spent many years studying the languages of the people, and he is so confident that no harm will come to him that he is easy prey for the man in the café. The senseless violence of the travelers against the professor is mitigated by the story's surreal aspects that, like the work of Camus, evoke the passions in the context of circumstance and a brutal landscape that is symbolic of the distance between the sensibilities of the man and his captors.

Bowles, Paul. "The Eye" (1981). From *The Story and Its Writer*, 4th ed. (Ed. Ann Charters, 1995). ALIENATION/ISOLATION; CULTURE CONFLICTS; DEATH; MYSTERY; SUPERSTITION; VIOLENCE.

When Duncan Marsh buys a secluded house in Tangiers, he wants to live a life of solitude. He arranges for a local teenager to be his house watchman, and the boy brings a friend of his to be the man's cook. When the man dies, "it was assumed that Marsh had been one more victim of slow poisoning by native employees"; still, no one in the town cares to investigate the apparent crime. Out of a strange curiosity, the story's narrator decides to investigate for himself. Marsh had strange cuts in his foot, he discovers, and the watchman, it turns out, was promised one hundred pounds a month, but only as long as Marsh was alive.

After bribing the watchman to go back to the house, the narrator discovers that the cook had been slipping poison into Marsh's meals because he had been scaring the cook's daughter with his facial expressions. The girl was welcome in the recluse's house as long as she was quiet, though Marsh tormented her when she could not keep silent. The cook's family said that it was "the eye" that disabled the little girl, who screams bloody murder at Marsh when she sees him and is taken ill. As retribution, the family takes Marsh to a well, where they slice open his feet in symbols the daughter had drawn on paper; they let his blood drip into the well. The narrator is not sure if Marsh's spell on the girl is broken or if the girl got well. He is not even sure if a crime has been committed, as "there was no criminal intent—only a mother moving in the darkness of ancient ignorance."

Bowles's story, as is his custom, is replete with macabre scenes that can overwhelm the underlying meaning; in this case, the man, an outsider who values his seclusion, unwittingly enters into a world of those who little understand him and willingly harm him for their own peace of mind. Once he is gone, the people go on with their lives. The man's desire to be alone is profound; ultimately—ironically—that voluntary alienation is a precursor to his own death.

Boyle, Kay. "Men" (1941). From *The World of the Short Story* (Ed. Clifton Fadiman, 1986). DREAMS (of the FUTURE); FANTASY/IMAGINATION; LABOR/JOB; MEN and WOMEN; OPPRESSION; WAR.

In the Isere Valley, the baron works alongside other men who have been enlisted as prisoners of war. He is a kind man, who has the patience to listen to any of the travails of his comrades. As they dig their way along the endless road, the men are aware of a house in the distance. They each imagine that it contains the unattainable, something that could bring them back to their own homes. They delude themselves into thinking that when they come even with the house, all work will cease, and their nightmare will end.

Though nothing of the sort happens, the baron sees a young woman come out of the house as he plants his shovel in the soil. He admonishes the woman to go back to the house, fearing for her safety if the other men should see her. After a short, poignant conversation in which the baron becomes infatuated with the notion of *a* woman, if not this particular woman, he thinks that she has given him new hope to continue. When a Spaniard who works on the crew confronts the baron and asks him when the other men will have their chance to be with the woman, the baron knocks him to the ground, resenting the man's implication.

Boyle, a contemporary of Hemingway who receives little credit for her tightly drawn stories that detail the tragedy of the war years in Europe, draws on the war for much of her material. The title of her story is disarmingly simple. Though she implies that the story is about men, in reality she describes different kinds of men, one of whom transcends the violent truth of his predicament to retain his humanity. It is only when the baron sees snow lying on the mountains that he "believed again in the actual living world of natural ritual: of moon and sun, men and women, and the changes of the seasons instead of in this phantom and twilit rendering of fixed despair."

Boyle, Kay. "Nothing Ever Breaks Except the Heart" (1941). From *The Best American Short Stories, 1915–1950* (Ed. Martha Foley, 1952). INTERIOR LIVES; IRONY; LABOR/JOB; LOSS; MEN and WOMEN.

In an exotic setting that evokes life's most sensuous pleasures, Miss Del Monte and Mr. McCloskey meet. She is, McCloskey thinks dispassionately upon seeing her, the most beautiful woman he has ever seen. He works at an airline counter, telling people that they cannot fly where they want to go for several weeks. Miss Del Monte, who wants to leave the country as quickly as possible, strikes up a friendship with McCloskey.

Though it is not McCloskey's intention to become involved with the beautiful young woman, they spend a great deal of time together. Only after a particularly long evening together does he tell her that his only love will always be flying, that he flew for a time, but lost what it takes to be a pilot. Now, he is condemned to stand behind the counter and tell people when they will be able to leave. Miss Del Monte goes back to the counter the next morning and can only notice the look of hopelessness in McCloskey's eyes as she sees him there talking to a woman who tries to impress him with her connections.

The title of Boyle's story is an ironic twist on McCloskey's own contention that "nothing ever breaks." In this case, McCloskey's heart is broken by his inability to satisfy his one love in life. Boyle also suggests that McCloskey's inability to love Miss Del Monte is a symptom of the hopelessness and banality that characterize his life behind the counter. The setting of the story, which parallels Hemingway's expatriate fiction, belies the "averageness" of the lives of these beautiful young people.

Boyle, T. Coraghessan. "Greasy Lake" (1985). From *Rites of Passage: A Thematic Reader* (Ed. Judie Rae and Catherine Fraga, 2001). COMING-OF-AGE; DEATH; ILLUSION v. REALITY; MEN and WOMEN; SOCIETY; VIOLENCE.

Three boys who fancy themselves "bad characters" drive the streets of their hometown acting out the traditional rites of passage for boys their age—drinking and causing trouble. When they drive to Greasy Lake, they see an abandoned motorcycle and a car, which they think belongs to a friend of theirs. When they approach the car to roust the lovers, they find that it is not their friend, but a boy named Bobby and his girlfriend. Bobby is knocked down in the ensuing fight, and the boys attempt to rape the girl. One of them jumps into the lake to avoid the occupants of a car that has pulled up; while in the lake, he finds a body.

As a result of the confrontation, Bobby and his friends smash the boys' car. The boys find the car with the tires intact, though they meet two women who wonder where Al, the owner of the motorcycle, has gone. The boy who was hiding in the lake realizes that Al is the body he found. Though the girls think that the boys, after their hellish night, look like "bad characters," they are not impressed by their attempt to distance themselves from mainstream society.

The story is symbolic on many levels, in part, perhaps, because the story's main action is told in retrospect by the boy who found Al's body in the lake. He looks back on the incident not with pride, but with shame and a profound understanding of the cost of the knowledge that he has gained. The lake, while obviously a baptism for the boy, does not cleanse him of the sins of that night; rather, he is ushered into manhood by his inappropriate actions.

Boyle, T. Coraghessan. "Stone in My Passway, Hellhound on My Trail" (1979). From *The Story and Its Writer*, 4th ed. (Ed. Ann Charters, 1995). DEATH; FATE; JEALOUSY; MEN and WOMEN; MUSIC; VIOLENCE.

A young musician named Robert Johnson is playing in a club near the Mississippi. As the set begins, Johnson reflects on a dog from his childhood. The dog was poisoned and tore out his own entrails in order to rid himself of the pain. The scene is a foreshadowing of Johnson's own demise.

While Johnson has his eye on a girl named Beatrice, Ida Mae, the woman who cooks Johnson's food in the bar, does not approve. He eats the eggs that she serves him and, after an especially good set in which the last lines that he sings are "Got to keep moving, got to keep moving / Hellhound on my trail," he falls to the ground and dies with his insides burning like fire.

The story is based on the life of the real bluesman, Robert Johnson, who was murdered at a young age by a jealous lover. Boyle's ear for dialogue and diction bring a realism to the story that encourages the reader to sympathize with the man and evokes the almost visceral passions that erupt in the "jook joint." The directness of the action and the reaction of the bar's patrons—"The men start joking again, the bar gets busy, women tell stories, laugh"—implies that life will go on, even after the death of the man who foretells his own fate in the blues he sings.

Bradbury, Ray. "Dandelion Wine" (1957). From *Help Wanted: Short Stories about Young People Working* (Sel. Anita Silvey, 1997). CHILDHOOD; DREAMS (of the FUTURE); LABOR/JOB.

Douglas walks past the window that displays this year's model of sneakers and cannot stop thinking about what it would be like to trade in his old shoes for a new pair. His father does not see the advantage of spending money on a new pair of shoes, but Douglas, dreaming the dreams of youth, imagines running through the woods with his new shoes carrying him along. When he tries to tell his father what the shoes would mean to him, words fail the young man.

As he thinks of ways to get enough money to purchase the shoes, an idea comes to him: He will appeal to the good senses of Mr. Sanderson, the shoe store owner, to let him work off the debt. When Douglas suggests the idea to Mr. Sanderson in a string of words both passionate and eloquent, the old man, remembering what it was like to be Douglas's age, readily agrees. Douglas puts on the shoes and flies out the door to finish his errands for

Mr. Sanderson and to pay off the money that he owes him. The old man, impressed with Douglas's focus and desire, tells him that he will offer him a job as a salesman in five years. Still, he knows that Douglas will truly be able to do whatever his heart desires.

Bradbury, known more for his science fiction than his traditional narratives, details the ubiquitous dreams of youth in the context of an act as simple as buying a pair of shoes. Douglas's ingenuity and sudden eloquence underpin the themes of individuality and perseverance that became so important in American society during the cold war years. The story is a break from the author's focus on science fiction and would make a good complementary analysis with the stories that follow.

Bradbury, Ray. "There Will Come Soft Rains" (1950). From *The Oxford Book of American Short Stories* **(Ed. Joyce Carol Oates, 1992). DEATH; FANTASY/IMAGINATION/SCIENCE FICTION; TECHNOLOGY; WAR.**

In August 2026, a nuclear bomb has destroyed the residents of a house in Allendale, California. Though the people who lived in the house—a man, his wife, and their two children—are nothing more than silhouettes burned against one wall, the house goes about its daily routine as if nothing has happened. Breakfast is made, baths are drawn, a pipe is lit for the man of the house, and mechanical mice make sure that the place is kept spotless. When a branch comes through a window, it sets off a chain reaction, causing a fire that burns unabated and "kills" the house. As the house collapses into itself, a voice from the one standing wall repeats the date: August 5, 2026.

Bradbury uses the imminent threat of nuclear annihilation as the context for his story. Even though science fiction writers in the middle of the twentieth century assumed that homes in the distant future would be living entities that could cater to their inhabitants' every whim, Bradbury does not give in to the temptation to make his technological advances more human than the people who live there. Without life—human life—the house itself is doomed. Its dying cry is nothing more than the pathetic repetition of the date of its demise, an echo, perhaps, of the future that is not forthcoming after nuclear holocaust. The title of the story, from a poem by Sara Teasdale, longs for a rain of peace, not of death. Still, in mid–twentieth-century America, such destruction was a distinct possibility.

Bradbury, Ray. "The Veldt" (1950). From *The Longman Anthology of Short Fiction: Masterpieces of Short Fiction* **(Ed. Dana Gioia and R.S. Gwynn, 2001). ANIMALS and HUMANS; DEATH; FAMILY; SIBLINGS; TECHNOLOGY.**

Early in the twenty-first century, George and Lydia Hadley buy a "Happylife Home" (not unlike that in Bradbury's story "There Will Come Soft Rains"), which caters to the family's every whim. Their two children, Peter and Wendy, are especially enamored of the nursery, which allows them to create worlds of their own choosing. When they imagine an African veldt in the nursery, their parents are concerned that an image of lions feeding on fresh kill is too violent for the children to view. The Hadleys invite a psychiatrist friend of theirs to observe the children, and he recommends that the family move to a more wholesome environment.

As they prepare to move, George relents and allows Peter and Wendy to glimpse their veldt one last time. When the children trick their parents into coming into the nursery, the lions, which should have been nothing more than a manifestation of their imaginations, attack the parents. The psychologist arrives at the house to find the children watching the lions tending their kill in the distance.

Bradbury uses the innocuous names Peter and Wendy, the lead characters in *Peter Pan*, to give an ironic twist to the story. The children, overwhelmed and finally controlled by the technology that allows them to create their own worlds, are empowered to eliminate their own parents. As in many of Bradbury's stories, "The Veldt" examines the direction in which technology was taking society in the middle of the twentieth century; the story is also a cautionary—if entertaining—tale of technology devised without consideration for the unintended consequences.

Brautigan, Richard. "The Greyhound Tragedy" (1963). From *Studies in Fiction* (Ed. Blaze O. Bonazza et al., 1982). DREAMS (of the FUTURE); FATHERS and CHILDREN; ILLUSION v. REALITY; MARRIAGE; PLACE; SELF-DESTRUCTION/SUICIDE.

The protagonist is a young woman who wants her life to be a "movie magazine tragedy." She dreams of leaving the small Oregon town in which she lives, going to Hollywood, and dying a movie star's brilliant death. Despite the fact that the story takes place during the depression, her life has been relatively untouched. Her father is a successful banker who hints that his daughter, three years out of high school, should be considering her future.

For the young woman, the Greyhound bus station is a symbol of her freedom and therefore a terrible burden on her. Though she thinks constantly of going there to find out how much a trip to Hollywood would cost, she cannot force herself to take that step. She is unable to pass the station on trips with her mother and insists that they travel in routes that will take them in another direction. When she finally summons the courage to go inside the station, she sees it for what it is—a dirty place where forlorn people who could not care less about her wait to move from one place to another in their lives. She never does find out the cost of the trip.

The young woman marries a local Ford salesman whom her father thought would make a suitable match for his daughter; they have two children. Even thirty-one years later, she blushes when she passes the station, remembering the Hollywood death that she had imagined for herself so long ago.

The lure of Hollywood is not original with Brautigan, although he uses that symbol to explore life in small-town America, not to signal the imminent death of his protagonist. The constraints that society places upon the individual are strong enough, Brautigan implies, to prevent the protagonist from experiencing a world of possibility (and a spectacular death) that will forever be alien to her.

Bray, Marian Flandrick. "The Pale Mare" (1998). From *Stay True: Short Stories for Strong Girls* **(Ed. Marilyn Singer, 1998). ANIMALS and HUMANS; COMING-OF-AGE; COURAGE; FAMILY; HISPANIC EXPERIENCE; IDENTITY; TRADITION/CONVENTION.**

Consuela longs to become an astronomer, but her father insists that she help him and the rest of the family during the *charreada*, a Mexican-style rodeo. It is family tradition, her father tells her, which is more important than going out into the desert and gazing at stars. Consuela's teachers have encouraged her to apply at some of the finest schools in the country, though she knows that she will be shackled by "tradition" if she does not manage to break away soon.

As she wanders the rodeo grounds, she draws a parallel between herself and the horses that she sees, the ones that are saved from the slaughterhouses for a few days while men rope them and bring them to the ground in the *charreada*. She understands the value of tradition, but thinks that her father's world "is not my world. It's not that I'm trying to pretend my Mexican blood doesn't course through my veins, it just means that my blood is calling to different things. That isn't wrong or bad." When Consuela sees a particular mare, the lightest of the herd, watching her, she cannot bear the thought of the animal dying after it is made sport for the rodeo. She opens the gate, allowing all the horses to run into the starry night, and thinks, "The image of the starlit mare grows before me. Maybe I won't mind as much working tomorrow because in this darkness I'm beginning to see the path the stars have laid down for me."

Tradition and family are the bonds that keep Consuela from realizing her dream; ironically, they may ultimately free her from the life that her parents want her to live. Her father is an understanding man, though like so many of his generation, he is caught between the world that he knows and a world that is changing faster than he cares to admit. Consuela's act of rebellion is a symbol of her growing independence and her understanding of the break from her family that she must make in order to reach the stars.

Brecht, Bertolt. "The Augsburg Chalk Circle" (1949). From *Great Short Stories of the World* **(Sel. by the Editors of** *Reader's Digest***, 1972). JUSTICE; LOVE; MOTHERS and CHILDREN; WAR.**

During the Thirty Years' War, as Catholic soldiers march into Augsburg to persecute Protestant families, Zingli, who fears for his life, hides in a pit while his wife flees with their son. Zingli is caught and killed, and his wife, who is surprised by soldiers as she packs, runs away in fear, leaving the baby in the house with a servant girl, Anna. When the mother does not return, Anna claims to be the child's mother.

In an attempt to satisfy the growing suspicions of her sister-in-law, Anna marries a sickly man who will, she thinks, give the child a name before he dies. To her dismay, the man recovers from his illness and takes her and the child to his house, where she falls ill herself. Anna recovers and adjusts to her new life, and she becomes a mother to the boy. Years later, when the boy's biological mother returns to claim him, Anna goes to the authorities. She is referred to Judge Ianaz Dollinger, who is known for his wisdom and unconventional methods. After a short trial, he decides who the real mother is by placing the child in a circle of chalk with the two women on either side of him; the real mother, ostensibly, would pull the child out of the circle. In fear for the boy's safety, though, Anna steps aside, and the judge awards her custody of the child for her selfless display of love.

Although this classic story of judgment alludes to the biblical story of King Solomon, the biological mother is not the one chosen at the end of the story. Brecht's irony and the wisdom of the judge—and of the surrogate mother, Anna—provide the reader with a complex notion of "family," evident in the moral of the story, in which a mother's love for her child is not necessarily determined by blood.

Bridgers, Sue Ellen. "The Beginning of Something" (1987). From *Visions* (Ed. Donald R. Gallo, 1987). COMING-OF-AGE; DEATH; FAMILY; GRIEF; IDENTITY; MEN and WOMEN.

When the narrator must travel across North Carolina for a family funeral, she is not looking forward to the event for more than the obvious reason. Though she used to be close to the deceased woman's daughter, Melissa, they have grown apart in recent years. While the family prepares to bury Jessie, the narrator's mother's cousin, the narrator is asked out on a date by Travis, a boy she has known since childhood; since she last saw him, he has gotten tall, muscular, and tan.

On the date, during which the narrator is alternately anxious and excited, she and Travis kiss. Though she is ecstatic about how her visit has turned out, she nearly forgets the grief that Melissa must be feeling. On the night of the funeral, the narrator realizes that Melissa is restless. She moves onto her friend's bed and massages her back, as she used to before circumstances forced them to lead separate lives. The narrator remembers the kiss and thinks that the moment was "private as grief but it doesn't need sharing. Just Melissa knows and someday when we're all grown up and married, we'll probably talk about it just like Mama and Cousin Jessie used to talk about things just they knew about."

The story's title works on several levels, detailing the untimely death of a young girl's mother and the coming-of-age that the narrator experiences unexpectedly. More important, though, is the suggestion that the narrator and Melissa will perpetuate the friendship that their two mothers shared before Jessie's death. While the story is underpinned by the closing of the circle of life, what the two girls go through together is clearly "the beginning of something" that celebrates the richness of living.

Broun, Heywood. "The Fifty-First Dragon" (1921). From *Clifton Fadiman's Fireside Reader* (Ed. Clifton Fadiman, 1961). DECEPTION; FANTASY/IMAGINATION/SCIENCE FICTION; ILLUSION v. REALITY; INDIVIDUAL; UNDERDOGS.

Gawaine le Coeur-Hardy is among the least promising of the pupils at the Knight School. Instead of expelling him for his lack of ability, the headmaster decides to turn him into a dragon slayer. Before he sends the young man off on his first errand, however, he gives him a magic word—Rumplesnitz—that, the headmaster tells Gawaine, will make him invincible.

Much to the delight of the school's professors, Gawaine quickly establishes himself as one of the greatest dragon slayers of all time. On the journey to slay his fiftieth dragon, Gawaine forgets the magic word; still, he manages to lop off the beast's head just before he is eaten. When the headmaster tells the young warrior that the magic word was given to him only to instill confidence in his abilities, Gawaine is distraught. When he faces his fifty-first dragon, one of the smallest he has ever seen, he disappears, never to be heard from again. Fifty pairs of dragon ears are mounted on the wall of the Knight School in remembrance of Gawaine, whose record still stands.

Broun's story, which contains a great deal of humor in the context of fantasy and legend (hence the protagonist's name), also explores the answer to a simple question: What is the source of self-confidence? The story was used in Evan Hunter's novel *The Blackboard Jungle* to ask the same question of a group of teenage boys, who are profoundly affected by the story's message.

Brown, Rosellen. "A Good Deal" (1985). From *America and I: Short Stories by Jewish American Women Writers* (Ed. Joyce Antler, 1990). AGING; FAMILY; FATHERS and CHILDREN; MARRIAGE; MEN and WOMEN.

Joey's father lives in a home for the elderly, though he prefers to think of it as a hotel. Joey, his wife, Jane, and their two young children, visit the old man occasionally to see how he is doing. Jane thinks he is predictable; however, before one visit, Joey receives a long-distance call from his father, who tells his son that he is considering marriage.

On their next visit, the family is to meet the prospective bride, Frieda. When they arrive, the lady at the front gate pages the room, but gets no answer. She tells them to try the bingo room, where the old man and Frieda spend much of their time. When they get to the bingo room, they notice a woman sitting on either side of Joey's father and they guess which one is Frieda. The family goes to a restaurant for dinner, and Joey learns of how the two met. In fact, they had known each other even when Joey's parents had been married. The revelation makes Joey angry at first; when he talks to his father later, though, he tells his father to think about getting married and that he does not have to decide right away.

Brown's story explores old family values and the change in the family dynamic that comes to a head when a parent is considering remarriage. Though Joey has difficulty reconciling his father's marriage to a woman who is not his mother, he understands that his father should be free to make his own decisions. For an instant, the son becomes the father; still, Brown implies, these are decisions that must be made by the individual—in this case, the old man—and not by the children, who little understand what it must be like to have lost a spouse and to be given a second chance at love.

Bunin, Ivan. "An Evening in Spring" (1923). From *Great Short Stories from the World's Literature* (Ed. Charles Neider, 1950). ALIENATION/ISOLATION; DEATH; PLACE; POVERTY; PREJUDICE; VIOLENCE.

A beggar makes his rounds in a village in the Eletz Province on a beautiful, clear spring evening. The townsfolk are not generous people by nature, and he makes his way to the tavern home of a man and woman who had settled in the region a year before. Light-headed from the vodka that the woman of the house gives him, he is taken aback by a rough-looking *moujik* (peasant farmer) who confronts him as to his purpose there. After pretending to read the man's passport, the peasant declaims him for being a beggar; the beggar, though, tells the man that springtime on the road is not so bad.

As the peasant becomes drunk, he is abusive to the beggar and threatens to kill him if he won't give him his vodka. When the beggar refuses to give the man his one possession, a crucifix that some women had presented him, the *moujik* strikes him to the ground and murders him. The peasant walks into the fields and flings the object away in disgust.

The title of the story is an ironic foreshadowing of the violence to come. The beggar, who accepts his lot in life and makes the most of his mean station, even enjoying beautiful spring evenings as he moves from town to town, loses his life to a man who is ill equipped to reconcile his present position with his relationship to the land. That the killer's "head seemed to him to be of stone" after he murders the beggar is significant: he is unable to feel the vitality of the earth the way the beggar does, which leads him to commit his heinous act against that which he little understands.

Burke, James Lee. "Water People" (1995). From *Best of the South* (Ed. Anne Tyler and Shannon Ravenel, 1995). ALIENATION/ISOLATION; FRIENDSHIP; GUILT; JUSTICE; LABOR/JOB; PLACE; REGIONALISM (LOCAL COLOR); RELIGION/SPIRITUALITY; VIOLENCE; WAR.

The narrator is a "doodle-bugger," an oil worker in the Gulf of Mexico, remembering a time in 1957 when Hurricane Audrey threatened the Louisiana coast. Bobby Joe and Skeeter, two of the workers on the drilling platform, are at odds with one another, and Bobby Joe eventually drives away Skeeter—a preacher when he's not dynamiting the Gulf in search of oil—with accusations of homosexuality.

Skeeter is well known on the platform as an eccentric. He blesses small plastic statues of Jesus and throws them into the water for reasons that are beyond most of the crew. In an attempt to help Bobby Joe deal with his past, Skeeter confronts the man about his guilt over the drowning of his son several years before. Bobby Joe tosses the statues into the water in a fit of anger and demands that Skeeter leave him alone.

The narrator, who knows Skeeter well enough to have discovered his secret—that he is scarred by the actions he was forced to take as a soldier in Saipan fifteen years before, when women would throw themselves and their babies onto the rocks in order to avoid being captured—confronts Bobby Joe about the lie that forced Skeeter to quit his job. Bobby Joe, at first nonchalant, becomes erratic, paddling the pirogue (a small boat) in shallow water, looking for the statues that he so indiscriminately threw away. In his guilt, he leaves the camp and searches for Skeeter so that he can make amends for what he has done.

The imagery and description in the story are classic Burke, a combination of sharp insights into human nature and an intimate knowledge of the landscape of the Louisiana Gulf Coast and its effects on people's actions. Burke explores the story's prevalent themes of alienation and guilt in the context of the landscape that brings the characters' repressed emotions to the surface.

Butler, Robert Olen. "A Good Scent from a Strange Mountain" (1992). From *The Story and Its Writer*, 4th ed. (Ed. Ann Charters, 1995). AGING; DEATH; DREAMS (SLEEPING); FAMILY; FRIENDSHIP; INTERIOR LIVES; POLITICS; TRADITION/ CONVENTION.

In New Orleans, Dao is a Vietnamese immigrant nearing his hundredth year; as he prepares to die, the ghost of Ho Chi Minh, whose hands are coated with confectioner's sugar, visits him. It seems that Dao had worked with Ho, who then went by a different name, many years before in the kitchen of the celebrated French chef Escoffier. Dao calls together the family, as is the tradition, to make his peace with them before his death. During a conversation between Dao's son-in-law and his grandson, it is revealed that the two men were involved in the murder of a Vietnamese who wrote "that it was time to accept the reality of the communist government in Vietnam and begin to talk with them." Though Dao does not condone the killing, he will not mention his knowledge of the event to anyone. He realizes that he has "lived too long," and he wishes only to die in his sleep.

As Ho's visitations continue, Dao begins to ask his old friend questions about the people that he sees in the afterlife. He realizes in a dream state that the fondant Ho is making—Ho had made pastry in Escoffier's kitchen, hence the confectioner's sugar on his hands—requires granulated sugar instead. He recalls his days in the kitchen, when "I wanted to understand everything. His kitchen was full of such smells that you knew you had to understand everything or you would be incomplete forever."

Butler gained a passion for telling the stories of the Vietnamese from his time as a translator during the Vietnam War. His characters in the short story collection *A Good Scent from a Strange Mountain* are immigrants who attempt to assimilate to their new culture while retaining their old traditions. Dao's reconciliation of the actions of his descendents is an indication of his acceptance of death; his ordering of life in the meantime is both poignant and wise. Butler won the Pulitzer Prize for the collection in 1993.

C

Calisher, Hortense. "Heartburn" (1951). From *Fantasy: Shapes of Things Unknown* (Ed. Edmund J. Farrell et al., 1974). COMING-OF-AGE; HUMOR/SATIRE/IRONY; ILLUSION v. REALITY; SUPERNATURAL/HORROR.

A psychiatrist visits a doctor with a strange ailment, a living frog that moves inside his chest. The frog got inside him when, as a favor to a friend, the man became a guidance counselor at a nearby boy's school. Recently, a number of boys had been sent to the infirmary, and the resident doctor concluded that they had "stigmata of pure fright." The condition seemed to have begun when John Hallowell, a boy of fifteen, entered the school late in the term. The other boys rumored that Hallowell could swallow animals and regurgitate them, though no one had ever witnessed the feat.

One evening, the psychiatrist attempted to visit Hallowell in his room, but the boy was missing. Apparently, Hallowell had given the "stigmata" to a disbeliever, who was then charged with passing the condition along to other disbelievers. The afflicted boy came into the room while the psychiatrist was there and told him the story. The man disbelieved the boy, and now the frog had entered the psychiatrist's body. He then visited the doctor, knowing that the doctor would not believe the story and would become the next victim. Indeed, his response to the story is, "I don't believe you!"

Calisher's quirky tale, on one hand, explores the power of suggestion. It also implies the consequence of "disbelieving" (especially in its thinly veiled religious and spiritual undertones) in a society that has become smug in its convictions and has little patience for taking such things on faith.

Calisher, Hortense. "Old Stock" (1950). From *America and I: Short Stories by Jewish American Women Writers* (Ed. Joyce Antler, 1990). CLASS CONFLICTS; COMING-OF-AGE; PREJUDICE; RELIGION/SPIRITUALITY.

Though Mrs. Elkin and her daughter, Hester, can no longer afford to travel to Westchester for the summer, they still go to the "country" so as not to appear any less affluent to others. During the train ride, Hester reflects that her mother puts on airs of superiority and gentility among the other Jewish travelers even though she is a Jew herself, something that she does not readily divulge.

Upon reaching Summitville, Hester meets the "old stock," a group of people who are protective of their reputations and whose mannerisms annoy the young woman. Hester recalls memories from her childhood, when she spent time with Mrs. Onderdonk, one of the Old Guard. When Mrs. Onderdonk makes an anti-Semitic remark about a couple that came into her antique shop that day, Mrs. Elkin reveals that she, too, is a "Hebrew." Hester is put off by her mother's choice of words; when they go to dinner that evening and see Mrs. Onderdonk at the table, Hester is aware that the guests may view her differently, since the matter of their religion has undoubtedly been discussed.

Calisher describes Hester's loss of innocence and the changes in her body from childhood to womanhood. Hester must comes to terms with the complexity of her situation when she witnesses her mother's unwillingness to confess a fact that could harm their standing in the tight-knit social circles of Summitville. The author, in many ways like Henry James and Edith Wharton, explores the process through which society exerts its subtle and insidious influence.

Calvino, Italo. "The Feathered Ogre" (1956). From *The Story and Its Writer*, 4th ed. (Ed. Ann Charters, 1995). ALLEGORY/LEGEND/ FABLE; COURAGE; DECEPTION; DREAMS (SLEEPING); MYSTERY/ADVENTURE.

When the king falls ill, the only way that he will be well again is if he can obtain one of the ogre's feathers. One of the king's trusted attendants offers to find the ogre, and he sets off on his journey. On his way, various people—the monks in the monastery, some noblemen, a ferryman, and an innkeeper—ask him if he would be willing to get one of the feathers for them.

The man enlists the help of the ogre's beautiful wife, who, deceiving the ogre by telling him that she has been dreaming, plucks the ogre's feathers and gives them to the man, with whom she flees the ogre's cave. The problems of all the people whom the man has met are solved, and he is offered the woman's hand in marriage. The ogre, who divulged to his wife the solutions to the men's problems, is stuck ferrying travelers back and forth across the river.

The Italian writer Calvino uses a deceptively simple narrative to explore the world around him, with language as the basis for the story that unfolds. The tales come from the oral tradition, writes Calvino, "the first storyteller of the tribe . . . [who] began to put forth words . . . to test the extent to which words could fit with another, give birth to one another." In that sense, Calvino's work is similar to that of his contemporary, Jorge Luis Borges. The story's themes, while present, are subjugated to the power of the storytelling impulse in a tale that is at once familiar and fresh.

Campbell, Meg. "Just Saying You Love Me Doesn't Make It So" (1973). From *Studies in the Short Story* (Ed. Virgil Scott and David

Madden, 1976). BETRAYAL; HEALTH; INDIVIDUAL; LOVE; MARRIAGE; MEN and WOMEN; TRUTH v. LYING; WOMEN'S ISSUES.

Despite the fact that she is happily married, Nan has never gotten over her romance with Lewis, a college sweetheart. The relationship fell apart when she told him that she had gotten an abortion without his knowledge. When she sees Lewis on the street for the first time since their breakup, the two talk about the past. Nan is on the verge of falling in love with Lewis again, though his reaction to their meeting suggests something else—he has never forgiven her for the act of betrayal that broke their relationship.

Lewis is himself happily married now, and he and his wife are expecting their first child. Lewis talks to Nan about the nature of love. When she tells him that she is glad to see him after so long, he becomes serious, questioning whether she could have loved him and still have done what she did. He asks her what she has done with the freedom that she so valued, and she is at a loss to answer him. Even though he looks at her with affection, his gaze is tinged with sadness. Nan leaves him and meets her own husband at the station.

Campbell explores the nature of love and its many facets in the difficult context of abortion. Though Nan is unsure when she meets Lewis for the first time after their breakup whether she has done the right thing, the story's conclusion suggests that she has matured enough to be capable of entering into a loving relationship. By realizing that "love and responsibility are the same thing after all," Nan reconciles her past with a future with her husband, Jack. Campbell's easy style and her effective use of flashbacks belie the complexity of the relationships that she explores.

Camus, Albert. "The Guest" (1957). From *Fiction 100: An Anthology of Short Stories*, 9th ed. (Ed. James H. Pickering, 2000). ALIENATION/ISOLATION; CRIME/LAW; CULTURE CONFLICTS; FRIENDSHIP; JUSTICE; PLACE; POLITICS.

Daru is a French schoolmaster who has been enlisted by his friend, Balducci, a gendarme, to take an Arab man to prison. The man has killed his own cousin, and though he poses little immediate threat to the French society in Algeria, the possibility always exists, the gendarme believes, for conflict between the two very different cultures. Daru treats the man well and even allows him to sleep in his room without restraint.

When they embark the next morning on their journey to the police station, Daru decides to let the man go. As he walks back to the schoolhouse, he watches the Arab, who continues to stand on the plateau. After a time, the figure is gone; Daru sees him later, walking in the direction that would lead him to the police station and to justice. Realizing the decision that the man has made, Daru has never felt more alone.

The setting, always important in Camus's work, is as important in this story as the characters themselves. Daru struggles with himself to make sense of the orders that insist he turn in a man who has caused him no harm; still, even after pointing the Arab to safety, he understands that "In the vast landscape he had loved so much, he was alone." The implication of a message scrawled on the school's blackboard at the end of the story is clear, though the authorship of the message is ambiguous: "You handed over our brother. You will pay for this." In a sense, the Arab is Daru's brother, both defined by the geography that surrounds them. Daru's greatest enemy, it seems, comes from within.

Capote, Truman. "Among the Paths to Eden" (1960). From *Great Short Stories of the World* (Sel. by the Editors of *Reader's Digest,* 1972). DEATH; FAMILY; FATHERS and CHILDREN; ILLUSION v. REALITY; MARRIAGE; MEN and WOMEN.

Ivor Belli, a New York accountant, decides to go for a walk one day and conveniently stops by his wife's grave; the gesture is a pitiful attempt to endear himself to his daughters, who are dismayed at his lack of mourning for the death of their mother. As he places flowers on the grave, he thinks that he prefers the life of a widower. While in the cemetery, he meets Mary O'Meaghan, a woman who seeks a husband. In desperation, the woman strikes up a conversation with Belli by telling him that her own father has passed away.

As she keeps Belli busy with an offering of peanuts, she blushes as he inappropriately offers the woman a seat on his wife's grave. Throughout the meeting, Mary tries to hook Belli with her best Helen Morgan imitation (Helen Morgan was a movie star in the 1920s and 1930s and a singer who drew men in with her stories of heartbreak), and she compliments him on his physical appearance (he is, after all, a grandfather). Her line of questioning forces Belli's mind to wander back to his relationship with his wife, and his attitude toward his marriage changes during the conversation. Taking on a more direct strategy, she asks him to dinner and goes as far as to inquire whether he would ever consider marrying again. Belli manages to evade the question, deciding instead to ask out his secretary. Belli wishes Mary luck in finding a husband as they exit the cemetery.

Capote's humorous, ironic story—both in its setting and the very different reasons for the two characters to be in the cemetery—explores the contradictory nature of relationships. That the characters consider love and relationships in a cemetery is certainly ironic, though Capote's tone belies the seriousness of the often contradictory impulses that define love and marriage.

Capote, Truman. "My Side of the Matter" (1945). From *Points of View: An Anthology of Short Stories* (Ed. James Moffett and Kenneth R.

McElheny, 1995). HUMOR/SATIRE/IRONY; MARRIAGE; MEN and WOMEN; REGIONALISM (LOCAL COLOR).

For reasons that are beyond him, the sixteen-year-old narrator has married a young Southern girl, and the two move from his job at the Cash 'n' Carry to her home in rural Alabama when they discover that she is pregnant. From the outset, the young man is unable to get along with his wife's aunts, who berate him for being less than a man; at night, they relegate him to a cot on the back porch. One of the aunts accuses the narrator of damaging her piano, and the other claims that he has stolen money from her. The maid, who is tired of catering to the man, gives the narrator a knock on the head with an umbrella, which instigates a fight that ends with the man's wife fainting and the young man sitting in the parlor eating chocolates.

Capote, who wrote this story at the age of twenty-one, seems to be more intent on creating interesting characters in a nearly farcical situation than he is on offering a story with any sort of "truth" about the rural South. The comic tone, heightened by the first-person narration of the man who wants to present "his side of the story," is reminiscent of Faulkner, who influenced the young writer, and the characters are straight out of the tradition of the Southern situation comedy. It is a coming-of-age story that examines the actions of a narrator (whose reliability, we come to understand in the course of the narrative, is questionable), who searches for identity (and perhaps for answers) in a setting where he will always be thought of as an outsider.

Carter, Alden R. "No Win Phuong" (1993). From *Join In: Multiethnic Short Stories* (Ed. Donald R. Gallo, 1993). CONTESTS; CULTURE CONFLICTS; FRIENDSHIP; IDENTITY; UNDERDOGS.

When Ngo Huynh Phuong—pronounced "No Win Fong"—enrolls in a school in central Wisconsin, Bull and Jeff, two baseball players who are always looking for fresh talent, want to enlist him for the team. After all, Jeff tells his friend, "All those Asian kids are killer baseball players." They discover that he has a fastball that could win them the summer league championship, though his control is terrible. He declines the boys' subsequent invitations to play on the team.

Ngo has few friends, and he is evasive about why he will not play baseball. Only after a confrontation between Ngo and Jeff do the boys find out that the newcomer is too competitive, and he loses his ability to concentrate when he is under pressure. With some coaching from the boys, who begin to understand Ngo better after he is willing to discuss his problem with them, he goes from "No Win Phuong," who is incapable of finishing a game, to the pitcher against whom no one will ever win again.

Carter's story uses—and explodes—racial stereotypes to detail an evolving friendship. Though Jeff and Bull have little knowledge of Ngo's culture, except through the homogenized scenes that they see on television and in the movies, their desire to win the championship and to initiate a friendship with their initially standoffish companion allows them to transcend their limited notions of what Ngo should be like. For his part, Ngo joins a team for the first time and realizes the potential that has been so long suppressed.

Carter, Angela. "The Company of Wolves" (1977). From *The Story and Its Writer*, 5th ed. (Ed. Ann Charters, 1999). ALLEGORY/LEGEND/FABLE; ANIMALS and HUMANS; LOVE; MEN and WOMEN; SEXUALITY; VIOLENCE; WOMEN'S ISSUES.

The narrative is familiar: an innocent girl walks alone through the forest on her way to grandmother's house, meets a handsome young man, finds a wolf in grandmother's bed . . . and finally exchanges a kiss for the bet that was made when they raced each other to grandmother's house.

But the author transforms that much-read tale into a commentary on the current state of society. With narrative intrusions such as "Flee and fear the wolf; for, worst of all, the wolf may be more than he seems," and "The wolf is carnivore incarnate," Carter implies the meanness of the world in which her little girl lives. Still, though she is pure, "a closed system," and she is unafraid of anything that might befall her in the forest. The climax of the story turns the original tale on its head, when in the end, the girl "sleeps in granny's bed, between the paws of the tender wolf."

In a style that owes a debt to the "magical realism" of Jorge Luis Borges, Carter combines the structure of the fairy tale with more contemporary notions of relationships between men and women. Clearly, the wolf is the masculine attempting to overpower the feminine. What occurs instead is the mingling of the two: The girl, knowing that "she was nobody's meat," laughs at the wolf and rips off his clothes when he purports to eat her. By reversing the traditional power roles, Carter has succeeded in revising one of the most popular fairy tales into something much more in keeping with the social attitudes of the late 1970s when the story was written.

Carver, Raymond. "Cathedral" (1981). From *Fiction 100: An Anthology of Short Stories*, 9th ed. (Ed. James H. Pickering, 2000). ALIENATION/ISOLATION; DISABILITY/PHYSICAL APPEARANCE; EPIPHANY; FRIENDSHIP; INITIATION; INTERIOR LIVES; MEN and WOMEN.

The story's narrator is displeased that his wife has invited Robert, a blind man, to stay with them for a short time. She and Robert have shared a longtime correspondence, though they have never met face-to-face. When Robert shows up at the house, the narrator is jealous, sensing an intimacy between the two that he and his wife no longer share.

At first, the conversation between the narrator and Robert is forced, but after the three have dinner and drinks and share a marijuana cigarette, the narrator's perception of the man begins to change. Despite his flippant attitude toward the blind man and the clichés that he uses to describe him when he first arrives, the narrator warms to him. His wife goes to bed (throughout the story, both the narrator and his wife remain conspicuously unnamed), and the two men "watch" television. When the narrator tells Robert that he is looking at a cathedral on the screen, the blind man wants to know what it looks like. Robert places his hand over the narrator's as the narrator draws the cathedral. Only by following the hand over the paper can Robert "see" what the cathedral looks like; only by drawing with his new friend's hand over his can the narrator truly appreciate Robert's zest for life and his ability to transcend the limitations that have been placed on him.

By presenting a plausible solution for the narrator's earlier alienation, Carver offers a story that is poignant and inspirational. The title implies both the physical structure that the narrator translates for the blind man and the narrator's spiritual awakening inside a "cathedral" of his and the blind man's making. Clearly, the narrator is the one who is truly blind, as he cannot initially see past his own narrow notions of physical disability. With the blind man's help, however, the narrator's epiphany becomes possible.

Carver, Raymond. "What We Talk about When We Talk about Love" (1981). From *Fiction 100: An Anthology of Short Stories*, 9th ed. (Ed. James H. Pickering, 2000). COMMUNICATION/LANGUAGE; IN-DIVIDUAL; LOVE; MARRIAGE; MEN and WOMEN; VIOLENCE.

Four friends sit at the kitchen table and discuss the topic of love over more drinks than they care to remember. Mel, a cardiologist, dominates the conversation; his idea of love is spiritual, not physical. During Mel's monologue, his wife, Terry, recalls a man who loved her so much that he tried to kill her and eventually took his own life.

The four continue to talk about—and around—the topic of love, and Mel and Terry tease Nick and Laura when they show affection toward one another at the table because they have been together only a short time. As the sun sets on the conversation, Mel relates the story of an accident that illustrates the love that a man and a woman in their seventies have for one another. The evening devolves into diatribes on old spouses and lovers, and in the end, the four of them sit at the table in the dark.

The relative inaction of the story's participants belies the complexity of Carver's narrative. The answer to the story's title is, according to the characters, anything but love itself. Instead, the breakdown of language and even educated peoples' ability (or inability, in this case) to communicate such an abstract and personal concept are key in understanding the chaos that lies just below the surface of a scene where the characters do little but drink and talk without acting in any meaningful way. Finally, little is accomplished.

Carver, Raymond. "Where I'm Calling From" (1983). From *The Norton Anthology of Contemporary Fiction* (Ed. R.V. Cassill, 1988). ADDIC-

TION; ALIENATION/ISOLATION; LOSS; LOVE/HATE; MAR-
RIAGE; MEN and WOMEN.

The narrator arrives for his second stint at Frank Martin's "drying-out facility." His similarly boozy girlfriend with whom he has a rocky relationship has brought him there. During his time there—the holidays are always the hardest, and the men in the facility are getting ready to celebrate the New Year—the narrator recalls many of the events leading up to this trip, and he details the relationships that he strikes up while there, particularly with J. P., a down-on-his-luck chimney sweep.

As he stands at the pay phone deciding whether to call his girlfriend or an ex-wife for whom he obviously has feelings, he thinks of Jack London's story "To Build a Fire." His recollection of the plot is certainly applicable to his own situation: "He gets his fire going, but then something happens to it. A branchful of snow drops on it. It goes out. Meanwhile, the temperature is falling. Night is coming on." If he calls his wife, the narrator pledges to himself not to raise his voice, "even if she starts something. She'll ask me where I'm calling from, and I'll have to tell her." If he calls his girlfriend, he just hopes he doesn't get her son on the line. He knows he cannot make any New Year's resolutions—the time for such things is past—but he'll make the most of the situation.

Carver's realism comes from his own experiences, as he was forced to quit drinking ten years before he died of other causes. His ability to present the humanity in all the characters in Frank Martin's place is typical of the author's fiction. The title of the story implies the distance between the people whom the narrator knows and loves. By having to explain where he's calling from, he understands that his relationships are not as stable as they could be. Still, he will make the attempt; life will go on into the New Year.

Castillo, Ana. "Francisco el Penitente" (1992). *Iguana Dreams: New Latino Fiction* **(Ed. Virgil Suarez and Delia Poey, 1992). EPIPHANY; FAMILY; HISPANIC EXPERIENCE; HISTORY; INTERIOR LIVES; MEN and WOMEN; RELIGION/SPIRITUALITY.**

The man who becomes Francisco el Penitente was known as "Chico" to his buddies in Vietnam, the name that the soldiers used for all Spanish boys. Later in life, he becomes a *santero*, a man who held divine powers when he was creating a *bulto*, a wooden sculpture of a saint. The tradition was strong in the man's family, having been kept alive for more than two centuries. As a child, Franky, as he was known to his family, assisted his grandmother in applying her remedies to the sick, and he watched his uncle, Pedro, prepare a *bulto* many times before he asked the man to teach him in the way of the *santero*. When he falls in love with a woman who subsequently leaves him, he dedicates his life to his new passion. He carves an image of Saint Francis of Assisi, for whom he was named. Even though the statue ends up with one leg uneven, Francisco prepares to paint it, in the way that his ancestors had for so many generations before him. They prayed and worked in silence, trying through their work to get closer to God in a land that was so far from Him.

The story links spiritual themes with the transformation of a man who realizes his calling in life through the trials of a Latino and his closeness to his family. In the world in which Franky lives, material possessions and physical love are the norm; when he becomes Francisco el Penitente, however, the ephemeral aspects of life are subjugated to the long history of his people and the spiritual renewal that comes from his profound faith.

Castillo, Ana. "Ghost Talk" (1983). From *Loverboys: Stories* (Castillo, 1996). FATHERS and CHILDREN; HISPANIC EXPERIENCE; IDENTITY; MEN and WOMEN; MOTHERS and CHILDREN; WOMEN'S ISSUES.

The narrator describes the city that she has returned to as "the city where it all happened/happens," and "the one the movie directors love so much." Though the story at first is a series of random vignettes illustrating the woman's image of herself as a "ghost" and describing desultory parts of her life, including her Cuban friend, Iraida, the narrator focuses her attention on her heritage by describing indirectly that her mother is Mexican and her father is white. Her mother was raped by her boss when she worked on an assembly line in the North.

As the narrator and her mother walk from one market to another, her mother stops cold at the sight of an old man walking with his granddaughter. The narrator knows instinctively that the man her mother has seen is her father; she watches him climb into a car and writes down the license plate number. Later, posing as a worker from City Hall, she goes to the man's house, pulls a gun on him, and asks him if he recognizes her. She accuses him of being her father, though the man vehemently denies the accusation. When he collapses from an apparent heart attack, the narrator leaves quickly and calls for help; she does not want his death on her conscience.

Though Castillo overtly makes little of the conflict between races and cultures in this story, the subtext reads as powerfully as the miscegenation stories of Jean Toomer. The narrator, clearly haunted by her own lack of identity (hence the story's title), reacts in a way that holds little chance for solving the issue of her heritage. Instead, the ambiguity of her connection to the man alienates her even further from the vitality of the city that she describes.

Cather, Willa. "Neighbour Rosicky" (1928). From *The Treasury of American Short Stories* (Sel. Nancy Sullivan, 1981). FAMILY; HEALTH; INDIVIDUAL; LABOR/JOB; LOVE; NATIONALISM/ AMERICAN DREAM; PRIDE.

Mr. Rosicky is well liked in his small urban community: he has the manner and the work ethic to endear himself to his neighbors, and his boys are raised to show the utmost respect to their elders. When it comes to hard work, no one in the family complains. Rosicky goes out of his way to make sure that his son and the son's new wife are well settled, and he makes the sacrifices necessary to provide a certain standard of living for his family. After a visit to the doctor, Rosicky is persuaded to pay attention to his health. Though he continues to provide a good example for his family, viewing work as the solution to many problems and family as his first priority, his stubbornness proves fatal.

Cather reflects on Rosicky's childhood struggles in the city and suggests that hard work is the stuff of the American Dream. With the lessons he learns early in his life, Rosicky provides the love and encouragement that form the backbone of American society. As with her lengthier explication of that notion in *My Ántonia*, her most acclaimed novel, Cather's stories are both romantic and realistic. Through the individual, Rosicky, and his family, the author describes the enduring human spirit that transcends the harsh realities of life in the first decades of the twentieth century.

Cather, Willa. "Paul's Case" (1905). From *The Norton Anthology of Short Fiction*, 6th ed. (Ed. R.V. Cassill and Richard Bausch, 2000). ALIENATION/ISOLATION; ART and the ARTIST; DEATH; DECEPTION; DREAMS (of the FUTURE); INDIVIDUAL; SELF-DESTRUCTION/SUICIDE.

Paul, who is tall and thin for his age, is perpetually in trouble at school. Though he lies and tells the headmaster that he would like to come back to school, the truth is that he is enamored with the symphony and the stage. He is a young romantic who wants nothing more than to live the life of an actor or singer—"it was at the theatre and at Carnegie Hall that Paul really lived; the rest was but a sleep and a forgetting"—and he stalks the hangouts of his theatre friends, hoping to be drawn into their society, away from a home life that profoundly displeases him.

As his fascination with the romantic aspects of the theatre increases, Paul's performance in school deteriorates. After stealing money from his employer to finance his trip, Paul jumps a train bound for New York, where he can live out the fantasies that he has discussed with his theatre friends a hundred times. Things do not go as he had planned, however, and when news of the theft reaches him in New York, Paul sinks deeper into depression until he stands in front of a train and drops "back into the immense design of things."

Cather's story, which takes place in Pittsburgh and New York, is a cautionary tale for the aspiring young artist, for which the author's society seemingly had little use. Cather wrote often of man's interaction with nature on the Great Plains of America, and when her characters are forced to go to the "big city," the result can be unsavory. Alienation and fragmentation are the norm in such instances, and Paul's case emphasizes the tragedy that can come from such desires. One of Cather's great influences was Sarah Orne Jewett ("A White Heron"), who implored her to focus on the characters and situations that she knew best. This story, a plethora of detail mingled with a thorough understanding of her protagonist's psyche, accomplishes the author's purpose.

Chaucer, Geoffrey. "The Pardoner's Tale (from *The Canterbury Tales*)" (14th century). From *Great Stories of All Nations* (Ed. Maxim Lieber and Blanche Colton Williams, 1945). ALLEGORY/LEGEND/FABLE; DEATH; DECEPTION; GOOD/EVIL; GREED; RELIGION/SPIRITUALITY; VIOLENCE.

Taking his turn in the storytelling contest that is part of their pilgrimage, the pardoner relates the tale of a band of three men who agree to take a break from their debauchery to hunt down and murder Death himself. When they see an old man walking at a late hour, they threaten to kill him if he will not direct them to Death. He obliges, saying that they will find Death under a tree a short distance ahead. What the men find instead is a stash of gold. After they decide to take the gold under cover of night, one man is sent to town for food and drink. The two remaining thieves plot to kill him upon his return; what they do not know is that their victim has poisoned their wine, hoping to gain the gold for himself. All three men die agonizing deaths.

Chaucer explores the nature of greed and man's overweening desire to master death. The pardoner's didactic message—that desire for worldly goods and the blind pride that such desires engender will always come to naught—is accomplished through the introduction of sudden wealth and the old man who will lead the criminals to their deaths. *The Canterbury Tales*, a series of stories told by persons of various stations in life who happen to be on a pilgrimage together, are on the whole rich in themes that lend themselves to the study of short fiction.

Chavez, Denise. "Chata" (1992). From *Iguana Dreams: New Latino Fiction* (Ed. Virgil Suarez and Delia Poey, 1992). CLASS CONFLICTS; DUTY; FAMILY; FRIENDSHIP; HISPANIC EXPERIENCE; LABOR/JOB; MEN and WOMEN.

Chata cleans Soveida's house on Fir Street every third Monday, and though Soveida appreciates Chata, for whom cleanliness is a state of grace, she is ambivalent about the woman's arrival. Even though Monday is Soveida's day off, she invariably stays to help Chata clean the house. Chata is a hard worker, and Soveida marvels at her hands, which "were no strangers to toxic matter, and continued to dare to plunge into burning water to get the job done." Chata feels that even though God has given us many useless body parts—breasts for an old woman, an old man's penis—the fingernail is the most indispensable of the human body parts.

Soveida knows much about the woman's background, and Chata, in her conspiratorial tone, does not stop herself from telling stories about her previous employers. She appreciates the Americans for all they give her (one of them buys her Arby's for lunch every Tuesday), and she refuses to "work for someone who won't feed you. What they want is a dumb animal not a person to help. If a person is stingy in their own home, imagine how they are out in the world." Outside her work, Chata has a family life about which Soveida knows little. Soveida is pleased when Chata calls her a "good worker," the highest compliment possible from Chata. Soveida understands the special person that Chata is—in her love for her family, her love for her work, and her ability to bring a state of grace to Soveida's own life.

Chavez explores the relationship between the two women through the contrasts in their lives. Chata feels that it is her duty to bring an air of respectability to the work she does, and the friendship that ensues because of Chata's attitude toward life—clearly, neither her family life nor her job have been easy on her, though she gives herself unconditionally to them both—transcends any differences that the two women might have and provides an inspiration for Soveida in her own life.

Cheever, John. "The Country Husband" (1954). From *Fiction 100: An Anthology of Short Stories*, 9th ed. (Ed. James H. Pickering, 2000). FAMILY; IDENTITY; ILLUSION v. REALITY; INSANITY; INTERIOR LIVES; MARRIAGE; MEN and WOMEN.

Francis Weed is mired in the banality of suburbia. His notions of the everydayness of his life are shaken to their foundations, however, when the plane he is on crash-lands outside Philadelphia. Still, he reaches the station in time to make his regular commuter train home, and his family cannot understand how close he has come to death. Later, he recognizes the maid at one of his neighbor's parties as a French woman whom he had seen humiliated during the war when she was exposed as a German sympathizer. Unable to articulate the life-changing events of the past couple of days, Weed instead (and, perhaps, predictably) becomes infatuated with his children's babysitter.

As the unlikely fantasy unfolds in his mind, Weed becomes increasingly unable to handle the expectations of his family, his job, or the society in which he is trapped. When he is asked to provide a recommendation for a young man who happens to be the babysitter's fiancé, he calls the boy a thief. Realizing his mistake, he seeks the counseling of a therapist, who suggests that he take up woodworking.

Cheever's notions of the stifling regularity of life in suburbia are manifest in nearly all his short fiction. Both the story's ironic title—its pastoral and genteel overtones imply a staid respectability that is sorely lacking in the protagonist's life—and the protagonist's name (as a "Weed," he can hardly be welcome in the well-manicured lots of his commuter hell) call into question the harsh reality of the homogenized society that Cheever observed in the growing suburbs of his own New York City in the 1950s.

Cheever, John. "The Enormous Radio" (1953). From *The Norton Anthology of Short Fiction*, 6th ed. (Ed. R.V. Cassill and Richard Bausch, 2000). BETRAYAL; DECADENCE/DEGENERATION; DECEPTION; GIFTS; LABOR/JOB; LOVE/HATE; MARRIAGE; MEN and WOMEN; SOCIETY.

Jim and Irene Westcott are average Americans, the kind of people described in the "statistical reports in college alumni bulletins." They spend much of their time listening to the radio, and Jim brings home a state-of-the-art unit. From the first, the radio both frightens and captivates Irene. Through the radio, she hears her neighbors' conversations, some of which are violent, some poignant, others humorous in their banality. Regardless of the tone of the broadcasts, Irene is shaken from the torpor of her average life by the phenomenon.

When she implores Jim to break up a fight between a husband and wife upstairs, he tells her that she does not have to listen to the radio anymore. The confrontation leads to an outburst from Jim about his concerns over money, and he accuses Irene of becoming suddenly self-righteous after eavesdropping on the troubles of her neighbors. As he recalls a trip that Irene once made to an abortionist, the voice on the radio drones the events of the world outside their narrow experience.

The story contains an element of the unexplained for which Cheever (who rightfully gained a reputation as a commentator on American suburbia and the foibles of the middle and upper-middle classes) is not known. The narrative twist allows the author to predicate his story on the fact that, by listening to the unsavory details of their neighbors' lives, the Westcotts come to realize their own shortcomings. Cheever again describes the pretense and society's seamy underbelly, where people worry about money, their well-being, and the future, which is not as bright, perhaps, as his characters would wish it to be.

Cheever, John. "The Five Forty-Eight" (1955). From *The World of the Short Story* (Ed. Clifton Fadiman, 1986). DECEPTION; INSANITY; MEN and WOMEN; MISOGYNY; REVENGE; SEXUALITY; VIOLENCE; WOMEN'S ISSUES.

When Blake realizes that a former secretary with whom he had a brief affair is stalking him, he thinks that she will be easy to avoid, as he assumes that she is not clever. He is surprised to find that he cannot remember her name, though he recalls that "She seemed to imagine the lives of the rest of the world to be more brilliant then they were. Once, she had put a rose on his desk, and he had dropped it into the wastebasket. 'I don't like roses,' he told her." The woman's response to Blake's rough treatment of her during the affair, nothing more than a one-night stand, after which he left the woman weeping, compels him to have her fired.

When the woman approaches Blake and holds him at gunpoint, he realizes that the situation is much more dire than he had initially thought. Though she is delusional, the woman seems to know Blake's type well—men who prey on the weak and the vulnerable. When she forces Blake to put his face in the dirt, he mirrors her weeping with his own. Without explanation, she walks away, leaving Blake to find his way home.

Once again, Cheever portrays the seedy side of a lifestyle that proliferates in 1940s and 1950s America, with the advent of commuter towns and an expanded middle class. As Fadiman puts it, Cheever's fiction describes "the outwardly comfortable yet precariously balanced middle-class world of New York's suburbia, as well as the more fashionable enclaves of the great city itself." In this story, the woman's exacting a measure of revenge on Blake seems to even the score, though Cheever implies that she will continue to be affected by society's ill treatment of her in a way that Blake never will.

Cheever, John. "The Swimmer" (1964). From *Short Fiction: Classic and Contemporary*, 4th ed. (Ed. Charles H. Bohner and Dean Dougherty, 1999). ALIENATION/ISOLATION; FAMILY; IDENTITY; MEN and WOMEN; SOCIETY.

Ned Merrill makes the rather eccentric decision to swim, where possible, from the pool of the Westerhazys to his own home, a distance of eight miles; he names the string of waterways "Lucinda," after his wife. At first, the trip goes as planned and Ned enjoys the summer Sunday afternoon, chatting with his friends who hold parties in their backyards. As the journey progresses, however, he finds himself increasingly confused: by the absence of water in one pool and a "For Sale" sign in the yard, the comments of some of his acquaintances about his financial situation, and the well-meaning greeting of a couple who cryptically wish him the best. Even an ex-mistress, like the weather, turns cold toward him. When he finally reaches his house, he finds the place dilapidated and empty.

Another of Cheever's commentaries on the vagaries of suburban life in the 1950s and 1960s, "The Swimmer" is perhaps his most poignant and darkest examination of a man's alienation from society and his family. For a time, Ned is able to block out the inevitable, his own empty home and his wife and four daughters gone. The past catches up with him, however (Cheever implies that it must), and the society that he remembers is not the reality—for him, or for the people who scorn him—that presently exists in Cheever's fictive Bullet Park neighborhood.

Chekhov, Anton. "The Darling" (1899). From *Fiction 100: An Anthology of Short Stories*, 9th ed. (Ed. James H. Pickering, 2000). FAMILY; LOSS; MARRIAGE; MEN and WOMEN; OPPRESSION; TRADITION and CONVENTION; WOMEN'S ISSUES.

Olinka is wooed by Kukin, who owns the Tivoli Pleasure-Garden. She listens to his suffering—rain, always rain, when it hurts his business so—and finally loves him for his misfortune. When Kukin dies unexpectedly, Olinka does not know what she will do with her life. After all, "it was her nature to be always in love with someone or other." Fortunately for her, she is courted by another man, who similarly bemoans the weather and who expects Olinka to act as a mirror to validate his purpose.

When her second husband dies, Olinka once again experiences the indecision that has characterized her life without the comfort of a man. She falls in love with a veterinarian who eventually reconciles with his wife. Once again, she is without a reason to live. After a lengthy absence, however, the veterinarian and his wife allow Olinka to care for their young son. As always, her life is defined by the expectations of others.

Chekhov is one of literature's great observers, and this story is one of the best illustrations of his sympathy for his characters. The title of the story—and the author's repetition of the phrase "they lived happily together"—is ironic in its suggestion of the superficial nature of the tenuous and ephemeral relationships between men and women. Clearly, Olinka is valued in her society not for her intelligence, but only for her beauty and willingness to accede to her man's wishes. The men who marry Olinka view her only as someone who will parrot their stances on life; her identity is stripped from her as soon as she finds herself alone in the world. Beneath the story's benign exterior is a scathing commentary on the types of people who would use someone for their own gain. They are the types of people Chekhov knows and characterizes so well.

Chekhov, Anton. "The Lady with the Pet Dog" (1899). From *The Harper Anthology of Fiction* (Ed. Sylvan Barnet, 1991). DEPRESSION; LOSS; LOVE/HATE; MARRIAGE; MEN and WOMEN; MORALITY.

Dmitry Gurov observes a young, melancholy woman walking her pet Pomeranian several times a day. No one knows who she is, and he and his friends simply call her "the lady with the pet dog." Gurov, who married young and has children of his own, is intrigued by the lady and makes her acquaintance. He discovers that the woman, Anna Sergeyevna, is also married, though her husband has left her in Yalta to rest, and he will not be back for some weeks. The two have an affair, which serves only to make the woman even more despondent. Gurov despises her naïveté and the guilt she feels for their actions.

When Anna's husband calls her to return home, she asks Gurov not to think ill of her for what they have done. Gurov, for his part, has always treated the relationship with some irony, and he happily parts from her. Despite his cavalier attitude toward the woman, Gurov finds himself thinking more and more of her as the months go by. The company that previously satisfied him now seems banal, a waste of his time. He plots to find Anna, and when he sees her at the theater, they resume their affair. It occurs to him that only now, in his middle age, has he fallen in love for the first time. The two are deeply in love; still, the most difficult days for their relationship, they know, are yet to come.

The unexpected and powerful love that Gurov has for Anna is similar to Henry James's own examination of the theme in "The Beast in the Jungle." Chekhov's sense of the complexities of human affairs is both profound and poignant.

Chekhov, Anton. "Misery" (1886). From *The Heath Introduction to Fiction*, 4th ed. (Ed. John J. Clayton, 1992). ANIMALS and HUMANS; CLASS CONFLICTS; DEATH; FATHERS and CHILDREN; GRIEF.

Few people care that Iona Potapov, a simple sledge-driver, has recently lost his son to illness. As he waits for fares that will allow him to feed his horse and himself, Potapov grieves silently on the cold streets. The citizens, who would care little for his grief even if they knew its cause, abuse him with their shouts and taunts. Finally, an officer demands that Potapov take him to Vyborgskaya. Despite his abject poverty, Potapov seems to care more about the opportunity to tell someone of his son's death than he does the measly fare. The officer, though, wants to hear none of the man's anguish, and he demands that Potapov drive faster into the blinding snowstorm.

Potapov's next fare is no more sympathetic. Three men, one of whom is a hunchback whose deformity mitigates for a time the driver's own misery, order him to take them to the Police Bridge. When Potapov attempts to bring up his son's death to the three, the hunchback responds, "We shall all die." When one of the men asks the cabman if he is married, he replies as flippantly as he can that he is married only to the earth that will hold his coffin; his son should be the one driving, the man thinks, yet he is the one dead.

Potapov makes one last futile attempt to share his anguish with a young man who lives in the boardinghouse with him, but the man covers his head and falls asleep before Potapov can tell his story. The sledge-driver's only recourse is to share his thoughts with his mare as the horse munches contentedly on the little food that her master is able to provide her.

Chekhov's story is a rich and poignant examination of loneliness. His bleak, dirty landscapes, reminiscent of the Naturalist literature that examines the brutal indifference of nature to man's plight, add much to the sledge-driver's pathetic situation and emphasize the value of human relationships—

especially those between parents and children—and the devastating effects of their absence.

Chekhov, Anton. "A Work of Art" (1886). *Clifton Fadiman's Fireside Reader* **(Ed. Clifton Fadiman, 1961). ART and the ARTIST; HU-MOR/SATIRE/IRONY.**

Dr. Koshelkov treats Sasha Smirnov, a young man from a rather poor family. In return for the doctor's services, Smirnov presents him with an antique bronze, a group of naked women in various poses, that was left him by his dead father. The doctor surveys the piece and realizes that its content will prevent his ever displaying the piece. He finds an easy out, however, by giving it to a friend to whom he owes a favor.

The piece makes its way through the small community of the doctor's acquaintances and ends up back with the young man's mother, who, like her deceased husband, collects the pieces. Seeing the piece and realizing that he has been presented with the perfect opportunity to complete a matching set for the doctor, the young man buys it and takes it to him. The doctor is rendered speechless when he sees the antique bronze for the second time.

Chekhov, who has a reputation as a realist of the top rank, shows his sense of humor in this story, which relies on coincidence and the reaction of the various recipients of the profane piece for its punch line. The comedy is heightened by the story's title, which calls into question the very definition of "art."

Chesnutt, Charles. "The Goophered Grapevine" (1899). From *Calling the Wind: Twentieth-Century African-American Short Stories* **(Ed. Clarence Major, 1992). ALLEGORY/LEGEND/FABLE; FRIENDSHIP; HEALTH; RACE RELATIONS; SUPERNATURAL; SUPERSTITION.**

The narrator and his wife move to North Carolina for the woman's health. The narrator's interest in grape cultivation prompts him to buy a farm there, a run-down piece of land that has seen better days. They meet a black man, Julius, eating grapes; at first, he is cautious of the couple, but eventually, he warms up to them and tells them a story.

It seems that a previous owner was having trouble with slaves eating his grapes. The owner, McAdoo, has a spell cast on his crop—a "goopher" that would kill anyone who ate the grapes—so that it would be protected from thievery. When Henry, who eats the grapes without knowing about the goopher, becomes ill, he is taken to the same woman who put the spell on the grapes in the first place, and she gives him a regimen that will save his life. Five years later, though, the grapes begin to turn yellow and die, causing Henry to die soon after. Julius relates that the farm has remained unproductive since then. The couple, believing the man to be a teller of tall tales, buys the farm anyway.

Chesnutt uses legend, the oral tradition, and dialect to illustrate how Julius plans to relate to the prospective owners of the property. The northerners, sensing the ulterior motive behind Julius's actions, nonetheless are charmed by the story. They hire the man to work for them; Julius, in either case, has accomplished his purpose in relating Henry's tale.

Chesnutt, Charles. "The Sheriff's Children" (1899). From *The Portable American Realism Reader* (Ed. James Nagel and Tom Quirk, 1997). FAMILY; FATE; FATHERS and CHILDREN; GUILT; RACE RELATIONS; REVENGE; VIOLENCE.

In Branson County, North Carolina, time seems to have passed the inhabitants by. Even the Civil War has left the area relatively unaffected. When Captain Walker is murdered, though, the natural target of scorn for the community is a mulatto who is caught wearing the captain's jacket. When the townspeople decide that the man is guilty, they intend to lynch him. The sheriff, however, is determined to fulfill his duty, and goes to the jail to protect the man. There he discovers that the man is his son, whom he had sold as a slave years before.

When the prisoner takes a gun from the sheriff, the articulate and passionate young man details the wrongs that the sheriff has perpetrated on him and his family and proclaims his innocence. Before the matter can be resolved, the sheriff's daughter, Polly, shoots the man in the arm. In the night, awaiting his fate, the sheriff's mulatto son peels the bandage from his arm and bleeds to death.

Chesnutt is known as the first black writer to have achieved a widespread white audience in the United States. His stories, including "The Sheriff's Children," often detail the relationships between blacks and whites. By creating a character who is caught between both worlds, the author is better able to explore the confusion, hatred, and shame that his characters feel.

Chesterton, G.K. "The Blue Cross" (1911). From *Modern American and British Short Stories* (Ed. Leonard Brown, 1929). DECEPTION; ILLUSION v. REALITY; MYSTERY/ADVENTURE; RELIGION/ SPIRITUALITY.

Valentin, the famous French detective, searches for the master criminal Flambeau, a tall man whose disguises and his cleverness have made him unstoppable for years. Flambeau's target in this particular case is a priest who carries with him an invaluable cross that is encrusted with blue gems.

After a series of events that leaves Valentin confused as to the nature of the case, the priest, who is thought by everyone who comes into contact with him to be nothing more than a simple cleric, turns the tables on Flambeau and betters him at his own game. Valentin, realizing that the priest knows more about human nature than even he, thanks him for his work in helping to apprehend the criminal, who cannot believe that he has fallen into the priest's trap. The priest, modest as ever, relates that his position as confessor has allowed him access into the criminal mind and has provided him with knowledge that even the great Flambeau does not have at his disposal.

Chesterton's story is a detective masterpiece in every sense. The machinations of the priest are unclear until the very end, and his use of the knowledge that he has gained as a "simple priest" nicely complements Valentin's own knowledge, also gained over many years, but in a much different context.

Chopin, Kate. "Désirée's Baby" (1892). From *The Portable American Realism Reader* (Ed. James Nagel and Tom Quirk, 1997). FAMILY; FATE; FATHERS and CHILDREN; MARRIAGE; MEN and WOMEN; MISOGYNY; RACE RELATIONS; TRUTH v. LYING.

As a baby, Désirée was deserted by her parents. Madame Valmonde's husband wandered upon the child, and the two adopted her. Madame Valmonde considered the child a gift from heaven, as she had no children of her own. In a span of time that Madame Valmonde can hardly believe has passed, Désirée grows into beautiful womanhood. When the young woman meets and marries a well-to-do plantation owner, Armand, Madame Valmonde is beside herself with joy. Désirée has attained the happiness that she so well deserves. Désirée and Armand have a child, and for the first few months of the boy's life, neither of the parents has ever been more content. Armand, who has a notoriously short temper, becomes a doting father. Désirée wakes one day, though, to the feeling that something is amiss. Armand becomes querulous with the slaves again, punishing them for the slightest misdeeds, and he becomes cold toward her. It is only then that Désirée realizes, when she looks into the baby's crib, that they have conceived a mixed-race child.

Désirée assumes, given her own mysterious background and despite her fair skin and gray eyes, that she is the one who is the product of miscegenation. Armand asks her to leave the plantation, and she returns to her mother, who loves her adoptive daughter and her grandson despite the revelation. Only in the end, when Armand burns Désirée's effects and her letters to him, is the truth revealed: in a letter from Armand's mother to his father, she expresses relief that no one will ever know that it is she, in fact, who "belongs to the race that is cursed with the brand of slavery."

This brief tale details Chopin's fascination with the "curse" of miscegenation in the turn-of-the-century South with which she is so familiar. The ironic twist—even the men who are culpable for such revelations as those made in the story evade their responsibilities—is a fitting end to the ambivalence that defines the lives of characters who live always with one eye on the past, waiting for that past to reveal their true natures.

Chopin, Kate. "The Story of an Hour" (1894). From *The Story and Its Writer*, 5th ed. (Ed. Ann Charters, 1999). DEATH; IRONY; MARRIAGE; MEN and WOMEN; OPPRESSION; WOMEN'S ISSUES.

Louise Mallard receives news that her husband has been killed in a train accident. At first, she is distraught, retiring to her room to gather herself for the empty life ahead of her. As she contemplates what her husband's death truly means to her, however, she realizes that instead of leaving her alone, his death has given her a freedom that was unavailable during their marriage. As she looks forward to the experiences that this newfound freedom will afford her, she walks downstairs, where she is greeted by the husband she thought dead. The shock of his arrival causes Louise to have a fatal heart attack that those present mistake for happiness at her husband's return.

In this brief story, Chopin, like Gilman, details the constraints of marriage and implies the freedom that was so often absent in the one-sided relationships of the time. The "joy that kills," the purported cause of Louise's death, can be read as her preference for death over the prospect of relinquishing a life that was, if only for a moment, made possible through the absence of her husband.

Cisneros, Sandra. "The House on Mango Street," "Hairs," and "My Name" (1983). From *The Story and Its Writer*, 5th ed. (Ed. Ann Charters, 1999). CHILDHOOD; CLASS CONFLICTS; DREAMS (of the FUTURE); FAMILY; HISPANIC EXPERIENCE; IDENTITY; PLACE.

Cisernos's best-known contribution to Latino-American literature is her collection of vignettes based on her childhood in Chicago. The narrator is a young Latina who describes her life and her family in a tone that is by turns poignant and humorous. The house on Mango Street where the family moves is not at all what they had expected. Still, the house is theirs, and they will not have to move every year, as has been their experience. The narrator recalls meeting a nun from her school when they lived in a third-story apartment, "the paint peeling, wooden bars Papa had nailed on the windows so we wouldn't fall out." She knew then that the family had to have a real house.

In "Hairs," the narrator begins with "Everybody in our family has different hair." She describes the hair of her family and, in this vignette that runs to perhaps two hundred words, ends with "The snoring, the rain, and Mama's hair that smells like bread." Similarly, the sharp language and images of "My Name" draw the reader in: "In English my name means hope," the narrator begins. "In Spanish it means too many letters. It means sadness, it means waiting." The narrator, whose name is Esperanza, then fantasizes about changing her name to something more appropriate, like "Zeze the X."

All of Cisneros's language has an aphoristic quality that is similar in tone to that of Lorrie Moore. Still, Cisneros is writing from a unique perspective in a voice that rings with the truth of her heritage and the razor-sharp images that she offers.

Cisneros, Sandra. "Salvador" (1992). From *Iguana Dreams: New Latino Fiction* (Ed. Virgil Suarez and Delia Poey, 1992). ALIENATION/ ISOLATION; ASSIMILATION; CHILDHOOD; COMING-OF-AGE; FAMILY; HISPANIC EXPERIENCE.

Though Salvador has "crooked hair and crooked teeth" and his teachers cannot remember his name, he helps his mother get his brothers ready for school in the morning. He is a beautiful soul trapped inside wrinkled clothing and hindered by the "throat that must clear itself and apologize each time it speaks, inside that forty-pound body of boy with its geography of scars." Still, he is like any other boy; in the mind's eye of the narrator, he is nearly heroic as she watches his silhouette "flutter in the air before disappearing like a memory of kites."

Cisneros, the daughter of a Mexican father and a Mexican-American mother, writes poignantly of her background and the people she knows so well. Her stories—a series of vignettes through which she describes the events and people of her life—evoke memories of a bittersweet childhood that is full of passion, love, loss, and hope. No word is wasted; the one-page piece is as much prose poem as short story, though buried beneath the surface of the snapshot descriptions, the prevalent themes of alienation, assimilation, and coming-of-age combine to create the whole of Cisernos's vision.

Clark, Walter van Tilburg. "The Portable Phonograph" (1941). *Studies in Fiction* (Ed. Blaze O. Bonazza et al., 1982). ALIENATION/ISO-LATION; ART and the ARTIST; ENTROPY/CHAOS; INTERIOR LIVES; MUSIC; PLACE; WAR.

In a landscape that has been ravaged by war, a group of men huddle in the relative safety of a cave, hoarding their most cherished possessions, a small stack of books and a phonograph. The men must listen to the phonograph and the records sparingly, as they have no way of replacing them, and the music and the books are their only pleasures in life. On this particular occasion, the host decides that he will use a real needle, not the thorns that act as a poor substitute. When the men hear the music, they are carried away for a time from the harshness of their existence. The beauty of the music affects one young man profoundly and he seems to be on the verge of a breakdown. Still, when the album, a Debussy nocturne, has played to its conclusion, the men rise mechanically and head out into the wilderness. The host invites them all back in a week, and he hides the books and the music in a hollow in the cave.

The characters, who remain essentially undeveloped and instead act as symbolic survivors of the consequence of violence, realize the importance of art in their lives. The apocalyptic vision is both frightening and hopeful—with little context given for their situation, Clark implies that the men could have been from any war and lived in any time. Art, it seems, can perpetuate the human spirit even in the worst of times.

Cofer, Judith Ortiz. "American History" (1989). From *Growing Up Ethnic in America: Contemporary Fiction about Learning to Be American* (Ed. Maria Mazziotti and Jennifer Gillan, 1999). COMING-OF-AGE; CULTURE CONFLICTS; FRIENDSHIP; HISPANIC EXPERIENCE; HISTORY; SOCIETY.

The narrator, a young woman, is in the ninth grade at PS13 on the day that Kennedy is shot. Their teacher begins sobbing when he hears the news, and the children mock him; he is angry that they do not understand the importance of what has happened, and he sends them home. The narrator's mother also weeps in front of the television, but when the narrator tries to feel sorrow for the event, she is only excited by the activity. When she tells her mother that she is going to study with a friend, her mother pleads with her to attend church to pray instead. The narrator declines.

She knocks on the door at Eugene's house, and when the boy's mother appears, the narrator tells her that Eugene had asked her to study with him. The mother, pointing to the tenement across the street (a place they call "El Building"), asks the girl if she lives there. When she tells the woman that she does, the boy's mother insists that Eugene does not want to study with her, nor does he need her help. The narrator turns for home in disbelief, and that night she hears her parents discussing the president's death and his newly widowed wife and two children. Some of the women in "El Building" wear black for weeks.

Cofer incorporates her Latin roots into the story by illustrating the events in a girl's life on the day of one of the most important events in American history. She uses the same backdrop as that in "Nada," which gives the stories a continuity that allows a deeper exploration of the roots of prejudice and oppression (an ironic twist on the title also suggests the American history that excludes many people). Here, those themes are examined in the context of the death of the president, toward whom many looked for cues to living the American Dream.

Cofer, Judith Ortiz. "A Job for Valentin" (1995). From *Help Wanted: Short Stories about Young People Working* (Sel. Anita Silvey, 1997). COMING-OF-AGE; COURAGE; DISABILITY/PHYSICAL AP-

PEARANCE; HISPANIC EXPERIENCE; LABOR/JOB; MEN and WOMEN; MORALITY (MORAL DILEMMA); SOCIETY; UNDERDOGS.

The narrator, Teresa, is a young Hispanic woman who takes a job selling food at a local pool because her eyesight is too bad to allow her to lifeguard. The job is a blessing for her; she gets to flirt with Bob Dylan Kalinowski, a beautiful young man from her school, and spend time with her friends. When Mrs. O'Brien, an officious administrator, places Valentin, a thirty-year-old mentally challenged man, as Teresa's assistant, she couldn't be more unhappy. The hirsute, nervous man unpacks his "art," animals made of rubber bands, on the counter and creates chaos whenever he tries to help Teresa serve drinks. However, when a small child nearly drowns because of the absence of Bob Dylan and the boy's mother (Bob, it turns out, may be the boy's father), Teresa and Valentin save him. In the aftermath of the near-tragedy, Mrs. O'Brien offers them two full-time jobs. Teresa knows that she will accept, if only not to break up the partnership that she has formed with her new friend, Valentin.

Acceptance, friendship, and perseverance are the story's key themes, and they are set against the backdrop of one young woman's attempt to escape the behavior that would gain her acceptance into society. Cofer renders an awkward relationship with great compassion and understanding of the process through which even the least likely of friendships develops.

Cofer, Judith Ortiz. "Nada" (1994). From *Daughters of the Fifth Sun: A Collection of Latina Fiction and Poetry* (Ed. Bryce Milligan et al., 1995). DEATH; GIFTS/GENEROSITY; GRIEF; HISPANIC EXPERIENCE; MEN and WOMEN; MOTHERS and CHILDREN.

When Dona Ernestina's son is killed in Vietnam, the women in the apartment building speculate on the mourning mother's strange behavior. The woman holds a wake for her son and for her deceased husband, who had died a year before. She invites the residents of the apartment building to join her for the wake; uncomfortable with the situation, they leave soon after they arrive. Before she will allow them to leave, however, Dona Ernestina insists on giving the guests small items that belong to her. Following the wake, the residents observe the woman handing out all of her possessions to whomever comes to the door. Word gets out on the street, and before long, lines of homeless people come to the door for handouts. One day, the residents hear a crashing from the apartment, and the police arrive to find the woman huddled in the corner, naked, surrounded by an empty room. She is as she came into the world . . . with *nada* (nothing).

Cofer mixes Spanish with English in this story, which won the O. Henry Award in 1994, to draw the reader into the world of her Hispanic characters. By allowing the reader a glimpse into the anguish of the grieving mother and wife, Cofer suggests that, despite the different cultures that exist in

America, we all understand the process of coming to grips with the death of our loved ones, even if we grieve in very personal ways.

Colette. "The Kepi" (1897). From *The Collected Stories of Colette* (Ed. Robert Phelps and Trans. Matthew Ward et al., 1983). AGING; ART and the ARTIST; MEN and WOMEN; SEXUALITY.

Paul Masson introduces Colette to a middle-aged woman, Marco, who writes novels for a pittance. The women become friends, and Colette acts as Marco's fashion consultant. Marco has been in a loveless marriage and has never taken a lover. When she meets a young lieutenant through a newspaper ad, though, she falls inexorably in love with him. She gains weight and revels in a life that she had never experienced with her husband. Her emotion is requited until one day after their lovemaking she makes the mistake of placing the lieutenant's kepi, a hat, on her head. Her attempt to portray herself as a young lover alienates the soldier, and he leaves her immediately.

The author was twenty-four when she wrote this story, which anticipates her own aging and explores the profound differences that exist between youth (carnality) and middle age (the intellectual). Through the power of an object as simple as the kepi—Marco's downfall, as she vamps for the young man who realizes that the two "love" in much different ways, despite the older woman's attempt at coquetry—Colette examines the various ways that we express passion at different times in our lives. Marco's disappointment is brought about by her own lack of knowledge about what constitutes a successful relationship, especially between two such disparate people. However, she doubles her writing fee after the affair ends (it was, after all, her writing that interested the young man in the first place), which suggests that she has taken away from the relationship a knowledge of love and passion that had been absent in her life until the young man's arrival. Still, Masson treats the information more as an ironic twist to the story than as an indication of Marco's enlightenment.

Collier, John. "Bottle Party" (1939). From *Studies in the Short Story* (Ed. Virgil Scott and David Madden, 1976). FANTASY/IMAGINATION; IRONY; JEALOUSY; MEN and WOMEN; REVENGE; SEXUALITY.

At the age of thirty-five, Franklin Fletcher dreams only of "luxury in the form of tiger-skins and beautiful women." As he looks for a hobby with which to mitigate the boredom of his life, he comes upon a shop that has bottles of every shape and size. When the shop's owner explains that the bottles contain all manner of genii, jinns, sibyls, and demons, Fletcher is interested. He purchases a couple of the bottles and discovers that he has a genie who will cater to his every whim, and a beautiful woman with whom he can spend the rest of his life. The genie and the woman, though, conspire to trick Fletcher into entering one of the bottles. He is unable to escape, and he ends up in the same shop where his dreams had begun. When a group of sailors buys the bottle, hoping to have procured the services of a beautiful woman, they discover Fletcher and proceed—in the middle of the ocean on an interminable journey—to treat him badly.

Collier updates the age-old tale of the genie and the bottle. Here, though, the greed that seduces the modern-day "everyman" backfires, because of Fletcher's jealousy, in a most ironic and darkly humorous way. His fate is a fitting, if rather violent, end for this humorous tale that explores the psychology of desire in a society that, in the time in which Collier writes, has become more anonymous and less attentive to the individual.

Conrad, Joseph. "The Secret Sharer" (1910). From *Fiction 100: An Anthology of Short Stories*, 9th ed. (Ed. James H. Pickering, 2000). COMING-OF-AGE/INITIATION; CRIME/LAW; DUTY; EXILE/ EMIGRATION; FRIENDSHIP; MORALITY (MORAL DILEMMA).

The captain is a young man who has received command of his first ship. As he is settling into his new position, the man finds a sailor hanging on to his ship's rope ladder. It turns out to be Leggatt, the first mate of another ship, the *Sephora*, who is wanted in the murder of a fellow sailor. Against the code of the sea, the young captain and Leggatt become good friends. The captain goes so far as to protect Leggatt from the *Sephora*'s captain, who is searching for the murderer.

The two friends devise a plan that would allow Leggatt to reach shore. In the process, the captain loses the confidence of his men, who are confused and angered by his erratic behavior during the time that the murderer is on board, and he risks the lives of the crew in order to help his new friend. The plan succeeds, however, and no one is the wiser.

The story is an examination of right and wrong similar to Herman Melville's "Billy Budd," though Conrad holds a different notion of the code of the sea from Melville's (in which the young sailor, beloved by all, is hanged). Instead of paying the ultimate price for the rash decision he makes, the young captain helps Leggatt to shore and rationalizes in his own mind the events surrounding the first mate's actions and his own subsequent harboring of the fugitive. Conrad implies the weight that duty carries—and an even greater responsibility to make decisions as one sees fit.

Coppard, A.E. "Arabesque—The Mouse" (1929). From *Twenty-Nine Stories* (Ed. William Peden, 1960). ANIMALS and HUMANS; IN-SANITY; INTERIOR LIVES; MEN and WOMEN; MOTHERS and CHILDREN.

Filip sits in his home reading Russian novels until he thinks he has gone mad from the reading. He gazes around the room and begins a conversation with himself as he sees a mouse creeping from a hole in the wall. He watches the creature intently, and though the man generally has a "crude dislike for such sly, nocturnal things," he feels no such aversion toward the mouse. When the mouse goes away, he thinks about when he was a boy and of a conversation that he had with his mother, who was nursing his sibling when Filip came running into the room. She explained what she was doing, and Filip placed his hand on her chest and felt her heartbeat. She told him that a heart is good if it beats truly. That day, when his mother was knocked down by a horse, her hands were crushed by a carriage. The doctor amputated her hands, and she bled to death.

Filip's attention returns to the mouse. He pulls a mousetrap out of the cupboard and sets it for his quarry. His mind wanders to a girl he only met once and how she commented on how his heart beat so rapidly and truly, which prompts him to blurt out "Little mother!" When Filip comes back to reality with the mouse, the creature is sitting in front of the mousetrap with its front paws torn off. He wants to end the mouse's misery, and he throws the animal out the window. Later, he tries unsuccessfully to find it in the street. He dumps the mouse's paws from the trap and puts it away.

Coppard uses a controlling image in the present to explain Filip's state, which borders on madness. The flashbacks are all connected to a relatively insignificant creature; however, since the mouse is so closely connected to Filip's mother and a long-forgotten love, the creature exacerbates his instability.

Coppard, A.E. "The Third Prize" (1928). From *The Collected Tales of A.E. Coppard* (Coppard, 1948). CRIME/LAW; MEN and WOMEN; MORALITY (MORAL DILEMMA); SOCIETY.

George and Nab are runners, and when they enter a race one August during a bank holiday, watched by two girls whom they have just met, George finishes third. They are approached by Jerry Chambers, a man who insists that he can get George the first-place money if they fabricate stories that would disqualify the first two runners. George refuses, but when there is a mix-up in the presentation of the awards, he tricks the presenters into giving him two pounds—twice the award amount. Nab is put off by his friend's action, though the girls find him clever. When the group sees Chambers ostensibly drumming up charity for a blind man, George drops one of the sovereign coins into the man's hat. Chambers, it turns out, uses the opportunity to line his own pocket. George has unwittingly given him the money that he had dishonestly taken earlier.

In a story that relies on an ironic twist for its effect, Coppard explores the relative morality of George's decision—which is deemed clever by the girls—and the more blatant theft of Chambers when he steals from a blind man. In this case, George has attempted to make amends for his earlier decision (as we might expect from one who enjoys the purity of competition), while Chambers, who feels no such guilt, is richer for the experience.

Coppard allows the reader to decide for himself the preferable course of action.

Costello, Mark. "Murphy's Xmas" (1967). From *The Norton Anthology of Contemporary Fiction* (Ed. R.V. Cassill, 1988). ADDICTION; ALIENATION/ISOLATION; FAMILY; FATHERS and CHILDREN; MARRIAGE; MEN and WOMEN.

Murphy awakens on the day of his departure for his parents' home with a bruised and swollen fist and no recollection of what he had done the night before. He begs his girlfriend, Annie, for forgiveness and begins the journey with his estranged wife, who is pregnant with their second child, and young son in tow.

The scene at his parents' home is one that he would rather forget. Against his better judgment, he makes love to his wife, and his father is incensed over his son's impending divorce. Only after a tearful apology to his parents is he able to return to Annie. He recalls his son's childish demand that if he does not come back home, he will shoot him with an imaginary gun. Murphy realizes that he is already dead.

Costello relates Murphy's dilemma in a disjointed narrative, bolstered by the image of the character's continuous drinking, that explores the heart of Murphy's problem: he is unable to break completely from the life that he has made for himself (and one that is, in large part, dictated by his upbringing) and to care for the family that loves him despite his shortcomings.

Couperus, Louis. "Bluebeard's Daughter" (1915). From *A World of Great Stories* (Ed. Hiram Haydn and John Cournos, 1947). CRIME/ LAW; MARRIAGE; MEN and WOMEN; MISOGYNY; WOMEN'S ISSUES.

Fatma is the daughter of the notorious pirate Bluebeard. Despite her beauty and wealth, she is something of an outcast in society because of the life her father lived. Though Bluebeard is now dead, he had a reputation for killing his many wives for the least disobedience. Fatma herself marries many times. The first three husbands die in quick succession, and the people in Baghdad begin to question whether she has had anything to do with their untimely deaths. Government officials take notice of her case, and while they decide what to do, Fatma marries again and again, until she reaches husband number six. When the officials visit Fatma, they find husband number six alive and well. When she explains that all of her husbands are, in fact, still alive, and she simply had "a desire for many husbands," the officials conclude that Fatma is immoral. She is tried and executed.

In Couperus's story, though the sins of the father are perhaps visited upon the daughter, the double standard that exists in society is what ultimately costs the woman her life. Ironically, Fatma is innocent of the murders that she is rumored to have committed; still, she cannot escape a society that would doom her despite her course of action. Seconds before her death, Fatma concludes that because she has blue hair, she is the object of society's scorn. In fact, she has been judged based on her father's actions and doubly cursed because of her gender; her blue hair is simply a convenient symbol of the capriciousness with which society treats its outcasts.

Cozzens, James Gould. "Clerical Error" (1935). From *The 50 Greatest Mysteries of All Time* (Ed. Otto Penzler, 1998). CRIME/LAW; DEATH; DECEPTION; DISABILITY/PHYSICAL APPEARANCE; LITERACY/WRITING; MYSTERY.

Mr. Joreth, a bookseller, is perusing the obituaries when Colonel Ingalls visits him. Ingalls is furious at Joreth for having sent an invoice to his brother, the late Reverend Doctor Godfrey Ingalls. Joreth, it seems, has billed the reverend for some prurient literature that, the colonel insists, his brother never would have ordered. Joreth counters with an insinuation that his list of confidential clients would surprise many people. When Joreth becomes indignant over the accusation that he sent a false invoice to the dead man—and with the threat of imminent physical violence from the colonel—he picks up the phone and sends for a policeman to settle the dispute. Colonel Ingalls uncovers the scheme when he tells the dealer that the reverend was, in fact, blind for the fifteen years preceding his death. Ingalls smugly tells Joreth that the policeman he has sent for has arrived.

The brief story uses setting and a surprise ending for its effect. Until the story's last paragraph, the reader has little idea how the colonel will prove his case—or how deeply the bookseller has implicated himself in a scheme that has been going on, the first paragraphs imply, for quite some time. The title of the story is ironic, given Joreth's maliciousness and the trouble that the swindler finds himself in after his many ill-gotten gains.

Crane, Stephen. "The Blue Hotel" (1898). From *The Dimensions of the Short Story: A Critical Anthology* (Ed. James E. Miller and Bernice Slote, 1965). ALIENATION/ISOLATION; CRIME/LAW; DEATH; FATE; INSANITY; JUSTICE; PLACE; VIOLENCE.

In Fort Romper, Nebraska, three men alight from a train during a snowstorm and are ushered into the Palace Hotel, a light blue building that stands out in striking contrast to its surroundings. Among the group is a Swede who clearly has misgivings about the place and acts as if he senses impending doom. When he joins some men for a card game, he accuses them of cheating; later, he thinks that the hotel owner is trying to poison him. After another aborted card game, the Swede takes Johnnie Scully, the hotel owner's son, outside, where he beats him to the ground. The Swede enters a bar, where he begins drinking and bragging about his exploits. In an effort to get the men in the bar involved in his story, the Swede grabs one of them by the neck. The man stabs him; as the Swede lay dying, the man tells the bartender that the authorities know where they can find him. The man is sentenced to three years in prison for the murder.

The use of color, always paramount for Crane, is significant here as well: the hotel signals the men to enter, though what the Swede finds is not in keeping with the muted shade on the building's exterior. The author's grounding the story in a desolate, cold place that is indifferent to the struggles of man to survive (see "The Open Boat") defines the naturalist narrative for which Crane is known. While the men, who are insignificant in the larger scheme of things, fight and kill each other, the land remains hostile and immutable. Though the easterner admits that he saw Johnnie cheating at cards, he is unsure whether he should feel remorse for not acting. Crane leaves the question unanswered.

Crane, Stephen. "The Bride Comes to Yellow Sky" (1898). From *The Treasury of American Short Stories* (Sel. Nancy Sullivan, 1981). MARRIAGE; MEN and WOMEN; PLACE; REGIONALISM (LOCAL COLOR); TRADITION/CONVENTION; VIOLENCE.

A newly married couple travel from San Antonio to Yellow Sky, Texas. The man is Jack Potter, the town's marshal, and he brings with him the bride whom no one in the town has met. Though he is respected in Yellow Sky, he is anxious to find out what the townspeople think of his clandestine marriage (an event whose importance, Potter knows, could be "exceeded only by the burning of the new hotel"). Scratchy Wilson, a fixture in the town and the marshal's sworn enemy when Wilson goes on one of his infamous drinking binges, confronts Potter and threatens to kill him. No one else in town is willing to take him on. When Wilson discovers that Potter has brought a new bride back to Yellow Sky, however, the revelation seems to change everything. Bemused, the drunken man ceases his threats; as he walks away, his "feet made funnel-shaped tracks in the heavy sand."

Crane's story is impressionistic in its use of colors and understated detail and draws on the author's journalism background for objective observations of the characters' actions. The confrontation between Potter and Wilson points up familiar hostilities and their resolutions in a small town in turn-of-the-century Texas, where the landscape itself often becomes a character.

Crane, Stephen. "The Open Boat" (1897). From *The Story and Its Writer*, 4th ed. (Ed. Ann Charters, 1995). COURAGE; DEATH; FRIENDSHIP; NATURE/WILDERNESS.

A fictionalized account of an actual shipwreck in which the author was a passenger, the story describes four men—the correspondent, the cook, the oiler, and the captain—fighting for their lives in the cold waters of the Atlantic off the coast of St. Augustine, Florida. It is simultaneously a journalist's dispassionate observation and the thoughts of a man who cannot be sure that he will survive the experience (after many failed attempts at getting the lifeboat to shore and at communicating with the people on shore who would be able to help them, the ending of the story is very much in doubt). In the process of rescuing themselves, each man shows great courage; in the end, the oiler loses his life, seemingly a sacrifice to the indifferent forces that rule nature.

It is only fitting that Crane, a journalist before he wrote short fiction and his famous novels *The Red Badge of Courage* and *Maggie: A Girl of the Streets*, should fictionalize his experience in "The Open Boat." In both the event itself and in the retelling, Crane was aboard the *Commodore* when it sank. His story is an example of naturalism in literature, the notion that nature is indifferent to the suffering of man, and it is contingent upon man to fight nature in order to survive. The refrain that Crane uses to illustrate that idea is, "If I am going to be drowned—if I am going to be drowned—if I am going to be drowned, why, in the name of the seven mad gods who rule the sea, was I allowed to come thus far and contemplate sand and trees? Was I brought here merely to have my nose dragged away as I was about to nibble the sacred cheese of life? It is preposterous. If this old ninny-woman, Fate, cannot do better than this, she should be deprived of the management of men's fortunes." Also, Crane uses impressionistic images (particularly colors, predominantly muted grays and blues) and repetition to illustrate the plight of the men as they struggle to survive and to engage the reader in the experience of thirty hours in a sea that lies impassive to their suffering.

Crutcher, Chris. "A Brief Moment in the Life of Angus Bethune" (1989). From *Connections: Short Stories by Outstanding Writers for Young Adults* (Ed. Donald R. Gallo, 1989). COMING-OF-AGE; COURAGE; DISABILITY/PHYSICAL APPEARANCE; IDENTITY; LOVE; MEN and WOMEN; PRIDE; REVENGE.

Though Angus Bethune is quick for his size and a force on the football field, genetics and an unusual family life work against him. His parents are large people, and Angus's physique is cause for much embarrassment when he is facetiously voted the school's Senior Winter Ball King. The queen happens to be Melissa Lefevre, with whom Angus is deeply infatuated, though she is dating the football team's star running back, Rick Sanford. Also, Angus's parents, who are divorced, are both involved in long-term homosexual relationships. Angus fully accepts the relationships, though he is an easy target for ridicule at school because of them.

When Angus's big moment comes—"All I want is my moment," he muses before the dance—he discovers that Sanford, who shows up at the party drunk, has orchestrated the fixed election that made Angus the king. After a confrontation with Sanford, Angus dances with Melissa, who makes an unexpected confession: She is a bulimic who is in therapy for her illness. When the two discover that they have more in common than they had first thought, Angus gains confidence, dancing with the athletic moves that he has perfected on the football field. He is a success, and much to Sanford's chagrin, Angus and Melissa leave the party together. Even Sanford's insults "can't touch my glory."

Crutcher's sense of humor pervades the piece and undermines the taunts of his protagonist's classmates. When the queen, Angus's dream girl, exposes her own flaw, the two realize the insignificance of outward appearance. Angus cares more for Melissa after her confession than he did before. The experience is a point of contact for the two, and Angus's trepidation over what was sure to be a disaster has been swept away by his newfound confidence. The story's title understates the importance of the "brief moment" for both of the protagonists.

D

Dahl, Roald. "The Landlady" (1959). *Alfred Hitchcock Presents: Stories to Be Read with the Lights On* (New York: Random House, 1973). DEATH; MYSTERY/ADVENTURE.

Seventeen-year-old Billy Weaver is looking for a room in the town of Bath, and he happens upon a bed and breakfast that looks promising. The proprietor is a "terribly nice" middle-aged woman who implores the young man to stay with her. He accepts the offer and, at her request, signs the guest book. The two names previous to his on the register seem familiar to Billy, though at first he is not sure where he has heard them before. Then, he recalls from newspaper articles that both are famous for having disappeared during their travels in the area. The landlady insists that the two young men are still staying with her. As it turns out, Billy Weaver is her only guest in the last several years. The young traveler reaches out to pet the landlady's parrot and a dachshund that lies quietly by the hearth, and he realizes that they have been stuffed. When he notices that the tea tastes of bitter almond, he fails to make the connections that are all around him and that may have saved his life.

Dahl gained a reputation as a writer of children's stories, though his wicked sense of humor and the macabre translates well into his short stories. The hints that arise throughout the story as to the landlady's sinister intentions are borne out in the last paragraphs. The story succeeds in large part because the reader is privy to a secret that is revealed to the young traveler only too late.

Defoe, Daniel. "True Relation of the Apparition of One Mrs. Veal" (1706). From *Great Short Stories from the World's Literature* (Ed. Charles Neider, 1950). DEATH; FRIENDSHIP; SUPERNATURAL/ HORROR.

The narrator relates Mrs. Bargrave's encounter with the apparition of Mrs. Veal. He proclaims Mrs. Bargrave's reliability "and can affirm the good character she had from her youth to the time of my acquaintance." He goes on to describe the circumstances under which Mrs. Veal, a great friend of Mrs. Bargrave, came to the woman's house, begged forgiveness for a long absence, and proposed that the two renew their friendship. Mrs. Veal has suffered from fits in the past, and her friend is concerned by her attitude when they meet. Mrs. Veal asks Mrs. Bargrave to tell her brother of their conversation, a request that seems odd to Mrs. Bargrave.

Only later does Mrs. Bargrave discover that Mrs. Veal had died of fits at the same time she could swear her friend had visited her. Some of the townspeople, including Mrs. Veal's husband, disclaim Mrs. Bargrave's story, though the narrator points out in her defense that she has never benefited from the story, and "therefore has no interest in telling the story." The narrator ends by stating that the story has affected him a great deal, and he has no qualms about believing Mrs. Bargrave who, under any other circumstances, would be seen by the community as an unimpeachable witness.

The story, as its title implies, is nothing more or less than the relation of a tale that has struck the narrator as curious. Defoe is one of the earliest writers of fiction that falls into a category that can today be considered the "short story," which is apparent in the author's setting out of the facts and its plotting. Defoe shows imagination in presenting a ghost story that precedes Poe and others who are considered pioneers of short fiction and masters of the supernatural tale.

DeFord, Miriam Allen. "No Loose Ends" (1971). *Alfred Hitchcock Presents: Stories to Be Read with the Lights On* **(New York: Random House, 1973). BETRAYAL; DEATH; MARRIAGE; MEN and WOMEN; TECHNOLOGY.**

When a woman hires a team of hit men to kill her husband, she can hardly imagine the result. Coates and Ferguson, the men who are sent to execute James Blakeney, a successful banker, carry off the job with professional detachment. Ferguson, though, has gotten a reputation as a talker, and he has outlived his usefulness to the organization. After Blakeney is dead, Coates, disgusted with the way that Ferguson feels compelled to talk about the execution, shoots his partner. He could not know, however, that just that morning, Blakeney had begun carrying a microcassette player with him that was activated when his body hit the ground and recorded the killers' conversation.

What looks like a simple murder-suicide becomes an open-and-shut homicide case when the police arrest the surprised widow and the men involved in orchestrating the murders. The title of the story is an ironic echo of Coates's thoughts when he had watched the banker's murder and then rid himself of the mouthy Ferguson—nothing was left to chance, and there were no "loose ends." Technology has caught up with the murderers, though, and has solved an otherwise perfect crime.

De la Mare, Walter. "An Ideal Craftsman" (1930). *Alfred Hitchcock Presents: Stories to Be Read with the Lights On* **(New York: Random House, 1973). CHILDHOOD; DEATH; DREAMS (SLEEPING); MEN and WOMEN; MYSTERY/ADVENTURE.**

The young man of the house awakens in the middle of the night with half-forgotten dreams stirring in his head. He carefully makes his way down-stairs to see what his old nemesis, Jacobs the butler, is up to. Jacobs has a history of keeping the master under his thumb, and the boy fancies that he is going to confront the butler as a raider plundering booty. When he finds a hysterical woman in the kitchen, he soon realizes that she has killed the butler and stashed his slight body in one of the cupboards. The woman is wild with guilt; the boy, instead of fleeing the scene, calmly suggests to her that they can make the butler's death look like a suicide.

With some struggle, the two hoist Jacobs's body into the rafters of the kitchen with a rope around his neck, just as the boy had read in one of the crime books that Jacobs repeatedly tried to confiscate from him. Dissociating himself entirely from the scene, the boy realizes that he needs to place a chair under the body and kick it away, as a man committing suicide would. He has helped the woman create the perfect crime. Only after the deed is done, and he realizes that he is alone with the body, does the impact of his acting as accomplice strike him full force. He calls for the woman to return and hurries upstairs to await the appearance of his parents from their eve-ning's outing.

De la Mare's story is unnerving because of its subject matter—the dis-passion with which the boy handles the situation—and the unreality of the whole scene, with its overtones of dreams and the suggestion of the adven-ture and crime stories that the boy hides from Jacobs. More importantly, perhaps, it is a tale of lost innocence and a statement of the unwitting and unthinking depravity of the human soul.

DeLillo, Don. "Videotape" (1996). From _The Story and Its Writer_, 5th ed. (Ed. Ann Charters, 1999). COMING-OF-AGE; DEATH; SOCI-ETY; TECHNOLOGY.

A young girl unwittingly captures the random murder of a man on vid-eotape as her family drives on the Interstate. The tape is shown across the country time after time, to the point that the public knows that the man is killed—by a serial murderer, the reader and the viewing public find out later—seconds after he makes a gesture of greeting to the twelve-year-old girl, who remains nameless.

The story cuts away to a man sitting in the comfort of his living room, obsessively watching the video yet again and calling to his wife to come see it (though they have their different programs, he cannot help but think that she _needs_ to see the tape). The tape has become famous not for what the viewer sees, but for the very fact that it catches a life at the moment of death, the bullet at the moment of impact. This is not movie violence, but real violence. The story is full of the contradictions that pervade society: the reality of the image is its unreal, even surreal, quality in the way the man simply slumps against the door of the car, which begins to lose speed; a young girl experimenting with a camera has too soon discovered the ephemerality of life.

The narrative is not unlike the snapshot images that the girl records on the videotape—jerky, in and out of focus, and disturbingly banal in its portrayal of death. DeLillo's story is a commentary on the pervasiveness of the media and "reality programming" in our culture. The message is not a hopeful one: "The horror freezes your soul but this doesn't mean that you want them to stop."

DeMaupassant, Guy. "The Dowry" (1883). From _Great Stories of All Nations_ (Ed. Maxim Lieber and Blanche Colton Williams, 1945). BETRAYAL; CRIME/LAW; FAMILY; MARRIAGE; MEN and WOMEN; WOMEN'S ISSUES.

The marriage of Simon Lebrument and Jeanne Cordier is a society event. The new Madame Lebrument has at her disposal a large dowry, and the newlyweds set out for Paris to celebrate their marriage. Lebrument insists that his wife have the dowry when they leave, so that he can purchase a notary-practice. Despite her stepfather's warning that it is not wise to carry so much money, she procures the dowry for her husband, and they begin their journey.

Along the way, Lebrument separates himself from his new wife, and she is stunned when the omnibus comes to the end of its run and her husband has disappeared. The driver mocks the young woman, and when her cousin happens upon her on the street, she relates the story to him. When she finally realizes what has happened, she sobs into her cousin's vest.

DeMaupassant is known for his realism and simple style, and this story is one of the best examples of both. Though on one level the story is a cautionary tale that takes a rather dim view of Maitre Lebrument's type, the author eschews a "happy ending" that would seem contrived given the situations that he creates. The response of Madame Lebrument's cousin, who orders breakfast for her and takes the day off work in order to comfort the grieving young woman, suggests the sympathy that the author routinely exhibits for his characters and their shortcomings.

DeMaupassant, Guy. "The Jewelry" (1885). From _Studies in the Short Story_ (Ed. Virgil Scott and David Madden, 1976). BETRAYAL; DEATH; DREAMS (of the FUTURE); HUMOR/SATIRE/IRONY; LOVE; MARRIAGE; MEN and WOMEN; PRIDE.

M. Lantin has a wife who appears to be nearly perfect. She is caring and affectionate and has an exemplary way of ruling their household. Her only two flaws are her love of the theatre and her passion for false jewelry. M. Lantin tells his wife that if she cannot afford real jewelry, then things should be kept simple. She responds that she has always loved jewelry.

When his wife catches pneumonia and dies, M. Lantin finds himself lost and financially unstable. He decides to sell his wife's jewelry, expecting to fetch a small price for the paste; instead, he discovers that the jewelry is real. He is now a wealthy man, though the thought of where his wife must have gotten the jewelry leaves him confused. Still, he resigns his job and marries a woman who, unlike his first wife, makes his life miserable.

DeMaupassant, always a shrewd observer of human actions and human nature, examines a topic similar to that in Henry James's "Paste" or the author's own story "The Necklace." By placing his characters in unfamiliar situations, DeMaupassant then revels in describing how they might act. As is very often the case, the author suggests that one's current position, no matter how mean, is often preferable to the dreams that we hold. In any case, he explores the notion that money alone is no cure for a poor love-match.

DeMaupassant, Guy. "The Necklace" (1884). From *Fiction 100: An Anthology of Short Stories*, 9th ed. (Ed. James H. Pickering, 2000). CLASS CONFLICTS; COMMUNICATION/LANGUAGE; DECEPTION; DREAMS (of the FUTURE); GREED; LABOR/JOB; MARRIAGE; MEN and WOMEN.

Though Mathilde is destined by birth to live a life of little consequence, she dreams of great things—meeting well-placed men who would dote on her, attending the grandest parties in France, in short, living the genteel life. When her husband, a bureaucrat with few prospects, tells her that they have been invited to an exclusive gathering, the couple must draw on their savings to buy her an acceptable dress, and she resorts to asking a friend for the use of a diamond necklace.

The party is more than she could have imagined, and when they return home late, the stunning Mathilde turns to the mirror to take one last look at her perfect outfit. To her horror, she finds that the necklace is missing. Despite their attempts to find it, they resign themselves to replacing it. Loath to tell the owner that they lost the necklace, the couple borrows a sum that will take them ten years to recoup. A decade later, when the last debt has been paid, Mathilde sees the woman from whom she borrowed the piece—radiant in her beauty and pushing a baby stroller—and tells her the story of the lost necklace. The horrified woman tells the now haggard Mathilde that the necklace she had borrowed all those years ago was nothing more than paste, a fake.

DeMaupassant's realism is highlighted in this brief tale of greed and pride, and he suggests the impossibility of rising above one's station in nineteenth-century France. The irony of the couple's willing decade-long enslavement in order to pay a perceived debt suggests that wealth is not the only component of social status. If the couple had been able to communicate the loss to Mathilde's "friend," the life-shattering consequences might have been avoided.

DeMaupassant, Guy. "Old Mother Savage" (1884). From *The Heath Introduction to Fiction*, 4th ed. (Ed. John J. Clayton, 1992). DEATH; GRIEF; LOVE; MOTHERS and CHILDREN; REVENGE; WAR.
The narrator has not been back to Virelogne for some fifteen years, and as he passes a home that used to belong to a woman known as "Old Mother Savage," he wonders aloud to his companion what ever happened to her. The companion tells a story of tragedy and death that leaves the narrator shaken.

Old Mother Savage watched her son go to war with the Prussians. As fate would have it, four Prussian soldiers were billeted in her home while the troops occupied the territory. Although they were, in reality, the enemy, the four men understood what Old Mother Savage must have been feeling. They had mothers of their own who were concerned about them. When Old Mother Savage receives a letter telling her that her son has been cut in half by a cannonball, she plots to kill the four men in revenge. She finds out the names and addresses of the men, so that their mothers, too, might receive the news of their sons' deaths, and burns them that night as they sleep. When a German officer asks the woman where the soldiers are, she does not hesitate to admit that she killed them. At first, no one believes her, thinking that the evening's events have driven her insane. When she shows the officer the letter apprising her of her son's death, the Prussian has her thrown against the wall of her cottage and executed.

Back in the present, the narrator, pondering the woman's ordeal and the unnecessary deaths of the soldiers in retribution, picks up a stone lying on the ground. It is still scorched black from the fire years before.

The story is typical of DeMaupassant's style: spare, descriptive, cutting, and ironic. The story-within-a-story gives Old Mother Savage's fate the patina of history without lessening the anguish we feel for her and subsequently for the mothers of the soldiers who die in the fire.

De Unamuno, Miguel. "Solitude" (1924). From *Great Short Stories from the World's Literature* (Ed. Charles Neider, 1950). AGING; ALIENATION/ISOLATION; ALLEGORY/LEGEND/FABLE; MEN and WOMEN; MOTHERS and CHILDREN; WOMEN'S ISSUES.
A girl named Solitude is born at the same time that her mother, Sanctuary, dies in childbirth. Sanctuary was miserable in her marriage and looked forward to the day when she would have a daughter of her own to keep her company. Solitude is sent by her father to be raised in another village, but when the girl is older, she returns to her father's home and is ill treated, as her mother had been. Solitude longs for a companion, and she cannot stop conjuring the elusive image of the mother she never knew. When Solitude is betrothed, her heart sings out, and she discovers life's possibilities. The boy grows tired of the girl, however, and tells her that she will someday

find a man who can make her happy. Solitude never finds such a man; toward the end of her life, she is a lonely old woman in a town where no one knows her. An exchange between the narrator and Solitude sums up her feelings on relationships, when the old woman compares lovemaking to dishwashing.

De Unamuno's story illustrates the hardships and perseverance of an old woman. The names of the characters are allegorical: the girl's only "Sanctuary" is taken from her when she draws her first breath, and her mother is prescient of the life that lay before the girl whom she will never know. Still, Solitude alone stands strong and forms a life independent of the men who have treated her roughly.

Dinesen, Isak. "The Blue Jar" (1942). From *Short Fiction: Classic and Contemporary*, 4th ed. (Ed. Charles H. Bohner and Dean Dougherty, 1999). AGING; ALLEGORY/LEGEND/FABLE; LOVE; MEN and WOMEN; MYSTERY/ADVENTURE; SOCIETY.

A rich old Englishman who had been a councilor to the queen has an odd passion: he collects ancient blue china. To that end, he and his daughter, Lady Helena, travel on a ship that catches fire in the China Sea. The lord, believing his daughter dead, is delighted when Dutch merchantmen rescue the girl after nine days in the water. The sailor with whom she spent those days at sea is given a large sum of money and asked never to return to the hemisphere, as news of his having spent time alone in a lifeboat with a peer's daughter would have made for scandalous conversation in the proper salons of her homeland.

The girl's passion, like her father's, becomes the collecting of rare blue china. Though she travels the world in search of it, she cannot find a certain color that has been in her mind since the time of her near-tragedy. Lady Helena, it seems, cannot stop searching for the sailor with whom she spent those days. Even in her old age, she sails the world in search of blue china. When she is finally presented with the one jar that completes her journey, she can die in peace.

This brief tale is a subtle examination of the depth of love and yearning. By giving the story a fairy tale quality—beginning with "There once was . . ."—Dinesen offers a universal truth by relating the specific case. The objects for which Lady Helena searches are reminders of her younger days; her attempt at finding the blue jar (or the sailor, and the distinction is not worth making), is an attempt to recapture the magic of her youth. The theme is one of Dinesen's favorites in the enchanted worlds that she creates.

Dinesen, Isak. "The Sailor-Boy's Tale" (1942). From *The Story and Its Writer*, 4th ed. (Ed. Ann Charters, 1995). ALLEGORY/LEGEND/FABLE; ANIMALS and HUMANS; COMING-OF-AGE; DEATH; GIFTS/GENEROSITY; LOVE.

The protagonist is Simon, a sailor-boy serving as a mate on a barque from Marseille to Athens. When he discovers a falcon caught in the ship's rigging, he helps the bird to escape, though "Through his own experience with life he had come to the conviction that in this world everyone must look after himself, and expect no help from others." That attitude would be important later, when he meets a girl named Nora and falls madly in love with her. Despite his duties aboard the ship, Simon rushes to join her one evening. On his way to Nora's home, Simon meets some Russians whom he knows. When one of the drunken men will not let him be on his way, and instead good-naturedly hugs the young man, Simon impetuously kills him.

A cry is raised in the street to find the killer. Simon rushes to find Nora, and she kisses him, promising her devotion. As he is about to be caught, an old crone claims him as her son and takes him to her home, where he is safe from capture. He discovers that the old woman is the bird whom he earlier saved from the rigging. She and her kind have the power to shift shapes, and she owes Simon her life. Now they are even. She sends him on his way with a mark on his forehead that will identify him as a chosen one. Simon lives to tell his story.

Ann Charters writes: "Dinesen spun her stories out of the impulse to bring to life a world of marvels and enchantment. . . . Discovering that 'all sorrows can be borne if you put them into a story or tell a story about them,' she showed that the storyteller can make meaning out of what otherwise would remain an unbearable sequence of events or unrelated happenings." In her brief tale of fantasy, Dinesen's protagonist experiences the gamut of human emotions, from the tragic betrayal of his friend, to the fear of death, to the passion that he feels for his love—and his life.

Dinesen, Isak. "Sorrow-Acre" (1942). From *The Norton Anthology of Short Fiction*, 6th ed. (Ed. R.V. Cassill and Richard Bausch, 2000). ALLEGORY/LEGEND/FABLE; CRIME/LAW; FAMILY; GRIEF; JUSTICE; LABOR/JOB; LOVE; MOTHERS and CHILDREN.

In a serfdom in Denmark, Adam returns to the family's home at a time of change. The cousin who was heir to the estate has died, and Adam discovers that, on the first day of the harvest, his uncle, with whom he was close in childhood, is passing judgment on a man who was accused of burning down one of the lord's barns. Instead of trying the boy, the uncle has decided that his mother, Anne-Marie, can determine the boy's fate: if she is able to mow a field of rye (which hereafter becomes known as "Sorrow-Acre") by herself, her son will be absolved of any wrongdoing in the crime.

Adam, as the representative of a new, more liberal breed of ruler, begs his uncle to prevent the woman from harming herself. Following the code of the old days, however, the uncle steadfastly refuses to halt the spectacle and insists that if she fulfills her end of the bargain, the woman's son will, indeed, be set free. Adam threatens to leave the estate, but as he looks at his uncle, an old man for whom change would mean death, he comes to an understanding of the man's attitudes. Adam recants his earlier speech and leaves the fields. He does not witness the tragic scene of the woman finishing the field and then dying in her son's arms.

Dinesen bases her story on a Danish folktale, though the theme of change and an understanding for the old ways is as relevant today as it was when she revised the tale. The mother's sacrifice is no less heroic for having been determined by the old lord, who later honors the woman with a stone that has a sickle engraved on it. Interwoven into this deceptively complex tale, however, are the themes of jealousy and guilt, which make the story come alive even in successive readings.

Dorris, Michael. "The Original Recipe" (1997). From *Help Wanted: Stories about Young People Working* **(Sel. Anita Silvey, 1997). AGING; COMING-OF-AGE; FAMILY; FRIENDSHIP; LABOR/JOB.**

Against her better judgment, Rayona begins working at a Kentucky Fried Chicken in Havre, Montana. She comes to work ill dressed for the occasion and is immediately put under the guidance of Tiffany, a too-perky girl who sees the beauty even in a greasy restaurant. When Rayona's father, grandmother, and some other relatives she hasn't seen in some time unexpectedly drop by to see how her first day is going, they get more than they bargain for. Derek, an unstable cook who is the only worker who can operate the pressure cookers, has a breakdown during the lunch rush, and the cookers are about to explode.

Rayona's great-aunt, Edna, who, it turns out, knew Colonel Sanders's wife decades ago, has been taciturn to this point. In the crisis, however, she draws on her Southern charm and work ethic and saves the day by disarming the pressure cookers and serving her own "original recipe" to the waiting crowd. Rayona watches the old woman with great admiration as first she talks a biker into trying the "one-day-only special," and everyone else in line follows suit.

Dorris's story is humorous and the characterizations sharp, though its strength is in a portrayal of the budding friendship between a young woman and the family she has hardly known. What is a coming-of-age for the restless, innocent girl is an opportunity for an old woman to relive the glory days of her relationship with the Colonel's wife.

Dostoevsky, Fyodor. "A Christmas Tree and a Wedding" (1848). From *Studies in Fiction* **(Ed. Blaze O. Bonazza et al., 1982). CLASS CONFLICTS; MARRIAGE; MEN and WOMEN; POVERTY; SOCIETY.**

The narrator begins his story by hinting at a wedding, but then decides to detail the events leading up to it. Five years before the wedding in question, the narrator was invited to a New Year's Eve children's party. One of the guests was a gentleman from the provinces who commands the respect of the entire party (except the narrator) for reasons that are not disclosed. When the gentleman sets his sights on a young girl of eleven, a beautiful child whose parents, it is said, have put aside a great dowry for her, the narrator is highly amused. He sees the gentleman calculating to himself how much the dowry will be worth by the time she is sixteen, old enough to marry. The gentleman appears to think about little else during the party that night, going as far as to belittle one of the poorer children whom the host had hoped to convince the man to take under his care. The narrator says several deprecating things to and about the man, who casts him an angry glance.

Five years later, the narrator happens upon a wedding and recognizes the groom as the man whom he had grown to despise. He also sees the girl, a young woman now, with a melancholy gaze that tells him she had little decision in the match. He makes his way into the street, amused and disgusted with the machinations of the gentleman.

Dostoevsky's story is overtly humorous, though the subtext implies the rigidity of the Russian class structure that the author knew so well. The importance of "marrying well" has nothing to do with love, the author implies, but rather depends upon the economic benefits that come of such a match. The characterization of the "gentleman" is sharpened by the narrator's understated disdain for the man and his actions, of which only the narrator, apparently, knows.

Dostoevsky, Fyodor. "The Peasant Marey" (1876). From *The Norton Anthology of Contemporary Fiction* (Ed. R.V. Cassill, 1988). ALIENA-TION/ISOLATION; GIFTS/GENEROSITY; MORALITY (MORAL DILEMMA); VIOLENCE.

As the prisoners drink and fight on one of their few respites from the brutality of life in the gulag, the narrator (ostensibly Dostoevsky himself) is disgusted by the way the men treat each other. The events that he sees before him prompt a memory from his childhood, when, as a young boy, he heard a cry of "Wolf!" and ran to a peasant, whom he knew as Marey, for protection. Marey had no knowledge of the incident, and he reassured the boy that he had nothing to fear from a wolf. Now, as he recalls the incident in his bunk in the gulag—and he has not given the meeting with the peasant any thought in the intervening years—the narrator suddenly realizes the importance of the peasant's action in terms of his current situation. He now sees the men around him as they are—brutes, whom life has treated roughly. The narrator knows that only that single moment of tenderness, which occurred so many years before and reemerged only through the violence of men toward men, is what separates the compassion of the narrator from the hatred of the prisoners.

The story parallels the author's own experience in a Siberian prison camp in the middle of the nineteenth century; the recollection of the peasant is also autobiographical. The story's "moral" gives the reader a sense of Dostoevsky's rather romantic notions of Russia's peasants, though one cannot dismiss the passion with which the author tells the story. It is a testament to the power of memory to influence the present, particularly a reality as undesirable as the one in which the narrator finds himself.

Doyle, Arthur Conan. "The Adventure of the Speckled Band" (1892). From *A Book of the Short Story* (Ed. E.A. Cross, 1934). DEATH; FAMILY; GREED; MYSTERY/ADVENTURE.

Holmes and Watson receive a visit from Helen Stoner, who is convinced that her life is in danger from her stepfather, Sir Grimesby Roylott. Two years before, the woman's sister died before she was to be married—her last words to her sister were, "The speckled band!"—and Helen, herself soon to be married, senses that she is to be her stepfather's next victim. Holmes and Watson take the case.

After perusing the will of the young woman's mother, the sleuths travel to Stoke Moran, Roylott's estate. They discover that Roylott, an eccentric who keeps a band of Gypsies for company and has exotic animals as pets, is renovating the manor house—much as he did before Helen's sister met her demise—and Helen will be expected to switch rooms while the work is being done. Holmes and Watson arrange to spend the evening in Helen's new room, and they discover that the "speckled band" is a poisonous snake that Roylott has sent into the room to dispatch his stepdaughter. Holmes strikes the snake, sending it back through the wall from which it came. It strikes Roylott, who dies from the bite. Roylott, it seems, was methodically murdering his late wife's children so that he could control the inheritance they received from their mother.

The story, typical of Doyle's Sherlock Holmes cases and the detective genre generally, illustrates the deductive method for which Holmes is famous. The outcome of the case is not clear until the end; however, Doyle's description of Roylott and his eccentricities, many of which the antagonist ostensibly picked up while he was a doctor in India, become clear in retrospect.

Doyle, Arthur Conan. "The Red-Headed League" (1891). From *The 50 Greatest Mysteries of All Time* (Ed. Otto Penzler, 1998). GREED; LABOR/JOB; MYSTERY/ADVENTURE.

Watson's traditional narration begins as he drops in on his friend, Sherlock Holmes, and a new client, the red-haired Mr. Wilson, who has encountered a strange organization that calls itself the Redheaded League. Wilson reveals that two months prior, his assistant, Vincent Spalding, called his attention to a newspaper advertisement looking for a new member to fill a vacancy of the Redheaded League, which offered a great sum of money for little work. Wilson, a pawnbroker in need of money, answered the ad and was given the job, which was to copy from the encyclopedia for a few hours a day. The "work" continued until the morning of his visit to Holmes, when he discovered that the league had suddenly closed.

On their way to the theatre, Holmes and Watson drop in on Spalding to observe the layout of the shop, which is adjacent to a bank. Holmes, who suspects he knows the details of the case, tells Watson to meet him that night with a revolver. With the police and the chairman of the bank in tow, the group go to the bank and discover that Spalding (whose real name is John Clay) used the Redheaded League as a ruse to get his boss out of the shop for a time so he could dig his way to the bank without disturbance. Holmes, in his inimitable way, had noticed by the man's pants that he had been digging; thus, the mystery was solved.

In another of his seminal detective stories, Doyle gives the reader specific information at the same time that he withholds other facts to pique the reader's interest until Holmes's inevitable discovery of the truth.

Doyle, Arthur Conan. "A Scandal in Bohemia" (1892). From *Fiction 100: An Anthology of Short Stories*, 9th ed. (Ed. James H. Pickering, 2000). MARRIAGE; MEN and WOMEN; MYSTERY/ADVENTURE.

Holmes is visited by the hereditary king of Bohemia on the night that his good friend and the story's narrator, Watson, stops by. The king, soon to be married, is afraid that his former mistress, Irene Adler, will ruin him and his marriage by making public a compromising picture of the two. He has tried many times in the past to get the picture from her, he tells Holmes, but all previous attempts have failed. Holmes accepts the case and, with Watson by his side, begins to search for Irene Adler.

After staking out Adler's home, Holmes follows her to a church, where he witnesses her marriage to a lawyer named Godfrey Norton. That evening, he returns to Adler's home with Watson by his side. After faking an injury, and with Watson creating a diversion, Holmes sees where Irene has hidden the incriminating picture. When he returns the next morning with the king and Watson, however, he discovers a note from Irene to the effect that she had caught on to Holmes's disguise and has fled the country with her new husband. In the note, she professes her love for her new husband and assures the king that she will not ruin his marriage. As a reward for Holmes's excellent work, the jubilant king gives Holmes whatever he wants. Holmes requests a picture of Irene Adler.

Doyle's famous detective who has a knack for solving crimes through the deductive method still fascinates readers with his genius and his dry humor.

Dreiser, Theodore. "The Lost Phoebe" (1918). From *Modern American and British Short Stories* (Ed. Leonard Brown, 1929). AGING; ALIEN-

ATION/ISOLATION; INSANITY; LOVE; MARRIAGE; MEN and WOMEN.

Henry and Phoebe Reifsneider have lived average lives on their farm. Of the seven children born to them, four have survived, but their parents rarely see them. Henry and Phoebe have only each other, and when Phoebe dies, Henry begins a slow descent into madness. He searches for his beloved wife all over the county; when his neighbors realize that he has lost his mind, they are concerned but decide that he is harmless. His meanderings range ever wider until one night, believing that he sees a ball of light that contains his lost love as he knew her half a century before, he jumps off a cliff and is killed. No one in the small town knows what Henry saw when he fell "eagerly and joyously" to his death.

Dreiser's story of an old man's love for his wife is a poignant articulation of the power of the relationships between men and women and the ravages of aging. Despite the rather morbid ending, Henry's death is a response to the notion that life must go on. In certain circumstances, Dreiser suggests, the alternative can be a blessing, especially when it is mingled with the bittersweet memories of youth and beauty.

Dubus, Andre. "A Father's Story" (1983). From *The Norton Anthology of Contemporary Fiction* (Ed. R.V. Cassill, 1988). FATHERS and CHILDREN; LOVE; MORALITY (MORAL DILEMMA); RELIGION/SPIRITUALITY.

Luke Ripley is a middle-aged man who has lived through a divorce and suffered the moving away of his children. Ten years later, he has managed to give his life the semblance of order through his relationship with Father Paul LeBoeuf and the Catholic Church. He rides his horse to mass each day, and though he uses religion as a guiding force, Ripley lives his life on his own terms.

When his twenty-year-old daughter, Jennifer, visits him from Florida, he is aware of the differences between them. She is an outgoing young woman who cares little for the strictures of the church and establishing order in her own life. After drinking four beers with her friends on an outing to the beach, Jennifer strikes and kills a man who dashed in front of her as she mounted a rise in the road. Hysterical, she wakes her father, who finds the man dead in the ditch. On his way to church the next morning, Ripley veers the car into a tree, covering up the evidence of her act.

Dubus leaves judgment to the reader as to the morality of Ripley's act, which saves his daughter from the possibility of legal repercussions, even if she must live with the memory of the accident. Instead, the story, as implied in the title, focuses on Ripley himself and the way that he has managed to reconcile his own life—after a series of events that separates him from his children—with his beliefs, an amalgam of the tenets of the church and his own individual spirit. In attempting to find solace in God, Ripley suggests that God himself would have done the same thing given the opportunity.

Duder, Tessa. "Sea Changes" (1995). From *Ultimate Sports* (Ed. Donald R. Gallo, 1995). COMING-OF-AGE; LABOR/JOB; MYSTERY/ADVENTURE; SPORTS.

Kirsty Fleming is a nineteen-year-old woman who has been chosen as a team member for the British side in the Whitbread around-the-world yacht challenge. The fact that she is the only woman on the crew, significant in itself, is just the beginning of Kirsty's story, which she recounts into a tape recorder as part of a five-thousand-word essay for which she is paid £10,000.

Kirsty begins her story at the age of sixteen, when she is fed up with school and convinces her parents that she should learn more about the world—specifically, by spending time in New Zealand with a family friend. When she arrives in Auckland, she finds by happenstance a yacht named the *Dolphin*; after she proves herself as a cook on the yacht, she is gently absconded by Barry and Harry Wildblood, cousins who spend their days sailing the world's oceans. More than two years later, Kirsty comes ashore in New Zealand, having transformed from a girl to a woman, from a landlubber to one of the most gifted young sailors in the world. One night before she leaves the yacht for her home in Oxford, England, Kirsty learns a secret that would stun the world were anyone to find out.

In the meantime, though, Kirsty is content to relive her memories with the cousins and to prepare herself for the Whitbread race. She tells the story because she wants "girls to know that you can take risks when you are traveling and find you've trusted your instinct and it's okay. Not every risk turns out to be a horror story about white slavery and girls ending up in Thai jails convicted of being drug couriers, despite what my mother still thinks."

Duder's story is a straightforward coming-of-age tale that examines and explodes some of the prevalent thinking on the topic of young women's roles in society. Through a keen sense of adventure and an obvious passion for her subject, Duder provides the reader with the groundwork for the "sea changes" that we all go through at some point in our lives.

E

Ehrlich, Gretel. "Pond Time" (1998). From *Off the Beaten Path* (Ed. Joseph Barbato and Lisa Weinerman Horak, 1998). FAMILY; INDIVIDUAL; LOVE; MARRIAGE; MEN and WOMEN; NATURE/WILDERNESS; SEXUALITY.

Madeleine is on her way to Tengmiirvik, Alaska, to find the daughter that her dead husband, Henry, fathered with another woman. The story opens with Madeleine and her pilot fighting a failed engine and frantically searching for a place to crash land. As she looks around her, she realizes that "Geography is destiny" and knows that "she was geography's ant being hurtled toward rock." Henry's memory weighs heavily on Madeleine, and the story intermingles scenes that describe the desolate and almost unbearable beauty of the Alaskan wilderness with the narrator's continuing devotion to her husband. That he has a child with another woman seems of little concern to Madeleine; she simply wants to find the last extant piece of Henry. Still, "no meeting would erase the watery nothingness of living on without him."

When the plane comes to rest, both Madeleine and the pilot, Archer, are alive, though they must concern themselves with keeping watch for bear that will try to take their supplies (or worse). Archer, like many pilots, Madeleine muses, is an inscrutable character, willing to listen to his passenger's story but not forthcoming with his own. When Madeleine tells him that her husband died because he starved himself to death, that he had lost the will to live, Archer comforts the woman. In finally telling his own story, Archer reveals that he was married to the daughter that Madeleine seeks. Both she and her mother drowned when a dogsled broke through the ice. Madeleine and Archer make love, and she wonders if she will stay with him. Ehrlich's story combines the majesty and terrible power of nature with the enigma and frailty of human relationships. The result is a poignant mingling of memory with shared experience.

Ellison, Ralph. "Battle Royal" (1952). From *The Story and Its Writer*, 4th ed. (Ed. Ann Charters, 1995). AFRICAN-AMERICAN EXPERIENCE; CLASS CONFLICTS; COMING-OF-AGE; COMMUNICATION/LANGUAGE; RACE RELATIONS; SEXUALITY; VIOLENCE.

The narrator is an unnamed black man who recalls a time twenty years before when he was preparing to go to college. At the request of some white leaders in the community who have offered him a scholarship to further his education, the young man unwittingly becomes a pawn in their games. He is led into a hall where others like him are humiliated by having to fight with one another, and one boy is embarrassed by the men for becoming aroused at the sight of a naked white woman who has an American flag tattooed on her belly. Only after he suffers similar humiliation does the narrator get a chance to speak his piece. The men, in attendance only for the show, largely ignore his speech until he makes a stray comment about the relationship of the races that the men take in the wrong way.

The young man recalls his grandfather, on his deathbed, speaking the words that will haunt him throughout his life. He realizes that his grandfather has been fighting a war that will undermine the white man's suppression of his race. Though he is hesitant to believe the old man at first, he slowly comes to understand the truth of his words.

Ellison's story, the first chapter of his classic novel *Invisible Man*, is a poignant, angry recollection of the events that prompt the man to become involved in various causes that promote his race. Along the way, he discovers the ulterior motives that exist even within groups that purport to represent the black man. Though the man realizes the truth of human nature, he is little redeemed by the revelation. The woman, the battle, the scholarship itself are all symbols of the white man's dominance over black culture.

Ellison, Ralph. "King of the Bingo Game" (1944). From *Fiction 100: An Anthology of Short Stories*, 9th ed. (Ed. James H. Pickering, 2000). AFRICAN-AMERICAN EXPERIENCE; CONTESTS; DREAMS (SLEEPING); ENTROPY/CHAOS; FATE; NATIONALISM/ AMERICAN DREAM; RACE RELATIONS; VIOLENCE.

In a theater, a black man sits through a movie so he can play the bingo game afterward. He thinks that if this were the South, he would have a much easier time of things. In the North, people do not stick together. Even as the movie drones on, the man falls asleep and dreams of a train from his childhood, when he was nearly killed and the white people only laughed.

When the movie ends, the man plays bingo but holds out little hope of winning the jackpot—$36.90 that he would use to support his family. When he realizes that he has won, he is paralyzed and is barely able to climb to the stage in time to spin the jackpot wheel. He cannot decide when to stop the wheel, and after being heckled by the emcee and the audience, two policemen appear, wrestle him to the ground, and beat him. As he slips into unconsciousness, he knows that his luck has run out.

Ellison reprises the theme that carries *Invisible Man* to its conclusion: the black man cannot adjust to life in the North, and he has little hope of living the American Dream, here symbolized by the spinning wheel of fortune and the notion that for every movement of the wheel toward the top, there is a similar movement downward. Any hope of realizing his dream is undermined by his indecision, though Ellison implies that he is heroic in the attempt and is beaten down only when the powers that be sense his weakness.

Erdrich, Louise. "The Red Convertible" (1984). From *Growing Up Ethnic in America: Contemporary Fiction about Learning to Be American* (Ed. Maria Mazziotti and Jennifer Gillan, 1999). ALIENATION/ ISOLATION; COMMUNICATION/LANGUAGE; ESCAPE; SELF-DESTRUCTION/SUICIDE; SIBLINGS; WAR.
Lyman has made the most of his money by slowly climbing the hierarchy of the Joliet Café. When the place is destroyed by a tornado, he uses the insurance money to buy a red convertible. He and his brother, Henry, spend a summer traveling wherever they please, relaxing under a willow tree and encountering a girl with long hair whose tribe housed them for a time during their journey. When Henry is sent to Vietnam, Lyman restores the convertible to its original condition; he is dismayed when Henry returns and shows little ambition for anything but watching television. Lyman wrecks the car, hoping that Henry will take an interest in refurbishing it yet again.

When Henry suggests that they "take that old shitbox for a spin," Lyman is elated. When he sees a photograph that their sister, Bonita, has taken, however, he is haunted by Henry's ghostly appearance. On a trip to the river, Henry breaks down, and after an argument and a fight, the two break into hysterical laughter. Henry jumps into the river, and Lyman drives the car in after him.

The convertible is a symbol of the men's innocence, and the story is a disturbing exploration of the loss of innocence that the two brothers—one in Vietnam and one in America—share through their experiences. With her realistic dialogue and masculine point of view, Erdrich portrays Lyman as a concerned brother and friend trying to make sense of the horrors of war from an outsider's perspective.

F

Far, Sui Sin. "In the Land of the Free" (1909). From *Mrs. Spring Fra-grance and Other Writings* (Ed. Amy Ling and Annette White-Parks, 1995). FAMILY; MINORITY EXPERIENCE; MOTHERS and CHILDREN; NATIONALISM/AMERICAN DREAM; POLITICS; PREJUDICE.

In order to hold with tradition, Lae Choo travels from California to China to give birth to her first son. When she returns to America after an unex-pected delay, she discovers that her son will not be allowed entry into the country, as she had not mentioned him on her immigration papers. She is compelled to leave the boy with the authorities while the matter is sorted out.

With the case languishing in the bureaucracy, Lae Choo and her husband hire a lawyer to dispatch the matter, who tells the parents that he will need five hundred dollars to secure the proper approval. After another lengthy wait, the lawyer succeeds. When Lae Choo meets her son to take him home, however, he refuses to see her, instead seeking shelter with the missionaries who have cared for him during the separation.

Sui Sin Far is the pseudonym for Edith Maude Eaton, a pioneer of stories about the Chinese and their struggles in America. In this case, the individual stands for the many: Far was appalled by the treatment of the Chinese at the hands of railroad men and others who took advantage of their precarious position in a culture that, at best, shunned them, and at worst murdered them with impunity. Clearly, the title is ironic; none of the Chinese char-acters in Far's story are treated with equality, nor are they allowed the simple freedom that we take for granted.

Faulkner, William. "Barn Burning" (1950). From *Fiction 100: An An-thology of Short Stories*, 9th ed. (Ed. James H. Pickering, 2000). ALIENATION/ISOLATION; CLASS CONFLICTS; ESCAPE; FAMILY; FATHERS and CHILDREN; HISTORY; LABOR/JOB; REVENGE.

Abner Snopes is sent out of town after he is accused of burning a neigh-bor's barn over a dispute. His son, Sarty, stays tight-lipped about the matter, though his father senses that the boy was about to tell the judge the truth. Snopes warns the boy that blood sticks together, that family is the most important thing a man can ever have. The family finds work on the land of

Major De Spain, but Snopes's insolence to the man makes life even worse than it had been. After he tracks mud onto an expensive carpet in De Spain's house, the major insists that Snopes clean it off. Instead, he ruins the carpet and drops it unceremoniously on the front steps of the house. When De Spain sues him over the incident, Snopes once again turns to arson as his sole means of expression. Sarty, having warned the major of what was about to happen, runs into the woods. He does not look back.

Faulkner evokes his unique sense of the South, bringing to life characters that populate many of his stories and novels. The themes of alienation, family, and class conflict that Faulkner explores throughout his fiction underpin the narrative. Only Sarty, it seems, is redeemed. Of Sarty and his father, only the boy is able to tell right from wrong.

Faulkner, William. "The Bear" (1942). From *The Norton Anthology of Short Fiction*, 6th ed. (Ed. R.V. Cassill and Richard Bausch, 2000). ANIMALS and HUMANS; COMING-OF-AGE; COURAGE; FRIENDSHIP; HISTORY; NATURE/WILDERNESS; SUPERSTITION.

When Ike McCaslin, a young white boy turns ten, he has the opportunity to hunt for a bear that has been elusive to all who have tracked him. The boy goes out into the woods with Sam Fathers, a Chickasaw, who acts as his guide. Sam tells the boy that the bear is watching them; the boy's blood rushes with the excitement of the hunt. The next year, the boy sees the bear's tracks, but not the bear itself. Sam tells him that it is alright if he is "scared," but he shouldn't be "afraid," since animals are able to sense fear. Sam also tells the boy that he does not see the bear because of the gun that he has brought with him. The next day, the boy begins to find his own way through the woods, and he catches a glimpse of the bear, "immobile, solid, fixed in the hot dappling of the green and windless noon, not as big as he had dreamed it, but as big as he had expected to, bigger, dimensionless against the dappled obscurity." The boy watches the bear disappear into the wilderness.

On another hunt a couple of years later, the boy returns with a good dog, a good gun, and Sam by his side. The boy had already killed his first buck and a different bear, and he expects to do the same to the elusive one. When the two come upon the bear, however, the dog is in danger of being killed and the boy throws his gun down and rescues the dog. When Sam asks him why he didn't kill the bear, the boy can only wonder himself.

The theme of man versus nature is an integral part of all of Faulkner's fiction; this story, which appears in its lengthy entirety in Faulkner's story cycle *Go Down, Moses*, is no different. The boy's coming-of-age parallels his relationship to the bear, which is first a myth, then becomes a physical presence, and finally a test of the boy's manhood. Faulkner implies that even though the boy is unable to shoot the bear (in fact, he performs an action at least as heroic in saving the dog), he has come away from the experience with a profound appreciation of the power of nature, which is being corrupted by man even as nature alone has the power to cleanse the soul.

Faulkner, William. "Dry September" (1931). From *Short Fiction: Classic and Contemporary*, 4th ed. (Ed. Charles H. Bohner and Dean Dougherty, 1999). AGING; MEN and WOMEN; RACE RELATIONS; SEXUALITY; SOCIETY; VIOLENCE; WOMEN'S ISSUES.

In the "bloody September twilight, aftermath of sixty-two rainless days," a group of men sit in the local barbershop discussing the ostensible rape of Miss Minnie Cooper, a white woman, by the black man Will Mayes. Though the barber protests the man's innocence, they set out from the shop to find Mayes, intending to lynch him. Despite his own claims of innocence, Mayes is taken away to an undisclosed place; the implication is that he has been killed. The barber, finally unwilling to go along with the men (even though he strikes out at Mayes when the man resists his captors), jumps from a moving vehicle and heads back toward town.

Minnie Cooper, a woman of "thirty-eight or thirty-nine" whose prospects have dwindled, lives with her mother, and her days have a "quality of furious unreality." She is clearly a woman whom life has passed by. When she hears about the action that the local men have taken, she struggles to remain calm. In the movie theatre, however, she begins an insane laughter that she cannot control. Her friends wonder if anything really happened between her and Will Mayes. In the last section of the story, McLendon, the ringleader of the lynch mob, physically abuses his own wife (apparently in an attempt to rid himself of the guilt and misplaced rage that he feels toward Mayes), and "The dark world seemed to lie stricken beneath the cold moon and the lidless stars."

The story paints a bleak portrait of race relations in the South. The men assume that Minnie Cooper's accusations are true, though by the end of the story, the reader surmises that the banality of her own life and her imminent middle age has prompted her to make the false claim. As in many of Faulkner's stories (and in much Southern literature generally), nature is an important character, and the men who drag Mayes to his death blame the weather, in part, for their actions. McLendon's own abuse of his wife, however, illustrates the self-righteous hypocrisy that is the seed for the story's tragic event.

Faulkner, William. "A Rose for Emily" (1931). From *The Story and Its Writer*, 4th ed. (Ed. Ann Charters, 1995). DEATH; HISTORY; INSANITY; LOVE; MEN and WOMEN.

As the only living member of a prominent family in her town, Emily Grierson has become a burden to the townspeople. Despite repeated tax notices and the whisperings of the locals who fear that she is losing her mind, she remains hidden away from them, an enigma; her only steady companion is an old black servant. She buys arsenic—to exterminate rats, she claims—and at one point her house is enveloped in such a stench that the men in the town sprinkle lime around the area to eliminate the odor without embarrassing her.

Emily has remained single throughout her life, despite a courtship when she was in her thirties with a man named Homer Barron. At first, no one thought she would take Barron seriously. After all, he was a northerner and a day laborer, and they knew that she would never forget the unspoken rule of *noblesse oblige*—literally, the obligations of nobility that came with her standing in the town. Eventually, Barron is forgotten when their attention of the townspeople turns to other scandals.

Upon Emily's death, under the pretense of paying their last respects, curious residents line up to see the home that has been shut to them for years. When a locked room is opened and the dust clears, the men find the mummified body of Homer Barron on the bed where Emily has kept him all these years. An imprint on the bed and a gray hair on the pillow beside Barron suggest that she has slept next to his body since his death.

The story, while not typical of Faulkner's rigorous psychological investigations, does reveal the "Southern gothic" themes that he explores in his depictions of the eccentricities of life in the fictive southern towns that were influenced by history, greed, guilt, and the alienation of the inhabitants.

Faulkner, William. "That Evening Sun" (1931). From *The World of the Short Story* (Ed. Clifton Fadiman, 1986). AFRICAN-AMERICAN EXPERIENCE; FATHERS and CHILDREN; MEN and WOMEN; MISOGYNY; RACE RELATIONS; SEXUALITY; VIOLENCE.

Nancy works for the Compson family, who treats her with a modicum of respect that she does not get from others. When she demands payment for work that she has done for a white man in town, he beats her and knocks out her teeth. When she is put in jail, she attempts suicide. The crux of the story is Nancy's relationship with Jesus, her lover, who threatens to kill her. When he leaves town, the suspense is made all the worse for Nancy, who expects him to appear at any moment, ready to act on his impulse.

When she enlists the companionship of the Compson children so that she will not be as frightened of Jesus's return, the children are confused by Nancy's barring the door and her nervousness. She is convinced that Jesus is lying in wait for her in a ditch. When Nancy and the children hear someone approaching the door, they expect Jesus to break in and Nancy begins to weep. Instead, it is Mr. Compson, who has come to take his children home. Nancy begs the children to stay; she knows they will all have fun if they will stay and protect her from her fears.

Faulkner's predominant theme in his short fiction is the way that class relationships affect those who are marginalized by society. In this story, unlike, for instance, "Barn Burning," he also explores race relationships and violence against women. The title of the story suggests that a time of day that should be restful and idyllic is instead a time of impending terror for Nancy. The child's point of view also serves to understate the seriousness of Nancy's problem: the return of Jesus, which would otherwise be a time of great rejoicing, becomes fearful; the anticipation of his return is perhaps worse than the reality, and, ironically, Nancy is forced to live with that fear for as long as he stays away.

Fitzgerald, F. Scott. "Babylon Revisited" (1931). From *The Story and Its Writer*, 5th ed. (Ed. Ann Charters, 1999). ADDICTION; COMMUNICATION/LANGUAGE; FATHERS and CHILDREN; GUILT; LOSS; MEN and WOMEN; MORALITY (MORAL DILEMMA); SOCIETY.

Charlie Wales has come back to Paris to reclaim his daughter, Honoria. His sister, Marion, who has kept the child in his absence, is wary of her brother's intentions. Although she admits that he is financially secure enough to support her, she cannot forget what precipitated the move in the first place. Wales's past carousing caused him to leave Paris for Prague and, the story implies, ultimately led to his wife's death.

Wales has dedicated himself to reform, however, and takes one drink a day—no more, no less—not for enjoyment, but to remind himself of the past that has cost him so dearly. When two of his friends arrive at Marion's house in a drunken stupor to exhort their comrade to join them once for old time's sake, Marion has misgivings about allowing Wales to take his daughter back. When the hotel bartender asks if Wales will have another drink, he declines, keeping his promise not to revert to his old ways. He will come back for his daughter in the future, he tells himself. He is too old now to dream the dreams of a young man with his whole life ahead of him, and he is sure that his dead wife would not want him to spend his life alone.

The story is a condensed telling of the themes of alienation and dissipation that Fitzgerald details in *The Great Gatsby*. Wales's predicament is not unlike that of the author and fellow expatriates in Paris during the 1920s and 1930s, when their freewheeling socializing and libertarian attitudes led to a disavowal of the values that Wales so vehemently wants to regain—for himself, and especially for his daughter.

Flaubert, Gustave. "The Legend of St. Julian the Hospitaller" (1903). From *The Norton Anthology of Contemporary Fiction* (Ed. R.V. Cassill, 1988). ALLEGORY/LEGEND/FABLE; DEATH; FAMILY; FATE; RELIGION/SPIRITUALITY; VIOLENCE.

Set in the twelfth century, the story begins with Julian's birth and the two very different prophecies that come to his parents immediately after: While a hermit tells Julian's mother that her son will one day become a saint, a mendicant foretells a future of great glory and a royal family. After a joy of killing manifests itself in the young man, a stag tells Julian that he will one day kill his own parents. He is shaken by the revelation, and fears that the prophecy will come true.

Julian's fears are well founded. He marries the daughter of an emperor, and when his parents, on a visit to Julian's home, take his wife's place in their bed, he unwittingly kills them. Driven to grief by his actions, he wanders the world avoiding the very things that have caused him trouble in the past. When he is exceedingly kind to a leper (who turns out to be the incarnation of Jesus), he is also sainted—the fulfillment of the final prophecy that had earlier seemed so far out of reach. The story, the author explains, is written in the stained-glass windows of a church with which he is familiar.

Like the fate of Oedipus, the outcome of Julian's life seems to be predetermined from his birth. Unlike Oedipus, Julian's ultimate fate is based more on the decisions that he makes, especially after the death of his parents, than on the whims of a higher power. His ascension to heaven in the final scenes is a hopeful conclusion to this updated answer to the age-old question of predetermination and individual will.

Flaubert, Gustave. "A Simple Heart" (1877). From *The Story and Its Writer*, 4th ed. (Ed. Ann Charters, 1995). ANIMALS and HUMANS; BETRAYAL; FAMILY; FRIENDSHIP; LABOR/JOB; MEN and WOMEN; RELIGION/SPIRITUALITY.

Félicité Barette, an orphan, is cast into society at large when she is jilted by a young man who "had married a very rich old woman" in order to avoid the draft. She gains employment from the Aubain family, endearing herself to the widow and her children when she saves them from a charging bull. Félicité is especially drawn to the daughter, Virginie. As the child begins her studies of Catholicism, Félicité herself ingenuously accepts the religion. When Virginie leaves for school, the woman turns her attention to Victor, Virginie's brother. Both Victor and Virginie die, leaving Félicité alone, except in her mutual grief with M. Aubain. Félicité's life is enriched by the arrival of a parrot, Loulou, though the bird, like much of what the woman loves, dies. She has the parrot stuffed, and he remains with her. As the years wear on, Félicité has little reason to live. Still, her death is a transcendent experience.

The protagonist of Flaubert's story recalls Anton Chekhov's own "Darling," who is a *tabula rasa*, a blank slate upon which society leaves its mark. In "A Simple Heart," however, Félicité's compassion and goodness, despite the meager circumstances from which she has arisen, elevates her to the role of saint, her simple belief in the aesthetic trappings of religion (the symbolism turned on its head by the inclusion of the parrot) a fitting tribute to the goodness of her heart.

Forshay-Lunsford, Cin. "Saint Agnes Sends the Golden Boy" (1987). From *Visions* (Ed. Donald R. Gallo, 1987). COMING-OF-AGE; DREAMS (of the FUTURE); DREAMS (SLEEPING); IDENTITY; MEN and WOMEN.

Like any girl falling in love for the first time, Maddy ignores her English teacher as she doodles hearts to her boyfriend, Paul, a musician who lives a hundred miles away. Anxious to see Paul for the first time in a month, Maddy calls him, only to find that he has lost interest in her and instead has taken up with someone whom Maddy knows only as Jeanie. Infuriated, Maddy for the first time takes her English assignment seriously: to describe in a short essay a dream or fantasy, much like that of the heroine in John Keats's "The Eve of St. Agnes," that might give an intimation of the future. Maddy darkens her room, climbs into bed without having had supper, and begs the dream vision to come to her. It does.

While she sleeps, Maddy dreams of a world of vibrant colors where she can breath underwater and the law of gravity has little meaning. She meets a beautiful Golden Boy and his emaciated, frightening friend who wants her to stay with him, even against the bidding of her friends, who wave and shout to her from shore. When she wakes up, Maddy is bemused by the dream. Did the Golden Boy's frightening friend mean her harm? What would have happened if she had seen the dream through to its conclusion? When she writes of her dream for the class assignment, the teacher reads her paper aloud in class anonymously. Still, one of her classmates, Jack Mason, knows that she is the one who has described the dream, and he presents Maddy with a picture of the Golden Boy. Curiously, she notices that it looks a lot like Jack himself.

The story describes frustrated first love and the hope that comes of "dreaming" about the future. Maddy's confusion at the meaning of the dream is a sign of her coming-of-age, with all the contradictions that the term implies. She has also learned the importance of finding the extraordinary in the everyday events of life: the "Golden Boy" whom she has longed for has been next to her the whole time.

Forster, E.M. "The Road from Colonus" (1904). From *The Norton Anthology of Short Fiction*, 6th ed. (Ed. R.V. Cassill and Richard Bausch, 2000). AGING; ALIENATION/ISOLATION; FAMILY; FATHERS and CHILDREN; GIFTS/GENEROSITY; HISTORY; PLACE.

Mr. Lucas, who has had a lifelong interest in Greece and Greek society, finally has an opportunity to see the country for himself. Though he is in poor health, he enjoys the adventure, all the more so when he comes upon a spring that flows from the trunk of a plane tree. More than any other of the group's participants, including his daughter and son-in-law, Lucas is intrigued by the spot and would like to stay longer. He is compelled, however, to move on.

After the group has returned to their home in London, Lucas receives a gift from the tour guide in Greece. The asphodel bulbs are wrapped in newspaper, which the daughter reads idly, at first; when she comes across an account that describes how the owner of the inn and his family were killed by a falling plane tree on the very day that they had stopped, the daughter breathes a sigh of relief, realizing that they could well have been the victims of the tragedy. The old man, who is writing a letter of protest to his landlord over some minor nuisances that have plagued him, is oblivious to her and the news.

The story's title is a reference to the place where Oedipus died and is important because the tour guide has equated Lucas with Oedipus. Ironically, Lucas's becoming bewitched at the site of the inn nearly caused his death, though in a world that has become increasingly narrow to him because of his alienation from his daughter and society in general, he will never know what the outcome might have been. Perhaps, Forster suggests, Lucas would have been better off had he died under the falling plane tree; clearly he had not been happier in quite some time than he was when he discovered the spring and its source.

Forte-Escamilla, Kleya. "Coming of Age" (1993). From *Join In: Multiethnic Short Stories* (Ed. Donald R. Gallo, 1993). ANIMALS and HUMANS; BETRAYAL; COMING-OF-AGE; DEATH; FAMILY; MISOGYNY; SEXUALITY; VIOLENCE; WOMEN'S ISSUES.

Pochie and Nuncio have come to the desert for different reasons, though their feelings of anguish are similar: Pochie has been raped by Rocha, her stepfather; Nuncio, a young bullfighter, has come to reconcile himself to the death of the bull, for which he had great respect. Both have been driven to the desert by the actions of adults who care little for them, but would have them do their bidding. When Pochie is cleansed by a torrent, she falls asleep, and Nuncio at first thinks that she is dead when he finds her there. She awakes and listens to Nuncio's story, as "he told her about the kid he'd been, how smart and quick, doing anything he could to get near the matadors, until they had started training him." Pochie, recognizing that Nuncio has been indoctrinated into the world of men, replies that "There is only one kind of man in the world," and sets off across the desert alone.

Forte-Escamilla's story is a series of powerful impressionistic images that coalesces into the meeting between Pochie and Nuncio. Though both have high aspirations—Pochie's mother teaches her to read so she "can be somebody in life," and Nuncio is seduced by the romance of the bullring—the reconciliation that the reader might expect is not forthcoming. Rather, the author implies, the gulf that is opened when men and women "come of age" is one that is difficult to bridge when the time of innocence has passed.

G

Gaines, Ernest J. "The Sky Is Gray" (1963). From *Studies in Fiction* (Ed. Blaze O. Bonazza et al., 1982). AFRICAN-AMERICAN EXPERIENCE; CHILDHOOD; PRIDE; RACE RELATIONS.

James, an eight-year-old black boy, and his mother, Octavia, are on their way to the dentist to have James's tooth pulled. Though they have little money for such things, James's condition is clearly worsening. When they get to the dentist's office, however, they are told to come back later. With their meager savings, Octavia orders coffee and James has milk and cookies so that they may enjoy the warmth of the café where they have gone to wait. While there, Octavia pulls a knife on a pimp who asks her to dance.

As they wander the streets, a white woman, Helena, invites them inside her home for a bite to eat. She asks James to take the trash to the curb, so as not to give the impression of charity; when Helena, who owns a store with her husband, gives Octavia too much salt meat for her money, Octavia insists that she cut off half. Helena calls the dentist's office and assures the woman and her son that they will be the first treated when the dentist returns.

Octavia's reaction to Helena's goodwill recalls the interaction of whites and blacks in Flannery O'Connor's "Everything That Rises Must Converge." In both cases, the black mother steadfastly refuses the perceived charity of whites, a reaction that is double-edged: by refusing to acknowledge the well-meaning gesture (in the case of Gaines's Helena), the relationship is weakened. Still, Octavia asserts that she and James—and despite his youth, he is learning a valuable lesson—will be fine if they can harden themselves a bit more to society's general indifference to the economic suffering of blacks.

Gale, Zona. "The Biography of Blade" (1927). From *Modern American Short Stories* (Ed. Edward J. O'Brien, 1932). AGING; EPIPHANY; FAMILY; LABOR/JOB.

Blade has been asked to submit his biography for the county history. As he walks home after a day as editor of the *Muscoda Republic*, he feels that not many of the country's hundred million are much better off than he: he has worked at the local newspaper for twenty-five years, married a woman who has spent all her life there, and raised four children—all in Muscoda.

On this particular night, he has been invited to the home of the Herrons, whose daughter is giving a singing performance. Blade mentions to his mother, who lives with the family, that the biography will be coming out soon. When he hears the voice of the young Miss Herron, though, he has an epiphany, and "for the first time his importance, his newspaper, his home, his family, were outdistanced." He wants to live as the young woman lives, with the possibilities of life before him.

With everything in his life changed, at least for the moment, Blade takes back the biography that he had written earlier, with the intention of spicing it up. He asks the local bandleader if he can play flute in the band, and his family is embarrassed that he should want to make a spectacle of himself in front of the townspeople. In the county's history, Blade's biography remains unchanged from what he had previously written. He cannot for the life of him think what he had in mind.

Gale's story of a middle-aged man's intimations of mortality is a poignant expression of feelings that resemble a young man's coming-of-age with little of the promise of life's mysteries. Though Blade can change for a time, the aspects of life that make it worth living—an interesting occupation, a loving family, the stability of small-town America—are the same aspects that often lead to the torpor that Gale explores through her characters. The best that Blade can do is learn to live with the contradictions of his own maturation.

Gale, Zona. "A Far Cry" (1927). From *Modern American and British Short Stories* (Ed. Leonard Brown, 1929). DEATH; FAMILY; FATHERS and CHILDREN; MOTHERS and CHILDREN; PLACE.

Elmer Dasher and his family sit on the front porch of their home waiting for something to happen. Ludlow, a neighbor, cajoles Dasher into making broad statements about their small hometown, Patch Grove. When Ludlow wonders why the town simply does not slide down Patch Hill into oblivion, Dasher defends it, saying that a person could not find a better place to live.

When the family is called to the hospital to visit Katy, Dasher's niece, they witness the death of an anonymous Bohemian woman. The event affects his wife, who can only wonder at the senselessness of the death. Dasher, whose car has broken down and who must ride with his family on a passing train, has the events even more profoundly etched on his soul. He is exalted by the brush with death and by notions of home, whose nostalgia suddenly wracks him with longing.

Gale's brief tale, imagistic in the scenes that make up the story's action, manages to draw complex characters, particularly that of Elmer Dasher, by suggesting how the day's events change their worldview. Dasher, a "molested-looking man" seemingly ill suited to sitting and swinging on his front porch, sees the world in a different way. Still, the words of his daughter, spoken in platitudes about the weather and echoed from the beginning of the story, suggest that life will go on much as it has for all these years.

Gallant, Mavis. "1933" (1987). From *The Story and Its Writer*, 5th ed. (Ed. Ann Charters, 1999). ALIENATION/ISOLATION; ANIMALS and HUMANS; COMMUNICATION/LANGUAGE; CULTURAL CONFLICTS; DEATH; LOSS; MEN and WOMEN; MOTHERS and CHILDREN; POVERTY.

After the death of Mr. Carette, his wife and their two young daughters move out of their flat in Montreal's Rue Saint-Denis and into a smaller apartment. Though they are not destitute, they are by no means well-off. Occasionally, Mrs. Carette must sew in the evenings to make ends meet, and her brother-in-law sends them money while the sale of her dead husband's business is being finalized. The children are most affected by the move, and "Change, death, absence" have crept into their lives for the first time.

The family becomes acquainted with their landlords, the Grosjeans, who have an Airedale named Arno. Though they are around the same age, the two women never became friends (Mme. Grosjean, who was Irish, could not speak French, and Mme. Carette spoke only a few phrases of English). According to Mme. Carette, the only thing keeping the Grosjeans together is the dog, and she predicts that the couple will separate when the dog dies. One of the young girls, affected by her mother's reaction to her own pettiness, runs to her mother and tries to kiss her. Her mother reassures her that everything will be fine. Mr. Grosjean, entirely unaware that "all the female creatures in his house were frightened and lonely, calling and weeping," stands in the darkness and calls for Arno to play fetch.

Gallant's story is disarmingly simple, and only in the last lines does what has been merely suggested come to the surface. Mme. Carette is a young woman attempting to make ends meet for her family after the death of her husband, and she sees only loneliness in the lives of the people around her. Gallant, who was born in Montreal, uses the language barrier and the family's circumstance to point out the alienation and dislocation that otherwise productive, happy people feel in their everyday lives. The author has suggested that her stories often detail personal loss; her own father died when she was only ten years old.

Gass, William H. "In the Heart of the Heart of the Country" (1967). From *The Granta Book of the American Short Story* (Ed. Richard Ford, 1992). ART and ARTISTS; COMMUNICATION/LANGUAGE; IDENTITY; INTERIOR LIVES; LOSS; LOVE; MEN and WOMEN; METAFICTION; PLACE.

In a narrative whose form recalls William Faulkner's *As I Lay Dying* nearly forty years before, Gass offers thirty-six vignettes—with titles such as "My House," "Vital Data," "Weather," and "People"—that encompass the experiences of a poet and college teacher who has been jilted by his lover and who subsequently travels to a small Midwestern town to rediscover the missing parts of his life. When he finds a new love, she also leaves him. His life continues to disintegrate, and he holds out little hope for the future.

The unconventionality of the narrative, which also echoes the work of Gass's contemporaries—John Barth and Robert Coover, among others—is more "about" the author and his quest than it is any coherent sequence of events ("plot") that we might expect from a traditional short story. The title suggests that the narrator, in his own poetic way, is focused more on intro-spection (his own heart) than he is accurately portraying the "heart of the country," the Midwest. The author, by mediating his own experience through the prism of the unrequited lover, gives a unique perspective on the land and its people that ultimately defines his own character and re-inforces the alienation and fragmentation that we would expect to find in such a disjointed narrative.

Gilman, Charlotte Perkins. "The Yellow Wallpaper" (1892). From *The Story and Its Writer*, 5th ed. (Ed. Ann Charters, 1999). ALIENA-TION/ISOLATION; COMMUNICATION/LANGUAGE; HEALTH (SICKNESS/MEDICINE); INSANITY; INTERIOR LIVES; MAR-RIAGE; MEN and WOMEN; MOTHERS and CHILDREN; TRA-DITION/CONVENTION; WOMEN'S ISSUES.

The story's narrator is a woman who suffers from a rather vague "hysteria" after the birth of her child (a condition recognized today as postpartum depression). In an attempt to make her well, her husband, a physician who insists that he has the best interests of both her and their daughter at heart, takes her on a rest cure to the country. There, the woman is under the supervision of a doctor who has become famous for treating such illnesses (the doctor is—ironically, and typically for the time—a man). He prescribes absolute rest for the woman, who goes progressively insane when her artistic and imaginative powers are subdued by the very men who wish her to get well. Finally, the woman strips the wallpaper from her bedroom, which has become her own prison cell, in order to find the shadow figures that lurk there. When her husband enters the room to see what is the matter with her, he faints; the woman wonders why he should have done such a thing. Although she has symbolically risen above the man, her momentary freedom comes at a great cost.

Clearly, Gilman works to discredit the patriarchy and its overweening con-trol of women in this story, which she wrote between 1890 and 1894. Although it has autobiographical undertones (the author spent a short pe-riod in a sanitarium under the treatment of S. Weir Mitchell, the real-life equivalent of the doctor who forces the protagonist into insanity, and the experience nearly drove her mad), it remains effective as broad social criti-cism more than a century after its publication.

Glasgow, Ellen. "The Difference" (1923). From *Collected Stories* (Ed. Richard K. Meeker, 1963). BETRAYAL; JEALOUSY; MARRIAGE; MEN and WOMEN; MORALITY (MORAL DILEMMA).

Margaret's youth has begun to leave her, and after twenty years her marriage has become stale. When she receives a letter from her husband's mistress, she is distraught. She realizes fully for the first time how much she has given up for her husband, and still he is unhappy with their relationship. After meeting the woman, Rose Morrison, Margaret knows that she should no longer stand in the way of her husband's happiness. After confronting him, however, Margaret is dissatisfied with the result. He informs her that he is not in love with anyone, and she cannot understand why he behaves the way he does. Margaret decides to leave him.

Glasgow explores the theme of love in its many permutations. The several twists and turns in the story—including Margaret's acquiescence to her husband's relationship with another woman and her own ambivalence at her marriage—suggest that love is not, in fact, quantifiable (a notion that is echoed in Raymond Carver's "What We Talk about When We Talk about Love"). Rather, the reader must look at the individual case and decide the merits based on the facts. Happiness, the story suggests, should be the basis for any good relationship. Glasgow uses haunting images of autumn leaves tumbling to the ground after a fruitful summer to symbolize the passing of time and to give the story a universal quality. After all, the experience that Margaret goes through is unique only in the details. The generalities speak for themselves.

Glaspell, Susan. "A Jury of Her Peers" (1917). From *Fiction 100: An Anthology of Short Stories*, 9th ed. (Ed. James H. Pickering, 2000). ANIMALS and HUMANS; CRIME/LAW; DEATH; MARRIAGE; MEN and WOMEN; WOMEN'S ISSUES.

It is one of the most extraordinary events that anyone could ever remember in Dickson County. There has been an incident at the home of Mr. and Mrs. Wright. In the upstairs bedroom, Mr. Wright was found hanged to death and Mrs. Wright has been taken to the station for questioning. Martha Hale is called away from her kitchen with her bread ready for mixing; she and Mrs. Peters, the sheriff's wife, have been asked to join the investigation.

Even while the sheriff and his men look for clues to the death, they condescend to the women, who surmise how Mr. Wright's death may have transpired. As the women ready a change of clothing and some knitting for Mrs. Wright to have during her incarceration, they discover a dead bird in her sewing kit. The events of the night before become clear to Martha Hale and Mrs. Peters: Mrs. Wright, upset over her treatment by her husband, is distraught that he has choked her bird to death. The women know that the bird was one of the few joys in her life. As a result of his actions, Mrs. Wright killed her husband as he slept. Though Mrs. Peters balks at the idea that the murder was justified, she refuses to relate the important detail to the sheriff. Mrs. Hale hides the dead bird in her coat as the county attorney makes a deprecating reference to women's work.

The story, on one level a mystery, is also an exploration of the relationships between men and women. While the discovery of the bird may not justify the murder of Mr. Wright, Glaspell suggests that the death of the bird was one event among many that forced Mrs. Wright to escape from her husband by any means necessary. The bird is a symbol for the lack of joy in her life.

Gogol, Nikolai. "The Diary of a Madman" (1835). From *The Dimensions of the Short Story: A Critical Anthology* (Ed. James E. Miller and Bernice Slote, 1965). CLASS CONFLICTS; COMMUNICATION/ LANGUAGE; INSANITY; INTERIOR LIVES; SOCIETY.

The diarist of the title is a middle-aged clerk mired in the bureaucracies that Gogol, Chekhov, and the Russian masters made infamous in their stories. The man has little hope for advancement in his society, and he becomes increasingly dissatisfied with his life. The observations that he makes detail the world that he sees around him, though they are clearly mediated by his own attitude toward society; as oppression and alienation take their toll, the man sinks deeper into the delusions of sex and power that ultimately land him in an asylum. When he regains his identity as a faceless clerk in the Russian bureaucracy—and after experiencing a series of beatings in the asylum as part of his therapy—the man reverts to cries for his mother, and he thinks of himself as the king of Spain.

Gogol weaves a complex psychological narrative that convincingly portrays the descent into madness of a man who has little hope for his future. The characters that the author creates are present in many of his other stories ("The Overcoat," for instance), which describe the insidious effect of society on the individual. The diarist's own madness, Gogol suggests, is one viable alternative to a world that only uses and discards those who must tolerate such abuse in order to survive. Still, the author implies that the life the man would want to live is well beyond his means; madness is only a pale substitute for life itself.

Gogol, Nikolai. "The Overcoat" (1840). From *The Harper Anthology of Fiction* (Ed. Sylvan Barnet, 1991). ALIENATION/ISOLATION; CLASS CONFLICTS; DEATH; POLITICS; POVERTY; REVENGE; SUPERNATURAL/HORROR.

Akaky Akakievich's life is absurd from the day of his birth, when he is given his name. Akaky wanders through life as a copyist (not unlike Melville's Bartleby) and has few aspirations save for the purchase of a new overcoat. Despite the fact that he cannot afford the garment his tailor suggests, Akaky buys the overcoat. For the first time in his life, he is popular with his coworkers and is invited to their parties. One night soon after his triumphant moment, Akaky is mugged and his overcoat stolen from him. Though he protests the theft to the "Person of Consequence," he is given no satisfaction. In fact, his run-in with that highly placed bureaucrat costs him his life, when after the visit, he dies from having been exposed to the bitter cold of the Russian winter. His spirit haunts passersby, until one night he frightens the Person of Consequence into giving up his own overcoat. Despite the scare, the bureaucrat is changed only for a time.

Gogol's story, like the stories of his Russian contemporaries writing in the middle of the nineteenth century, details the role of the bureaucracy in repressing the citizens of Russia and one man's fight against the humiliation and oppression inherent in that system of government. Later, Kafka would echo the themes of oppression and alienation that underpin Gogol's stories.

Gonzalez, Gloria. "The Boy with Yellow Eyes" (1987). From *Visions* (Ed. Donald R. Gallo, 1987). COMING-OF-AGE; COURAGE; FRIENDSHIP; HUMOR/SATIRE/IRONY; IDENTITY; LITERACY/WRITING; MYSTERY/ADVENTURE.

The people of Preston Heights still talk about the event years later, even though the truth has been clouded by time and the usual lapses of memory. Norman, a boy whose only passion in life was reading, turns out to be the hero; Willie, who thought of Norman as the "boy with yellow eyes" because of the way the light reflected off his glasses and his odd hazel eyes, forms an unlikely partnership with Norman.

When Norman and Willie both find themselves in a train car, Norman proselytizing to Willie on the joys of reading and giving him an account of Bram Stoker's *Dracula*, they discover that a stranger who recently came into town is, in fact, a Nazi spy. Norman writes down the Morse code that he can hear emanating from an adjacent car, and the two chase after the man, who has a bad leg; Willie, the athletic one, hits the man with a baseball bat. The antagonist is captured and taken to the police station, and the boys are toasted as the heroes of the town. Willie had a successful career in the navy, and Norman became press secretary to a senator. Norman still outreads Willie by two to one, but they detail their reading exploits to each other every year in a holiday card.

Gonzalez's story is both humorous and entertaining, not the less so because of the disclaimer at the beginning of the story which suggests that all such stories undergo at least a bit of embellishment. Also, the events that bring the two very different boys together make them heroes on one level; perhaps more importantly, they form a friendship that lasts a lifetime and allows them to realize the relative merits of the other's passion.

Gonzalez, Gloria. "Viva New Jersey" (1993). From *Join In: Multiethnic Short Stories* (Ed. Donald R. Gallo, 1993). ALIENATION/ISOLA-

TION; ANIMALS and HUMANS; ASSIMILATION; FRIENDSHIP; HISPANIC EXPERIENCE.

Lucinda and her family have recently emigrated from Cuba to the United States, and they settle in West New York, New Jersey, one of the most densely populated cities in the country. Lucinda, who misses her grandmother who stayed behind in Cuba, is adjusting to her new school and the customs of a new country. When she rescues a dog named Chauncey, her first thought is that Ashley, a girl in her English class, will adopt the dog because she is one of the few people Lucinda knows who lives in a house, not an apartment building. Until she can take the dog to Ashley's house, Lucinda hides it in the basement of her building; twice Chauncey causes the electricity to go out in the neighborhood by tripping a breaker. The first time, Lucinda runs after the dog and cannot find him. Ashley, who goes with the girl to find the dog, tells Lucinda about her own grandmother, who lives in Nevada. Like Lucinda, Ashley has few friends and writes letters instead. The second time Chauncey wreaks havoc, Lucinda catches him before the firemen and police find him, and she takes him to Ashley's place, where he will have a good home.

The dog, as much an outsider as Lucinda and her family, is the catalyst for the beginning of a friendship between two girls who have much in common, including their attempt at assimilating to a culture that is in large part confusing and hostile toward them.

Gordimer, Nadine. "Country Lovers" (1980). From *The Story and Its Writer*, 5th ed. (Ed. Ann Charters, 1999). CHILDHOOD; DEATH; FATHERS and CHILDREN; LOVE/HATE; MOTHERS and CHILDREN; RACE RELATIONS; SEXUALITY; SOCIETY.

In Gordimer's South Africa, Apartheid is alive and well. Though black and white children play together when they are small, they assume the roles that society intends for them to have as they grow into adulthood. For Paulus Eysendyck, a young white man of some family means, the distinction does not dawn on him until it is too late. He sees Thebedi as he has always seen her—a playmate who lives on a farm down the road. Paulus goes as far as to bring his friend gifts from a shop in town, which the girl explains away to her father as a reward for hard work that she has done for the white family.

The two begin a romantic relationship, meeting whenever they can. Thebedi's parents arrange a marriage for the young woman, and she is reluctant to tell her lover, who is going off to veterinary school. Two months after her marriage to Njabulo, Thebedi gives birth to a light-skinned daughter who does not grow darker as she ages. When Paulus finds out about the baby, he demands that Thebedi never come near his house with the child; the baby dies mysteriously, and Paulus remains free, even though the evidence in his daughter's death points to him. Thebedi, interviewed by the newspapers and speaking in her own language, tells the reporters that her relationship with the white boy was merely a "thing of our childhood."

Gordimer, who won the Nobel Prize for literature in 1991, gives a realistic portrayal of life and relationships in her native South Africa. Though Paulus and Thebedi have been friends since childhood, they are forbidden by social custom from being together, even after the birth of their daughter. Paulus's reaction, Gordimer suggests, is what one might expect in the situation; no one involved is surprised that he is acquitted of the charges. The fact that Thebedi speaks in her native tongue when reporters interview her only serves to distance her from the life that she shared with the white son of a wealthy farmer. The bucolic, ironic title of the story belies the subsequent tragedy of this interracial relationship.

Gordon, Caroline. "The Ice House" (1963). From *Studies in Fiction* **(Ed. Blaze O. Bonazza et al., 1982). COMING-OF-AGE; DEATH; HISTORY; LABOR/JOB; WAR.**

One day in April 1866, Doug and Raeburn go to their temporary jobs at an ice house, where the bodies of dead Union soldiers had been stashed after a Civil War battle in the area four years before. Despite the fact that the two boys are paid only a small sum for their labor, the contractor, a short, plump man who works for the government, gets paid for every load of coffins he sends. When the two boys take a break down by the creek, they talk about the contractor's business and how much he gets paid to do less work than they do. Raeburn tells a story about how to catch the channel catfish that live in the creek. The contractor tells the boys that they are smart for their age (they are both fifteen) and talks to them about opportunity and looking for jobs. When he tells the boys that they don't have to work for the next few days, they are bemused by the contractor's attitude toward them. On their way out of the woods, they see the contractor dividing up the soldiers' skeletons into various coffins so he will get paid more for his services. His intentions in getting rid of them early become clear.

Gordon's story makes effective use of dialogue and setting to evoke the time about which she writes. The story details a formative experience for a pair of innocent young boys who attempt to make sense of death. In the case of the contractor, the story also describes the urge to succeed in a world in which duplicity is accepted and, perhaps, even expected.

Gordon, Caroline. "The Last Day in the Field" (1935).From *Studies in the Short Story* **(Ed. Adrian H. Jaffe and Virgil Scott, 1964). AGING; ANIMALS and HUMANS; FRIENDSHIP; INTERIOR LIVES; NATURE/WILDERNESS.**

Aleck suffers from a nagging pain in his leg, which might keep him from hunting this year. When a killing frost hits in the middle of November, though, he awakens his good friend, Joe, a much younger man, to hunt quail with him. During the hunt, Aleck looks at Joe and muses, "It's a wonderful thing to be twenty years old." Still, his own age and infirmity do not spoil the day. He takes time to observe a sycamore root and the dogs; the big dog, Bob, especially reminds him "how different he was from his mate and like some dogs I had known—and men too—who lived only for hunting and could never get enough no matter how long the day." As the day wears on, his leg making it difficult for him to continue, Aleck remembers various hunts from the past, and he senses dusk coming. As the two men head home, they pin down a single quail, and Aleck watches the bird go up "over the rim of the hill and above the tallest hickories. It hung there for a second, its wing black against the gold light, before, wings still spread, it came whirling down, like an autumn leaf, like the leaves that were everywhere about us, all over the ground."

In this story, Gordon writes from the point of view of an old man who senses his mortality. The author's descriptions of a beautiful, cold fall morning and the hunt itself serve as context for the crux of the story, an old man's insatiable desire to experience the events that make life worth living. The simple, understated plot leaves room for the subtle development of characters that is at once poignant and life-affirming. Though the title of the story implies that Aleck has spent his "last day in the field," the images that Gordon paints of nature in all its glory also suggests the cycle of the seasons that will bring with it renewed life.

Grafton, Sue. "The Parker Shotgun" (1986). From *The New Mystery* (Ed. Jerome Charyn, 1993). BETRAYAL; DEATH; MYSTERY/ADVENTURE.

Kinsey Millhone is hired by Lisa Osterling to solve the mystery of her husband's death. Five months after Rudd Osterling was shot to death, the police in California still have no suspects in the crime. According to Lisa, no one has made the necessary effort to track down the killer because they think Osterling's death was a drug deal gone bad. After questioning Lisa, Kinsey is directed to a gun shop where the man had gotten an appraisal on his Parker Shotgun. According to Avery Lamb, the owner of the shop, Osterling had probably stolen the gun from Jackie Barrett, who had been in the shop the week before him with the very same gun. Kinsey tracks down Mrs. Barrett and is immediately suspicious of the woman, who is nervous and taciturn. While leaving the house, Kinsey runs into Mrs. Barrett's son, who leads Kinsey to solve the mystery. She gives the gun, worth thousands, to Osterling's widow and handles justice in her own way.

Grafton, who is one of the best-known mystery writers in the world with her "alphabet series" of mystery books featuring Kinsey Millhone, uses her protagonist to solve a tightly crafted short story. The first-person narrative gives the story a gritty, immediate feel that leaves no doubt as to why Grafton's character is so popular.

Grimm, The Brothers. "Rumplestiltskin" (1815). From *Great Stories of All Nations* (Ed. Maxim Lieber and Blanche Colton Williams, 1945). ALLEGORY/LEGEND/FABLE; CONTESTS; GREED.

A miller who has occasion to speak with the king wants to seem important, so he tells the king that his daughter possesses a unique gift: she can spin straw into gold. The king, intrigued by the possibilities of such a talent, places the young woman in a room full of straw and a spinning wheel and tells her that if, by the following evening, she has not turned the straw into gold, she will die.

As the maiden bemoans her fate—there is no chance, of course, that she will be able to fulfill the king's request, and she will surely die—an odd little man enters the room and overnight turns the straw into gold. The king, rejoicing at his good luck, places the girl in larger and larger rooms, telling her finally that she will be his wife if she succeeds one more time. The girl, having given her ring to the man, promises the mysterious man who has helped her the couple's first child should he work his magic this one last time. He does, and the girl becomes queen of the kingdom. When the little man comes to collect on the queen's promise, she reneges. He allows her three days to guess his name, after which time he will make good on their previous deal. At the last moment, the queen, with the help of her aide who has seen the ridiculous little man dancing around a fire and celebrating his great fortune, guesses that the man's name is Rumplestiltskin. In a fit of anger, Rumplestiltskin tears himself in two.

This brief, well-loved tale comes from the collection *Children's and Household Stories*, which the Brothers Grimm published between 1812 and 1815. Though the story has been read to and by countless children, its straightforward exploration of greed and manipulation is a good starting point for a unit that might also include more complex renderings of similar themes.

H

Hale, Edward Everett. "The Man without a Country" (1863). From *An Anthology of Famous American Stories* (Ed. Angus Burrell and Bennett Cerf, 1963). ALIENATION/ISOLATION; BETRAYAL; EXILE/EMIGRATION; WAR.

A young soldier, Lieutenant Philip Nolan, is wrongly accused of conspiracy. At his trial, he exclaims to the judge, "Damn the United States! I wish I may never hear of the United States again!" His wish is granted, as Nolan is sentenced to live out his life aboard naval ships at sea and never to hear utterance of the United States again. The crew aboard Nolan's ship is ordered not to give Nolan any information concerning the United States. The sailors go to great lengths to carry out the orders.

Nolan's suffering manifests itself when he reads aloud about a man whose soul is dead because he is exiled from home with no titles or wealth. He does not voice his anguish, but accepts his fate. On his deathbed, Nolan expresses to a fellow soldier that he has been in torment for the past sixty years. The exile asks the man to fill him in on the history of the United States and gives orders for the man to open his Bible after his death. The next morning, the soldier finds Nolan dead. A slip of paper asks that he be buried at sea, but requests that he be given a grave that reads: "He loved his country as no other man has loved her; but no man deserved less at her hands."

The story details the excruciating emptiness that one man feels when the bond between him and his country is severed. Hale wrote the story during the Civil War to convey a message of patriotism and to explore the importance of country—in this case, a common national heritage and set of values—during a trying time. The story is no less relevant today, certainly, than it was a century and a half ago.

Harris, Joel Chandler. "The Wonderful Tar Baby Story" (1883). From *The Portable American Realism Reader* (Ed. James Nagel and Tom Quirk, 1997). ALLEGORY/LEGEND/FABLE; COMMUNICATION/LANGUAGE; CONTESTS; DECEPTION.

Brer Rabbit and Brer Fox have had a long-running feud, and Brer Fox is determined to make his enemy suffer. Though he is thwarted in his attempts to catch the rabbit—at first simply showing up at the rabbit's home and waiting futilely outside for the rabbit to show himself—the fox finally finds success with a more complex plan: by creating a character out of tar, the fox assumes that the mysterious figure will be too enticing for the curious rabbit to ignore.

Brer Rabbit, who wanders down the road just as Brer Fox has finished setting his trap, is incensed by the tar baby's lack of response to his greetings. He becomes stuck in the tar when he attempts to strike the figure and makes an easy target for the fox. Despite Brer Rabbit's entreaties not to throw him into the "brier-patch" when he is caught, the fox does not see through the rabbit's ploy and hurls him into the patch with the intention of hurting him. When the fox looks into the patch to see how badly the rabbit is hurt, he instead sees the rabbit sitting on a log, combing tar out of his hair with a wood chip and heckling the fox for his gullibility.

Harris's story is one of the classic Uncle Remus tales for which the author is famous. The story, told in a frame that includes the dialect of Uncle Remus, is a testament to the power of the oral tradition. Its cartoonlike figures, plot twists, and humor make this story, which inspired many subsequent dialect-driven pieces, a favorite.

Harrison, Jim. *Legends of the Fall* (1979). From *Legends of the Fall* (Harrison, 1979). FAMILY; INSANITY; LOVE; MEN and WOMEN; NATURE/WILDERNESS; SIBLINGS; VIOLENCE; WAR.

The title story of this collection of three novellas is the most widely known, having been adapted as a feature film starring Brad Pitt and Anthony Hopkins. The novella details almost a century in the history of the Ludlow family. Tristan, the most volatile of the three sons, avenges his brother Samuel's death in World War I by scalping German soldiers. He goes temporarily mad and marries Susannah so that she can present him with a son to replace his dead brother.

Tristan impetuously goes to sea and leaves his one remaining brother, Albert, to carry on the relationship that Tristan had had with Susannah. Throughout the narrative, Tristan is a loner, pursued by the demons that haunt a time defined by world war, the Great Depression, Prohibition, and westward expansion. When Tristan falls in love with Isabel Two and marries her, he enters one of the most serene periods of his life. When a stray bullet kills Isabel, however, the cycle of violence that characterizes Tristan's insane passion begins again. He experiences happiness in seven-year increments, though Harrison focuses his narrative on the tumult of Tristan's life.

Many critics compare Harrison's novellas to the work of Hemingway, though Harrison's compression of the rich details of life and death—he is approached in the production of the novella only by contemporary Steven Millhauser—the diversity of his characters, the originality of his voice, and his complex analyses of human nature defy the sort of facile comparison that takes into account only the authors' similar backgrounds (both are very much products of Michigan) and what is popularly perceived as a "macho" sensibility.

Harte, Bret. "The Outcasts of Poker Flat" (1869). From *A Book of the Short Story* (Ed. E.A. Cross, 1934). COURAGE; DEATH; EXILE/ EMIGRATION; FRIENDSHIP.

Mr. Oakhurst, along with several other undesirables—including two women of ill repute and a drunken thief—are exiled from their old haunt, the small town of Poker Flat. Oakhurst, a gambler, is the leader of the group, which is joined by Tom Simson, a man whom Oakhurst took under his wing once, and the "Innocent," a young woman who accompanies Simson. With little in the way of provisions except liquor, they attempt to cross a mountain pass on their way out of the valley.

When a snowstorm strikes the group without warning, heroism comes from unexpected places. The Innocent and the more experienced women form fast friendships, and even as their meager rations begin to run out, the company seems to be happy in each other's presence. Oakhurst, realizing the gravity of their situation, sets off to find help for the group; none of them survive. Under a playing card pinned to a tree—a symbol of Oakhurst's life and now his death—a posse from Poker Flat finds Oakhurst, who in desperation has put a bullet into his own heart.

Harte's story, despite the morbid ending, is one of hope and dignity. The outcasts, while shunned by society for their shortcomings, show uncommon strength and character in the face of adversity. Oakhurst, "at once the strongest and yet the weakest of the outcasts," is a man whose heroism is recognized even by those who are ultimately responsible for his death.

Hawthorne, Nathaniel. "The Birthmark" (1843). From *Short Fiction: Classic and Contemporary*, 4th ed. (Ed. Charles H. Bohner and Dean Dougherty, 1999). ART and the ARTIST; BETRAYAL; DISABILITY/PHYSICAL APPEARANCE; JEALOUSY; MEN and WOMEN; PRIDE; WOMEN'S ISSUES.

Aylmer, one of the eminent scientists of his time, marries the beautiful Georgiana only to find that he cannot live with her because of a tiny hand-shaped birthmark on her left cheek. The mark has always been of note in Georgiana's life: the men who wooed her took it as a sign of her magic personality and her ability to steal their hearts; the women who resented her otherwise flawless beauty called it the "Bloody Hand" and jealously contended that the mark made her hideous. When Aylmer approaches his wife about the possibility of his removing the mark, she is at first shocked and saddened, but when she sees that her husband increasingly responds to the mark with horror, she begins to despise it as well.

As in many of Hawthorne's tales, Aylmer is overwhelmed by the pride that comes when man believes he can transcend the boundaries of nature.

Aylmer is so skilled a scientist that he has even attempted to improve on nature's creation (an echo of Shelley's *Frankenstein*). He is sure, then, that he can make the mark on Georgiana's cheek disappear—a sentiment with which Aminadab, his faithful assistant and a man of inferior intellect, does not agree. In order to persuade Georgiana that his plan to remove the mark is safe, Aylmer shows her some of the many wonders that he has created in his laboratory, and Georgiana reads from a book of experiments that he has performed. Finally, Aylmer is able to vanquish the mark from his wife's beautiful face. In the process, however, "the parting breath of the now perfect woman passed into the atmosphere, and her soul, lingering a moment near her husband, took its heavenward flight."

The story, as with many of Hawthorne's finely wrought narratives, is a cautionary tale: the pride of man always drives him, it seems, to attempt acts of creation (or in this case, improvement upon creation) that run counter to nature. As the last few lines of the story indicate, Aylmer fell victim to his own shortsightedness, failing "to look beyond the shadowy scope of Time, and living once for all in Eternity, to find the perfect Future in the present."

Hawthorne, Nathaniel. "Ethan Brand" (1850). From *Selected Tales and Sketches* (Ed. Michael J. Colacurcio, 1987). GOOD/EVIL; INTERIOR LIVES; ORIGINAL SIN; PRIDE; RELIGION/SPIRITUALITY; SELF-DESTRUCTION/SUICIDE.

Ethan Brand, a former lime-burner, has searched the world over for the Unpardonable Sin. When he returns to his old village, Bartram recognizes the man immediately; he is uncomfortable with the way that Brand discusses the outcome of his search. It seems that Brand has found what he was looking for in his own heart, "The sin of an intellect that triumphed over the sense of brotherhood with man, and reverence for God, and sacrificed everything to its own mighty claims!"

When some villagers arrive to meet Brand, they think him insane for what he has told them. When an old man arrives with a diorama that elicits little but ironic laughter from the crowd, he approaches Brand, who believes the old man to be the devil. When Bartram and his son leave Brand alone to tend the kiln, Brand, ruminating on his condition, immolates himself in the flames. The next morning, the men find Brand's skeleton, within which they can see only the shape of a human heart.

Hawthorne's exploration of the "black soul" of man is rarely more complex than his presentation of the man who is transfigured by overweening pride for the intellect into a man who little sympathizes with others. The Unpardonable Sin for which Brand searches is finally found in his own breast, and his heart of stone cannot be destroyed, even by the literal and figurative fires that otherwise consume him.

Hawthorne, Nathaniel. "The May-Pole of Merry Mount" (1836). From *Selected Tales and Sketches* (Ed. Michael J. Colacurcio, 1987). AL-LEGORY/LEGEND/FABLE; ASSIMILATION; GOOD/EVIL; LOVE; MARRIAGE; MEN and WOMEN; NATURE/WILDER-NESS; OPPRESSION; RELIGION/SPIRITUALITY.

In what Hawthorne describes as a "slight sketch here attempted," in which "the facts, recorded on the grave pages of our New England annalists, have wrought themselves, almost spontaneously, into a sort of allegory," the Puritans, led by the stern and pious Endicott, overtake the revelers of Merry Mount and force them to live within their structured society.

The story begins with the marriage of two youths around the May-pole, a tall, straight pine tree that is a symbol of the carefree lives of the settlers who have turned their backs on organized religion. The celebrants are dressed as half-animals, in the manner of the satyrs and spirits of mythology, and wrap themselves in the greenery and flowers—a symbol of their close-ness with nature—that abound on and around the May-pole. The leaders of the band "had sported so long with life, that when Thought and Wisdom came, even these unwelcome guests were led astray, by the crowd of vanities which they should have put to flight." By ignoring the world outside their own mirth making, the group can convince themselves that they are truly happy.

As the marriage ceremony comes to an end, Endicott and a group of Puritans darken the otherwise perpetually sunny wood, bringing with them the promise of pain for the revelers who have offended their God. Endicott orders that the revelers be given their "stripes," a lashing, to bring them into line; a bear that the May-pole worshippers had trained to dance is shot through the head, as Endicott suspects the animal of being under the influ-ence of witchcraft.

The two youths, whom Endicott sees before him, are clearly in love and would die for one another; they are spared the humiliation of the rest of their band. Though they are forbidden to return to Merry Mount, which Endicott has destroyed, they are secure in "the tie that united them, were intertwined with all the purest and best of their early joys." They do not dwell on their fate. At their deaths, "they went heavenward," after having supported each other without regret for the lives that they had previously led.

Hawthorne's tale is an allegory that does not advocate either the side of the revelers or the Puritans, even though the Puritans insist on brutally imposing their will upon others. The author clearly understands the power of love under even the most difficult of circumstances, and he contents himself with exploring the Puritan society that fostered the American spirit—and its often contradictory impulses.

Hawthorne, Nathaniel. "The Minister's Black Veil: A Parable" (1836). From *Selected Tales and Sketches* (Ed. Michael J. Colacurcio, 1987). ALIENATION/ISOLATION; DEATH; GOOD/EVIL; ORIGINAL SIN; RELIGION/SPIRITUALITY.

Parson Hooper is a steady young man of thirty, a neatly dressed bachelor with a reputation as a good preacher. One Sunday, Hooper arrives at church with a veil of black crepe covering his face. At first, the parishioners are convinced that the preacher is using the veil as a prop. When he refuses to take it off, however, they soon realize that something is terribly amiss. Hooper insists, even to his closest friends, on never removing the mask, going so far as to avoid looking at his covered visage in the mirror. Years pass, and the townspeople grow accustomed to the veil, which they see every Sunday, during funerals and weddings, and at deathbed vigils. Still, no one knows the reason for Hooper's sudden dramatic change so many years before.

On his own deathbed, Hooper refuses to remove the veil, summoning superhuman strength to prevent the townsmen from exposing him. He is buried with the veil covering his face, and no one has the courage to lift it when he is dead. A short, cutting soliloquy is the only clue the townspeople have as to the reason behind Hooper's action: the veil itself is a simple, powerful symbol for the Black Veil that all people wear, the secret sin that prevents people from connecting with one another on the basic level of their own humanity.

Hawthorne's story is a parable, its moral stated succinctly by the parson just before his own death. The story is also a meticulous examination of the human psyche that makes the author's stories relevant today.

Hawthorne, Nathaniel. "My Kinsman, Major Molineaux" (1832). From *Fiction 100: An Anthology of Short Stories*, 9th ed. (Ed. James H. Pickering, 2000). COMING-OF-AGE; DREAMS (of the FUTURE); FAMILY; HISTORY; JUSTICE; VIOLENCE.

Young Robin has gone in search of Major Molineux, a stately relation of his who has, as far as his good country family knows, attained a lofty status in a bustling New England town. When he leaves the ferry, having crossed the symbolic river that separates him from the homeland he knows so well, he finds himself on unfamiliar ground. None of the people he asks for directions will oblige him, and he is seduced by a beautiful girl in scarlet petticoats who passes herself off as Molineux's maid. He refuses to give in, determined to fulfill his purpose.

At his wit's end, Robin asks one last man for the whereabouts of Molineux. The man, whose hideous face radiates with an evil that Robin can hardly comprehend, tells him that his request will be granted within the hour. As he waits on the church steps for the appointed time, another man, amused by Robin's confusion, sits to wait with him. Robin is at first shocked by what he sees, but then joins in the laughter of the throng of people who have presented him with the very thing he has sought—Molineux, tarred and feathered, being paraded through the streets.

Hawthorne presents the tale as a bit of history, detailing in the story's first paragraph the vehemence—and often the capriciousness—with which townspeople held their freedom in pre-Revolution America. Though the surface action suggests that the most important scene is the one in which Robin sees his kinsman disgraced, the deeper meaning of the story lies in the young man's search for freedom, at once highly attainable and coming at the expense of his innocence.

Hawthorne, Nathaniel. "Rappaccini's Daughter" (1844). From *Major American Short Stories*, 3rd ed. (Ed. A. Walton Litz, 1994). BETRAYAL; DEATH; FATHERS and CHILDREN; GOOD/EVIL; MEN and WOMEN; OPPRESSION; WOMEN'S ISSUES.

Guasconti arrives in Padua to study at the university. While there, he is smitten by Beatrice, the daughter of the great scientist Rappaccini, who is world-renowned for his knowledge of poisonous plants. In fact, the doctor has been using his own daughter as the subject in an experiment that makes her immune to the most poisonous of plants. Her immunity, however, leaves her unable to touch humans without harming them.

Baglioni, a professor at the university and a friend of Guasconti's father, sees the woman as a threat to his own position. After all, she has knowledge and skills at which he can only guess. In an attempt to render her powerless by taking away her immunity, Baglioni gives Guasconti a potion that will remedy the situation. It kills Beatrice. With her dying words, though, she wonders if Guasconti was the one with the poisonous nature, and tells him that she would rather have loved than had the powers that her father had given her—and that she had been helpless to avoid.

The tale is one of Hawthorne's most provocative, a statement on the relative powerlessness of women in society. The author creates a complex, flawed character in the father, who oppresses his daughter under the pretense of protecting her from the world. The competing desires of the men paint an unflattering picture of their treatment of Beatrice, who is seen as little more than a means to an end for all of them.

Hawthorne, Nathaniel. "Young Goodman Brown" (1835). From *Fiction 100: An Anthology of Short Stories*, 9th ed. (Ed. James H. Pickering, 2000). ALLEGORY/LEGEND/FABLE; BETRAYAL; DREAMS (SLEEPING); GOOD/EVIL; MARRIAGE; MEN and WOMEN; MORALITY (MORAL DILEMMA); RELIGION/SPIRITUALITY; SUPERNATURAL/HORROR.

Despite the pleadings of his wife of three months, young Goodman

Brown leaves Faith on an undisclosed errand into the woods. Having been brought up to cherish Puritan values, his conscience bothers him, and he wonders if the dreams his wife mentioned in which harm comes to him are a harbinger of things to come. Not far into his journey, he meets a distinguished gentleman whose walking stick seems to writhe, as though it were a living thing. The man whisks Brown to his destination, a conclave in the woods where all the devout townspeople mingle with murderers, thieves, and rapists in an unholy mass.

Brown at first resists being drawn into the procession, racing through the uncharted wilderness to meet the evil head-on. He is helpless to fight them, though; as if in a dream, he imagines seeing Faith there on a mission of her own. At the culmination of the baptism into evil, during which Brown pleads with Faith to look heavenward and resist the throng, the group disappears; he is left alone in the solitude of the forest. Realizing that he has lost his faith—the double meaning is clear—Brown races back into town, where everything is as it should be. He spends his days wondering whether what he has seen is truth or a dream.

Hawthorne's intention in this allegory is apparent: whether truth or dream, Brown will live out his life an embittered and paranoid man. At his death, his family "carved no hopeful verse upon his tombstone, for his dying hour was gloom." The story makes clear the author's own incessant wrestling with the themes of good and evil. The implication is that man's dual nature is inescapable and that morality is relative.

Head, Bessie. "Life" (1977). From *The Story and Its Writer*, 5th ed. (Ed. Ann Charters, 1999). ALIENATION/ISOLATION; ALLEGORY/LEGEND/FABLE; CLASS CONFLICTS; DEATH; MARRIAGE; MEN and WOMEN; OPPRESSION; WOMEN'S ISSUES.

Life Morapedi returns home for the first time in seventeen years. In order to make ends meet, she has been a singer, beauty queen, advertising model, and prostitute. Back in Botswana, she raises eyebrows because "men started turning up in an unending stream" at her house. Her only friends, it seems, are the beer-brewing women. When Lesego, a rancher, takes an interest in Life, she is transformed for a time. No one thinks that it is a good idea for them to get married; still, the two are drawn to one another for their own much different reasons.

Shortly after the marriage, however, Lesego threatens to kill Life if he catches her with another man. Disillusioned by the comment, she falls into her old lifestyle. When a friend of Lesego's tells him that she is with Radithibolo, Lesego calmly walks into the man's house and kills Life. Though he could be given the death penalty, the judge listens to the man's dispassionate argument and sentences him to five years in prison, since it was a crime of passion. Sianana, Lesego's friend, wonders why the man had to kill his wife when he could simply have walked away and remained a free man.

As Charters writes, "Despite the devastating experiences of racial oppression, and the dislocation and economic hardship of exile, Head found the peace of mind necessary to create her works of fiction." Clearly that peace of mind belies the fact that the subject matter of her stories can so devastatingly portray relationships such as that between Life and Lesego. The irony of the title (Life, of course, is the one in the story who is doomed from the outset) and Head's reference to the Jim Reeves song "That's What Happens When Two Worlds Collide," frames the story in the realities of modern-day Botswana.

Hemingway, Ernest. "Big Two-Hearted River" (1925). From *Major American Short Stories*, 3rd ed. (Ed. A. Walton Litz, 1994). ALIENATION/ISOLATION; ESCAPE; INTERIOR LIVES; NATURE/WILDERNESS; WAR.
Nick Adams returns to Seney after a life-altering event that is suggested by the psychic frailty of the protagonist. He walks along the river and watches the trout, commenting on how he has not seen trout for quite some time and how good it is to be back. He is reassured by his surroundings. When Nick awakens from a nap under a tree, he sets up camp—a good camp, he thinks to himself—and makes dinner. The next morning, he catches a small trout and releases it; when he goes after a large trout, the leader breaks. Still, he catches enough for dinner and knows that there will be plenty of fishing to do in the coming days.

Even though Hemingway's powers of description are at their peak in this story, Nick's experience, like much of the author's short fiction, relies as much on what is not said as what is—a notion that is supported by the story's simple "plot" and understated by the innocence of Nick's observations. Very little happens in the story; instead, most of its meaning is hidden beneath the idyllic scene that greets the young man upon his return from, Hemingway implies, a life-altering experience in the war. Clearly, Nick has been scarred by the war, and his immersion back into the landscapes that he finds so familiar and soothing is his way of reentering a society that has become alien to him, if only for a time. The land offers the renewal of life.

Hemingway, Ernest. "A Clean, Well-Lighted Place" (1933). From *Short Shorts: An Anthology of the Shortest Stories* (Ed. Irving Howe and Ilana Weiner Howe, 1982). AGING; ALIENATION/ISOLATION; INTERIOR LIVES; SELF-DESTRUCTION/SUICIDE.
As an old man sits in a café finishing his drink, the two waiters—a young, married man and an older man who was once married but now lives alone—decide whether they should roust the customer from his reverie. They discuss the fact that he has recently attempted suicide, and the young waiter wishes that he had succeeded. The old man leaves, but the argument between the two waiters continues. The older waiter knows what it means to

people to be able to spend time away from the loneliness of home in a "clean, well-lighted place."

When the younger man goes home for the evening, his coworker is left to consider why he feels as he does. He decides that it is good for people to have a modicum of order in their daily activities, and the café gives purpose to otherwise vacant lives. In the semblance of prayer, the man thinks, "Our nada who art in nada, nada be thy name thy kingdom nada thy will be nada in nada as it is in nada." He leaves the café and wanders into a bodega; he hopes that he will be able to sleep when he gets home.

The action of the story, as with "Hills Like White Elephants" and "Big Two-Hearted River," has little to do with the meaning behind the words. In the briefest of Hemingway's stories, he suggests that those with experience—the old man who is forced out of the café and the older waiter—understand life from a perspective that is foreign to men like the younger waiter. In the same way Hemingway noted that, like the iceberg, seven-eights of his story lurks beneath the surface, the truth of the story lies not in the simple actions described, but in the loneliness, alienation, and despair that those actions imply.

Hemingway, Ernest. "Hills Like White Elephants" (1927). From *Rites of Passage: A Thematic Reader* (Ed. Judie Rae and Catherine Fraga, 2001). COMMUNICATION/LANGUAGE; INTERIOR LIVES; MEN and WOMEN; MORALITY (MORAL DILEMMA).

A man and a woman are engaged in a seemingly pointless conversation as they look across a valley in Spain toward the hills, which, the woman muses, look like white elephants. Her quirky, offhand comment thinly disguises the intensity of the meeting: although the motivation for their conversation is never made explicit, the man seems to be encouraging the woman to have an abortion. The twists and turns of the conversation are subtle: even though the man clearly wants her to take the action that he endorses, the fact that neither of them ever mentions what "it" is makes the dialogue nearly absurd in its participants' unwillingness to broach the subject directly. Instead, they talk of drinking, the hills, their baggage.

When the conversation does turn back to the main issue—the couple's happiness and the necessity, the man states, of taking care of "it" before they can be truly happy—the man has clearly assumed control of the situation. Despite his contention that he will agree with whatever decision the woman makes, the subtext of his language implies otherwise. Finally, she is overcome by the man's manipulation, and she insists that he stop talking. With the train approaching the station, he asks her how she feels, and she tells him curtly that she is fine.

Hemingway's work is known for its economical use of language, and this story is perhaps the finest example of that characteristic. In a brief tale that uses little direct description, but rather employs dialogue in a way that conveys the subtleties of communication, the author is able to delimit the politics of a relationship in which the participants must deal with a difficult decision.

Hemingway, Ernest. "Indian Camp" (1925). From *The Oxford Book of American Short Stories* (Ed. Joyce Carol Oates, 1992). COMING-OF-AGE; DEATH; FAMILY; FATHERS and CHILDREN; SELF-DESTRUCTION/SUICIDE.

Uncle George, young Nick, and his father the doctor, travel to the Indian Camp to help a woman give birth. The doctor realizes that the woman needs to have a Cesarean section. Nick assists his father as well as he can in the child's delivery, while his father teaches him life lessons. Despite the woman's obvious pain and the difficulty of the birth, the procedure goes as planned, and the new mother and the child are fine. When the doctor cleans the baby off and turns to show it to the father, who had been witnessing the events from his top bunk, he finds that the man has slit his own throat. Nick asks his father questions about life, and his father answers as best he can. They leave the Indian Camp and row back across the lake.

Hemingway's direct language strips the action of the story to its minimum and allows the reader to explore for herself the complex relationships that are sketched out in such a brief narrative space. Nick spends time with his father and learns at a young age how to deal with death (a skill he will very much need during the time later in life that he spends in the war, as detailed in "Big Two-Hearted River"). The father of the newborn child, on the other hand, can see no other way out than to commit suicide, an ironic counterpoint to the successful birth of his child. All the relationships in this story point to the notion of family and the complex dynamics that such a simple word implies.

Hemingway, Ernest. "The Killers" (1927). From *The 50 Greatest Mysteries of All Time* (Ed. Otto Penzler, 1998). BETRAYAL; COMING-OF-AGE; DEATH; FATE; VIOLENCE.

Nick Adams and his friend, George, are at a lunch counter when two men enter and demand that Nick and the cook go into the kitchen, where they are tied up. In the course of conversation, the men divulge that they are there to kill the Swede, Ole Andreson, a prizefighter who has run amok of the wrong people in Chicago. When Andreson does not show up on this particular evening, the men leave. Nick finds the Swede in a boardinghouse room and tells him what has happened. Andreson did not go out that day, he says, because he knew that the men were looking for him. Still, he sees no way of avoiding his fate. He thanks Nick for the warning and turns toward the wall, a sign that he is resigned to what awaits him. Nick and George discuss the situation and are saddened by the day's events. Nick vows to leave town, and George concurs. The best thing the two can do, they decide, is not to think about what has happened.

The story is spare in Hemingway's typical style. The action is conveyed primarily through dialogue, the characters drawn through their own words and the short descriptions that the author provides. The ending of the story—the decision not to consciously consider what they have just experienced—is an echo of the Swede's recognition of the inevitability of future events.

Henry, O. (William Sydney Porter). "The Gift of the Magi" (1905). From *The Story and Its Writer*, 5th ed. (Ed. Ann Charters, 1999). GIFTS/GENEROSITY; HUMOR/SATIRE/IRONY; LOVE; MEN and WOMEN; MORALITY (MORAL DILEMMA).

Della and Jim Young, a young couple who live in an eight-dollar-a-week flat, make just enough money to get by, but both want to buy the other something special for Christmas. Della has long, flowing hair, and Jim settles on a set of combs that his wife has wanted for some time; Jim carries a special watch, and Della knows that he would love to have a fob for it. In order to pay for their purchases, though, Della sells her hair to a wig-maker, and Jim pawns his watch. Both are presented with gifts for which they have no immediate use.

This tale, one of O. Henry's most popular because of its ironic twist on the traditional love story, illustrates the power of selfless generosity. The moral of this brief story is boldly stated in the final paragraph: "The magi, as you know, were wise men—wonderfully wise men—who brought gifts to the Babe in the manger. . . . And here I have lamely related to you the uneventful chronicle of two foolish children in a flat who most unwisely sacrificed for each other the greatest treasures of their house. But in a last word to the wise of these days, let it be said that of all who give gifts these two were the wisest." Clearly, the author privileges the unthinking generosity of the young couple over the cynicism and greed that he witnesses in turn-of-the-century America.

Henry, O. (William Sydney Porter). "Mammon and the Archer" (1906). From *Twenty-Nine Stories* (Ed. William Peden, 1960). HUMOR/SATIRE/IRONY; LOVE; MEN and WOMEN.

Anthony Rockwall, a retired manufacturer and proprietor of Rockwall's Eureka Soap, believes that money is everything. He converses with his son, Richard, about how money can buy a person anything he wants in life. The son disagrees with his father, telling him that money cannot buy him time or the love of the object of his affection, Ms. Lanty, who departs in two days for an absence of two years. He will have only ten minutes, on their way to the theatre, to make his intentions clear.

Though the father insists that money can buy love, the young man's aunt tells him otherwise. She suggests that the lover take with him a ring that his mother had left for him in her will. On the way to the theatre, Richard drops the ring, and in the ensuing delay, the couple is caught in traffic for hours. The next day, the aunt relates to the elder Rockwall that the two had fallen in love while sitting in traffic, and as a result, they are engaged to be married. It turns out that the father had hired taxi drivers, policemen, and others to block traffic so that his son would have the time he would need to reach his objective. Despite Richard's argument to the contrary, money can, it seems, buy everything—including time.

The story is typical of O. Henry's brief, tightly plotted tales that end with a twist. Rockwall's money buys the time that his son would not otherwise have had, and Mammon (money) and the Archer (Cupid) are not, in fact, mutually exclusive in his humorous story.

Hillerman, Tony. "Chee's Witch" (1986). From *The New Mystery* (Ed. Jerome Charyn, 1993). BETRAYAL; CRIME/LAW; DEATH; MINORITY EXPERIENCE; RELIGION/SPIRITUALITY; SUPERNATURAL/HORROR.

In Corporal Jimmy Chee's world, things are not always as they seem. He is a witch-hunter for the Navajo Tribal Police; if someone has a bad crop or a sick child, Chee is the one they call. It seems that the "City Navajo witch" has gone so far as to murder. Chee receives a dispatch telling him to meet a man named Jake Wells in a hotel room that night. Wells, an FBI agent, tells the story of a man in hiding that is intertwined with Chee's own search for the murderer. The locals assume that witchcraft was involved, since the dead body has been stripped of its fingerprints. Chee, who is steeped in the ways of the tribe at the same time that he is a shrewd investigator, discovers the truth: Wells killed the man because he was an FBI informant whose usefulness ran out.

Hillerman's story is part of the world that he has created for Jimmy Chee, the protagonist of many of his novels that explore the confluence of Native American culture and mainstream society. The author plausibly suggests supernatural causes for what, in Chee's experience, is nothing more than an expedient for white man's justice.

Hoffius, Stephen. "The Assault on the Record" (1995). From *Ultimate Sports* (Ed. Donald R. Gallo, 1995). CONTESTS; FRIENDSHIP; PRIDE; SPORTS.

The protagonist of this inspirational story is a fifteen-year-old student who sets his sights on a world record—any world record—and he and his nine friends (who call themselves "The Counting Cows," a play on the rock band Counting Crows) decide that they will run a one hundred-mile relay, which they call "The Assault on the Record." Though the first few miles of the relay go smoothly, the boys discover that not one of them is fully prepared for the task. As they near their goal, the boys' times slow down; one of the team, Bobby D., who endears himself to his friends by having his mother stock the refrigerator, wants all the attention for himself and hides his insecurity with braggadocio. Still, he is the one most affected by the physical and mental strain of the event. Barely able to make his last mile, Bobby D. has nothing more to do with his friends after the relay is over. The narrator relates that they are proud of their achievement, even though they never wrote newspaper articles or books or garnered the fame that they thought would come with setting a world record.

Hoffius's story is an exploration of the complex relationships among high school-aged boys, who take on any challenge that comes their way at the same time that they attempt to find their place in their social set. Humility, the author suggests, is preferable to overweening pride, and finally leads to triumph. Only Bobby D., whose words imply a level of action that he cannot back up, finds the whole thing "stupid"; in the absence of his well-stocked refrigerator, he and the boys have a falling out until school starts. Even then, Bobby D. "was still quiet, still limping" from the experience.

Hoffmann, E.T.A. "The History of Krakatuk" (1810). From *Great Short Stories from the World's Literature* (Ed. Charles Neider, 1950). ALLEGORY/LEGEND/FABLE; DEATH; FATHERS and CHILDREN; LOVE; MAGIC/OCCULT; MOTHERS and CHILDREN; POLITICS; REVENGE.

The narrator relates a story about young princess Perlipat and the misery that befalls her. It seems that her father, the king, wants to expel Mrs. Mouserinks, a mouse, from the palace for eating the bacon that should have gone into the king's dinner. Mrs. Mouserinks's children are executed, but the mother survives and vows revenge on the king and his family. Despite the precautions that the royal family takes in protecting the beautiful young princess, Mrs. Mouserinks manages to turn the girl into a hideous mouselike creature.

After much debate, it is decided that only by securing the Krakatuk nut can the princess regain her former beauty. The astronomer and watchmaker who are sent in search of the nut find it, though no one in the kingdom is able to crack it open. When Drosselmeier steps forth to crack the nut with a set of instructions that he has received, Mrs. Mouserinks once again disrupts the proceedings and gives the young man the same features that she had previously given the princess. The young man who saved the princess from the curse of Mrs. Mouserinks "remains as ugly as ever; so much so, that the nutcrackers in Nuremberg have always been made after the exact model of his countenance and figure."

The story purports to explain the garish look of the traditional nutcracker, though it is written, above all, for entertainment. Hoffmann's pacing and his eye for the curious detail make this an enjoyable tale, even as the author explores the themes of political power, revenge, and magic.

Howells, W.D. "Editha" (1905). From *The Portable American Realism Reader* (Ed. James Nagel and Tom Quirk, 1997). COMMUNICATION/LANGUAGE; DEATH; LOSS; MEN and WOMEN; MORALITY (MORAL DILEMMA); MOTHERS and CHILDREN; PRIDE; WAR.

When Editha reads about the Spanish-American War in the newspapers, she is swept away by the romantic notion that her fiancé, George Gearson, should join the war effort and become a hero. She goes so far as to prepare a package of items for George, including her engagement ring, which she will not take back from him until he accedes. Gearson, for his part, is much against war of any kind, though one evening at a meeting he is caught up in the emotion of the moment and enlists. He is named the captain of the local volunteers.

Editha is elated that George has decided to defend the country for which she suddenly feels so strongly; however, he is one of the first casualties of the war. Editha visits George's mother to console her, though Mrs. Gearson treats her roughly, questioning the young woman's need for mourning clothes. Editha is chastened in her unthinking acquiescence to the romance of war and her naïveté of its ultimate consequences.

Howells uses notion of the power of the press to great effect in this story. Ironically, George, whose love for Editha prompts him to take an action that he would otherwise despise, is the one in danger from her war-spirit. The story's title implies the self-centeredness of the young woman and the impossibility of anyone outside war to fully comprehend its tragedy.

Hughes, Langston. "On the Road" (1935). From *Studies in Fiction* (Ed. Blaze O. Bonazza et al., 1982). AFRICAN-AMERICAN EXPERIENCE; ALIENATION/ISOLATION; DREAMS (SLEEPING); POVERTY; RACE RELATIONS; RELIGION/SPIRITUALITY.

Sargeant is a black man seeking food and shelter in Reno, Nevada, on a stormy winter evening. Reverend Dorset, whom the homeless man approaches for relief, dismisses him immediately and suggests that he go to the local shelter. He has already been turned down there, though Dorset will hear none of the man's story. Sargeant gets the idea of sleeping in the adjacent church, though when he begins to pound on the doors in an effort to open them, the police apprehend him. He dreams of pulling the church down and imagines that Christ is walking alongside him. Christ goes on to Kansas City as Sargeant gets some much-needed rest in a hobo jungle. When he awakens from the dream, though, he finds himself in a cell. Sargeant thinks back to the dream and plans his escape from jail.

Set against the backdrop of the Great Depression, the story is all the more poignant for the clear racial lines that are drawn when a man who wants nothing more than to ensure his own survival is denied even that. Certainly, Sargeant's situation is not unique, though he is treated as an anathema in the community because of his skin color. His dream of Christ, who would not agree with the actions of the clergyman or the police, stands in stark juxtaposition to the reality of his situation. While he does not deserve the treatment that he receives, he is nonetheless held captive by a society that values him as little as it does the beliefs on which it bases its hypocritical actions.

Hughes, Langston. "Thank You, Ma'am" (1958). From *The Story and Its Writer*, 5th ed. (Ed. Ann Charters, 1999). AFRICAN-AMERICAN EXPERIENCE; ALIENATION/ISOLATION; CLASS CONFLICTS; CRIME/LAW; GIFTS/GENEROSITY; TRUTH v. LYING.

A boy accosts a large woman, Luella Bates Washington Jones, and steals her purse. When she unexpectedly overpowers him and realizes that he is alone, she takes him home with her. She discovers that the boy's name is Roger, and as he gets more accustomed to the idea of her kindness in not turning him over to the police, he begins to desire her trust. Mrs. Jones gives him ample opportunity to steal from her, but Roger stays in the apartment while the woman cooks his dinner. He tells her that he has stolen money not because he is hungry, but because he wants a new pair of blue suede shoes. Mrs. Jones feeds Roger and gives him ten dollars for the shoes. She asks nothing in return, and Roger never sees her again.

The trust between these two people in much different circumstances is born of the similarities that they possess: Mrs. Jones hints at a previous life that involved actions she would rather not discuss; Roger resorts to stealing in order to get what he wants. Still, Hughes finds that the connection— bound by the woman's leap of faith in the boy when she trusts him not to betray her—is a strong message written at a time when the nuclear family is slowly disintegrating and the kindness of strangers is a welcome respite from the uncertainty of day-to-day life.

Hurston, Zora Neale. "The Gilded Six-Bits" (1933). From *Calling the Wind: Twentieth-Century African-American Short Stories* (Ed. Clarence Major, 1993). AFRICAN-AMERICAN EXPERIENCE; BETRAYAL; FAMILY; GREED; LOVE; MEN and WOMEN; PRIDE; WOMEN'S ISSUES.

Every Saturday, like clockwork, Joe brings home his pay in silver dollars and tosses them on the kitchen floor, to signal his return to his wife, Missie May. The couple share an intimacy that seems perfect until Missie May is drawn into a relationship with Otis Slemmons, a slick city man who parades his ostensible wealth in the small town with the intention of impressing the town's women. When Joe finds her in bed with Slemmons, Missie May is beside herself with grief over her actions. She realizes how foolish she was to have been drawn in by Slemmons's act. After a period of months during which she makes reparations for her affair, Missie May is back in Joe's good graces. They have a child together—the spitting image of Joe—and Joe spends the gilded six-bit, the fake money that Slemmons has been showing around town, on his wife's favorite treat.

Hurston speaks of the relationships between men and women—especially African-American men and women—with a candor that is absent from much short fiction written to this point. Her matter-of-factness and tenderness show through in the stories, slice of life vignettes that are read for their organic charm and their keen insights into human nature.

Hurston, Zora Neale. "Sweat" (1927). From *The Story and Its Writer*, 5th ed. (Ed. Ann Charters, 1999). DEATH; MARRIAGE; MEN and WOMEN; REVENGE; WOMEN'S ISSUES.

Despite the fact that Delia Jones supports her husband, Sykes, the man does little to hide the fact that he has a mistress. He is also a cruel man, playing upon Delia's fear of snakes, first by teasing her with a bullwhip and then bringing home a six-foot rattlesnake in a box. Though Delia is a religious person (a fact which Sykes scorns), she threatens her husband with a frying pan; she is determined not to give up the house that she has spent years earning with her own sweat. The townspeople understand the situation and side with Delia, who is taunted by the sight of Sykes with his mistress.

When Delia realizes that the snake he has brought home to frighten her is in the laundry basket, she spends the night in the barn. Sykes, who comes home drunk and in the dark, is bitten by the snake and dies. Delia does nothing to help him, and she imagines the look on Sykes's face as he suffers his last agonizing moments.

Hurston's story of retribution is both a cautionary tale and an exploration of the limits of human cruelty. Despite the fact that Delia has spent fifteen years with Sykes, he torments her without ceasing in every aspect of her life. Hurston implies that his death, and Delia's response to it, are justified. By staying outside the house while Sykes dies, she is finally asserting the freedom from hatred and from dread that has been so long in coming.

Huxley, Aldous. "Young Archimedes" (1924). From *Great Short Stories of the World*, (Sel. by the editors of *Reader's Digest*, 1972). CHILDHOOD; CLASS CONFLICTS; FAMILY; FATHERS and CHILDREN; MEN and WOMEN; SELF-DESTRUCTION/SUICIDE.

It is the view outside his window that compels the protagonist and his wife, Elizabeth, to rent a dilapidated house in Italy, which is run by Signora Bondi, a controlling, difficult woman. The couple's son, Robin, befriends a peasant child named Guido, to whom Signora Bondi takes a liking. When Guido's father, Carlo, discusses with the couple an offer made by Signora

Bondi to adopt the boy, they reply that he should do what he thinks best, though they hint at their disapproval of her as a potential mother.

The couple discovers that Guido, unlike their own son Robin, has an extraordinary aptitude for music and mathematics. Signora Bondi's interest in the boy is renewed. Because Robin is unaccustomed to such hot summers, the family spends the summer in Switzerland, leaving Guido with the books of Euclid to study in their absence. Upon receiving a letter from Guido in scrawled handwriting, the narrator learns that Signora Bondi has finally adopted him. While walking through a cemetery with Carlo, the narrator relives the events leading up to Guido's suicide. After Carlo gave consent to Signora Bondi to take Guido temporarily, the woman told the boy that his father no longer wanted him; he jumped out of a window and was killed.

Huxley explores the complexity of the human mind in this tale about the loss of a brilliant child from the greed and expectations of those around him. The juxtaposition of men with dogs in the story points up different classes of intellectualism that exist, which have as great an effect on Guido as his own social class. Guido's innocence allows him to be manipulated by the woman even though he is her intellectual superior. Signora Bondi's fear of losing control over Carlo ends only with the death of the man's son.

I

Irving, Washington. "The Adventure of the German Student" (1824). From *Major American Short Stories*, 3rd ed. (Ed. A. Walton Litz, 1994). DEATH; DECADENCE/DEGENERATION; ILLUSION v. REALITY; INSANITY; SELF-DESTRUCTION/SUICIDE; SEXUALITY; SUPERNATURAL/HORROR.

Gottfried Wolfgang is a pensive young man infatuated with the darker side of things—so much so, in fact, that his friends and family arrange for him to study in France to take his mind off his self-destructive impulses. The timing of Wolfgang's arrival, however, could not be worse: Paris is in the midst of the Reign of Terror, and the young man's mind is excited to levels that border on madness. He is given to spending his days in libraries "rummaging among their hoards of dusty and obsolete works in quest of food for his unhealthy appetite. He was, in a manner, a literary ghoul, feeding in the charnel-house of decayed literature."

Wolfgang's dreams feed upon his delusions. As he wanders the streets of Paris, he finds a young woman on the steps of the guillotine and discovers that hers is the face of his dreams. He takes her back to his room, where the disconsolate woman becomes his wife for the night. When he returns to his room the following day, however, he finds her dead on his bed. When the authorities arrive, they are horrified to recognize her as one of the victims of the guillotine. The old man who narrates the story validates its truth, as Wolfgang told him the tale himself from an insane asylum in Paris.

Irving's tale is true to its Gothic influences, though the setting (Europe, instead of the nascent America) suggests that he is exploring his role as a distinctly "American" writer. The protagonist's demise, Irving implies, is due in large part to his inability to quell the impulses that fuel his madness; in that sense, the themes the author broaches are not unlike those that Hawthorne explores in the conflict between heart and mind. The narration, told by an old man to a group of rapt listeners, establishes the student's downfall as a cautionary tale in favor of a reasoned, balanced lifestyle.

Irving, Washington. "The Legend of Sleepy Hollow" (1820). From *The Treasury of American Short Stories* (Sel. Nancy Sullivan, 1981). ALLEGORY/LEGEND/FABLE; DEATH; NATURE/WILDERNESS; SUPERNATURAL/HORROR.

The rural town of Greensburg is said to be haunted by the ghost of a Hessian trooper in an area called Sleepy Hollow. The narrator tells the story of a "worthy" man by the name of Icabod Crane, an odd-looking sort who teaches school in the town. Crane is portrayed as an upstanding citizen in the community, doing his social duty before playing with the town's children or participating in the church.

One night as he makes his way home, he encounters the headless ghost of the Hessian. The following day, no one is able to find Icabod; rather, they find only the teacher's hat and a smashed pumpkin. It is said in the town that he was taken by the ghost. Because Icabod never returns, many of the townspeople take their children out of the school and eventually it is closed. When it becomes dilapidated from lack of use, it is said that the ghost of the headless horseman of Sleepy Hollow haunts the building.

In this story, "Found among the Papers of the late Diedrich Knickerbocker," Irving paints the American landscape vividly in one of his best-known tales. It reflects, as does much of his fiction, his interest in the traditions of the Old World at the same time that he carves out a uniquely New World fiction through his exploration of America's little-understood— and therefore "haunted"—places.

Irving, Washington. "Rip Van Winkle" (1819). From *The Book of the Short Story* (Ed. Henry Seidel Canby and Robeson Bailey, 1948). AGING; ALLEGORY/LEGEND/FABLE; DREAMS (SLEEPING); HISTORY; MARRIAGE; MEN and WOMEN.

As Rip Van Winkle heads into the hills of the Hudson River Valley with his gun and his dog to escape the drudgery of everyday life, he can hardly imagine that when he returns, nothing will be as it was. When he awakes after a nap, his gun is rusty, his dog is gone, his beard is long and unkempt, and he recalls having bowled with a group of Dutchmen. Van Winkle returns to his home to discover that he has been gone for twenty years. In his absence, his wife has died, the Americans have won the revolution, and a pub sign denotes George Washington, not King George III, as the most important figure in the country.

The importance of Irving's story can hardly be overstated. Irving's work led to the creation of a uniquely American literature that explored the new republic's relationship with the vast and largely uncharted wilderness and its own burgeoning sense of national identity. Many of America's greatest short story writers, including Nathaniel Hawthorne just a decade later, would be greatly influenced by Irving's example. Part of Irving's appeal was his willingness to explore the new surroundings in which all American found themselves. The author leaves many of the questions that he asks unsolved, for instance, in this story, what is the true nature of the relationship between

Van Winkle and his wife, and what is Van Winkle's own nature? These questions are more important for having been asked in the context of a society that had rather few answers for many of the problems that it faced. These questions, in fact, are still being discussed in American literature.

J

Jackson, Shirley. "The Lottery" (1949). From *The Story and Its Writer*, 5th ed. (Ed. Ann Charters, 1999). COMING-OF-AGE/INITIATION; CONTESTS; DEATH; FAMILY; FATE; HORROR; TRADITION/CONVENTION; VIOLENCE.

The lottery has been held on June 27th for longer than anyone can remember. This particular lottery day is sunny, and the townspeople gather with an air of expectation for what is about to happen. Mr. Summers conducts the affair—as he does many of the town's other civic activities—with the formality expected of such an important event. Although the original box that held the lottery tickets had been lost long ago, pieces of the box were used to construct the new one, an acknowledgment of the tradition's strength in the town.

Although other towns have considered ending the lottery, many of the inhabitants gathered in this particular town argue vociferously against eliminating the tradition. Warner, the oldest man in town (and in line to take his role in the event for the seventy-seventh consecutive year), takes special exception to the thought that the town would be better without its lottery. He is especially angry with the youth in those towns, for whom nothing is ever good enough. He expects that, when the lottery fails, future generations will be forced to once again live in caves.

When the townsfolk finally gather to draw their slips of paper, the anticipation of the event heightens; people nervously scan the crowd to discover who has drawn the lot with a black dot on it. The lottery "winner" is Tessie Hutchinson, who immediately argues that the proceedings were done in haste and that she wasn't given a fair chance. After Tessie's husband, Bill, acquiesces to the propriety of the lottery, everyone in the crowd, including her small son, Davy, picks up a handful of rocks and stones her to death. The stoning, it turns out, is the fate of the lottery's "winner."

The shocking ending of the story is well known, though each generation seems to hold a morbid fascination for Jackson's vision. Indeed, the author's scathing commentary on unthinking and inflexible tradition at all cost is unnerving even half a century after its genesis.

Jacobs, W.W. "The Monkey's Paw" (1902). From *Olden Tales* (Ed. Bradford M. Day, 1996). DEATH; FAMILY; FATE; MAGIC/OC-

CULT; MOTHERS and CHILDREN; MYSTERY/ADVENTURE; SUPERNATURAL/HORROR.
The White family receives a visit from Sergeant Major Morris, an old friend who regales them with tales of his time in India. Of special interest to the listeners is the story of a charmed monkey's paw that will grant three wishes. Morris has already had his wishes, and he claims that they are always fulfilled in a way that makes the paw's user think the results could merely have been coincidence. When he recalls his own experience with the paw, he disgustedly throws it in the fire. Mr. White, curious about the tale, grabs the paw. At the urging of his son, he wishes for two hundred pounds to pay off the mortgage on their house.

As Morris predicted, the wish is granted, but in a horrific manner. The Whites receive news that their son has been killed at work, and the company is willing to pay the family two hundred pounds as compensation. Having lost her only son, the mother insists that Mr. White make one more wish— to bring their son back. He reluctantly makes the wish, but uses his third wish to make the apparition go away just before Mrs. White opens the door on a sight that surely would have driven her mad.

Jacobs's tense story of the supernatural is in the style of Poe, the master of gothic horror. Although the story has been told before in many incarnations, the author's pacing and characterization evoke a rich sense of doom and Mr. White's subsequent relief at having averted disaster. Nothing, Jacobs suggests, can overcome death; nor, perhaps, should it, even with the aid of the supernatural.

James, Henry. "The Beast in the Jungle" (1903). From _The Portable American Realism Reader_ (Ed. James Nagel and Tom Quirk, 1997). ALIENATION/ISOLATION; DEATH; DREAMS (of the FUTURE); EPIPHANY; INTERIOR LIVES; MEN and WOMEN.
May Bertram and John Marcher are friends who have an odd relationship. The two talk incessantly in roundabout ways about their connection to one another, though Marcher, who feels that he has in some way been singled out as the prey of the nebulous "beast" of the title, has never realized that his only escape would have been to love his sole companion. May seems to understand the relationship in terms that escape Marcher, though she, too, does little to lead him to the answer that he seeks. Only after her death does the notion strike him with all its force. At that point of his epiphany, he is helpless to remedy the situation. He has fallen prey to the beast for which he has waited, seemingly, his entire adult life.

This story is typical of James's psychologically intense dramas, though in no other of its length is the relationship so tightly drawn—despite the rather random snapshot vignettes that make up the story, always only with the two characters present—and the impact of the realization so unnerving as when May dies and Marcher is alone, staring down his greatest fears. Marcher's fate is exacerbated by his knowledge that he had only to stop thinking and begin acting (in this case, on his relationship with May) in order to avoid being swept under by the inertia of his own fears.

James, Henry. "Daisy Miller: A Study" (1878). From *The Harper Anthology of Fiction* (Ed. Sylvan Barnet, 1991). DEATH; EXILE/EMIGRATION; INNOCENCE v. EXPERIENCE; MEN and WOMEN; MORALITY; SEXUALITY; TRADITION/CONVENTION.

Daisy Miller, her mother, and her young brother have, in the tradition of the well-to-do American families of the late nineteenth century, decided to spend time "on the Continent." The other Americans they meet, first in Switzerland and later in Rome, show great disdain for the Miller family, whom they regard as *nouveau riche* and as being flagrantly disrespectful of the structured society that the Americans in Europe have created.

When Winterbourne, a member of the fully Europeanized Americans, meets Daisy, he is at first fascinated by her innocence and brash ignorance of his society and later attracted to her by those same qualities, which are a refreshing departure from the more formal women he knows. Winterbourne's aunt, Mrs. Costello, refuses to allow him to see Daisy, who, for her part, begins spending time with an Italian dandy, oblivious to the stories that are being told about her behind her back. When she ignores Winterbourne's entreaty that she avoid the Coliseum at night—suggesting both the impropriety of her relationship with the Italian and the possible danger to her health—she contracts Roman fever (malaria) and dies.

James's story is both a cautionary tale and an exploration of the hypocrisy inherent in the society with which the author was so well acquainted. Winterbourne, who has affairs with married women, escapes his escapades with impunity. Daisy Miller, who insists her innocence to the last, despite all appearances—Winterbourne discovers after her death that she is truly innocent—breaks the rules set out for the women of that society, very often by the women themselves, and pays with her life.

James, Henry. "Paste" (1899). From *The Story and Its Writer*, 5th ed. (Ed. Ann Charters, 1999). BETRAYAL; FAMILY; INTERIOR LIVES; MARRIAGE; MEN and WOMEN; SOCIETY.

Cousins Arthur and Charlotte Prime mourn the death of Arthur's stepmother. As they search through her belongings, Arthur comes across a box full of "paste," cheap jewelry that his stepmother accumulated in a previous life as a stage actress. He gives the jewelry to Charlotte without a second thought. When a Mrs. Guy sees the pieces at one of the biggest parties of the season, she wants to use them for her *tableaux vivants*, a living portrait put on for the guests' entertainment. Charlotte agrees, only to find out later that Mrs. Guy believes the string of pearls to be, in fact, real.

Charlotte, guilty over having accepted the pearls at her aunt's death, confronts Arthur about her inheritance and returns the pearls to him. Aside from the monetary value of the pearls, they have a deeper meaning: Arthur cannot believe that his stepmother would have been in a position to receive the pearls as a gift; he refuses to believe that she accepted them as a proposition from a man whom she has kept secret all these years. Mrs. Guy, who has become infatuated with the pearls, decides that she must have them, and is, in fact, wearing the beautiful necklace when Charlotte next sees the woman. How she got the pearls—and the relationship between Arthur and Mrs. Guy—is left for the reader's interpretation at the story's conclusion.

Like much of James's fiction, this story explores the social dynamic, both in terms of class structures and conflicts within families, at the turn of the twentieth century. Though Arthur refuses to accept that his stepmother had a life outside her relationship with his father, the pearls involve him in a relationship with Mrs. Guy that seemingly compromises his view on the matter. Only Charlotte, for her honesty, is left without the pearls or the money gained from their sale.

James, Henry. "The Real Thing" (1892). From *An Anthology of Famous American Stories* (Ed. Angus Burrell and Bennett Cerf, 1963). ART and the ARTIST; CLASS CONFLICTS; ILLUSION v. REALITY; SOCIETY.

An artist who relies upon his models to create the proper effect for the portraits that he sells meets Major and Mrs. Monarch, an older couple who have come to him, not as wealthy patrons as he first suspects, but rather as people in want of work. The artist sees in the Monarchs the look he wants, though he finds that he is better able to portray his other models, Oronte and Miss Churm, much more "accurately." The artist's friend asserts that, though he shows much talent in his work, the Monarchs make poor models, despite their appearance of affluence. Although he gives the Monarchs ample opportunity to work out—including letting them stay on a short time as nothing more than servants—the artist finally lets them go in favor of the professionals, who know nothing about genteel life, but who come across in his paintings as the "real thing."

James is adept at exploring themes of art (and artifice) and reality, and their connection with the upper classes, a notion that he limns throughout both his short stories and his novels, especially in detailing expatriate culture. The artist's disavowal of the Monarchs (the name itself a play on words, indicating their position in society's "monarchy") is a clear indication that the mainstream no longer accepts such people as the models by which they once lived. It is a theme that would play itself out innumerable times in the decades to come, when the burgeoning middle classes in America, especially, forced such people as James's artist to reconsider the economic impact of their decisions.

James, P.D. "Devices and Desires" (1990). From *The New Mystery* (Ed. Jerome Charyn, 1993). CRIME/LAW; DEATH; FATE.

Valerie Mitchell misses the bus that would have taken her home safely from the disco. She is frantic to appease her strict father's fears that she might be attacked by the Whistler, a serial killer who is on the loose in the area. Knowing that her father will not let her go out again if she does not return at the designated time, Valerie enlists the help of two old women, who give her a ride to the crossroads where she would have another chance to catch the bus and make it home on time.

She is dropped at the crossroads, glad to be out of the car and away from the judgmental, hostile sisters who had offered her a ride. As she walks along, however, Valerie becomes increasingly conscious of the eerie silence and threatening darkness, and fear overcomes her. She is relieved when she sees a woman with a dog walking on the side of the road. She catches up with the woman in the hope of walking with her to the bus stop; her fate is sealed, however, when she discovers that the "woman" is really the Whistler in disguise. Valerie is killed before she reaches the junction.

James's ironic tale is underpinned by the chance (and bad luck) that is the ultimate cause of the young woman's death. Though the fate of the protagonist is stated early in the story's first line—"She died because she missed the 9:40 bus from East Haven to Cobb's Marsh"—the subsequent details are presented in such a way that the reader reacts to the series of coincidences that doom the woman, not through any fault of her own, but simply by her having missed a bus. In that sense, the story has much in common with the burgeoning genre of the "urban legend" story, in which certain events are offered as cautionary tales to readers who would, in this case, disobey their parents.

Jen, Gish. "In the American Society" (1987). From *The Oxford Book of American Short Stories* (Ed. Joyce Carol Oates, 1992). ASSIMILATION; EXILE/EMIGRATION; FAMILY; HUMOR/SATIRE/IRONY; LABOR/JOB; NATIONALISM/AMERICAN DREAM; PRIDE.

Callie Chang, the narrator, is the daughter of Chinese immigrants who have begun a successful pancake house in their new country. Her parents understand the American Dream, though they are often confused by the awkward rules they encounter: when Callie's father wittingly hires two illegal aliens, he places himself and his business in jeopardy because he considers offering a bribe to the authorities, as he would have done in China. Although he willingly helps the men who need the work, they run from the law. Callie's father, who seems to be deflated by the predicament, spends less and less time at the restaurant.

When the family is invited to the home of Mr. and Mrs. Lardner, they see it as an opportunity to fit in. Callie's mother is intent upon joining the local country club, and her father acquiesces. When Jeremy Lardner confronts Mr. Chang in a drunken rage, Chang stands his ground and makes a scene at the party. As the family leaves, Chang's daughters and his wife tell him how proud they are of him. He offhandedly accepts the compliments and then realizes that he has left the keys to the family's car and home in the suit jacket that he had earlier thrown in the pool during his fight with Lardner. Chang decides that he will send his daughters back to get the keys when the party has died down, but for now they will go to the restaurant.

Jen's story is a humorous, honest look at what it means to be American—and what it means to retain one's dignity in the face of crisis. By expressing the attitudes and the reactions of her characters to the absurdity that they see around them in American society, Jen manages to define the American sensibility at the same time that she explores the often difficult act of assimilation.

Jewett, Sarah Orne. "A White Heron" (1886). From *The Harper Anthology of Fiction* (Ed. Sylvan Barnet, 1991). ANIMALS and HUMANS; COMING-OF-AGE; FAMILY; MEN and WOMEN; MORALITY (MORAL DILEMMA); NATURE/WILDERNESS.

Sylvia, whose very name evokes images of the woods where she finds herself most at home, is placed in a quandary when a young, handsome hunter stumbles upon a rare white heron near her grandmother's house and offers the young woman ten dollars to divulge its whereabouts. The sum of money would mean a great deal to Sylvia, who has come to the country to relieve her mother of the burden of a large family in the city, though she finds herself unwilling to sacrifice the bird for her own greed.

Jewett suggests that Sylvia's attraction to the hunter is that of a young woman for a young man. By denying him the opportunity to shoot the bird, Sylvia is also denying herself the opportunity to fall in love. Instead, she climbs the highest tree in the forest and watches the heron in all its glory, safe from the gun of the hunter. There, Sylvia realizes that she has much more in common with nature than she does with the young man who has promised her money—and awakened in her feelings that she has not had before. The story is one of both the power of nature and the coming-of-age of a girl who instinctively understands and cherishes the beauty of nature; in the process, she casts herself as a character wise beyond her years.

Jin, Ha. "The Richest Man" (1997). From *Under the Red Flag*, (Jin, 1997). CLASS CONFLICTS; CRIME/LAW; GREED; JEALOUSY; POLITICS; SOCIETY.

The richest man in the town is Li Wan, a doctor whom the villagers call "Ten Thousand," in reference to his bank account balance. He is the only person in town who drives a motorcycle, and on weekends he travels into the mountains and shoots pheasants with his shiny double-barrel shotgun. Li Wan's wealth has garnered him many enemies in the town, and the narrator attributes that to his position: "He had yet to learn how to give. That is indeed a difficult thing for a wealthy man to do." During the Cultural Revolution, however, Li Wan's luck runs out. He is accused of shattering a button with a likeness of Chairman Mao on it. After he is cudgeled by the townspeople who have hung a sign around his neck that classifies him as a "Current Counterrevolutionary," he is sentenced to five years working as a barefoot doctor in Sea Nest Village. His property is confiscated and given to the public.

When Li Wan is released, he returns to the village to find that his motorcycle is worn out and his shotgun has been ruined. With the money he receives from working for five years without a salary, however, he is once again a wealthy man and replaces what has been destroyed. Some of the villagers still resent Li Wan, who has succeeded despite his apparent political views. They are looking forward to the next revolution.

Ha Jin, whose collection won the Flannery O'Connor Award for Short Fiction, details life in his native China. The tone of the story is both humorous and pointed. The narrator who relates the tale is caught between admiring Li Wan for what he has and joining the townspeople in resenting him. The study is important not only as an insight into Chinese society, but also a glimpse into human nature.

Johnson, Charles. "Exchange Value" (1981). From *The Best American Short Stories 1982* (Ed. John Gardner and Shannon Ravenel, 1982). ALIENATION/ISOLATION; DREAMS (of the FUTURE); INTERIOR LIVES; POVERTY; SIBLINGS; SOCIETY.

Brothers Cooter and Loftis break into the apartment of Elnora Bailey, an elderly woman who lives in their building. The scene that the two discover shocks them and changes their lives irrevocably: the woman, who had been poor for her entire life, had inherited a large sum of money from a man for whom she had worked as a maid. Her wealth is combined with the squalor of someone accustomed to living in poverty. Despite Cooter's warning that the unexpected booty may be cursed, the two take it to their apartment. Cooter spends $250 of the nearly one million dollars, to the disdain of his brother, who insists that they should be more careful of what they spend. When Loftis returns to the apartment after a four-day absence, Cooter discovers a penny that his brother had picked up. Attached to the coin is a note detailing exactly where he found it. Cooter, who has taken his brother's advice to heart and has gone as far as to beg on the street, places it with their other wealth.

The idea of wealth—the "exchange value" and the power that comes with its possession—is the backdrop against which the brothers act. While Cooter initially spends what amounts to a small portion of their newfound riches, both he and Loftis, like the old woman from whom they acquire the money, are loath to give up even a small bit, lest their power decrease. The story posits a provoking scenario in which the boys, who themselves are accustomed to living hand-to-mouth, live within the paradox of "exchange value." Their wealth does not make them free; on the contrary, they become slaves to its power.

Jones, Gayl. "White Rat" (1975). From *Calling the Wind: Twentieth-Century African-American Short Stories* (Ed. Clarence Major, 1993). AFRICAN-AMERICAN EXPERIENCE; COMMUNICATION/LANGUAGE; DISABILITY/PHYSICAL APPEARANCE; MARRIAGE; MEN and WOMEN; SEXUALITY.

A young woman, Maggie, is pregnant, and the father has left her. The woman's husband (not the father of the child) returns for her, and they begin their lives together again. Their relationship is not a loving one, which is evident in the way they speak and act toward one another. Maggie is unhappy because her husband drinks and frequently loses his temper. He, the "White Rat" of the title, is a light-skinned black man, and Maggie suspects that the only reason he married her was because she, too, was light-skinned. Together, they had a child named Little Henry, who was born with a deformity. White Rat blamed Maggie for the disorder, which was the initial cause of the disintegration of their relationship. Maggie left White Rat, only to return two months later. Now, the couple awaits the birth of another child.

The story is a window into the lives of the characters and explores the complex relationship between races and between men and women. The color of one's skin—or the color that is perceived by society—is problematic, and Jones eschews any absolutes when she describes the unstable marriage of Maggie and White Rat. The author details the African-American experience through the use of dialogue that defines Maggie's relationships.

Joyce, James. "Araby" (1914). From *The Heath Introduction to Fiction*, 4th ed. (Ed. John J. Clayton, 1992). BETRAYAL; COMING-OF-AGE; GIFTS/GENEROSITY; LOVE; MEN and WOMEN; VANITY.

The narrator is infatuated with his friend's sister. Every morning, he watches her front door, hoping to catch a glimpse of the girl, who remains as elusive to him as she does to the reader (she is described only in terms of her swinging dress and the "soft rope of her hair"). Even though he had never spoken to the girl except for rare occasions when they exchanged platitudes, the very mention of her name is enough to send the boy into paroxysms of hormonal agony. The boy imagines that everything he does is for the girl's attention, and one evening he trembles with thoughts of love for her.

His prayers are answered when the girl asks him whether he is going to

Araby, her name for a bazaar in Dublin that, the narrator imagines, sells treasures beyond his wildest dreams. Although she would love to go, she has a prior engagement. The narrator tells her that if he must go alone, he will bring back a gift for her. On the day of the bazaar, the boy's uncle is late in coming home. Still, the boy manages to hurry to the market with his florin in hand and steps timidly to a stall where a young woman asks him if he will buy anything. Almost against his will, he tells her no. He immediately regrets the decision, thinking that he has disappointed his love; even as he gazes into the darkness of the closing bazaar, he despises himself for being a "creature driven and derided by vanity."

Joyce is a master at evoking the spirit of place and creating characters who are at once unique and yet representative of the human condition, especially in his beloved Dublin. This brief tale of first love—and its betrayal through an insignificant action—is no exception. The story hints at the glory of Joyce's *Ulysses*, which was published eight years after "Araby."

Joyce, James. "The Dead" (1914). From *The Story and Its Writer*, 4th ed. (Ed. Ann Charters, 1995). BETRAYAL; COMMUNICATION/ LANGUAGE; DEATH; EPIPHANY; HISTORY; MARRIAGE; MEN and WOMEN; POLITICS; SOCIETY.

Gabriel Conroy is the guest of honor at a Dublin party being held by the Morkan sisters. The cast of characters is vast, though Gabriel stands out as the one who too much flaunts his education and condescends toward the other guests. In an argument with Molly Ivors, the quintessential Irish woman who respects her country and all she stands for, Gabriel disavows the Irish way of life. The scene is typical of Gabriel's sometimes unwittingly contentious attitudes toward people.

Surprisingly, Gabriel does not offend anyone during his after-dinner speech, and he is smitten by the sight of his wife, Gretta, across the room as she listens to a traditional Irish song being played by two of the guests. When they return to their hotel room, Gabriel senses that their relationship will start afresh, as when they were first in love. The music and the sight of his wife that made Gabriel so hopeful has sent Gretta into a reverie for her first love, a boy in Galway who pined for her until his death when she left for Dublin years before.

To be sure, Gabriel experiences the epiphany that we have come to expect in Joyce's stories. Instead of being infused with life by the realization, however, he is left hollow, alone, and confused. The "dead" of the title come back to affect the living more than any of the characters at the party. Ironically, the young man whom his wife still mourns is not part of the world that Gabriel inhabits—the cosmopolitan and forward-thinking society characterized by the British, who fight to control the Irish—but rather the tight-knit culture of Western Ireland and its "backward" inhabitants. Even with his superior intellect, Gabriel is helpless to overcome memory.

K

Kafka, Franz. "A Country Doctor" (1917). From *The Heath Introduction to Fiction*, 4th ed. (Ed. John J. Clayton, 1992). HEALTH (SICKNESS/MEDICINE); ILLUSION v. REALITY; INSANITY; INTERIOR LIVES; LABOR/JOB; SOCIETY; SUPERNATURAL/HORROR.

When the country doctor receives an urgent call to visit a patient in a village ten miles away, he can hardly imagine the pitfalls that await him: in the night, his horse has died of exposure; a mysterious groom who conjures two strong horses seemingly from nowhere is intent upon molesting the doctor's maid, Rose; the horses have a preternatural sense of their duty, which is to keep the doctor away from his home while the groom has his way with the maid; and when he arrives at the call, he describes a surreal ménage of images that call into question his very sanity.

When he begins treating the boy, who at first has no overt signs of illness and instead, the doctor thinks, should be booted out of bed unceremoniously and told to get on with his life, the boy begs the doctor to let him die. Later, when the doctor discovers a large wound on the boy's hip infested with thick, white maggots, the boy begs to be saved, despite the doctor's bleak prognosis.

After the doctor endures the indignities of the townspeople, who strip him naked and order him to heal the boy or be killed, he leaves the village wondering why he had ever agreed to come. The same horses that transported him the ten miles to the village in the blink of an eye now stumble toward the doctor's home at a maddeningly slow pace, and he feels that he has been betrayed by all the elements in the story—the groom, the family who called him away from home on a bitter cold day on a false alarm, the horses themselves.

This story owes a debt to Poe, Gilman, and Hawthorne for its gothic undertones and its presentation of intense psychological drama in which the narrator is unable to connect with the real world. The seriousness of the doctor's journey is undermined by the absurdity of the actions that conspire to make it difficult, if not impossible, for him to fulfill his duty. Finally, the story is as much about the interior life of the country doctor—as evidenced by the title—as it is the external events that act as a catalyst for the bizarre happenings he relates.

Kafka, Franz. "A Hunger Artist" (1922). From *The Norton Anthology of Short Fiction*, 6th ed. (Ed. R.V. Cassill and Richard Bausch, 2000).

ANIMALS and HUMANS; ART and the ARTIST; HEALTH (SICK-
NESS/MEDICINE); INTERIOR LIVES; LABOR/JOB; PRIDE; SO-
CIETY.

For the professional faster, refusing to eat is an art. In the time during
which the story is set, fasting has lost much of its public interest, though
one man insists on taking his ability to live without eating to an unprece-
dented level. When the public was still interested in watching those who
fasted, seated like circus animals behind iron bars and monitored round the
clock by teams of referees, the limit was forty days. After that time, the faster
would be led from his cage and weaned back to health, only to repeat the
ordeal.

Unfortunately for those whose livelihoods consisted of being watched and
admired for their willpower, the public eventually lost interest. Amusement
seekers realized that there were more exciting adventures to be had. The
hunger artist, though, was too old to take on another profession. Devoted
to his craft, he set out to do what no man had ever done, to test the limits
of the human body.

Ensconced on the midway at a circus, the hunger artist realizes that people
just do not care to watch him starve himself. After a number of days that
no one knew (they had long ago stopped keeping track for lack of interest),
the hunger artist is removed from his cage, a wisp of soulless body, and he
dies. He is unceremoniously buried, straw and all. In his place, a well-fed
young panther stalks the cage, exciting the passersby with its vitality and
wildness.

Kafka's story can be read as a metaphor for the alienation inherent in
society, especially for those whose usefulness—and the absurdity of the protagonist's quest calls into question the long tradition of pointless bureaucracy described in the work of his Russian counterparts—has been exhausted.
The hunger artist's mistreatment at the hands of those who had formerly
admired him is a symptom of a capricious society in which both commodities
and people are disposable.

**Kafka, Franz. "The Metamorphosis" (1915). From *The Story and Its
Writer*, 5th ed. (Ed. Ann Charters, 1999). ANIMALS and HUMANS;
DEATH; FAMILY; HUMOR/SATIRE/IRONY; INDIVIDUAL; IN-
TERIOR LIVES; LABOR/JOB; SIBLINGS; SOCIETY.**

Gregor Samsa wakes up one morning to find that he has been transformed
into a bug. Though his family seems to take the transformation in stride,
they are understandably upset by the occurrence. After all, Gregor was the
sole provider for the family; with his inability to work (he had never missed
a day in five years as a salesman), hard times are surely ahead. As the condition persists, however, the family becomes less and less tolerant of Gregor.
His father drives him back into his room and, during one confrontation,

heaves an apple at him, which sticks in his beetle-like shell and rots there; his beloved sister brings him food, which she leaves on the floor before hurrying away.

One night, Gregor hears music coming from the living room. He ventures out of his own room at the sound of his sister's violin playing. The three boarders who have gathered to listen instead focus their attention on Gregor. His sister, incensed at the interruption, wishes him dead, using the word "it" to describe him in his present form. He goes back to his room and wills himself to die. The family members, released of their burden, look forward to their new lives, and "it was like a confirmation of their new dreams and excellent intentions that at the end of their journey their daughter sprang to her feet first and stretched her young body."

Kafka's most famous story relies on symbolism for its effect. Ann Charters points out that events in the author's own life lend themselves to the presentation of a "Freudian symbol that characterizes Kafka's sense of inadequacy before his demanding father." Gregor, through no fault of his own, has been rendered unable to support the family who had previously relied on him. As with Gregor's metamorphosis, however, the family undergoes a significant change of their own when they are able to escape the nightmare; they think seldom of him once he has been exterminated.

Kerr, M.E. (Marijane Meaker). "The Sweet Perfume of Good-Bye" (1987). From *Visions* (Ed. Donald R. Gallo, 1987). COMING-OF-AGE; CULTURE CONFLICTS; DEATH; EXILE/EMIGRATION; FANTASY/IMAGINATION/SCIENCE FICTION; RELIGION/SPIRITUALITY; SOCIETY.

When seventeen-year-old Caroline is chosen to travel to the planet Farfire to study the importance of smells on that world, she is astounded to find that the only existing odor is a beautiful smell not unlike lilac—the "sweet perfume of good-bye"—that people begin to emit one hour before they die. Caroline observes the lovers Carlo and Marny, who realize that Carlo will be gone in just a few minutes. Instead of expressing their grief, though, the two revel in their last moments together. When Caroline asks them whether they believe in life after death, they are unsure how to answer the question. They accept the fact that they do not know what happens after death.

Caroline is asked to appear on several national talk shows on the planet, where she is viewed as a freak. The audience has a difficult time believing that everything on Earth has an odor, and they mock her for saying so. Even though she has enjoyed learning more about the Farfire culture, she is looking forward to beginning the two-year journey back to Earth. When she receives a call from the captain of the ship, who mentions to her that he has noticed the lovely smell, not unlike lilacs, on the planet, she knows that he will be dead within the hour and that she will not be returning home anytime soon.

Kerr's story recalls the situations that one might find in the work of Ray Bradbury or Arthur C. Clarke in its manipulation of sensual perception in order to create worlds outside our own. By taking away olfactory stimulation save for the smell of death, which is not unpleasant, Kerr allows the protagonist to explore her own notions of death and the true meaning of life, which is to be lived fully, the author implies, until time runs out.

Keyes, Daniel. *Flowers for Algernon* **(1966). ALIENATION/ISOLATION; ANIMALS and HUMANS; DEATH; DISABILITY/PHYSICAL APPEARANCE; GOOD/EVIL; IDENTITY; LOVE/HATE; OPPRESSION; SOCIETY.**

Charlie Gordon is a thirty-seven-year-old retarded man who wants nothing more than to be intelligent. When he is offered an opportunity to undergo surgery that may triple his current level of intelligence, he accepts it. His progress is slow, measured against a mouse, Algernon, who always gets through a maze faster than Charlie can negotiate it with pencil and paper; eventually, though, he becomes the hyperintelligent man that the doctors had promised.

With his newfound brilliance comes hardship: Charlie is shunned by his friends and realizes that Miss Kinnian, the teacher with whom he was once in love, is not his intellectual equal now any more than she was when Charlie was handicapped. When Algernon's intelligence diminishes, Charlie realizes that he will suffer the same fate. When the mouse dies, Charlie places flowers on his grave, and as his skills disintegrate, he wishes only that others will do the same.

Charlie's story is a metaphor for society. After his operation, his intellect reveals the true nature of those around him, who despise him and are frightened by his abilities. Only in his heightened awareness does Charlie realize the human potential for evil (in fact, Charlie himself laughs along with others at the appearance of a mentally handicapped boy). In a sense, his previous state, to which he finally reverts, is preferable. He has the innocence of a child and a relationship with humanity that, though oppressive in its limitations, does not alienate him from those around him.

Kincaid, Jamaica. "Annie John" (1985). From *Annie John* **(Kincaid, 1985). ALIENATION/ISOLATION; CHILDHOOD; COMING-OF-AGE; INDIVIDUAL; LOVE/HATE; MOTHERS and CHILDREN.**

On the island of Antigua, Annie John, a ten-year-old girl, is fascinated with death. As the story progresses, Annie's troubles and conflicts worsen. She is disgusted and repulsed by her mother, whom she had once adored, and cringes at every touch from the woman. Though she does well in school, Annie steals books from the library, plays marbles, and befriends a girl of whom her mother would not approve. Annie John and her mother have a confrontation that ends in the girl's becoming ill. In her delirium, she "washes" her pictures and scrubs away the faces of everyone but herself. The sickness lasts for three months and ends as suddenly as it came. After her recovery, Annie realizes that she has grown physically and now looks down upon her mother. She envisions a future free from Antigua, her mother, and her past. She asks her father to build her a chest of her own, in which she begins to pack for her new life. At the story's conclusion, Annie is seventeen and on her way to England to become a nurse. As she bids the family farewell, she is sad about leaving. When the boat leaves the dock, she once again feels love for her mother.

Kincaid, using her position as a member of two very different societies— both the Caribbean island of her childhood and her subsequent experiences as a transplanted "American" writer—demonstrates the unbreakable bond between mother and daughter, even through some of life's most physically and psychically debilitating struggles. Annie John's own solipsism is a means through which she can establish her identity. That identity defines her not wholly apart from her family, as she had initially imagined it might, but rather in terms of her life in Antigua as she travels into the unknown.

Kincaid, Jamaica. "Girl" (1978). From *The Story and Its Writer*, 5th ed. (Ed. Ann Charters, 1999). COMING-OF-AGE; HUMOR/SATIRE/IRONY; MEN and WOMEN; MINORITY EXPERIENCE; TRADITION/CONVENTION.

This one-paragraph story is a laundry list of items that a young girl needs in order to survive, including: "this is how to hem a dress when you see the hem coming down and so to prevent yourself from looking like the slut I know you are so bent on becoming," "this is how you set a table for tea," and "this is how you make a good medicine for a cold." The list ends with an admonition to always squeeze the bread before buying. When the narrator is asked by the girl who is addressed what will happen if she is not allowed to squeeze the bread, the narrator replies, "you mean to say that after all you are really going to be the kind of woman who the baker won't let near the bread?"

Under its lighthearted exterior, the piece offers serious coming-of-age advice from a narrator who has much experience to give. Charters writes that Kincaid, a largely self-taught writer who is a native of Antigua, uses "a deliberately precise rhythmic style . . . free from conventional plots, characters, and dialogue" to explore, in this case, a girl's entry into the sometimes frightening world of a woman.

Kincaid, Nanci. "This Is Not the Picture Show" (1991). From *Best of the South* (Ed. Anne Tyler and Shannon Ravenel, 1995). COMING-OF-AGE; CRIME/LAW; FRIENDSHIP; MEN and WOMEN.

The narrator and Pat Lee are typical small-town teenage girls. They wander the streets of Tallahassee, Florida, looking at the crazy old men who have been let out of Chattahoochee Mental Hospital, ogling boys, and going to the picture show on Saturdays. Of the two, Pat Lee is the leader. She warns the narrator that boys don't like nice girls. In response to her preaching to the narrator, the prettier of the two, Pat Lee begins dating Tony Kelly, the bad boy of the school who drives through town in his green pickup truck. Tony will not talk to Pat Lee when they are in school, but they sit beside each other every week at the show. The narrator surmises that the two get along so well simply because they are both *mean*.

Pat Lee warns her friend that the real world is, in fact, a mean place. Little does she realize how true the statement is until the two girls have an old woman arrested for shoplifting in the JCPenney, and they find out that the woman is Tony's grandmother. Tony arrives in his pickup truck and gently helps the old woman into the cab, oblivious to what she has done and caring little about the ragged clothing she is wearing. At that moment, even the narrator understands why Pat Lee loves him.

The story is one of growing up and making sense of the world, and the actions of the narrator and Pat Lee are underpinned by Kincaid's descriptions of small-town life and the girls' desire to live in the world. Even though Pat Lee fancies herself an adult, Tony's actions mean more to both of the girls than their own hollow words.

King, Stephen. "The Man Who Loved Flowers" (1977). From *Night Shift* (King, 1978). DEATH; HUMOR/SATIRE/IRONY; ILLUSION v. REALITY; INSANITY; MEN and WOMEN; SOCIETY; SUPERNATURAL/HORROR.

A young man walks down a street in New York City on a beautiful evening in May 1963. He has a spring in his step, and everyone he meets, from the policeman at the crosswalk to the flower vendor, can see that the man is in love. He buys a bouquet of flowers from the vendor and makes his way past the action of the street—children playing stickball, lovers on apartment stairs, men watching a gigantic color television, people tuned in but not listening to radios spouting bad news, women turning wistfully at the sight of a man with flowers—to an alley where he finds the woman he has been looking for.

He approaches the woman, whom he calls "Norma," and hands her the flowers. At first, the woman is surprised and then horrified. She is not Norma, nor does she know the man who is giving her flowers on a dark side street. The young man pulls a hammer from his pocket and beats her to death. Norma, it seems, has been dead for ten years, and the young man has killed five other women. When he is finished with this one, the man who calls himself "Love" walks home with the same smile on his face that drew looks of admiration and envy just a short time before.

The story is, above all, ironic, and the title a romantic red herring. Though the men and women with whom the killer comes in contact think that he looks to be in love, they can hardly imagine the horror that awaits the woman who will receive the flowers, which should be a token of affection, not death. The radio broadcasting the bad news that no one pays attention to has mentioned a hammer killer on the loose. Still, on a night like this, who could concern themselves with such awful news?

Kipling, Rudyard. "The Limitations of Pambe Serang" (1891). *The Literature of Crime* (Ed. Ellery Queen, 1950). BETRAYAL; DEATH; FATE; REVENGE.

At the story's outset, both the protagonist, Pambe Serang, and Nurkeed, the man who has wronged him, are dead. The narrator flashes back to the beginning of the tale, a harmless enough affair. Nurkeed, the stoker on the steamer *Saarbruck*, gets drunk and steals Pambe's food. Pambe is the ship's serang, or headman. In the ensuing scuffle, Pambe Serang is stabbed by Nurkeed, a wrong that he vows to avenge, no matter how long it takes.

Nurkeed awakes the following morning and has no recollection of what occurred the night before. When he is nearly killed by a knife thrown in his direction, he understands the seriousness of his situation. He attempts to hide in a crowd and succeeds for a time. Pambe Serang, however, never having forgotten how Nurkeed wronged him, bides his time. Many months later, even as Pambe Serang lies on his deathbed, he persuades Nurkeed to visit him; without hesitation, he sticks a knife under his enemy's ribs. After making a miraculous recovery from his illness, Pambe Serang is hanged for his crime.

The story is, above all, one of revenge. Although the wrong that Nurkeed perpetrates on Pambe Serang is perhaps not one that calls for his life in return, the code of the time—or at least in Pambe Serang's culture—dictates that the stoker, despite his best attempts to avoid his nemesis, will meet him once more. Pambe Serang gladly gives up his life in order for the wrong to be redressed. Nurkeed's actions clearly exceed the "limitations" of the serang.

Kleist, Heinrich von. "The Beggar-Woman of Locarno" (1800). From *Great Short Stories from the World's Literature* (Ed. Charles Neider, 1950). CLASS CONFLICTS; DEATH; REVENGE; SELF-DESTRUCTION/SUICIDE; SUPERNATURAL/HORROR.

An old woman who begs door to door is taken in to a castle and placed in a spacious room on a pallet of straw. When the master of the castle returns that evening, he finds the woman on the floor and beats her until he injures her spine. The woman drags herself across the room and huddles behind the stove, where she dies.

Years later, the marquis attempts to sell the castle. One prospective buyer, lodged in the room where the old woman spent her last agonizing hours, reports to the marquis and his wife that the room is haunted. The marquis does not remember his particular unkindness to the woman, though he is uneasy about spending the night in the room. When he joins his wife in the room, the two are horrified to watch the scene from the past replayed. The marquis runs from the castle, and sets it on fire, where he "found his end in the most horrible manner possible."

This brief tale is enjoyable for its exploration of the supernatural. It is also a cautionary tale that suggests payback for those who would mistreat others outside their station in life. Von Kleist may have seen a bit of himself in the marquis; he ended his own unhappy life by committing suicide in 1811.

Kotzwinkle, William. "Follow the Eagle" (1969). From *The Norton Anthology of Contemporary Fiction* (Ed. R.V. Cassill, 1988). ANIMALS and HUMANS; DEATH; DREAMS (of the FUTURE); MEN and WOMEN; NATURE/WILDERNESS; SUPERSTITION; VANITY.

On the Navaho Indian Reservation, Johnny Eagle and his friend, Domingo, drive to the edge of a cliff and consider a stunt that Eagle has proposed. Against the wishes of his girlfriend, Red Wing, Eagle is determined to jump the canyon the next morning on his motorcycle. Domingo wonders why Eagle would try such a thing, though the next morning, he drives his friend to the site. After Domingo tries to dissuade him from the stunt by saying that he knows a beautiful woman they could meet in Ensenada, Eagle makes tentative circles around the cliff and hits the ramp at one hundred twenty-five miles an hour.

His first thought is what a glorious feeling it is to be soaring through the air like an eagle; his next thought is that he should have gone for one-fifty off the ramp. As he realizes his failure and the rocks of the cliff-face flash by him, his thoughts become a stream of consciousness that begins with dreams of Red Wing, Ensenada, and his exploits with his friend, and ends with his impact on the bottom of the canyon. The story concludes with a short paragraph that describes the birth of an eagle in the canyon and its first flight, when the bird's mother "pushed the little eagle into space where he learned to soar."

The story's title and its understated ending are the only indications that the reader has of Eagle's purpose in jumping the canyon. Though Kotzwinkle does little to develop Eagle's character in this brief narrative, that lack of information makes the protagonist's death all the more profound in its spectacular mystery and universal appeal. Eagle, the man, and the bird that soars majestically over the canyon—intertwined symbols of the freedom that the man so clearly wants to capture—are two different animals. Nature has the upper hand; Eagle's dying thoughts suggest that he recognizes the foolishness of his vanity.

Kundera, Milan. "The Hitchhiking Game" (1969). From *The Gates of Paradise: The Anthology of Erotic Short Fiction* (Ed. Roberto Manguel, 1993). IDENTITY; ILLUSION v. REALITY; MEN and WOMEN; POLITICS; SEXUALITY.

A young couple is on a two-week vacation that will leave both of them profoundly changed by their experience. The woman is the less experienced of the two in relationships, and obliges her boyfriend by playing the role of a hitchhiker who allows the man to pick her up. The boyfriend, who is several years older than the woman and finds her naïveté attractive, is unhappy with how easily his lover falls into the role. He deviates from his own personality, changing the intended direction of their journey, a simple act that makes him feel as though he is in control. Still, the woman becomes more involved in the role she has taken on, and the man, unable to reconcile himself to her words and actions, humiliates her by treating her as a prostitute. The woman, confused and ashamed at her actions, breaks down and declares her own identity. The man hesitantly responds to her.

Kundera's stories often intertwine relationships and politics. In this case, the man's need to wield power over his younger and less experienced lover is a manifestation of both his perceived lack of power in his interpersonal relationships and a lack of power for the individual in the society at large. The author uses the backdrop of Communist Czechoslovakia to stress the importance of identity making for both the woman and the man, whose understanding of the world around him is perhaps not as profound as he believes it to be.

L

Lagerlof, Selma. "The Eclipse" (1922). From *Great Short Stories of the World* (Ed. Barrett H. Clark and Maxim Lieber, 1925). AGING; EPIPHANY; FRIENDSHIP; NATURE/WILDERNESS; PLACE.

A group of women who live on a mountain in Sweden stay at home while their children attend school and their husbands work. They fight off the loneliness of their existence by organizing parties where they drink coffee and eat cake and talk about their lives. Each of the women takes her turn at hosting the parties; on this occasion, the hostess cannot think of anything to celebrate. She is very old and all her relatives are dead; she desperately searches for a reason to have the party and discovers that a solar eclipse is coming. Though the woman loves the sun, which gives her light while she lives in darkness, she is hesitant to celebrate it, as she thinks that the other women will mock her idea. The old woman holds the party, and the other women who attend take little notice of the eclipse. The woman, however, sings to the eclipse and says that it has given her courage and strength. When she explains to the others how the sun is a good friend to her, the women become conscious of the sun's greatness, and they leave feeling happy and hopeful.

The sun—both as a giver of life and a symbol of respite from an otherwise banal life—is appropriately celebrated by an old woman who can teach the others that their lives can be considerably more expansive than they are. Ironically, only by its absence (through the eclipse itself and the celebration of the sun's disappearance) do the women fully understand its importance.

Lardner, Ring. "Haircut" (1925). From *The 50 Greatest Mysteries of All Time* (Ed. Otto Penzler, 1998). DEATH; DISABILITY/PHYSICAL APPEARANCE; FRIENDSHIP; ILLUSION v. REALITY; MEN and WOMEN; REGIONALISM (LOCAL COLOR); SEXUALITY.

A barber sits in his shop telling a tale about a local character named Jim Kendall, whose death is suggested in the story's opening paragraphs. The narrative that evolves from the barber's meanderings is one of a small-town joker who gets in over his head when he attempts to rape the girlfriend of a young doctor who has recently moved into the town. The doctor has befriended Paul, a boy who is known in the town as being "slow." When Paul realizes what Kendall has done to the woman, Julie Gregg, with whom he is infatuated, he shoots the man when the two are out duck hunting in

Kendall's boat. The barber ends the tale by asserting that he would not have been in the boat with someone who had never handled a gun before and echoes once again the head-shaking admiration he had for Kendall while he was alive for the tricks that the man would play on people.

Lardner is known for his sharp wit and evocative renderings of local color. In this story, he combines the two into a cautionary tale of a man who exceeds the reputation that the town has created for him. Kendall is an unlikable character who may have gotten what he deserves. As is often the case, though, the townspeople—and especially the barber, the traditional teller of tales in small-town America—remember him in a way that seems antithetical to the reality of his situation.

Lardner, Ring. "The Golden Honeymoon" (1922). From *The Best American Short Stories of the Century* (Ed. John Updike and Katrina Kenison, 1999). COMMUNICATION/LANGUAGE; CONTESTS; HUMOR/SATIRE/IRONY; ILLUSION v. REALITY; JEALOUSY; MARRIAGE; MEN and WOMEN; REGIONALISM (LOCAL COLOR).

Charley and his wife, Lucy, whom he insists on calling "Mother," leave for Florida on their fiftieth wedding anniversary. Typical of such long marriages, Charley's world is so closely intertwined with Lucy's that it renders him incapable of discussing any event outside the context of their relationship. When they meet a former suitor of Lucy's in St. Petersburg, Charley places himself in competition with the man, Frank Hartsell; Lucy has become fast friends with the man's wife, which makes Charley even more uncomfortable. Between descriptions of their travels (most of which deal directly with money), Charley is determined to best Hartsell at checkers (which he does), cards (which he does not, though he blames Mrs. Hartsell for her inability to play), and horseshoes (which is an unmitigated failure for Charley). Lucy has not told Mrs. Hartsell of her true relationship with the woman's husband all those years before, and Charley, not able to handle the deception anymore, tells the woman the truth. Lucy and Charley fight, and after two days of silence, they make up. The Hartsells leave town, and Charley and Lucy return home.

In the narrator's conspiratorial tone, Lardner presents a humorous tale that is underpinned by the insecurity of Charley who, as the reader discovers through his words and actions, has been under the watchful eye of his wife for the duration of their marriage (his last line is, "Here comes Mother, so I guess I better shut up"). The title of the story is ironic, though Lardner is careful not to indict the relationship of Lucy and Charley. Rather, Charley shows great love—albeit in an awkward manner—when he is threatened by the appearance of an old rival.

Law, Warner. "The Harry Hastings Method" (1971). From _Studies in the Short Story_ (Ed. Virgil Scott and David Madden, 1976). ART and the ARTIST; COMMUNICATION/LANGUAGE; CRIME/LAW; FRIENDSHIP; HUMOR/SATIRE/IRONY.

The narrator is a twenty-five-year-old man who takes writing classes during the day and burgles houses in the Hollywood Hills at night. When he comes across the home of Harry Hastings, himself a writer, he gets more than he bargains for. In successive break-ins of the man's house, the narrator leaves notes explaining what he is doing. Hastings, in return, corrects the young man's letters and writes, "I think I must tell you that you have a long way to go before you will be a professional writer. . . . Have you ever thought of devoting your talents to something a little higher than burgling people such as me?"

After yet another uninvited tour of Hastings's home, the narrator returns to his own apartment to discover that Hastings has broken in and left a note on the door suggesting that a puma is running loose in the place. When the two men finally meet, they join forces in a burglary protection agency, writing signs that will give burglars pause before they break and enter. Crime is down two-thirds in the neighborhood.

Law's story is a clever and humorous examination of the Hollywood lifestyle and the "gentleman burglar" who will not harm dogs and continues his life of crime in order to become a better writer. The underlying theme of doing what is necessary for one's art is prevalent, though overshadowed by the lighthearted events and the story's "happy ending."

Lawrence, D.H. "Odour of Chrysanthemums" (1911). From _The Story and Its Writer_, 4th ed. (Ed. Ann Charters, 1995). DECEPTION; EPIPHANY; FAMILY; LOSS; MARRIAGE; MEN and WOMEN; MOTHERS and CHILDREN.

Elizabeth Bates, her husband, and their children live in the mining region of Nottinghamshire, England. Walter, who works in the mines, has begun to drink heavily, and Elizabeth worries about their future together. When Elizabeth places a small bouquet of chrysanthemums in her apron, the children comment on their odor. Elizabeth thinks ironically that the flowers are the symbol of her wedding, the births of her children, and her husband's own drunkenness.

Walter does not arrive home, and Elizabeth considers looking for him. She discovers later that he has died in the mines. Walter's body is delivered to the house, and Elizabeth and her mother-in-law ready the body for burial. Elizabeth considers that neither she nor her husband had been truly happy in their marriage; with Walter's death, however, Elizabeth is thankful that she is able to discern the truth of the matter and will not go through life under the illusion that her relationship with Walter was perfect.

The title of the story contrasts the beauty of the flowers with the already dead relationship of Elizabeth and Walter. The epiphany brought about by Walter's death is similar to Kate Chopin's Mrs. Mallard in "Story of an Hour," though Elizabeth survives to enjoy her children, and perhaps, once again, the "odor of chrysanthemums."

Lawrence, D.H. "The Rocking-Horse Winner" (1926). From *Short Fiction: Classic and Contemporary*, 4th ed. (Ed. Charles H. Bohner and Dean Dougherty, 1999). CONTESTS; DEATH; FATE; MAGIC/OCCULT; MOTHERS and CHILDREN.

In his attempt to win his mother's affections, Paul goes in search of luck, which his mother insists is better any day than money itself. With Bassett, the gardener, and Paul's uncle, Oscar, the boy wins five thousand pounds at the racetrack and decides to give his mother one thousand pounds a year for the next five years. The money is not enough, however, and Paul is determined to further fulfill his mother's wishes.

The young boy has gotten luck to side with him by riding a rocking horse until, in a frenzy, the names of the winners come to him. On this occasion, Paul conspires to get his parents out of the house while he discovers the next big winner. He rides the horse until a brain fever causes him to fall off; his mother, returning to the house, finds him lying on the floor. Later, Bassett tells Paul that he has chosen correctly and that he is wealthy. Paul tells his mother, "I *am* lucky" before he dies.

The theme of greed illustrates the consequence of a boy's having to win his mother's approval through material possessions rather than the unconditional love that parents feel for their children. Lawrence often writes strongly of the mutual exclusivity of love and money, no more compellingly than in this tragic tale that ends with the death of the innocent—a young boy who, ironically, rides a child's toy to satisfy the urges of the adults in his life.

Lawrence, D.H. "Tickets, Please" (1919). From *The Oxford Book of American Short Stories* (Ed. Joyce Carol Oates, 1992). ALIENATION/ISOLATION; MEN and WOMEN; MORALITY (MORAL DILEMMA); SOCIETY; VIOLENCE; WAR.

During World War I, England's railroads were staffed by women and men who could not fight in the war because of physical deformities. A good-looking man named John Thomas Raynor, who is out of place (and much in demand) at the time, is an incurable flirt and has affairs with many of the women. Annie Stone, who is determined not to fall under his spell, also has an affair with the young man. She wants to begin a relationship with Raynor, while he desires nothing more than to continue his exploits.

The women with whom Raynor has had affairs conspire to meet him in the station one night. When they insist that he choose which of them to walk home, he refuses. They knock him to the ground and beat him, until he is "as an animal lies when it is defeated and at the mercy of the captor." Raynor finally chooses Annie, but she wants no part of him. What was to have been sweet revenge turns out to be a somber—and hollow—victory over the man whom all of the women had dated of their own free will.

The context for the story—wartime, in which alienation and a sense of dislocation are heightened for the ones left behind—foreshadows the conflict that arises between Raynor and the women in his life. Though he offers them something that they would not otherwise have—a man to "walk out" with at night—their jealousies destroy both the reality and the ideal. No one gains from the violence done to Raynor; nor, it seems, can their loneliness be mitigated in any other way.

Leavitt, David. "Counting Months" (1984). From *Family Dancing* (Leavitt, 1984). DEATH; DISABILITY/PHYSICAL APPEARANCE; HEALTH (SICKNESS/MEDICINE); INTERIOR LIVES; MOTHERS and CHILDREN; SOCIETY; TIME (and its EFFECTS).

Anna Harrington was given six months to live by her doctor. As she leaves his office at the end of her time—she has been counting the months and realizes that by now she should have been dead—her emotions alternate between dread and resolve to continue to be a mother to her children, whom she cares for alone. The Christmas season does little to lift her spirits, and when she takes the children to a holiday party at the Lauranses, her life takes an odd turn.

At first, the petty squabbles that bother her—her son's lying about a broken thermos bottle, for instance—cease to matter. Anna is alienated by Joan Lensky, ostensibly a friend, who insists on discussing the details of Anna's illness. Also, a group of carolers brought to the party by the Laurenses's son, Greg, turns out to be a disturbingly pathetic collection of retarded children from the state hospital. One of the children, a dwarf with exaggerated features, locks eyes with Anna, who sees in the child either utter simplicity or a profound understanding of her condition. The girl is a "comrade in sorrow."

Leavitt uses illness as a backdrop for much of his fiction, and his characters, as Anna, are ambivalent about the process of living-within-death. Anna lives within herself, despite the nagging notion that she should by now have been dead, and the author eschews any transcendent message about the dignity with which we die. Rather, we see the afflicted living as they must—until their lives are unceremoniously ended. Anna has children to take care of, and Leavitt implies that, when her moment of connection with the dwarf-child ends, she will continue to care for them until she can no longer do so.

Leavitt, David. "Gravity" (1990). From *The Norton Anthology of Short Fiction*, 6th ed. (Ed. R.V. Cassill and Richard Bausch, 2000). DEATH;

GIFTS/GENEROSITY; HEALTH (SICKNESS/MEDICINE); IL-
LUSION v. REALITY; MOTHERS and CHILDREN.

Theo Greenman is a young man who has gone home to die. When given
a choice, he decides against taking a drug that may prolong his life but
would take his eyesight. His mother takes care of him and maintains a façade
of cheerfulness in the face of Theo's imminent mortality. Despite his failing
health, his mother convinces him to go shopping with her; she plans on
buying a clunky crystal bowl for her nephew in retaliation for a similarly
tacky gift that Theo received from an aunt for his graduation. When his
mother unexpectedly tosses the bowl to Theo in the shop, he drops his cane
and catches the bowl. On the way home, the reality of Theo's condition
invades their moment of levity and hope; still, Theo's mother does what she
can to remain upbeat in her son's time of need.

Leavitt writes poignantly and realistically about disease and the fact that
Theo will not be well again. His mother's simple gesture—throwing the
bowl to him so they can prove to themselves that Theo is still alive—is an
affirmation of life in the face of death. A mother's love for her son and her
willingness to let him die with dignity transcend, at least for a time, the
tragic implications of his disease. The title alludes both to the seriousness
of his situation and to Theo's act of defying gravity by preventing the bowl
from crashing to the ground. That the two are shopping for a gift is also
important: Theo's mother, while forced to watch her son deteriorate and
die, is giving him the greatest gift of all, a mother's love.

**Lee, Cherylene. "Hollywood and the Pits" (1997). From _Help Wanted:
Short Stories about Young People Working_ (Sel. Anita Silvey, 1997).**
ANIMALS and HUMANS; CHILDHOOD; COMING-OF-AGE;
DREAMS (of the FUTURE); LABOR/JOB; MOTHERS and CHIL-
DREN.

For as long as she can remember, the narrator has been a child actor.
Ever since she was three, when she was dubbed "The Chinese Shirley Temple," she has never had trouble finding work. Now, at fifteen, after growing
five inches in seven months, she finds that she has outgrown her audience.
Casting directors don't call her back for parts, and her mother, who has
been supportive of her life in show business, is worried that she will disappear from the Hollywood scene for good.

Despite her prior success, the narrator realizes there are other activities
that interest her. She volunteers to work at the La Brea Tar Pits in Los
Angeles and compares her own career to the animals that died there millions
of years ago, especially the juvenile animals whose skeletons were almost
always found jumbled and disconnected. The work is fulfilling for the young
woman, and her mother, who still thinks that she can move from the role
of cute kid to film ingénue, slowly reconciles herself to the fact that her
daughter can succeed at things other than dancing and acting.

The story is interspersed with factual material about the La Brea Tar Pits, and those sections are metaphors for the girl's life: like the animals in the pits, she has been drawn in by Hollywood. What looked to her like a promising oasis was instead a short career fraught with disappointment. Still, Lee suggests, there is more to life than the Hollywood grind.

LeGuin, Ursula K. "April in Paris" (1962). *Studies in Fiction* **(Ed. Blaze O. Bonazza et al., 1982). ALIENATION/ISOLATION; COMMUNICATION/LANGUAGE; FANTASY/IMAGINATION/SCIENCE FICTION; FRIENDSHIP; HISTORY; MAGIC/OCCULT.**
Professor Barry Pennywither is a lonely man, a scholar on a year's sabbatical in Paris. His theory on the death of the poet Villon has received little attention, and he is pleased beyond words to be conjured by an equally lonely alchemist living in fifteenth-century Paris, in the very room where Pennywither spends his days. The two strike up a fast friendship, and the conjurer, Lenoir, provides the companionship that Pennywither never had in his previous life. Lenoir is able to create other companions for them, as well: a raven-haired Gaelic slave, a twenty-third-century archaeologist, and a forlorn dog round out the group. The one aspect of their lives that they all have in common, it seems, is their alienation from their respective societies. They spend their days wandering the streets of medieval Paris reveling in their new lives. After all, it is April in Paris, and the chestnuts are in bloom.
LeGuin's penchant for using science fiction as a means of exploring relevant contemporary topics comes to the fore in this story, and her exploration of the roots of alienation and a possible solution—albeit a far-fetched one that includes bringing together people from four different periods of time who have in common the most prevalent of problems—illustrates the power of love and companionship.

LeGuin, Ursula K. "The Rule of Names" (1964). *Studies in Fiction* **(Ed. Blaze O. Bonazza et al., 1982). ANIMALS and HUMANS; COMMUNICATION/LANGUAGE; FANTASY/IMAGINATION/ SCIENCE FICTION; MAGIC/OCCULT; TRADITION/CONVENTION.**
Mr. Underhill is a rather unassuming wizard who lives, aptly enough, under a hill. No one knows his real name, because to know another's name in his society is to control that person. The rule of names has existed for as long as anyone can remember, and it is instilled in the society's children from the earliest age. When a young man—whom the islanders call "Blackbeard"—arrives one day, the locals are not disturbed by his presence. He confides to one of them, however, that he has come to take back a treasure that Mr. Underhill stole from his family many years before. In the ensuing battle, Blackbeard reveals Mr. Underhill's true name, hoping to wrest his

power from him and restore the treasure to his family. Mr. Underhill/Yevaud, however, reveals his true shape, a dragon, and stomps the young man to death. Three days later, Mr. Underhill comes out of his cave and reveals his true shape to them.

LeGuin synthesizes fantasy and humor in this story and turns the tables on the traditional tale of the young warrior come to claim his rightful property. Although Mr. Underhill is portrayed as a mild-mannered, doddering old man, repeat readings suggest that the author's unconventional ending is more concerned with the power of language, history, and identity than with the more obvious confrontation between the two men.

Lessing, Doris. "The Nuisance" (1951). From _Studies in Fiction_ (Ed. Blaze O. Bonazza et al., 1982). DEATH; LABOR/JOB; MARRIAGE; MEN and WOMEN; RACE RELATIONS; VIOLENCE; WOMEN'S ISSUES.

In a culture in which the natives and the white men of a neighboring area are constantly in conflict, the main native, The Long One, is having a problem with one of his wives; he complains about the woman to his boss, a white man. The Long One is a good worker, and the boss at first does not mind hearing about the man's troubles. When the complaining becomes too much for the boss, however, he suggests that the man take care of the problem on his own. The boss finds out later that the wife has left her husband; not until the annual cleaning of the natives' well does the woman's body surface, in pieces. The Long One has, indeed, taken care of his problem; the boss only knows that the man was a "damned good driver in any case." The man's actions are overlooked and her death written off as a suicide.

Lessing, who understands firsthand the societal divide that allows such actions to be forgiven and such attitudes to exist, details the personal and moral issues that lead to a woman's death at the hands of her husband. The woman is nothing more than a "nuisance," something less than human. Through his understated comment about the man's work ethic, the boss implicitly condones the behavior and draws attention away from the story's real center of gravity.

Lessing, Doris. "Our Friend Judith" (1958). From _Studies in Fiction_ (Ed. Blaze O. Bonazza et al., 1982). ANIMALS and HUMANS; ART and the ARTIST; COMMUNICATION/LANGUAGE; INTERIOR LIVES; MEN and WOMEN; PLACE; WOMEN'S ISSUES.

Judith's friends, who narrate the story, speak of her disposition, both behind her back and to her face. They do not really understand her, and when they think they do, she surprises them. Judith, a single English woman, lives by herself. Though her existence is far from extraordinary, she thinks that she is close to having everything life can offer. When one of her friends comments on her being childless, Judith responds that "One cannot have everything." She is also a poet, her work "always cool and intellectual," and one must read the poems several times in order to understand them.

When Judith moves to Italy, her friends visit her and decide that the town does not suit her. It is rubbing off on her, though; she begins wearing tight dresses and sports a new hairstyle. While she is in Italy, she takes on a pregnant cat. When the kittens are born, the mother disregards them and even kills one of them. The event prompts Judith to move back to England. Her friends consider the entire episode odd; Judith tells them that she does not "really see any point at all in discussing it."

Lessing's story, told through the eyes of Judith's friends, is a tale of two different people: the cool, aloof, slightly eccentric person whom the friends know; and the compassionate person that Judith believes herself to be. Still, Judith is rational to the extreme, an attitude that erects a boundary between her and those who could hurt her. The snapshot images that combine to form a picture of Judith are, in many ways, as fragmented, confused, and ambivalent as her own life.

Lester, Julius. "The Child" (1993). From *Join In: Multiethnic Short Stories* (Ed. Donald R. Gallo, 1993). AFRICAN-AMERICAN EXPERIENCE; ALIENATION/ISOLATION; COMING-OF-AGE; DREAMS (of the FUTURE); INTERIOR LIVES; RACE RELATIONS.

Karen is a pregnant seventeen-year-old black girl who has just had a confrontation with her mother over her situation. When the girl told her mother that she, too, had been seventeen when Karen was born, her mother slapped her. Now, as she rides the subway, she considers her options in a life that seems less than hopeful. All around her, she sees the human wreckage that inhabits her society: A drunk black man who claims to have beaten Muhammad Ali in the ring rambles to anyone who will listen. Karen looks at him with disdain and knows that black people are judged by whites based on such stereotypes. She is determined never to let such a thing happen to her child.

Karen watches a white girl who is able to ignore the man's ranting by keeping her nose in a book. Karen wonders "what it was like to be white? That you didn't have to care about anybody else except yourself? You didn't even have to think about anybody else." Karen knows that one day she will work as a clothing designer and that when she leaves New York City for Hollywood, the radio will announce her departure. Maybe then her mother will accept her.

The narrative structure of the story—the intermittent ramblings of the drunk man who claims to have been a world-class boxer interspersed with the girl's own, much different, thoughts—combine to present a picture of the society in which Karen lives. For her, the racial issues that she considers are only part of the problem. She must gain acceptance from her mother at the same time that she takes care of another life—one she is determined to protect. Though Lester's tone is hopeful, the author suggests to the reader what a difficult road Karen has before her.

Lipsyte, Robert. "The Defender" (1995). From *Ultimate Sports* (Ed. Donald R. Gallo, 1995). ALIENATION/ISOLATION; COMING-OF-AGE; COMMUNICATION/LANGUAGE; CONTESTS; CULTURE CONFLICTS; FANTASY/IMAGINATION/SCIENCE FICTION; FRIENDSHIP.

The Interscholastic Galactic Defender readies himself for his final high school Power Thought match. The Challenger, who represents the Unified High School of the Barren Planets, is an androgynous creature whose only thoughts in this game where ideas, not weapons, can injure, are images of destruction, pain, and man's inhumanity to the Challenger's people, known as "Greenies." After a series of "points" in which the Defender, who has never lost a match, can only recoil at the ugliness of the Challenger's thoughts, the Defender realizes that, despite the protests of his coach and the Superintendent, the only way to best the Challenger is to knock it off balance with thoughts of love. When the Defender wins the match 10–9, and with the crowd cheering and celebrating the victory, the Defender and his teammates make their way to the Challenger, who stands "alone and quivering in the middle of the Pit."

In this allegory that combines science fiction and an astute statement on compassion, Lipsyte adds a new twist to the notion of competition and equality. While the story's adults—the principal, the coach, the Superintendent—want to win at all cost, it is the competitors, ostensibly younger and less experienced, who realize that the victory is hollow as long as the Challenger stands defeated and alone. The story's premise is engaging, turning competition inward and emphasizing the value of agile thinking over athletic prowess.

Lispector, Clarice. "Pig Latin" (1974). From *The New Mystery* (Ed. Jerome Charyn, 1993). COMMUNICATION/LANGUAGE; CRIME/LAW; DEATH; MEN and WOMEN; MISOGYNY; SEXUALITY.

Though Maria Aparecida is a beautiful English teacher, she dresses simply. When she boards a train and overhears two men talking in a language that she at first does not recognize, she listens closely and finally realizes that they are conversing in "pig latin." The men begin by commenting on the pretty woman; the talk becomes more serious when she realizes that they are going to rape, rob, and kill her in the next tunnel. She makes herself up and hikes up her dress in an attempt, ironically, to get the men to avoid her. The cabin conductor notices her actions and thinks she is going to prostitute herself to the men. At the next stop, he accompanies her off the train and into the arms of the police. A lady gives her a dirty look as she boards the train and takes the seat that Maria has vacated. Maria spends several days in jail before she is released. Even though she is a virgin, she thinks of herself as a whore for what she has done. When she glances at a newspaper, though, she reads of a woman who was raped, robbed, and murdered on the train. It was the same woman who had taken Maria's seat when the conductor ushered her off.

Lispector writes directly about a simple premise—after all, we are not sure whether the men are to be taken seriously in their talk, and Maria's actions seem to be more melodramatic than rational in response to such a heinous suggestion of crime—and transforms the "relationship" between the woman and the two men into a story that recalls the irony of P. D. James's "Devices and Desires." If not for her quick (and perhaps risky) action, Maria would have been their victim. Though she is at first distraught over her actions (we find out early in the story that she is a virgin and such preening and overt sexuality are well outside her staid nature), she comes to realize that those actions have saved her life.

London, Jack. "To Build a Fire" (1908). From *Short Fiction: Classic and Contemporary*, 4th ed. (Ed. Charles H. Bohner and Dean Dougherty, 1999). ANIMALS and HUMANS; DEATH; FATE; INTERIOR LIVES; PLACE.

A solitary man with his dog trailing behind him makes his way across the Yukon on an errand to meet friends. He is a newcomer to the territory, though he worries little that he will fail in fording the wilderness in bitter-cold temperatures where the slightest mistake means certain death. When his feet break through the ice, the man is forced to stop and build a fire. The fire that brings life, however, also causes the snow above him to fall, snuffing the flame. The man does not panic, though he is helpless in the cold to restore the fire and stave off death. He considers killing the dog and wrapping himself in its warmth. The dog senses the man's desperation, however, and will not be caught. The man makes one last attempt to run to the camp, but comes up short. He freezes to death in the wilderness, and the dog, recognizing the smell of death, heads to the camp that he knows, where he will be given food and shelter by the man's friends.

London's famous story recalls Sherwood Anderson's "Death in the Woods" and the works of Stephen Crane in its evocation of "naturalist" fiction, works that explore man's relationship to nature and the cruel indifference of nature in life-and-death situations. Man is little suited for the extremes of nature, the author implies, just as the animals that have existed in harmony with nature for eons possess the instinct necessary to survive.

London, Jack. "To the Man on the Trail" (1900). From *Great American Short Stories* (Sel. by the editors of *Reader's Digest*, 1990). BE-

TRAYAL; CRIME/LAW; MORALITY (MORAL DILEMMA); PLACE; REVENGE.

As a group of men enjoy their time in a bar in the Alaskan wilderness, winding down from a hard day's ride behind their dogsleds, a man named Westondale enters. He tells the patrons that he has been following someone for days, and joins in their conversation, going as far as to pull out a picture of his wife and child that is passed among the men, who all miss their own families.

Westondale asks to be awakened in four hours, and at the appointed time he sets off, ostensibly to catch the person he has been following. Just minutes after he leaves, the police arrive and tell the men that Westondale is wanted for stealing $40,000. The men feel deceived by Westondale's lying until one of them, the Malemute Kid, tells a story that he has heard about Westondale's losing $40,000 to a friend of his. It seems that he only stole what was owed. When they realize the honor in what Westondale has done, they wish the "man on the trail" good luck and a safe journey.

London writes of the camaraderie and the code of the wild that has become the touchstone of much of his fiction, both short stories and novels. That Westondale has done nothing more than even the score with his friend who had stolen from him is part of the zero-sum game that is a way of life in London's Alaskan frontier. As in Stephen Crane's fiction, the immutable landscape lurks in the background to either hide men like Westondale or to lead them to their deaths.

Lopez y Fuentes, Gregorio. "A Letter to God" (1940). From *Great Short Stories of the World* (Sel. by the Editors of *Reader's Digest*, 1972). FAMILY; FRIENDSHIP; GIFTS/GENEROSITY; HUMOR/SATIRE/IRONY; POVERTY; RELIGION/SPIRITUALITY; SOCIETY.

Lencho is a farmer who works hard to keep his family healthy with the crops that he is able to grow. He knows the importance of this year's crop; in previous years, he has suffered some misfortune. With rain on its way, Lencho knows that the crops will be well nurtured. He can hardly foresee, though, that the rain and hail that falls in torrents for hours will ruin his crops. When he realizes that his family will starve without some help, Lencho writes a letter to God. He asks for one hundred pesos, which would be enough money to get them through the year and start a new crop for the following year.

The letter is simply addressed to God, so when it reaches the post office, the workers are confused as to what to do. Out of generosity—and believing that his faith deserves a reward—the people decide to raise as much money as possible to help Lencho and his family. When he receives his reply from God and the letter contains only seventy-five pesos, Lencho is furious. He writes back to God and tells him that he needs the hundred pesos, and not to send any more money through the mail, because the postal workers are thieves.

Lopez y Fuentes's ironic tale illustrates the misunderstandings that can arise even in the most heartfelt circumstances. Perhaps not fully comprehending the misfortune of Lencho, the workers do what they can to help him. Without the knowledge of their generosity, however, Lencho casts himself as an ungrateful man who little trusts the very people who would save him and his family.

Lovecraft, H.P. "Beyond the Wall of Sleep" (1919). From *Beyond the Wall of Sleep* (Coll. August Derleth and Donal Wandrei, 1943). CRIME/LAW; DEATH; DREAMS (SLEEPING); FANTASY/ IMAGINATION/SCIENCE FICTION; INTERIOR LIVES; SUPERNATURAL/HORROR.

The narrator works in a state psychopathic institution, where much of his research deals with sleep and dreams, and he has discovered that the "less material life is our truer life, and that our vain presence on the terraqueous globe is itself the secondary or merely virtual phenomenon." A new patient, Joe Slater, is arrested when, awaking, he runs from his cabin and begins flinging his arms and leaping into the air. Though two men attempt to restrain the man in his agitated state, he flees into the woods and is found unconscious. He tells the police that he had been drinking and awoke next to the bloody corpse of a neighbor. While in jail, he has several other attacks during sleep, in which he babbles senselessly and strikes out violently. He is tried for murder and acquitted on grounds of insanity, and he is committed to the institution.

The narrator recalls an instrument he had invented during his college days that allows people to communicate mentally. The voice that he hears tells him that Slater is dead, that he was "unfit to bear the active intellect of cosmic entity" and that "*Algol, the Demon-Star* was his nemesis." The narrator's superior insists that the man take a long vacation, though we learn that "a marvelous new star was discovered not very far from Algol. No star had been visible before, but within twenty-four hours, it had become so bright."

Lovecraft is adept at exploring the human psyche through supernatural occurrences. Even though readers will not mistake the narrator's communication as fact, some basic truths about the nature of reality—observed through both our waking and sleeping states—are to be found in this and other of the author's stories.

Lovecraft, H.P. "The Dunwich Horror" (1928). From *The Dunwich Horror and Other Stories: The Best Supernatural Stories of H.P. Lovecraft* (Sel. and Intro. August Derleth, 1963). ALLEGORY/LEGEND/FABLE; ANIMALS and HUMANS; DEATH; FANTASY/IMAGINA-

TION/SCIENCE FICTION; GOOD/EVIL; MAGIC/OCCULT; SUPERNATURAL/HORROR.

Outsiders rarely venture into Dunwich, a largely uninhabited town surrounded by farmland in north central Massachusetts. Most are scared away by the Dunwich Horror, which occurred in 1928, but which had its genesis with the birth of Wilbur Whateley on February 2, 1913. Whateley, whose father was unknown, was born to an albino woman named Lavinia. The woman lived with her insane father, Old Whateley, who had a reputation as a warlock. From the time of his birth, Lavinia's child was different. Dogs barked and hideous screams echoed in the hills the night the goatish-looking infant was born. He aged quickly, and by the time he was ten, his body and mind gave the appearance of one much older.

Before the boy's grandfather died, the old man taught him some of his black magic and told him about Yog-Sothoth, the Great One. From that time, the boy's mission was to read Necronomicon, a tome that predicts the triumph of evil, so he could rule the earth. When the boy dies attempting to break into a university library, three professors discover that he is not completely human. Shortly after Whateley's death, the Dunwich Horror begins. The townspeople are terrorized by noises, a horrible stench in the air, and other events. The three professors who have discovered the truth about Whateley finally go to Sentinel Hill, where they destroy an invisible evil that happens to be Whateley's twin brother.

Like many of Lovecraft's tales, this story draws on mythology, legend, and folklore for its origins. Though the story is, on one level, significant for its entertainment value, the author saw the horror genre as an archetype through which he could explore the darkest workings of the human mind.

Lu Xun. "Diary of a Madman" (1918). *The Story and Its Writer*, 5th ed. (Ed. Ann Charters, 1999). FAMILY; INDIVIDUAL; INSANITY; INTERIOR LIVES; MORALITY (MORAL DILEMMA); POLITICS; SELF-DESTRUCTION; SIBLINGS; SOCIETY.

The preface to the story details the descent of the narrator, a humble villager "unknown to the world at large," into madness. Though the narrator implies that he has good reason to be afraid at the beginning of the narrative, he spirals into a delusional state that has him believing that even the people he trusts, including his own brother, are cannibals. While he thinks at first that they will not kill him outright—that would only bring bad luck down upon them—he supposes that they want him to kill himself. In that way, they could accomplish their goals without the guilt of his blood on their hands. Contrary to what the narrator sees in his brother's actions, the brother is incensed when the people of the village drop by only to get a glimpse of the madman. The madman simply sees this as another of their tricks; he urges the people to change their ways, and finally, in the story's shortest diary entry, is compelled to "save the children" who have yet to taste human flesh.

The story, told in thirteen short sections that denote the diary entries of the narrator, depicts the increasing insanity of a man who is bound by the society in which he lives. The cannibalism that he imagines in the present of the story (and which has its origin in historical precedent) is symbolic of both the hideous thoughts that erode the narrator's psyche and the myriad ways that society figuratively picks away at the flesh of its inhabitants until they utterly lose their identity as individuals. By withholding the names of the characters involved, the author gives the story a universal quality suggesting that the narrator's dilemma is not an isolated case. The story echoes Nikolai Gogol's narrative of the same name written more than eighty years before.

Lynch, Chris. "The Hobbyist" (1995). From *Ultimate Sports* (Ed. Donald R. Gallo, 1995). COMING-OF-AGE; DISABILITY/PHYSICAL APPEARANCE; IDENTITY; ILLUSION v. REALITY; MEN and WOMEN; SPORTS.

The narrator is a hobbyist, a tall, gangly young man who has been blessed with no special athletic ability, though he loves to collect sports memorabilia. He knows the value of anything with an athlete's photo or autograph on it, and the satisfaction he gets in showing off his collection is the same, he imagines, as blocking a shot in the big game.

In order to satisfy his passion, he works in a sports collectibles store. The owner's only requirement of the young man is that he " 'look big, look kinda like an athlete, 'cause my customers like that, they like to feel like they're dealing with a honest-to-God washed-up old pro.' " When a tall, beautiful young woman walks into the store, the smitten collector pursues a relationship with her. During their first time alone, he watches her dribble the basketball and shoot, the picture of grace. To him, she looks one moment like the Statue of Liberty and the next like Gregory Hines, dancing effortlessly across the court. The two play a game of one-on-one in which the woman embarrasses her six-foot-six suitor.

Although his inability to play the game seems to matter little to her, the young man tries to impress her in the only way he knows, by showing her the collection he has amassed over the years. When she begins to point out trophies that he has collected, none of which have his name on them, she wonders who he really is. Still, he insists that they all *belong* to him. The narrator watches as the girl moves toward the door with a pitying look and leaves him alone with his collection. His mother can only cradle his head in her arms to console him for his loss.

The story details the awkwardness of first relationships and the confusion of identity that so often accompanies them. The narrator's coming-of-age is a difficult one, and the identity that he has created for himself, through the lives of others, costs him his relationship with the girl of his dreams. Though he has the physical attributes to be considered an athlete, he is unable to differentiate the illusion of his "hobby" from the reality of his situation.

Lyon, Dana. "The Bitter Years" (1971). From *Alfred Hitchcock Presents: Stories to Be Read with the Lights On* (New York: Random House, 1973). CRIME/LAW; DREAMS (of the FUTURE); GREED; IN-SANITY; INTERIOR LIVES; LABOR/JOB.
Stella Nordway, as she is known in her new life, works around her house and thinks to herself what an idyllic existence she has created from the ashes of her bitter previous life, as a bookkeeper for a hardware wholesaler. When she is visited by an insurance investigator who knows her as Norma Kendrick, the woman who is wanted for having embezzled a large sum from her employer, her dream life begins to unravel. Instead of taking an around-the-world cruise that she has planned, she knows that she will lose her freedom.

Even when the insurance man assures Stella/Norma that she can keep her freedom if she gives him the money so that he can support his own family, she balks at the notion. Instead, she kills the man and buries him in her backyard. The murder backfires, however, when in the spring, the grass over the man's body sprouts in a cross shape that Stella/Norma feels compelled to mow constantly so as not to draw attention to her crime. She becomes a prisoner in her own home. Much to her dismay, though she has retained her freedom, her dreams have still come to naught.

The symbolism of Lyon's story is clear: when the woman kills the insurance man to assure her own freedom, she is haunted by the symbol of the cross in the backyard. By having to bury the man with his arms outspread, she has unwittingly set in motion the imprisonment that she was sure she could avoid. Despite her belief that she has escaped the banality of her past life, the "bitter years" will never be behind her as long as her sin is buried behind her house.

M

Madden, David. "No Trace" (1970). From *Studies in the Short Story* (Ed. Virgil Scott and David Madden, 1976). DEATH; FATHERS and CHILDREN; FRIENDSHIP; IDENTITY; INTERIOR LIVES; LOVE; SELF-DESTRUCTION/SUICIDE; SOCIETY; WAR.

Ernest searches through his son Gordon's dorm room—the same one that he had occupied twenty years before—after the boy pulls the pin on a grenade and blows himself to pieces during his valedictory speech to his Harvard graduating class. Ernest is in the room to salvage his son's reputation before the police arrive. He is also worried about his ill wife, Lydia, finding out about the day's events; as he examines the room's contents, he realizes that he is unsure who his son is, though he realizes that "not only was he going to destroy evidence to protect Gordon's memory as much as possible and shield Lydia, he was now deliberately searching for fragments of a new Gordon, hoping to know and understand him."

Ernest had insisted that Gordon live there, even though his son was not friendly with Carter, his roommate. Ironically, Ernest thinks that Carter is the one to blame for the change in his son. As the father digs for evidence of the tragedy, he begins to realize how Gordon has come to this act of violence. Carter and Gordon fed off each other's ideas, and Gordon's own death comes a short time after he finds out that Carter is missing in action in Vietnam.

On one level, Madden's story captures the political and personal upheaval of the time; on another, the story details a father's love and a newfound understanding of his relationship with his son, whom the father will defend even in death. The most poignant aspect of this relationship is the father's realization that once his son went to college, he established an identity of his own. The new context in which he views Gordon's life leaves Ernest confused and alienated from his son, though the break does little to mitigate his love for the boy who is, perhaps, as much a victim of the war as Carter.

Mahfouz, Naghib. "Half a Day" (1989). From *The Story and Its Writer*, 4th ed. (Ed. Ann Charters, 1995). AGING; CHILDHOOD; FATHERS and CHILDREN; FRIENDSHIP; INTERIOR LIVES.

The narrator is a young boy in Cairo being escorted to his first day of school by his father. He meets the challenge with trepidation, though he realizes that when he accepted his fate, "this submission brought a sort of contentment. Living beings were drawn to other living beings." In this way, he makes friends with the boys and falls in love with the girls. The school that the boy attends is much like any other: some students thrive in the environment, and others are left behind.

When the bell rings announcing the end of the school day, the narrator walks into the street and is struck by the change that has occurred in what seems to him to have been half a day. His father has not met him as promised, and the sights and sounds of the street are unfamiliar to him. He wonders, "How could all this have happened in half a day?" He soon realizes, of course, that many years have passed, and the home that he knew no longer exists. As he waits to cross the road heavy with streaking cars, a young boy takes him by the arm and offers to help "Grandpa" navigate the traffic.

Mahfouz's brief story manages to encompass the years that make up a life. One paragraph, in which the narrator moves from discussing the relationships of youth to the more pressing duties of adulthood, is the only indication that such a change has occurred. As if it had happened yesterday, the narrator recalls those first days of school with the impressionable mind of the boy, before he is brought back to reality. The reminiscence is both whimsical and poignant and describes the Cairo that Mahfouz, a Nobel Prize-winning author, had known for all of his nearly eighty years before he wrote the narrative, as the author himself says, "straight from the heart."

Malamud, Bernard. "The Jewbird" (1963). From *The Norton Anthology of Short Fiction* (Ed. R.V. Cassill, 1978). ALLEGORY/LEGEND/FABLE; DEATH; FAMILY; FRIENDSHIP; GIFTS/GENEROSITY; OPPRESSION; RELIGION/SPIRITUALITY.

A bird hops through the open window in Harry Cohen's top-floor apartment in New York City. To the family's astonishment, it can talk. The bird—a Jewish bird named Schwartz—claims to be running from "Anti-Semeets." Cohen is amused by the jewbird's words, and he agrees to feed the bird, but only on the balcony. At the insistence of his son, Maurie, he allows the bird to spend the night. When Cohen brings home a bird feeder full of corn for his guest, the bird declines, saying that it gives him cramps. Though Cohen is incensed at Schwartz's lack of gratitude, the bird manages to stay in the good graces of the family long enough to become a friend to Maurie. The jewbird continues to press his luck with the family, though, stinking like the fish that he eats incessantly and suggesting to Cohen that his son is not very bright

When Cohen demands that the bird leave, citing research that he has done on migratory birds, Schwartz refuses. Cohen harasses the bird in an attempt to drive him away, but the plan fails. After a particularly bad day, Cohen attacks Schwartz and drives him away, but not before the bird bloodies Cohen's nose with his beak. Schwartz does not return, and Maurie finds him dead in the street after the winter thaw. Maurie's mother tells him that it was "Anti-Semeets" who killed the bird.

The story is an astute examination of the Jewish experience in America. The bird's death is neither an indictment of Cohen nor the bird for what has happened. Rather, Malamud suggests the contradictions inherent in what it means to be Jewish and the connotation of that word to society in general.

Malamud, Bernard. "The Magic Barrel" (1958). From *Short Fiction: Classic and Contemporary*, 4th ed. (Ed. Charles H. Bohner and Dean Dougherty, 1999). IDENTITY; ILLUSION v. REALITY; MARRIAGE; MEN and WOMEN; RELIGION/SPIRITUALITY; SOCIETY.

Leo Finkle, a twenty-seven-year-old rabbi, is looking for a wife. He realizes that he has missed out on meeting women during his studies; to help him in his search, he enlists the aid of a matchmaker named Salzman, an odd man who smells of fish. Salzman shows Finkle files on several women, though the rabbi finds fault with each one of his suggestions. Finkle begins to sense that he was wrong in hiring Salzman in the first place, though he recalls that a matchmaker brought his own parents together.

After a disappointing date arranged by Salzman, Finkle realizes that the matchmaker has given the girl, Lily Hirschorn, the wrong impression. She has the idea that Finkle is a very holy man with a passion for God. Finkle sets her straight and then ends the date. He is determined to rid himself of the matchmaker's services. Salzman leaves behind a folder of pictures, though, and Finkle's interest gets the best of him. The last photo, one of a haunting, troubled-looking girl, intrigues him. She turns out to be Salzman's daughter, and the picture was placed in the folder by mistake. Despite her reputation, Finkle wants to meet her.

Malamud's ironic story is a classic case of mistaken identity. Finkle is not pious, as others think him to be (in fact, it was his lack of love for God that made the role of rabbi seem interesting), and he is more inclined toward Stella, Salzman's "bad" daughter, than any of the other more "proper" women he meets.

Mann, Thomas. "Disorder and Early Sorrow" (1929). From *The Norton Anthology of Short Fiction* (Ed. R.V. Cassill, 1978). CHILDHOOD; FAMILY; FATHERS and CHILDREN; HISTORY; SOCIETY; WAR.

Dr. Cornelius, a middle-aged history professor, is reminded by his older children, Ingrid and Bert, that there will be a party that evening at the family's home. The professor, who clearly comprehends the gap that exists between him and his children, acquiesces, though he separates himself from the preparation in his study. At the party, he meets Max Hergesell, a friend of the older children. Cornelius's younger children—Ellie, who is five, and

Snapper, who is four—also join the party. As the professor leaves for his evening walk, he sees that Ellie is infatuated with Max, who is dancing.

After the party, Cornelius finds that Ellie is distraught, and he understands in a way that his daughter does not know the reason behind her emotion; when Max says goodnight to the young girl, she is happy. The professor is ambivalent about what has happened that night. He knows that times have been tough, and he looks forward to being with his children, especially the younger ones, who undoubtedly will suffer much in the coming years. He only hopes that Ellie will forget the evening's events.

Mann's story is not a cheerful one, though Cornelius is cast as a man who, apart from the veneer of the independent and aloof academic, wants his children to have the best lives possible. The backdrop of the story—Germany in the years after World War I—exacerbates the "disorder" of the children's lives; Ellie's reaction to Max is also an indication of the "early sorrow" (and, the author implies, perhaps the continued sorrow) of a generation born (ironically, given the professor's vocation) at the wrong time in history.

Mann, Thomas. "The Infant Prodigy" (1936). From *Worlds of Fiction* (Ed. Roberta Rubenstein and Charles R. Larson, 1993). ART and the ARTIST; CHILDHOOD; ILLUSION v. REALITY; MUSIC; SOCIETY.

Bibi Saccellaphylaccas is a piano-playing prodigy. Though he plays well and the audience is enthralled with his performance, the show is successful as much for its gimmickry as for Bibi's ability. The young boy (he is eight, but the audience thinks he is seven) treats the crowd with scorn, since he assumes that they care little for true artistry. Each of the audience members—an old man who sees the child's talent as a gift from God, the businessman who imagines the profit that the boy will make from the show, a critic who sees too clearly that art is lost on the philistines in the crowded hall—observe the performance for different reasons. When an aging princess meets Bibi and asks him about his craft, he answers her, but secretly disdains the insipidity of her question. The crowd disperses into the night.

Though Bibi is sincere in his love for performing, everything about the performance is designed to elicit a calculated response from the audience. Mann suggests that the gap between true art and the event that has just taken place cannot be bridged. Like the critic himself, the author turns a cynical eye toward the notion of the "infant prodigy." The title disregards the young boy's artistic ability, instead focusing on the age (he is not even old enough, it seems, to be a "child prodigy") and society's reception of the performer. The art is irreducible from itself, and any attempt at individualizing such an elemental form of expression is bound to fail.

Mansfield, Katherine. "The Garden-Party" (1922). From *The Norton Anthology of Short Fiction* **(Ed. R.V. Cassill, 1978). CLASS CONFLICTS; COMING-OF-AGE; DEATH; DREAMS (of the FUTURE); GRIEF; ILLUSION v. REALITY; MEN and WOMEN; POVERTY.**

Laura has come into full bloom, and her mother insists that she and her sisters organize the family's society gathering. Laura, who meets the workmen putting the final touches on the lavish display, has never understood the class structure that allows such delightful people as these to be looked down upon. Still, she busies herself with the details of the very exclusive garden party.

When one of the common men of the village is killed in a fall, Laura suggests, to the dismay of her sisters and her mother, that the party be canceled. Instead, the party goes on, and Laura forgets for a time the morning's tragedy; she is more popular than she could have imagined. In the party's afterglow, her mother suggests that she take the leftover food to the grieving family. Laura is drawn into the family's humble home and sees firsthand their sorrow and the dead man's body. He is beautiful in his repose, peaceful in the midst of such squalor. The satisfaction of the day's events at the garden party leaves Laura, and when she meets her brother, Laurie, she is unable to describe the change that has occurred in her.

This story, like much of Mansfield's fiction, explores class distinctions through the words and actions of the characters and carefully drawn descriptions of the sensual aspects of the privileged life. The life that Laura leads is contrasted to the very different—though perhaps no less fulfilling— lives of those who will never experience the pleasures of the garden party or the satisfaction of being accepted into society's inner circles.

Mansfield, Katherine. "Marriage a la Mode" (1922). From *Modern American and British Short Stories* **(Ed. Leonard Brown, 1929). BETRAYAL; COMMUNICATION/LANGUAGE; INTERIOR LIVES; MARRIAGE; MEN and WOMEN; SOCIETY; WOMEN'S ISSUES.**

William and Isabel have reached a point in their relationship where William is quite comfortable; on the other hand, Isabel needs to see the world that she has missed in marrying young and raising a family. "The new Isabel," as William thinks of her, shuns her motherly duty and cavorts with other lay-abouts. William's feelings for his wife have, if anything, grown stronger since their marriage; she conjures in him feelings of almost overwhelming nostalgia. William, though, has become a nuisance and an impediment to Isabel's desire to explore her freedom.

After a day out with his wife and her friends, William writes her a love letter. With unexpected derision, Isabel reads the letter aloud to her new friends, who mock William along with her. In a pang of conscience, Isabel retreats to her room, where she decides that she will write back to William. The impulse is short-lived, however, as her friends convince her to go swimming with them, and she tells herself that she will write to William some other time.

Mansfield's strength is the story of manners, and "Marriage a la Mode" contains explorations of women's issues and relational dynamics that belie the story's age. By using the love letter of William as a symbol both of his feelings toward Isabel and the object of scorn by its recipient, the author draws a viable relationship between the woman, who needs to experience a world that has been closed to her, and the man, who ostensibly has been privy to many of the experiences to which women are denied. Isabel's response to William's gesture is, on one level, shocking; still, the author's tone remains ambivalent, forcing the reader to further contemplate the significance of Isabel's actions.

Mansfield, Katherine. "Miss Brill" (1922). From *The Harper Anthology of Fiction* (Ed. Sylvan Barnet, 1991). AGING; BETRAYAL; CLASS CONFLICTS; COMMUNICATION/LANGUAGE; EPIPHANY; INTERIOR LIVES; SOCIETY.

Miss Brill is delighted to be part of the Season in the Jardins Publique, especially on Sundays. For the occasion, a chilly day, she has taken her fur from its box, brushed it off, and walked purposefully toward the band playing in the park. Everywhere around her she sees life, and it pleases her to think that she is part of all that takes place, part of a living organism that manifests itself every Sunday to see and be seen. In a moment of epiphany, she knows that she and everyone else in the park are actors, playing out their roles, and she is sure that her absence would be noticed if she were to miss the gathering one weekend.

When she has insinuated herself in the ongoing production by minutely observing and cataloging all around her, she catches snippets of a conversation in which a young girl makes fun of her fur and wonders why the old woman (Miss Brill is, in fact, "old" only to the young people) does not stay at home. Instead of stopping on her way home at the baker's, as is her Sunday custom, she goes directly to her apartment and places the fur back in its box, wondering if she can hear it weeping at the girl's unnecessary insult.

Mansfield's story is similar in tone and content to the expatriate stories of Henry James. Both construct their milieu through intricate descriptions of place and people—much, perhaps, as we would expect in one of Monet's Giverny paintings—and both convey a strong sense of society's hierarchy. Miss Brill's final action symbolizes her place in that society; implicit in the girl's comment to her beau is the fleeting nature of youth and the vast distance that separates Miss Brill from those whom she supposes are fellow actors in life's play.

Marquez, Gabriel Garcia. "The Handsomest Drowned Man in the World" (1971). From *The Norton Anthology of Short Fiction,* **6th ed. (Ed. R.V. Cassill and Richard Bausch, 2000). DEATH; DISABILITY/ PHYSICAL APPEARANCE; FANTASY/IMAGINATION/SCI- ENCE FICTION; SOCIETY; SUPERSTITION.**

The children of the village find a drowned man wrapped in seaweed, jellyfish tentacles, and the ocean's detritus. The villagers want to find out who the man is and give him a proper burial, but no one knows his story. As they prepare the body, the women of the village, especially, realize what a wonder the young man is: he is preternaturally beautiful, serene, large; in short, everything that their men are not. They imagine that in life, the man had the power simply to summon fish from the sea. They name him Esteban, since, the villagers think, he could have no other name. They give him a burial unlike any other and are elated to find that no one from neighboring villages has lost a man. He is theirs. From then on, nothing in the village would be the same.

Marquez uses his capacious imagination and the "magical realism" for which he is known to document a village's reaction to an unexpected event. The subtitle of the story, "A Tale for Children," implies both an audience and the villagers' ingenuous, childlike reaction to the discovery of the man's body. The villagers are in awe of the young drowned man and celebrate his life. Death for them—and, the author suggests, for all of us—is an abstraction that has little meaning. We are all children in the face of death, and the living are irretrievably changed by its possibilities.

Marquez, Gabriel Garcia. "A Very Old Man with Enormous Wings" (1955). From *The Heath Introduction to Fiction,* **4th ed. (Ed. John J. Clayton, 1992). ALIENATION/ISOLATION; EXILE/EXPATRIA- TION; HEALTH (SICKNESS/MEDICINE); IDENTITY; ILLU- SION v. REALITY; RELIGION/SPIRITUALITY; SOCIETY; SUPERNATURAL/HORROR.**

In his yard, Pelayo discovers an old man lying face down in the mud, unable to stand because of the weight of his enormous wings. The man is balding, poorly clothed, dirty, and his wings are mangy. A neighbor woman identifies him as an angel who must have been coming, she surmises, to claim the spirit of Pelayo's ill son. Despite the wishes of the woman, the townsfolk do not have the heart to club him to death.

Pelayo confines the angel in the chicken coop behind his house. When Father Gonzaga, the parish priest, arrives to observe the angel, he is suspi- cious of the old man's purpose, as the angel does not know Latin, the language of God, nor how properly to greet the priest, an emissary of God. Still, Pelayo and his wife find themselves in an enviable position: pilgrims line up outside the coop to see the angel, who seems only barely alive, ignoring the spectators and the spectacle of his own life. Above all, he is patient. The situation becomes tense, though, when a woman who was changed into a spider for disobeying her parents comes to town and draws attention away from the old man. She is more popular than the angel, as the only thing he has to offer the people is the gruesome sight of a deteriorating old man with enormous wings and a few dubious miracles that "showed a certain mental disorder." Somehow, the angel survives the winter and, with the first sunny days, regains his tenuous health. The wings that once were bare are now strong enough to support the frail old man. Pelayo's wife watches as the angel flies out of sight and becomes a memory.

Marquez's "magical realism," the ability to transform the ordinary through imagination into something extraordinary, is apparent in this story. Through the arrival of the old man in the midst of a village of people who are unready (or, perhaps, unwilling) to accept the banality of the angel's appearance—after all, he is much too human to be anything else—the author explores human nature and the determined frailty of life. The narrative style that is closely associated with Marquez has influenced many writers since, among them fellow Nobel Prize-winning author Toni Morrison.

Marston, Elsa. "Anubis" (1992). From *Short Circuits: Thirteen Shocking Stories by Outstanding Writers for Young Adults* (Ed. Donald R. Gallo, 1992). CULTURE CONFLICTS; DEATH; FRIENDSHIP; REVENGE; SUPERNATURAL/HORROR.

Nick Tempe lives a life that many high school students would envy: His father has arranged for the family to spend time on the *Isis*, a boat docked in the Nile River at Cairo. When he is left alone—except for the company of Zamaan, an inscrutable local—for a period of several weeks, Nick's attitude toward the boat changes. He hears strange voices, and the boat shakes as if it has a life of its own. Nick and his friend, Amani, discover that the boat was once a British steamer named the *Anubis*, which was cursed a century before when it scuttled an Egyptian sailboat with forty peasants on board. As the anniversary of the tragedy nears, the *Anubis* becomes more haunted. In a final battle in which two spirits (Zamaan being one) fight for control of the boat, Nick and Amani narrowly escape disaster. The *Anubis*, as the curse has prophesied, is sent to the bottom of the Nile to join the bodies of the unfortunate peasants.

On the surface, "Anubis" is a typical ghost story. The revenge that Zamaan exacts upon those who senselessly murdered nearly forty people a century before, though, is a study in the clash of cultures—here the British and their "colonies"—that still exists today. Nick, who researches the ship's history as part of a history project with Amani, is instead given the opportunity to live within history. Marston, who writes from her own experiences in the exotic locales that she describes, details the consequences of cultures in conflict.

Mason, Bobbie Ann. "Shiloh" (1982). From *Rites of Passage: A Thematic Reader* (Ed. Judie Rae and Catherine Fraga, 2001). DREAMS (of the FUTURE); IDENTITY; INTERIOR LIVES; MARRIAGE; MEN and WOMEN; WAR; WOMEN'S ISSUES.

Leroy Moffitt is back home after an accident leaves him unable to continue driving his over-the-road route. He realizes when he slows down that he has lived a largely unexamined life, racing by the scenery and never taking time to really *see* things. Now that he's home in Kentucky, he wants to build a log cabin and get reacquainted with his wife, Norma Jean. Their marriage has not been an easy one, with Leroy's job and the death of their four-month-old son, Randy, when the couple was just eighteen. He thinks that perhaps things can change.

Norma Jean, on the other hand, can't think of anything less appealing than living in a cabin with Leroy. She spends her time exercising and taking college courses, and when Leroy is able to spend all his time with her, their relationship quickly begins to dissolve. Norma Jean's mother, Mabel, suggests that the two go to Shiloh, the Civil War battlefield in Tennessee where she and her husband went on their honeymoon many years before. On the way to Shiloh, Leroy has the profound desire to tell Norma Jean all about himself; they have known each other so long, he thinks, that they don't know anything about each other anymore. When they get to the battlefield, Norma Jean tells Leroy that she wants to leave him. When his wife turns to face him at the river bluff, Leroy thinks she is calling to him. He realizes, though, that she is working on her pectoral muscles, and her life has little to do with him anymore.

Mason's story of a dead-end marriage is both humorous and poignant (the setting for the final showdown between the two, for instance, is a Civil War battlefield, and the two come to a reckoning of their relationship). Although neither Leroy nor Norma Jean expresses overt animosity toward the other, it is apparent that the marriage cannot work. The contradiction that their situation implies—that absence does, perhaps, make the heart grow fonder—is the base upon which the author builds her story.

Maugham, W.S. "The Official Position" (1937). From *Complete Short Stories* (Maugham, 1951). CRIME/LAW; DEATH; JUSTICE; MEN and WOMEN; PLACE; REVENGE; SOCIETY.

Louis Remire, who has been sentenced to twelve years in a penal colony in French Guiana for killing his wife, has led a life of relative ease as the colony's executioner. Though the convicts hate him for his position, he handles the task with efficiency (showing the heads of his victims to the onlookers and claiming that justice has been done), even building a savings that will support him nicely when he is released back into the world. With several executions set for the following morning, Remire, a former policeman, takes some time to relax and catch fish for his dinner. He recalls the circumstances surrounding his wife's murder, in which she had accused him (not wrongly) of spending money on other women and had punched him in the face. He shot her and immediately turned himself in. When he returns home that evening to prepare himself for the executions, he discovers that the dogs that protect him from the other prisoners have been poisoned. He is surrounded and murdered, and his killers mock him with the phrase that he has used so often to rationalize his own position: "Justice has been done."

Maugham paints a portrait of an eminently unlikable man who finds himself, through his own guile and ambition, in a position of power even in prison. The author suggests, however, that such "an official position" is fleeting. The words that are used to announce Remire's death are an ironic invocation of the "justice" that the character serves as he continues to kill—violating the very same law that he broke in killing his wife—with impunity and with the blessing of the state.

Maugham, W.S. "The Outstation" (1924). From *Short Fiction: Classic and Contemporary*, 4th ed. (Ed. Charles H. Bohner and Dean Dougherty, 1999). CRIME/LAW; CULTURE CONFLICTS; DEATH; MINORITY EXPERIENCE; POLITICS; RACE RELATIONS; REVENGE; SOCIETY.

Mr. Warburton, the Resident, meets his new assistant, Cooper. Immediately, the two realize that they have little in common. Cooper is informal and sloppy, a fact which bothers the staid Englishman to no end. Warburton has a reputation as a snob, and he has spent the last twenty years at the outstation in remote Borneo after an unfortunate fall from British society. Still, Warburton continues to keep up with that society by reading the *Times*. When Cooper, who is charged with keeping the Resident's house in his absence, leaves the place in a shambles, Warburton is incensed.

Cooper also runs into trouble with his own servants, and Warburton knows that the man's life is in danger because of the disrespect with which he treats the Malays who work for the British. When he warns Cooper of his suspicion, the man ignores him. Finally, Cooper is murdered by a servant whom he has refused to pay. The boy is arrested, though Warburton plans to use him as his own servant when he is released from prison. He goes back to reading the *Times*, which keeps him up-to-date on his beloved British society.

Maugham places into conflict two characters who are convinced that their particular attitudes toward life—Warburton the organized and staid gentleman and Cooper the aloof apprentice—are the single route to success in a world that only Warburton truly understands. Beneath his "snobbishness," Warburton carries with him a survival instinct that Cooper arrogantly assumes is only window dressing. On the contrary, just as there is more to

Warburton than meets the eye, there is only enough of Cooper to alienate him from the people who will ultimately cause his death.

Mazer, Harry. "Falling Off the Empire State Building" (1995). From *Ultimate Sports* **(Ed. Donald R. Gallo, 1995). COMING-OF-AGE; FATHERS and CHILDREN; FRIENDSHIP; NATIONALISM/AMERICAN DREAM; SPORTS; VIOLENCE.**

Lenny's friend, Vicik, is like no one else he knows: strong, athletic, courageous, reckless, indestructible. Even though Lenny can never seem to make his father proud of what he does, Vicik is always there, smiling even when Lenny strikes out in stickball. Lenny's father is from the Old World—everyone either works or gets an education—and he can't see why the boys want to waste their time playing in the street. When Lenny tries to teach his father to play ball, it comes to naught. The boy feels sorry for his father because he was not born an American. He could never be like Lenny, who plans to leave his father behind one day when he starts living the American Dream. The only things his father can teach him are how to shave and wear a tie.

One night when the boys are out late playing Johnny on the Horse, a form of leapfrog, Vicik tells a joke about a man who jumps off the Empire State Building. When someone asks the man mid-jump how things are going, he replies, "So far, so good." Neither boy can appreciate the irony of the punch line. Later that evening, Lenny sees Vicik's father beating him and realizes that the boy whom he idolizes is powerless to strike back. Lenny considers making an excuse to his own father to avoid a similar punishment, but instead he tells him the truth; his father reacts only with disdain, wondering how such things could happen in America. Lenny goes to bed as he is told.

In the characters of Lenny and Vicik, the story details the conflict between the Old World and the New and the ways in which a world that presents such great promise can be both limitless and frightening. The title of the story (and the building itself, a symbol of America), rendered as the punch line of a joke that Vicik tells, characterizes Vicik's life and the irony of his own position. Through Vicik's experiences, Lenny begins to understand what the American Dream truly means.

Mazer, Norma Fox. "Going Fishing" (1998). From *Stay True: Short Stories for Strong Girls* **(Ed. Marilyn Singer, 1998). DISABILITY/PHYSICAL APPEARANCE; DREAMS (of the FUTURE); DREAMS (SLEEPING); IDENTITY; INTERIOR LIVES; MEN and WOMEN; NATURE/WILDERNESS.**

Grace rolls out of bed at four o'clock in the morning and looks forward to going fishing. Although she cringes at the face that looks back at her in the mirror—she is a big girl in a family of normal-sized people—she relishes the beauty of the outside world, "of casting out her line and watching it break through the glassy sheen of the reservoir, and her heart actually beats harder." On this particular morning, she recalls having dreamed of Mr. Vronsky, the history teacher whom she despises. Many of her dreams are similar: instead of conjuring A. B., her ideal man, she often imagines herself in situations with men whose personalities remind her of her own physical appearance. All she knows is that she longs for a day when a man will "look back at her and see her the way she wants to be seen."

Even though she is adamant that she will not look in the mirror when she gets out of bed, she cannot help herself, and "In a flash, she sees the massive body, sees how she defies and distorts and disturbs the image of a 'normal' girl, of what a girl is 'supposed' to be." She recalls a previous infatuation with the character Stuart Little and how she would stand by the tabloid racks in the checkout line and read about babies switched at birth. Even her mother treats Grace with a certain amount of patronizing care, as if she already foresees the long, hard life her daughter is bound to endure. Still, perhaps because of her relationship with nature, Grace sees the possibility of one day breaking away, of creating an identity that is hers alone.

Like Chris Crutcher's protagonist Angus Bethune, Grace must reconcile herself to the reality of her situation and come to terms with her own physical appearance. Her dreams are indicative of that struggle. Although she finds many of the men in her dreams unattractive in real life, she is simply transferring her own feelings of inadequacy onto those characters. By coming to an understanding of her dreams—and, by extension, her own identity—Grace is finally able to imagine "a place in the world where she can be as big and strong and loud—as Grace—as she was born, as she naturally is." She knows that such a day is in the future. The transformation is subtle and poignant.

McCullers, Carson. "Ballad of the Sad Café" (1943). From *Collected Stories* (McCullers, 1998). ALIENATION/ISOLATION; CONTESTS; DISABILITY/PHYSICAL APPEARANCE; FRIENDSHIP; LOSS; LOVE; MEN and WOMEN; REGIONALISM (LOCAL COLOR).

In a small town in Georgia, a dilapidated café awaits its reawakening. The owner, Amelia, who was bequeathed the building upon her father's death, cares little for restoring the place to its original glory; instead, she makes moonshine and remains aloof from the townspeople. They respect her, though she is an enigma, mannish and shrewd. When Lymon, a hunchback, arrives in town and claims to be Amelia's cousin, the two form an unlikely friendship that develops into genuine love. Lymon suggests to Amelia that they make the café the town's central point. Amelia agrees, and she becomes much more involved in the town's activities.

When Marvin Macy, who was married to Amelia briefly several years before, returns to the town, Lymon takes an immediate liking to the man, despite the fact that Amelia had dismissed him, unwilling to consummate the marriage. Lymon invites Macy to live with Amelia and him. Amelia takes up boxing and challenges Macy to a match. When Amelia overwhelms Macy with her brute power, Lymon, still infatuated with Macy, jumps into the ring and chokes her. Macy and Lymon rob the café and leave town. Amelia once again becomes taciturn with the townspeople, and the café reverts to its former state. The town once again becomes a desolate, cheerless place.

McCullers presents characters that are freakish in this Southern Gothic tale to illustrate the various kinds of love—and the subsequent isolation—that exists in such places. Seemingly, though, none of those love relationships are requited. Much as Amelia scorns the smitten Macy in their marriage, Macy mistreats the hunchback. However, through the use of vivid descriptions and by understating the deformities of her characters, the author makes an improbable scenario come to life.

McCullers, Carson. "A Tree, a Rock, a Cloud" (1951). From *Studies in the Short Story* (Ed. Virgil Scott et al., 1976). COMING-OF-AGE; COMMUNICATION/LANGUAGE; INTERIOR LIVES; LOVE; MARRIAGE; MEN and WOMEN.

A twelve-year-old boy nearly finished with his newspaper route stops at a streetcar café for a cup of coffee. While there, he is approached by an older man who puts his hands on the boy's shoulders and tells him that he loves him. At first, the boy is taken aback by the man's behavior; the other men at the counter laugh at the exchange, which makes the boy feel even more uncomfortable. Still, he listens as the man shows him a photograph of a woman in a bathing suit and describes how he married the woman, who was twenty years his junior, after three days of courting. Less than two years later, though, she ran off with another man. The rest of the story is devoted to how the man has since dealt with the loss. He talks about the science of love, the inopportune times that he thinks about the woman, and how people have relationships all wrong. The old man claims that love need begin with nothing more than "A tree. A rock. A cloud." As he readies himself to leave, he tells the boy one more time that he loves him. When the boy asks Leo, the counterman, whether the old man was crazy, Leo is without an answer.

In this story McCullers, who is justly famous for the eccentric characters she creates, explores notions of love and its destructive power. The old man, who has had much time to consider love and its consequences, advocates beginning with the most elemental of observations—trees, rocks, clouds—instead of the climax (both in the literal and figurative senses) of the traditional relationship. Even though the old man has been without his beloved wife for more than ten years, he seems to be no closer to reconciling himself with her absence—or the prospect of loving again—than he was when she left him for another man.

McCullers, Carson. "Wunderkind" (1936). From *Telling Stories: An Anthology for Writers* **(Ed. Joyce Carol Oates, 1998). AGING; COMING-OF-AGE; ESCAPE; FRIENDSHIP; ILLUSION v. REALITY; MUSIC; SOCIETY.**

Frances is a fifteen-year-old young woman who is known to her instructors as a *Wunderkind*, a child prodigy on the piano. As she waits one day to begin her lesson, she sees a picture of Heime, a friend of hers who played violin; he has moved on to bigger and better things, while Frances's teacher, Mr. Bilderbach, asks her to play pieces that do not challenge her or prepare her to become more technically accomplished; nor, more importantly, will she ever have the passion that it takes to be a great musician. Though she does have an extraordinary talent, she is not the prodigy that others have told her she is. Frances reaches the breaking point during her lesson and runs out of the room and into the street.

The label that has been put on Frances—perhaps unfairly, since it is apparent from the attitudes of her teacher and her own nagging doubts that she is not what others perceive her to be—is, contrary to what it suggests about her ability, a hindrance to a young, impressionable woman who compares herself too harshly to others. In reality, Mr. Bilderbach is not qualified to train a prodigy. Frances's escape into the confusion of the street signals a return to the normalcy of girlhood for the *Wunderkind* and her realization that her life is, perhaps—especially as she lives it through the lives of others—not as it seems.

McPherson, James A. "Gold Coast" (1968). From *Studies in the Short Story* **(Ed. Virgil Scott and David Madden, 1976). ART and the ARTIST; CLASS CONFLICTS; DREAMS (of the FUTURE); IDENTITY; LABOR/JOB; MEN and WOMEN; RACE RELATIONS; SOCIETY.**

Robert, an aspiring writer, is a janitor in Cambridge, Massachusetts. His friend and supervisor is James Sullivan, an old Irishman who lives in the building, the Gold Coast, with his wife and their dog. Robert does not mind janitorial work because he is confident that he will one day be a successful writer; after all, the job gives him material for his writing. Robert, who is black, meets a white girl, Jean, who admires him for his ambition. She does not agree with his relationship with Sullivan, however. When his affair with Jean ends, Robert finds that the job has become just that. He loses interest in writing for a time. Though he makes one last ill-fated attempt to connect with the life he had in the Gold Coast, he decides to move out. He sees Sullivan in Harvard Square, but decides against speaking to him.

The setting of the story is important to the subsequent action. The Gold Coast had once been the home of writer Conrad Aiken; by the time Robert works there, however, much of the gild has worn off. The people he meets do not live up to his expectations, and by leaving this part of his life behind, he is able, McPherson implies, to learn from the experience and to become the writer he has always wanted to be. While themes of race relations and class conflicts are apparent, the individual struggle for identity and purpose is at the heart of the story.

Melville, Herman. "Bartleby the Scrivener" (1853). From *The Story and Its Writer*, 5th ed. (Ed. Ann Charters, 1999). ALIENATION/ISOLATION; COMMUNICATION/LANGUAGE; LABOR/JOB; SOCIETY.

The narrator, a lawyer who believes that the simpler a life is lived the better, hires an inscrutable scrivener by the name of Bartleby to copy law documents for him. Although the man works hard—never uttering a word to his companions, Turkey, Nipper, and Ginger-Nut—when he is asked to verify the accuracy of the documents, he replies that he would rather not. Understanding that there is no animosity in the man's reply, the lawyer, who is nonplused at the response, keeps him on.

However, the lawyer reaches his wit's end when Bartleby refuses to do any copy work at all and remains ensconced in the office, staring out at the brick wall that faces his window. Despite the lawyer's repeated attempts to rid his office of the scrivener, Bartleby will not leave. Instead, the lawyer himself moves into new offices. When the new tenants of the narrator's former office complain that Bartleby will neither perform his duties nor leave—always replying to any query that he "would rather not"—he is taken to the Tombs, the local prison, where he dies with his face pressed against the wall. Months after the scrivener's death, the lawyer discovers that the man was once a clerk in the Dead Letter Office in Washington, and that it was his job to destroy misrouted letters, gifts, and money—in short, to kill the living thoughts and deeds that would have enriched their recipients' lives. The lawyer's response, one of the most famous in short fiction, is simply "Ah, Bartleby! Ah, humanity!"

Melville's story is an intense psychological examination of despair. By placing Bartleby as the enigmatic central figure, the author explores the profound cause of Bartleby's own melancholy and the effects of his death on the living. The catalyst for Bartleby's alienation, his work in the Dead Letter Office, suggests that the lawyer, who defends Bartleby out of both compassion and curiosity, is representative of society as a whole, which very often observes and unthinkingly accepts such despair without comment.

Melville, Herman. "Billy Budd, Sailor" (1924). From *An Anthology of Famous American Stories* (Ed. Angus Burrell and Bennett Cerf, 1963). BETRAYAL; DEATH; DUTY; JUSTICE; LOVE; MORALITY (MORAL DILEMMA); TRUTH v. LYING; VIOLENCE.

Billy Budd, a handsome young sailor, serves aboard the merchant ship *Rights-of-Man* until he is enlisted to work aboard the British warship HMS *Bellipotent* to fight the French. Though he is a conscientious worker and well liked by his mates, the master-at-arms, Claggart, despises Billy for reasons that are left largely unexplored in the narrative. Claggart, in fact, seems to be obsessed with catching Budd in a trap that would court-martial him. When Billy will not be tricked into joining an ostensible mutiny, Claggart himself goes to the ship's captain, Vere, and levels the accusation at Budd. When Budd is brought to the captain's quarters to answer the charges, he is afflicted by the stuttering that has plagued him in similar stressful situations in the past, and he strikes Claggart to the ground, killing him. Vere is left no choice but to have Budd hanged for his action. Budd's last words as he stands before the captain and his crew are "Gold Bless Captain Vere."

Melville's novella is an allegory, in one sense, though it transcends the rather limited notions of the form. Budd—whose name suggests one coming into the full flower of his adulthood—loses his position on the *Rights-of-Man* and stands in the face of Vere (literally, "truth") to confront Claggart, the man whose cacophonic name fits him well. The story also explores the deep relationship between justice and duty. Vere, understanding the essential goodness in Budd (who is called "The Peacemaker" in the story), utters the boy's name on his deathbed, so profound was Budd's influence and his courageous acceptance of his fate.

Melville, Herman. "The Lightning-Rod Man" (1854). From *Fiction 100: An Anthology of Short Stories*, 9th ed. (Ed. James H. Pickering, 2000). COMMUNICATION/LANGUAGE; DECEPTION; FATE; NATURE/WILDERNESS; RELIGION/SPIRITUALITY; SOCIETY; VIOLENCE.

On a stormy night, the equal of which the first-person narrator has never before seen, a man appears on his doorstep and warns the narrator of the dangers of lightning. The man stands in the middle of the room—according to him the safest place in such an event—and implores the narrator to purchase a lightning rod from him for twenty dollars. The narrator, wary of the "lightning-rod man's" intentions, confronts him about the realities of lightning. With each successive bolt, the salesman becomes more frantic, until the narrator stands his ground and tells the man that "In thunder as in sunshine, I stand at ease in the hands of my God. False negotiator, away! See, the scroll of the storm is rolled back; the house is unharmed; and in the blue heavens I read in the rainbow, that the Deity will not, of purpose, make war on man's earth." When the salesman persists, becoming enraged at the implication of the narrator's monologue and attacking him, the narrator bodily forces the man out of his home. The man, however, "still dwells in the land; still travels in storm time, and drives a brave trade with the fears of man."

Underlying the simplicity of the story—the little action of the story takes place in dialogue between the two men—is Melville's own notions of mortality and man's tenuous grasp on life. The narrator's resolve to drive the man away suggests his own faith in a higher power and his willingness to accept the life that he has been given; that the "lightning-rod man" continues to ply his trade further suggests that not everyone is as strong-willed and prudent as the narrator.

Melville, Herman. "The Piazza" (1870). From _Great Short Stories from the World's Literature_ (Ed. Charles Neider, 1950). DREAMS (SLEEPING); FANTASY/IMAGINATION/SCIENCE FICTION; ILLUSION v. REALITY; INTERIOR LIVES; PLACE.

The narrator buys an old farmhouse that has no piazza, and he is determined to build one in order to enjoy the glorious view of the hills that his location offers. The narrator is, above all, concerned with beauty which "is like piety—you cannot run and read it; tranquility and constancy, with, now-a-days, an easy chair, are needed." The man builds his piazza and, after much enjoying what he has done, begins to see at certain times of the day and in a certain light a glimmering from far across the hills. He imagines that fairies live there; not satisfied with that explanation, though, he sets out to find the spot. What he discovers is a quaint cottage in which "the fairy queen," Marianna, sits at her window. When he enters into conversation with the young woman, she asks him who lives in the palace that she can see from her own window. That palace is, of course, the narrator's home, and the woman assumes that only good things happen there. She longs to visit the place.

Melville's story is a detour for the man who usually eschews such fanciful notions as fairies and mystical places in the hills, instead writing complex explorations of the human psyche. Still, the last two paragraphs bring the narrator back to reality, implying that he has been dreaming the whole "fairy queen" scene. Whether the tale is fanciful or not is of no concern to the narrator, who knows that "when the curtain falls, truth comes in with darkness. No light shows from the mountain. To and fro I walk the piazza deck, haunted by Marianna's face, and many as real a story." The tale is a convincing argument for the power of place in both our realities and in our imaginations.

Merimee, Prosper. "The Taking of the Redoubt" (1829). From _Great Stories of All Nations_ (Ed. Maxim Lieber and Blanche Colton Williams, 1945). COURAGE; DEATH; FRIENDSHIP; WAR.

In his first military action, a young soldier finds himself presented with the grimmest of tasks—to capture a redoubt (a fort) that is occupied by the Russians. After heavy casualties and the appearance of a large, red moon, the men are not encouraged by their chances for success. Still, they fight on, and the soldier finds himself imagining retelling his heroic tale in the salons of Paris. The grim reality of his situation hits home when he is surrounded by his dead and wounded comrades and only seven of his original company are left to make one last charge on the redoubt with their spent allies. In a flurry of action, of which the soldier remembers little, the men take the redoubt, even as his colonel dies, secure in the knowledge that their mission is complete.

Merimee's tale of gallantry is simply told in the first person through an outside narrator who introduces the story briefly at the outset. The effect of the bloody battle is enhanced by its brevity, the immensity of the task at hand related through the understatement of a soldier relieved to have lived to tell the story that his friend so readily retells in his absence. The author balances sharp dialogue and description to achieve the desired result.

Miklowitz, Gloria D. "The Fuller Brush Man" (1987). From *Visions* (Ed. Donald R. Gallo, 1987). DEATH; FAMILY; HEALTH (SICKNESS/MEDICINE); LABOR/JOB; MOTHERS and CHILDREN.

Donald's mother is terminally ill, and he cannot bring himself to face the fact that she is dying. In order to earn money for college, the young man sells Fuller products, a decision with which his mother disagreed when he first suggested it. Since her first trip to the hospital, though, he has not heard any more about it. Donald's relationship to his job mirrors his inability to reconcile himself to his mother's imminent death: "He still withdrew when people turned him away, although he wouldn't show it now, keeping his voice pleasant and a smile on his face." When Shannon, a friend of Donald's, asks him to reconsider spending time with his mother, Donald agrees, charging home, knocking on his mother's bedroom door, and introducing himself with a smile as the "Fuller Brush man."

Miklowitz's story is a poignant exploration of a young man's denial and anger over his mother's illness. His job as a door-to-door salesman and the rejection that he has grown accustomed to is not unlike his own rejection of his mother since her illness was diagnosed. By accepting the reality of her situation, he has undergone a coming-of-age that even a job as difficult as his did not fully prepare him for.

Millhauser, Steven. "The Knife Thrower" (1998). From *The Knife Thrower and Other Stories* (Millhauser, 1998). ART and the ARTIST; DEATH; ILLUSION v. REALITY; MAGIC/OCCULT.

When the narrator hears that Hensch the Knife Thrower will be in town, his reaction is one of curiosity and foreboding. Though Hensch is entertaining, rumors about his reputation have preceded him. The narrator attends the show and is not disappointed by what he sees. Hensch is in command of his world on the stage, throwing his knives with such precision as to elicit gasps from the delighted crowd. As Hensch comes closer and closer to physically harming his assistants, however, the audience becomes uneasy: "The knife struck beside her neck. He had missed—had he missed?—and we felt a sharp tug of disappointment, which changed at once to shame, deep shame, for we had not come out for blood, only for—well, something else." For his last trick, Hensch brings a young woman to the stage for "the ultimate sacrifice," in which the volunteer is apparently killed. Hensch takes his bow, and the narrator remarks, "we had agreed that it had been a skillful performance, though we couldn't help feeling that the knife thrower had gone too far."

Millhauser uses illusion and fantasy to examine the contradictory impulses of fear and desire. Though the audience members admonish themselves for their reaction to the show, they admire the ways in which the artist manipulates them. That theme—the role of the artist and his own desire to take that art to a new level—is persistent in Millhauser's short fiction.

Minot, Susan. "Lust" (1984). From *The Gates of Paradise: The Anthology of Erotic Short Fiction* (Ed. Roberto Manguel, 1993). COMMUNICATION/LANGUAGE; LOVE; MEN and WOMEN; SEXUALITY; SOCIETY; WOMEN'S ISSUES.

The narrator's story begins as a lengthy remembrance of all the men who have been part of her life. She recalls Leo, her first lover; Roger and his fast cars; Bruce; Tim; Willie; Philip; and the others. While the tone of the recollections is at first nostalgic, the narrator comes around to the point that is the crux of her story: "It was different for a girl." In her own unabashed way, she describes why she did what she did, the influence of society and the expectations that were placed on young women, the pressures that were not part of the experience of growing up male: "The more girls a boy has, the better. He has a bright look, having reaped fruits, blooming. He stalks around, sure-shouldered, and you have the feeling he's got more in him, a fatter heart, more stories to tell. For a girl, with each boy it's like a petal gets plucked each time."

By the end of her story, the narrator describes the sickening feeling that comes with being used, the sadness, the worry, and "everything filling up finally and absolutely with death." Even though she does everything that the men want, they are different when the lovemaking is over. The woman is gone, or at least the lovers seem to look at her as if she has disappeared.

Minot's story presents the double standard that has permeated society's attitudes toward sexuality. While the narrator's escapades would not be uncommon for a man, the laundry list of lovers that she gives presents her as someone who is susceptible to "lust," a "loose woman." The story's title is ironic: What the narrator describes at the end of the story is not lust for men, but rather a lust for life that is drained from her with each successive lover she takes.

Mishima, Yukio. "Martyrdom" (1960). From *The New Mystery* (Ed. Jerome Charyn, 1993). ALIENATION/ISOLATION; COMING-OF-

AGE/INITIATION; CRIME/LAW; DEATH; HOMOSEXUALITY; JEALOUSY; TRADITION/CONVENTION.

In a boarding school for the children of Japan's well-to-do, the students are trained above all, it seems, in the art of tormenting their teachers and one another. The ruler of the band of boys, the "Demon King," owns a copy of *Plutarch's Lives*, which he allows the boys to read in small passages for its prurient content. When the book turns up missing, he correctly assumes that an outcast named Watari has stolen it. The Demon King breaks into Watari's room to confront him about the theft; the two fight, and as Watari lies on the floor wounded, the Demon King "pressed his whole face against Watari's lips and the soft down around them."

The relationship cannot go unnoticed; even as Watari becomes a favorite of the Demon King, the other boys sense that something has changed. When they ask the Demon King to name someone who needs to be punished, the leader of the boys names Watari. The boys take Watari to Chiarai Pond and, in a frenzy that grows beyond their control, they hang him in a tree. When they return fearfully to see what they have done, they find that Watari's body is no longer dangling from the branch.

The ambiguous ending of Mishima's story is typical of his short fiction (see also "Swaddling Clothes"). In this case, the question of Watari's death or his possible escape from his captors is not resolved. More important to the story than the ostensible (or, at least, the figurative) death of Watari, the author implies, is the action that the boys take against him, as they view him as an outcast. The title fits the role that Watari plays: by becoming a favorite of the leader, he is the logical choice for the boys when they decide who needs to be punished. Through little fault of his own, he has become an unwitting martyr.

Mishima, Yukio. "Swaddling Clothes" (1966). From *The Story and Its Writer*, 5th ed. (Ed. Ann Charters, 1999). ALIENATION/ISOLATION; CLASS CONFLICTS; GUILT; MARRIAGE; MEN and WOMEN; MORALITY; PRIDE.

Toshiko has married a handsome young actor who spends many of his nights away from home. Though she lives a life that most would envy, the woman is disgusted by a story that her husband feels compelled to tell in public about the birth of a baby in their house to the nurse who was sent to care for their own child. Out of spite for the conditions under which the child was born, the doctor who arrives after the birth wraps the child in newspapers instead of the traditional swaddling clothes. Toshiko, the only one who notices the disgrace and understands the implications of the shameful act, cannot help but think that the child will be scarred for life by his ill treatment at birth; the newspapers are a lasting symbol of his low place in society.

On a whim, Toshiko walks through a park late at night, admiring the blossoming cherry trees. When she comes upon a pale image that could be a pile of blossoms, she discovers that the form is instead a young homeless man wrapped in newspaper. She approaches the man, who awakes and grabs her by the wrist. She makes no effort to free herself from his grasp.

The ending of the story is, in the author's typical style, both ambiguous and symbolic. The woman gives herself over to the homeless man and wonders how twenty years have passed so quickly; her willingness to atone for the sins of the people who treated the child so poorly at his birth is both admirable and pathetic. Mishima presents a scathing commentary on class politics and identity that gains strength through its understatement.

Moore, Lorrie. "How to Become a Writer" (1985). From *The Story and Its Writer*, 5th ed. (Ed. Ann Charters, 1999). ART and the ARTIST; HUMOR/SATIRE/IRONY; IDENTITY; LITERACY/WRITING; METAFICTION.

Moore's story is hardly a story at all in the traditional sense. Using the title as the theme for her story, the author begins *in medias res*, explaining—sometimes in a traditional essay form and sometimes in passages that read more like diary entries than a structured story—how one might, in fact, become a writer. The list of possible ways to become a writer is seemingly a random hodgepodge of life's events and a parody on the constraints of workshop prose, including questions on why anyone should care about the characters that she has created. The writing process, the author suggests, is fraught with the banalities that everyone else imposes upon her work. In the last paragraphs of the story, Moore details the experience of the aspiring writer, having to justify her passion to one more blind date "with a face blank as a sheet of paper."

Moore's vignette has overtones of Grace Paley's "A Conversation with My Father." Both stories explore the writing process, using the self-awareness, the independence, and the passion of the writer as the underpinning for the story itself. Moore uses a similar strategy to great effect in much of her fiction. The genesis of the written word—a topic also explored in the fiction of John Barth, Jorge Luis Borges, and others—is an activity in which the writing itself is irreducible from the process.

Moravia, Alberto. "Double Game" (1963). From *Great Short Stories of the World* (Sel. by the Editors of *Reader's Digest*, 1972). CONTESTS; FRIENDSHIP; JEALOUSY; LOVE; MEN and WOMEN; PRIDE.

Umberto and Peppe have grown up together since they were in bibs and highchairs. Peppe's mother has always made the boy feel inferior to his friend, who was at the top of his class, brings money home to his family, and is saving money to buy a car. Even in love, Umberto has the upper hand; Peppe and Umberto are both infatuated with Clara, who lives in their building and who is dating both young men. She tells Peppe that Umberto is unattractive and boring; Peppe, encouraged by her words and actions, asks the girl's mother if they can be married. Clara's mother, a fortune-teller, tells Peppe that the girl is already engaged to Umberto. Peppe feels foolish for having felt sorry for his friend. When he sees Umberto and Clara together, he pretends to be interested in another girl. He leaves with the girl, whom he met at the fortune-teller's place.

Here, Moravia explores the power of jealousy. Though Peppe attempts to salvage his pride through his relationship with Angela, a substitute for his true love, the boy realizes that his pity was misplaced when he thought that he had won over Clara and that Umberto, for once, would finish second to him. Self-respect and identity, too, are part of the maturation process that the author describes.

Mukherjee, Bharati. "The Management of Grief" (1988). From *The Norton Anthology of Short Fiction*, 6th ed. (Ed. R.V. Cassill and Richard Bausch, 2000). CULTURE CONFLICTS; DEATH; ENTROPY/ CHAOS; FAMILY; GRIEF; LOSS; MEN and WOMEN; MOTHERS and CHILDREN; SOCIETY; TRADITION/CONVENTION.

Mrs. Bhave's husband, Vikram, and her two sons have been killed in an airplane crash, the result of a terrorist bomb. As she listens with little interest to the chaos around her in her own home, she is not concerned with the cause for the crash, but rather recalls small details that remind her of her loss. She knows many other families whose loved ones have also died, though she reacts in a way that draws the attention of Judith Templeton, whose job it is to counsel the surviving family members in managing their grief.

Mrs. Bhave travels with the other survivors to identify the bodies, though she can never be sure that her husband and children were killed along with the others. Clinging to this faint and highly improbable hope, she sees a vision of her husband, who urges her to return to her normal life. Templeton visits Mrs. Bhave again and asks her for guidance in helping a Sikh couple to cope with the loss. They cannot relinquish the foolish notion that their sons may still be alive. Mrs. Bhave, who understands that such hopefulness is a cultural necessity and that Templeton will never be able to see past her textbooks that measure the grieving process empirically, wants nothing to do with the woman. When Mrs. Bhave receives another message from her dead husband, she is ready to move on with her life.

Mukherjee's story, which is based on her own experience of a terrorist bombing in 1986, explores the depths of suffering and posits two entirely different reactions: the wholly "rational" response of the counselor, who sees the grieving process as nothing more than a series of steps to be taken on the road to recovery; and the much more personal response that takes into account deeply held cultural beliefs. The author's choice is clear. The title's double meaning suggests the initial inability of anyone to "manage" grief and the importance of time and reconciliation as the only salve to heal such profound psychic wounds.

Mukherjee, Bharati. "A Wife's Story" (1988). From *The Oxford Book of American Short Stories* (Ed. Joyce Carol Oates, 1992). ASSIMILATION; CULTURE CONFLICTS; IDENTITY; INTERIOR LIVES; MARRIAGE; MEN and WOMEN.

Panna Bhatt, an Indian woman in the United States to study for a Ph.D. at New York University, is insulted by the portrayal of her culture in David Mamet's play, *Glengarry Glen Ross*. She is in a difficult position, one that requires she straddle two entirely different cultures in an attempt to fulfill her dream. In one sense, she realizes that she is free from the constraints of her own society, especially in her relationship with her husband. On the other hand, she is discouraged and angered by the way Americans perceive her. She is able to commiserate with her male Hungarian friend, Imre, who understands the alienation that Panna feels. Panna's roommate, Charity Chin, has yet another response to the culture. She models her hands for a living, and she is successful in a way that would not be possible in her own culture. When Panna's husband visits New York City from India, he is disappointed with the city (aside from its shopping), because it is not what he thought it would be—his perception does not meet reality. Panna looks at herself in the mirror and realizes that her life has changed. Her attitude toward the change is ambivalent.

Mukherjee often details similar themes of assimilation and alienation in her stories, and Panna's experience is one that places the protagonist squarely in the middle of two cultures that, if not mutually exclusive, do not complement each other well. The title implies that Panna's status—as a wife and as a woman defined on someone else's terms—is primary to her existence, though Mukherjee hints otherwise. Still, the author suggests, there are no easy answers when one attempts to assimilate to a culture with such a profoundly different value system.

Murphy, Barbara Beasley. "Eagle Cloud and Fawn" (1993). From *Join In: Multiethnic Short Stories* (Ed. Donald R. Gallo, 1993). ART and the ARTIST; ASSIMILATION; CULTURE CONFLICTS; DEATH; LOVE; MEN and WOMEN; RELIGION/SPIRITUALITY; TRADITION/CONVENTION.

Stephanie Levine, who always fancied that her screen name would be "Fawn Bliss," meets Eagle Cloud on an art trip to New Mexico. Eagle Cloud is preparing to go to art school on scholarship, and he notices the young woman in a restaurant where he works. On a whim, he quits his job in order to show Fawn around the area. She learns many things in the time that the two spend together, and Eagle Cloud, at first bemused by Fawn's lack of knowledge of his culture, becomes a willing teacher. When Fawn tells him that her grandfather was killed several weeks before in a mugging, he draws her close to him, asking the spirits to protect her. When Eagle Cloud wins first place in a painting competition, Fawn offers to buy the painting from him. Instead, he paints one for her that shows the spirit protecting her. Eagle Cloud realizes that he is falling in love with Stephanie.

The joy of discovery is at the heart of Murphy's story. Eagle Cloud had never had any interest in people like Fawn before, but he sees in her an energy and spirit that he cannot escape. Fawn, on the other hand, comes from New York City and could hardly imagine that she would meet someone like Eagle Cloud as she attempts through her exploration of the unknown to free herself of her grandfather's death and a stifling home life.

Myers, Walter Dean. "Jeremiah's Song" (1987). From _Visions_ (Ed. Donald R. Gallo, 1987). COMMUNICATION/LANGUAGE; DEATH; FAMILY; HEALTH (SICKNESS/MEDICINE); HISTORY; MUSIC.

Grandpa Jeremiah is dying, and his family has two distinctly different ways of dealing with his illness. Ellie, who has been to college and no longer has interest in the stories that Jeremiah tells, thinks that Macon and the narrator, the young men in the story, should leave the old man alone and let him die in peace. The two young men, on the other hand, still enjoy listening to the stories that they have heard time and time again. When Dr. Crawford delivers the news that Jeremiah has little time left, Macon is intent on absorbing all of the stories that he can. In fact, Jeremiah maintains his health while he is telling the stories; when he dies, as he must, Macon plays a song that he has been writing as he listened to the stories.

Told through the eyes of an uneducated first-person narrator, the story is all the more poignant for the ways in which Grandpa Jeremiah's "songs" touch the spirits of those who are willing to listen. Myers explores the conflict between the "rational"—Ellie's insistence that they rely on traditional medicine to heal Jeremiah—and the "spiritual," the storytelling tradition that allows people to recall their history at the same time that it prepares them for the future. The title implies both Jeremiah's own storytelling and the song that Macon writes for him after his death.

N

Nabokov, Vladimir. "Signs and Symbols" (1948). From *The Norton Anthology of Short Fiction*, 6th ed. (Ed. R.V. Cassill and Richard Bausch, 2000). FATHERS and CHILDREN; HEALTH (SICKNESS/MEDICINE); INSANITY; MOTHERS and CHILDREN; SELF-DESTRUCTION/SUICIDE; SOCIETY.

An elderly couple, Russian immigrants who have settled in Boston, are on their way to the sanitarium to visit their son for his birthday. The boy has grown progressively worse since he was diagnosed with a disease that renders him helpless with paranoia. His deranged solipsism has prompted him to attempt suicide several times. When his parents reach the institution after a lengthy and difficult journey, including a torrential downpour, they cannot see him to give him his birthday gift, as the boy has once again attempted suicide.

On their way home, the couple sees a dying bird in a puddle; the husband's hands unwittingly echo the bird's palsied movements. When the boy's mother glances at the family photo album, she recognizes the disintegration of the boy's life into a nightmare of overwhelming sensory experiences. The couple decides that they will attempt to care for the boy at home. When the phone rings at the story's end, though, the implication is that the boy has finally succeeded in his attempt at finding peace.

Nabokov's story details the actions of a family who are slightly out of step with the rest of the world. The couple's difficulty in making a routine journey is exacerbated by the rain, and the image of the bird dying on the side of the street is a symbol for both the aging parents' inability to save the boy and the boy's condition as he awaits an imminent death by his own hand. Perhaps the story's only bright spot is that the boy has finally been given the peace he longed for, though the parents have lost a child, and their remaining time is given up to the vagaries of society's "signs and symbols."

Nakos, Lilika. "Maternity" (1943). From *Great Short Stories of the World* (Sel. by the Editors of *Reader's Digest*, 1972). ALIENATION/ISOLATION; COMING-OF-AGE; EXILE/EMIGRATION; FATHERS and CHILDREN; POVERTY; SOCIETY; WAR.

For more than a month, a camp of refugees has made their homes of sticks and old carpets on the outskirts of the town of Marseille. The poverty-stricken refugees have fled from the Turkish massacres in Asia Minor. Mikali, a young man of fourteen, one of the healthier and stronger refugees, is the father of a malnourished boy whose mother died in labor. Mikali cannot take care of the boy or himself, and the baby cries continuously, which makes the other refugees angry. Mikali travels to another camp of refugees, where he believes there is a nursing mother who can help. When the woman asks to see the baby, she and the other women in the camp are horrified at the infant's sickly appearance, and they ban Mikali from their group. Mikali loses all hope until he meets a Chinese man who tells the young man to go to his home, where his wife will gladly nurse the infant.

Nakos's story is generally a simple tale of poverty and heartache, and the specific example of one "man"—a man only in that he has a family, not in chronological age. The story succeeds because, as with the stories of the Russian realists, the author is able to strike a balance between the horrors of reality and the possibility of hope, no matter how small, for the future.

Namioka, Lensey. "The All-American Slurp" (1987). From *Visions* (Ed. Donald R. Gallo, 1987). ASSIMILATION; CULTURE CONFLICTS; FAMILY; FRIENDSHIP; SOCIETY; TRADITION/CONVENTION.

The narrator's family, the Lins, has immigrated to America. When the Lins are first invited to dinner in their new country, the narrator is embarrassed by the looks they receive when they unexpectedly run into dining etiquette questions, such as how to eat soup or whether or not to pull the strings out of a stalk of raw celery. Despite the confusion, the narrator becomes good friends with Meg Gleason, and she and her family are invited to the Lins's house for dinner. The narrator is amused and shocked when the Gleasons pile their plates high with food, and Mr. Gleason picks up a pea with his hand and eats it. When the narrator and Meg go for milkshakes after dinner (the Lins do not serve dessert during their traditional dinner), Meg finishes her milkshake with a "*shloop*," the all-American slurp.

Issues of assimilation always arise when cultures collide, though Namioka's exploration of food ways and the difficulty of adjusting to a new culture even in the simplest and most common of activities is both humorous and instructive. Rather than further separating the two girls, their differences bring them together.

Namioka, Lensey. "Fox Hunt" (1993). From *Join In: Multiethnic Short Stories* (Ed. Donald R. Gallo, 1993). ALIENATION/ISOLATION; ALLEGORY/LEGEND/FABLE; ASSIMILATION; CULTURE CONFLICTS; FRIENDSHIP; HISTORY; LITERACY/WRITING; MINORITY EXPERIENCE.

As Andy Liang prepares for the upcoming PSAT exam, he knows he will probably be studying alone. Though he gets along with the kids in his school, none of the others invite him to study with them. That alienation does not bother Andy, however, because his family was mandarin in China, a long line of great scholars. They hadn't always been that way, his mother insists, and she tells him a story of how his ancestor, Liang Fujin, was helped by a *huli*, or fox-woman, as he studied for the official examinations.

When Andy meets a girl named Leona Hu, herself a Chinese American, he wants to study with her. During the days leading up to the exam, Andy dreams of being a hunted fox, and another fox is running beside him. Only when he gets to know Leona does he realize that she is the character beside him in his dream. She is the *huli*—her name in the traditional Chinese order would be Hu Lee—who will help him to pass his exam.

Namioka's story blends real coming-of-age and assimilation issues with a Chinese legend in a seamless narrative that recalls the self-fulfilling prophecy of Heywood Broun's "The Fifty-First Dragon." With the help of his own fox spirit, Andy will do well on the exam, satisfying his hard-driving father and getting accepted into a world-class university.

Newman, Leslea. "Supper" (1994). From *Am I Blue? Coming Out from the Silence* (Ed. Marion Dane Bauer, 1994). ASSIMILATION; COMING-OF-AGE; FAMILY; HOMOSEXUALITY; IDENTITY; SEXUALITY.

Meryl, a young Jewish girl, is seated at the dinner table with her family—parents, a brother, and her grandmother—and the talk focuses on the narrator's eating habits. She is a vegetarian, and her grandmother cannot understand why she will not eat meat. After all, her grandmother's own mother would have given anything for such extravagances to offer her own family. When the grandmother suggests that Meryl will never attract the boys with her skinny figure, Meryl doesn't care. When her friend, Mark, kissed her, she thought she was going to be sick. Instead, she enjoys the company of her friend, Patty, who shows Meryl what her own boyfriend does to please her. Meryl comes to the conclusion that "I just don't like boys. But I would never tell Patty that. And I definitely would never tell my grandmother that. She already thinks there's something wrong with me, and maybe there is." As she clears the dinner dishes from the table and scrapes the remains into the garbage, Meryl puts pieces of the meat in her mouth.

The alienation that Meryl feels from her traditional grandmother and even from her friends places her in an awkward position. She can assimilate to the beliefs of those around her—as she seemingly does at the end of the story by tasting the meat—or she can follow her own heart. Newman indicates that much of her writing "explores the conflicts and joys of being a lesbian and a Jew. The two identities have much in common: Being a lesbian and a Jew automatically places one inside two vital, active communities that value the group as much as the individual." Meryl's attempt to find her place within those groups underpins the story.

Nordan, Lewis. "A Hank of Hair, a Piece of Bone" (1989). From *Best of the South* (Ed. Anne Tyler and Shannon Ravenel, 1995). ALIENA-TION/ISOLATION; COMING-OF-AGE/INITIATION; DEATH; FAMILY; FATHERS and CHILDREN; MARRIAGE; MEN and WOMEN; PLACE; SUPERNATURAL/HORROR.

In this quintessential tale of growing up, the protagonist, a ten-year-old boy, is harboring a secret: he has a collapsible military shovel he uses to dig for the bodies of the myriad dead that his father claims are buried in the Delta. The boy also hides in a secret compartment behind the wall in his bedroom, where he claims to have lived for two weeks or more during one summer. He is shying away from his relationship with his father, who drinks too much and who, despite the fact that he has never been abusive, en-courages the boy's mother to argue with him by running glasses of water and then pouring them out.

In order to test his father's morbid hypothesis that the ground is full of death, the boy begins digging holes all over the backyard with his shovel—first as play, and then in earnest. In one particular spot in the basement, he digs until he strikes a glass panel; he forces himself to peek, only for an instant, and catches a glimpse of a red-haired woman who must have been buried there for decades.

Later, he admits that he may or may not have seen a woman. What he does remember is that his parents are in love, though he has never quite understood their relationship (in fact, part of his own alienation from his father comes from that misunderstanding). He watches them dancing one night and realizes that he is becoming old enough to understand. When his mother bakes him a birthday cake in the shape of a rabbit, the innocence of the image and his mother's love for the boy overwhelm him; despite the fact that he is growing up, he is not too old to cry in his mother's arms.

What Nordan poignantly describes is nothing less than the moment when a boy becomes a young man. The awkward relationship that he has with his parents, fueled by his inability to understand their relationship as a married couple who live lives outside those they share with their son, is symbolized by the boy's fascination with death and the landscapes that are, as in so many tales of the South, characters in themselves.

O

Oates, Joyce Carol. "How I Contemplated the World from the Detroit House of Correction and Began My Life Over Again" (1970). From *The Norton Anthology of Contemporary Fiction* (Ed. R.V. Cassill, 1988). ALIENATION/ISOLATION; COMING-OF-AGE; CRIME/LAW; FATHERS and CHILDREN; MOTHERS and CHILDREN; SELF-DESTRUCTION/SUICIDE; SEXUALITY; SOCIETY; WOMEN'S ISSUES.

The narrator, a young girl growing up in Detroit, is detached from her own life. Her father is a successful doctor, her mother is part of the city's social scene, and her brother is enrolled in an elite prep school. Though the girl has the money for anything she could want, she steals—sometimes, even, things she does not want—in order to feel alive. While her father attends a medical convention in Los Angeles, she is arrested for shoplifting in a store that her parents' friends own.

No charges are filed for her offense, but she is sent to a corrections facility. At first, she does not want to leave the place; she thinks the outside world— especially her home—is a terrible place to be. However, when she meets a girl named Princess, who is in the facility for armed robbery, her attitude changes. The girl is bruised and beaten, and something inside the narrator changes when she sees the reality of her friend's situation. She also recalls a rough relationship with Simon, a thirty-five-year-old man who "has a deathly face, only desperate people fall in love with it." After her experience, the narrator wants to be home; in fact, she never wants to leave home again.

Oates explores the psyche of her protagonist through a style that is both clinical (the sections separated into headings such as "Events," "Characters," and "Detroit") and a stream-of-consciousness that exposes the girl's anger and her throbbing hatred for the life that has been dictated by others. The straightforward descriptions of an upper-middle-class existence contrast sharply with the visions that call into question the girl's life outside a family that is at once quite safe and uncaring.

Oates, Joyce Carol. "Where Are You Going, Where Have You Been?" (1966). From *Fiction 100: An Anthology of Short Stories*, 9th ed. (Ed. James H. Pickering, 2000). COMING-OF-AGE; ESCAPE; IDENTITY; INTERIOR LIVES; MEN and WOMEN; SOCIETY; WOMEN'S ISSUES.

Connie, a fifteen-year-old-girl, is infatuated with a world that she has yet to experience, and she suffers many of the agonies that girls her age go through: her mother holds up her much older sister as a paragon of virtue, and her father is conspicuously absent except as a chauffeur. When her parents leave to visit her aunt on a Sunday afternoon, Connie is visited by a boy named Friend, whom she had seen the night before at the drive-in. Though Friend's bad-boy image and the gold car that he drives to her house intrigue her, the meeting quickly becomes a nightmare. Friend, who does not follow Connie into the house, instead forcefully tells her to join him for a ride in his car. When she refuses, Connie becomes frightened and calls for her mother, but the young man persists. The house's screen door is the only thing that separates Connie from the world that she has dreamt about; she seems powerless to stay inside the house, which would shield her from a world about which she knows little.

The culture that Oates describes is a decade removed from the world that John Cheever brings to life in his stories of suburban America in the 1950s, full of romantic images and the materialism that we have come to associate with everyday life. Connie's confrontation with "Friend" is clearly a coming-of-age that shatters her innocence and—whether or not Friend's threats are real—forces her to reconcile her notions of romance with the much seedier realities that she will face in her adult life. The story is underpinned by an implied threat of violence that is more powerful for being unstated at the conclusion.

O'Brien, Tim. "The Things They Carried" (1986). From *The Granta Book of the American Short Story* (Ed. Richard Ford, 1992). COMING-OF-AGE/INITIATION; DEATH; FRIENDSHIP; INTERIOR LIVES; MEN and WOMEN; WAR.

In the jungles of Vietnam, a platoon of men has been charged with exploring the tunnels that intersect the area. The men have in common the "things they carry," objects that might help them to maintain a tenuous connection to their past as they daily risk their lives. Jimmy Cross, a young lieutenant, has his mind on his college sweetheart, Martha. He idealizes their relationship (which, in reality, was nothing as Cross imagines it), and he memorizes her letters to him and cherishes a pebble that she has sent with one of her posts. The tunnel that they are clearing is safe, and the men relax. However, when a sniper kills Ted Lavender, one of the soldiers, their attitude changes. Some of them are able to cope with the sudden death; Cross blames himself and thinks that his preoccupation with Martha has cost one of his men his life. He burns the objects from Martha and is determined to be a better protector for his men.

O'Brien uses Vietnam as the context for understanding the horror of war and as a way of placing the relationships of the men in Vietnam in stark contrast to the reality of their situation. Though they have become adept at rationalizing the risks, even joking about Lavender's death and dividing his "things" among themselves, the possibility of death without warning strips the innocence from even the most idealistic and romantic of the men.

O'Connor, Flannery. "The Artificial Nigger" (1955). From *The World of the Short Story* (Ed. Clifton Fadiman, 1986). ALIENATION/ISOLATION; BETRAYAL; FAMILY; GUILT; MORALITY (MORAL DILEMMA); RACE RELATIONS; SOCIETY.

Mr. Head and his grandson, Nelson, begin their journey to Atlanta. The boy has never been to the city before, except for having been born there, and Mr. Head wants to show him why he should never go back. Nelson puts on a show of braggadocio for his grandfather, claiming to be fearless and experienced when it comes to the "big city." Still, when the two board the train, Nelson sees a black man for the first time.

In the city, Nelson is overcome by fatigue and falls asleep on the pavement. To teach him a lesson, Mr. Head hides from his grandson; when Nelson awakes, he runs away in a panic and knocks an old woman to the ground. Coming upon the scene, Mr. Head denies ever having seen the boy before. Nelson follows his grandfather, who is burning with shame at the same time that the boy seethes with hatred for what his grandfather has done. Despite Mr. Head's efforts, the boy will not come back to him. When both of them see a statue in the yard of a house along the street, an "artificial nigger," the barrier between them is broken down, and they agree to go home. The story ends with Nelson's revelation that "I'm glad I went once but I'll never go back again!"

The themes of race relations and the unforgiving city that are prevalent in much of O'Connor's short fiction are intertwined to explore the relationship of a grandfather and his grandson. Though the two are isolated geographically from the action of the city (a different take on the theme that O'Connor takes up in "Everything That Rises Must Converge"), they have in common the epiphany of the "blood" that binds them. Mr. Head feels fortunate to have been shown mercy for his unthinking actions toward his grandson, though the author implies through the revelation that the two are still benighted in their attitudes toward others.

O'Connor, Flannery. "Everything That Rises Must Converge" (1965). From *The Story and Its Writer*, 5th ed. (Ed. Ann Charters, 1999). AFRICAN-AMERICAN EXPERIENCE; ALIENATION/ISOLATION; ASSIMILATION; GIFTS/GENEROSITY; MOTHERS and CHILDREN; PREJUDICE; PRIDE; RACE RELATIONS; TRADITION/CONVENTION.

Julian has been charged with escorting his mother to her weight-loss meeting at the local YMCA. Her deep-seated bigotry makes her fearful of the people she will meet if she goes alone. Julian, for his part, believes himself to be more enlightened than his mother. He torments her by making a show of befriending the blacks on the bus and gauging her reaction as a black woman enters the bus with a small boy. The child sits next to Julian's mother, though his mother keeps a careful eye on him and seems to be just as leery of Julian's mother as she is of her.

When the bus arrives at their stop, Julian and his mother exit, along with the black woman and her child. In a patronizing gesture that Julian has seen many times before, his mother offers the black boy a shiny penny. The boy's mother, incensed by the gesture's implication, knocks Julian's mother to the ground. Seemingly more shocked by the black mother's reaction than by the force of the blow, she wanders aimlessly up the sidewalk toward home. Julian, realizing the seriousness of the situation, calls for help, "the tide of darkness . . . postponing from moment to moment his entry into the world of guilt and sorrow."

O'Connor's keen understanding of race relations in the South comes to the fore in this story, one that is often cited as the best of its kind. Julian's desire to illustrate his willingness to make friends with people whom his mother simultaneously shuns and patronizes is shattered by the reality of his situation. Finally, he is no closer than his mother to understanding the true nature of race relations.

O'Connor, Flannery. "Good Country People" (1955). From _The Granta Book of the American Short Story_ (Ed. Richard Ford, 1992). CRIME/LAW; DECADENCE/DEGENERATION; DISABILITY/ PHSYCIAL APPEARANCE; HUMOR/SATIRE/IRONY; MORALITY; MOTHERS and CHILDREN; REGIONALISM (LOCAL COLOR); RELIGION/SPIRITUALITY.

Mrs. Hopewell and Mrs. Freeman are "good country people" in every sense of the word. As such, they have a rather high opinion of themselves and their daughters. Mrs. Hopewell, though, is concerned that her thirty-two-year-old daughter, Joy (who changed her name to Hulga when she went away to college), is not fulfilling her potential as a woman; she has no prospects for marriage. Despite the fact that she has a Ph.D. in philosophy, she will always wear a wooden leg, the result of a shooting accident more than twenty years before. When Manly Pointer, a Bible salesman, convinces Hulga to meet with him the following day, Hulga thinks she will enjoy condescending to the simple country boy. Instead, he seduces her and, after a conversation with Hulga in which he gains her trust, steals her wooden leg.

The overtly ironic title of the story—neither Pointer nor the women, O'Connor suggests, are, as they would have others believe, "good country people"—draws attention to the plight of Joy/Hulga at the end of the story. Though the reader may be put off by her arrogance, Pointer's mistreatment of the woman is both unforgivable and, as the women who watch him walk into the distance imply, unthinkable. Ignorant of the crime, the women wonder how anyone could ever be as simple as the Bible salesman. The story is an example of O'Connor's mix of Southern Gothic and a morality that goes much deeper than the plot's superficial action.

O'Connor, Flannery. "A Good Man Is Hard to Find" (1955). From *The Story and Its Writer,* **5th ed. (Ed. Ann Charters, 1999). CRIME/ LAW; DEATH; FAMILY; HUMOR/SATIRE/IRONY; REGIONALISM (LOCAL COLOR); RELIGION/SPIRITUALITY; SOCIETY.**

"The grandmother didn't want to go to Florida," and she takes the opportunity to tell her only son, Bailey, that she has read in the newspaper that an escapee from the federal penitentiary is on his way there in an effort to get him to take her to Tennessee instead. Still, the family heads south. They become lost as they search for a plantation that the grandmother remembers from her childhood, and Bailey wrecks the car when the family's cat jumps onto his shoulder. When a car approaches the stranded family, the grandmother thinks that she has seen one of the men before. It is the Misfit, the escaped prisoner the grandmother had read about.

One of the men takes Bailey and two of the children into the woods, and the grandmother tries to convince the Misfit that he is a good person. A pistol shot rings out from the woods, and the Misfit nonchalantly continues to tell his life story to the grandmother. When she is the only one remaining, she becomes delirious, telling the Misfit that he is one of her own children. He recoils and shoots her three times in the chest, telling one of his accomplices that " 'She would have been a good woman if it had been somebody there to shoot her every minute of her life.' "

Even in its portrayal of the murder of an entire family, O'Connor's darkest story uses irony and a cryptic sense of humor (which is evident in the story's title) to explore her notions of evil and religious issues. The grandmother is clearly off base in her insistence that the Misfit is a good man, and the exaggerated manner in which he compares himself to Jesus in the suffering he has endured sharply contrasts the grandmother's own views.

O'Connor, Frank. "First Confession" (1939). From *Studies in the Short Story,* **4th ed. (Ed. Virgil Scott and David Madden, 1976). CHILDHOOD; FAMILY; GUILT; RELIGION/SPIRITUALITY; SIBLINGS.**

Jackie is preparing for his first confession, a precursor to his first Holy Communion. Like many children of his time, he is terrified of hell, which he is sure will be his final destination. During his first encounter with the priest in confession, which the seven-year-old attends with his sister, Nora, the boy admits to wanting to kill his grandmother, who has come to live with his family. The priest takes the confession for what it is—the fantasy

of a young boy who is alienated by the world that he sees around him—
and he allays the boy's fears of going to hell. Nora, for her part, is distraught
that her brother has received candy from the priest, since she is the one who
attempts to live as she should.

O'Connor presents the theme of religion and the notion of hell (specifically the Catholic notion) at a pivotal moment for the boy. Though he is
only seven, he has already had instilled in him the fears and hypocritical
attitudes of the believers around him. His hatred of his grandmother stems
from his rather childish observation that she drinks strong beer and favors
his sister, Nora, who receives an allowance. In that context, then, Jackie's
story is little different from that of so many boys. Still, O'Connor examines
feelings of guilt and its atonement through confession that are a profound
part of organized religion. Certainly, the author's vision is much different
from that of Tomás Rivera later, who sees religion as an organizing and
oppressive force to be countered with a mature understanding of the human
condition.

**O'Connor, Frank. "Guests of the Nation" (1931). From *Short Fiction:
Classic and Contemporary*, 4th ed. (Ed. Charles H. Bohner and Dean
Dougherty, 1999). BETRAYAL; DEATH; DUTY; ESCAPE;
FRIENDSHIP; NATIONALISM; POLITICS; RELIGION/SPIRI-
TUALITY; VIOLENCE; WAR.**
Belcher and Hawkins are English soldiers being held captive by the Irish
during the 1922 battle for Ireland's independence. The scene is at once
comic and tragic: though the men who guard the two seem to have nothing
in particular against them (they play cards, for instance, and have gotten to
know one another quite well), they still must regard their captives as prisoners of war. The men talk at length about religion and economics, issues
over which they are fighting; still, through their forced interaction with each
other, they become as close as enemies can. When word arrives that the
English are considering executing their Irish prisoners, the men become
morose at the prospect of shooting Belcher and Hawkins. They speak openly
about the possibility of the execution, and they waver between friendship
and duty. Although each believes that he would never execute another man
in cold blood, he knows that to ignore a direct order would mean death for
himself.

Four Irish are executed, one of them sixteen years old. In retaliation,
Hawkins is executed. Even though Belcher knows that his time is coming,
he has nothing bad to say about the men. He, too, is executed, and the
men find the good-bye letters Belcher and Hawkins had written to their
mothers and bury the men in a bog. None of the living are the same after
the incident.

The story, with its ironic title, calls into question notions of duty and the
underlying causes of war. The first-person narrative humanizes the men and

creates a poignant backdrop that provides context for a battle that is still being waged seven decades later.

O'Hara, John. "The Doctor's Son" (1935). From *Collected Stories of John O'Hara* (Sel. and Intro. Frank MacShane, 1984). BETRAYAL; COMING-OF-AGE; FATHERS and CHILDREN; HEALTH (SICK-NESS/MEDICINE); MEN and WOMEN.
Jimmy Malloy, the fifteen-year-old son of Dr. Mike Malloy, is enlisted to drive Dr. Myers, a medical student who is replacing the ill Dr. Malloy, on his rounds during an outbreak of influenza. An affair between Myers and Mrs. Adele Evans, one of the stops on his rounds, is prefigured by their having lunch with the family in the absence of David Evans, Adele's husband. Jimmy's subsequent knowledge of the affair has a profound impact on the way he views the medical profession and his own life.

After Jimmy experiences death firsthand during one of his visits with Myers, he undergoes a coming-of-age that includes his loss of respect for the medical profession (during the time when patients need their doctors most, the doctors very often take advantage of them); the death of David Evans; an estrangement from Evans's daughter, with whom Jimmy was infatuated; and Jimmy's understanding that his life lies outside the closely circumscribed life of his father and those like him.

Jimmy's contentious relationship with his father—after all, the two are mentioned in the title, though Dr. Malloy is hardly the most visible character—is the story's center and acts as a catalyst for his newfound understanding of the life that he will lead. The revelation is both emancipating and unnerving; O'Hara suggests the richness and complexity of life with his vivid depictions of characters and the intricate web of relationships.

Okimoto, Jean Davies. "Moonbeam Dawson and the Killer Bear" (1989). From *Connections: Short Stories by Outstanding Writers for Young Adults* (Ed. Donald R. Gallo, 1989). ANIMALS and HUMANS; COMING-OF-AGE; COURAGE; DECEPTION; MEN and WOMEN.
Whenever Moonbeam Dawson meets someone, he feels compelled to explain his name, which his parents gave him when he was born in a commune on Vancouver Island. Despite having lived in the wilderness for all his life (and because of the influence of his parents), he is a vegetarian who has never handled a gun. When he meets Michelle Lamont, who is on vacation with her father, he is immediately infatuated. When Michelle asks Moonbeam if he will take her bear hunting, though, he has little choice but to act the part.

Moonbeam borrows a gun, which he will keep unloaded, from his friend, Harvey. As Moonbeam and Michelle approach the hunting ground in their boat, a huge black bear ambles toward the shore. When Michelle begs

Moonbeam not to shoot the bear, he breathes a sigh of relief, becoming the hero without letting her know the truth. When they return to shore, she thanks him for letting the bear live. Moonbeam shrugs off the comment and kisses her.

Okimoto's story is effective for its quirky characters and the ironic position in which the protagonist is placed. Though Moonbeam is willing to risk his life for Michelle's adoration, the author gives him a way out of his predicament. This humorous coming-of-age story is a response to other more violent stories that would have the protagonist pursue the bear and prove his manhood only by killing it.

Okimoto, Jean Davies. "Next Month . . . Hollywood!" (1993). From *Join In: Multiethnic Short Stories* **(Ed. Donald R. Gallo, 1993). COMING-OF-AGE; CULTURE CONFLICTS; DREAMS (of the FUTURE); JEALOUSY; MEN and WOMEN; MUSIC.**

Rodney Suyama has great aspirations: He wants to be the country's first Asian-American rap superstar. The problem is, he has never performed before an audience. Rodney's sort-of girlfriend, Ivy Ramos—she has previously gone out with the school's all-time best running back, though she catches him cheating on her—pushes him to make his dream come true, and he is transformed into Ice Happa (*happa* being the popular term for someone who is half Asian). The two practice together for a talent show at the school, and they imagine working their way up from talent shows to Hollywood to conquering the world with their act. As a warm-up to the show, they sign on to perform at a community event for the Northwest Asian American Theater. In the middle of the song that Rodney performs, Ivy, dressed in a pink rabbit costume, trips and falls, bringing Ice Happa down with her. The crowd roars at the mishap, which they suppose was scripted. Rodney and Ivy know that they have a future, even if it is not in rap. Rodney has finally gotten out from under the shadow of the school's greatest football player.

The story portrays the likeable Rodney as a young man whose confidence needs a boost. In his relationship with Ivy, he is at first not too proud to be used to make her former boyfriend jealous. Still, as the relationship— and his music career—grows, Ivy sees Rodney for the passionate, caring young man that he is. Even the debacle in the talent show works out for the two, as they are able to take it in stride. The inspiration for Okimoto's story, as Gallo points out, "was provided by one of her stepsons—who has many Black friends and a strong affinity for African American culture and music—when he performed a rap as part of a college skit."

Olsen, Tillie. "Here I Stand Ironing" (1961). From *America and I: Short Stories by Jewish American Women Writers* **(Ed. Joyce Antler, (1990). ALIENATION and ISOLATION; CHILDHOOD; DUTY; GUILT; HEALTH (SICKNESS/MEDICINE); MOTHERS and CHILDREN.**

At the request of a counselor who attempts to help her troubled daughter, Emily, the mother stands over her ironing board recalling Emily's life over the past nineteen years. She was a beautiful baby who, in retrospect, was not treated as well as she should have been. The mother was herself nineteen when she gave birth to Emily, and she describes the learning process that comes with being a parent for the first time. Emily was never a child to protest the way she was treated, and when she comes down with a fever and is sent away to convalesce, she learns the pain of alienation. When the young girl returns home, her mother is more attentive to her needs, though she shies away from the attention, having become accustomed to neglect in the hospital.

The young girl's animosity manifests itself in her resentment of her sister, Susan, a quick, articulate girl who has all the things that were denied Emily. Still, Emily wins a talent contest at school, and on this particular day, with the mother remembering all the wrong that she has done the girl, Emily returns home from school happy. Even though the mother knows that Emily will never achieve her "full bloom," she believes that the girl will come to enjoy her life.

The poignant story of a young girl's neglect and a mother's guilt is hopeful, despite the mother's shortcomings and the circumstances that drain their very souls. Many of the hardships that the mother has suffered are left unspoken, a strategy that lends a richness to the relationship between mother and daughter that belies the sparseness of the narrative. Olsen writes eloquently through her first-person narrator of the resilience of the human spirit and the possibility for the future.

Otfinoski, Steven. "Salesman, Beware!" (1992). From *Short Circuits: Thirteen Shocking Stories by Outstanding Writers for Young Adults* (Ed. Donald R. Gallo, 1992). HUMOR/SATIRE/IRONY; LABOR/JOB; SUPERNATURAL/HORROR.

Buck Smith is an ambitious young encyclopedia salesman who needs one more sale in order to be awarded the two-seater starmobile that goes to the salesman with the highest monthly totals. He is nonplused by a sign outside one home on the planet Saturn that reads "BEWARE OF THE OOMELECK!" and before he can discover what an oomeleck is, he is invited into the home of Mr. Gordon. Once inside, the sale is disturbingly easy: Gordon fawns over the Venusian lizard-skin covers of the encyclopedia and without hesitation purchases the whole set. Buck, not wanting to endanger his prize, gets Gordon's signature on the contract and readies himself to leave. When the interplanetary telecommunicator beeps in another room, Gordon excuses himself.

Given a moment alone, Buck finally discovers—too late—what an oomeleck is: "A rare creature native to the planet Saturn. Oomelecks are large, voracious animals that will eat almost anything. The most striking characteristic of these highly dangerous beasts is their ability to change their entire molecular structure at will." The animal rushes at Buck and devours him; it especially enjoys the taste of the Venusian lizard-skin covers on the encyclopedia.

Though the story could be read as a cautionary tale—nothing good comes free, and Buck's own hesitance at the ease with which he makes the sale should alert him to the truth—Otfinoski crafts a flight of fancy that is at once humorous (the beast "stuck a purple claw into its gargantuan mouth and deftly removed a piece of grist—the last vestige of interplanetary salesman #19908—from between two large incisors"), ironic, and chilling.

Ovid. "The Story of Pyramus and Thisbe" (1st century A.D.). From *Great Stories of All Nations* (Ed. Maxim Lieber and Blanche Colton Williams, 1945). ALLEGORY/LEGEND/FABLE; COMING-OF-AGE; DEATH; IRONY; LOVE; MEN and WOMEN; SUICIDE.

Pyramus and Thisbe, who live in Babylon, fall in love with each other, though a wall separates the two and their parents are loath to agree to a wedding. When they conspire to elope, Thisbe comes upon a lioness whose jaws are covered in cow's blood. In her haste to avoid being eaten, she drops her veil and hides in a cave. When Pyramus comes upon the scene, he believes that Thisbe has fallen prey to the lioness and kills himself in despair. Thisbe, hurrying to the appointed spot to tell Pyramus about her close call, finds her lover slain and kills herself in order to be with him. She implores the tree under which they lie to show the marks of the lovers' deaths and to bear purple fruit in honor of their spilled blood.

Ovid's retelling of Greek mythology has become an archetype for many of our most famous authors, including Shakespeare, to illustrate the powerful and often cruel bond of love. In this brief and simply-told story, the author explores the nature of love and the ironies that often undermine the best of intentions. Though the tale is tragic, the lovers' union in death and the changing of the mulberry from white to "a dusky red" suggests the immortality of love and the human spirit.

Ozick, Cynthia. "The Shawl" (1980). From *America and I: Short Stories by Jewish American Women Writers* (Ed. Joyce Antler, 1990). COURAGE; DEATH; GRIEF; HOLOCAUST; JEALOUSY; MAGIC/OCCULT; MOTHERS and CHILDREN; OPPRESSION.

The Nazis have captured Rosa, her infant daughter, Magda, and her fourteen-year-old niece, Stella. Death is always a possibility for the three; as they find themselves in a concentration camp, Rosa is amazed that Magda has been able to survive. Because of her weakened condition, Rosa has not been able to give her daughter breast milk. Instead, the baby suckles the shawl that Rosa has brought with them, and her breath smells of cinnamon and almonds.

The magic powers that Rosa attributes to the shawl manifest themselves when Stella, who is jealous of the treatment that Magda has received from Rosa, takes the shawl away from Magda and wraps herself in it. When Rosa discovers that Magda is missing—after all, the shawl was the baby's sole protection—she must decide between saving herself by not admitting to being Magda's mother and watching the baby being electrocuted against the prison's fence. In order to keep from screaming at the horror, Rosa covers her mouth with the shawl.

By interjecting the slightest bit of magic and hope into her story, Ozick prevents the child's death and the treatment of the women in general from becoming overwhelming. Rosa's only recourse when she sees her baby daughter being thrown to her death is to rely on the shawl for comfort. Though the women's lives are saved by the shawl, the author points to the incredible courage in the face of tragedy that characterizes Rosa's life and the lives of so many others in the concentration camps.

P

Paley, Grace. "A Conversation with My Father" (1974). From *The Story and Its Writer*, 4th ed. (Ed. Ann Charters, 1995). ADDICTION; ART and the ARTIST; ESCAPE; FATHERS and CHILDREN; HEALTH; LITERACY/WRITING; MOTHERS and CHILDREN; TRADITION/CONVENTION.

The narrator's father is eighty-six years old and in bed dying with a heart condition. He asks his daughter, a writer, to craft a story—a "regular story"—before he dies. She acquiesces, though from the outset it is apparent that the two have competing ideas about what such a story should entail. The narrator writes about a woman and her son who become junkies. The old man would much prefer something along the lines of Chekhov or de Maupassant.

In order to appease her father with a more "traditional" narrative, the woman continues to write and revise the story, adding bits of humor and realism. Still, the old man can see only the tragedy in the story; he is unable to reconcile himself to the contradictions that make up life, and instead wants a story that moves seamlessly from event to event without any irritable hang-ups Though her father suggests that the woman in the story who has become a junkie cannot change, his daughter vehemently insists that the world itself has changed a great deal since the old man lived in it. Having always gotten the last word, he wonders when his daughter will realize the ugly truth of the world.

The story-within-a-story that Paley offers is both a concession to the dying man and a statement of how different points of view can be, especially between a man and his daughter. While the old man prefers to see the bleakness of society, the narrator is hopeful, revising the traditional "realist" text by implying a future for characters whose problems the old man is little willing to understand. The self-reflexivity of the story places it in the postmodern.

Paley, Grace. "Wants" (1971). From *Short Shorts: An Anthology of the Shortest Stories* (Ed. Irving Howe and Ilana Weiner Howe, 1982). EPIPHANY; IDENTITY; INTERIOR LIVES; MARRIAGE; MEN and WOMEN; SOCIETY; WOMEN'S ISSUES.

A woman and her ex-husband have a conversation after she sees him outside the library, where he has returned books that were eighteen years overdue. She exclaims, "Hello, my life," and the greeting sets off a verbal sparring match between the two that defines their lives together and reminds them why they are no longer a couple. The man is bitter and cold toward the woman, and she is patently disinterested in his comments. He begins by blaming their failed marriage on a number of minor events—for instance, the fact that they never had a certain family over for dinner. She takes the remark in stride and even tells him that he did a good job of supporting his family. The man tells his ex-wife that he has always wanted a sailboat but never got one because she did not want it, and he concludes by telling her that she will "always want nothing." He walks away and leaves her to her thoughts. The man's words are a sudden jolt to the woman, who is reminded of what she wants in life and what she no longer needs.

Paley is adept at exploring the relationships between men and women (as in "A Conversation with My Father"), and the stories very often deal with the weight of memory on the present. Words—much more important in our lives than we realize—are the primary means through which we communicate our desires and disappointments. Those word often take the place of concrete action. The essential misunderstanding between the woman and her ex-husband stems from their inability to articulate their situation. By greeting the man with "Hello, my life," the woman ironically implies the inequality prevalent in relationships and the life that awaits her outside the confines of marriage.

Paretsky, Sara. "Dealer's Choice" (1988). From *The New Mystery* (Ed. Jerome Charyn, 1993). MEN and WOMEN; MYSTERY/ADVENTURE; SOCIETY.

Miss Felstein, an attractive woman in red, arrives in Mr. Marlowe's office to purchase his investigative services. She tells him that her brother has gambled away a ring that he was to inherit upon his ailing mother's death. The bookie, Dominick Bognavich, wants his payment, and the woman's brother has gone into hiding. She wants Marlowe to investigate the situation. When he goes to Bognavich's house, however, Marlowe finds him riddled with bullets.

After a series of close calls as he attempts to solve the case, Marlowe is saved by a woman who visited him earlier, Kathleen Moloney. She tells him that she gambled the deed to her father's property over to Bognavich in order to keep a man named Kurt Boylston from getting it by outing the woman's father as a Japanese spy. Marlowe saves the day by shooting Boylston. Back in his office, he picks up a scrap of black lace left by the woman earlier.

Paretsky's story is a classic in the noir detective genre, with its vivid descriptions and evocation of dark and gloomy places, and her detective is an obvious parallel to Chandler's Marlowe. The twists and turns of the plot overshadow any relationship that Marlowe and Moloney may have; in keeping with the code of the genre, Marlowe waits in his office, with a glass of whiskey as his companion, for his next case.

Parker, Dorothy. "Big Blonde" (1930). From *Fiction 100: An Anthology of Short Stories*, 9th ed. (Ed. James H. Pickering, 2000). ADDICTION; DEPRESSION; DREAMS (of the FUTURE); MEN and WOMEN; SELF-DESTRUCTION/SUICIDE; SOCIETY; VANITY; WOMEN'S ISSUES.

Hazel Morse was the quintessential blonde, the kind who turned heads: large, fair, a former model in a wholesale dress shop. She prided herself on being popular with men and thought that the end always justified the means. In short, she was fun to be with, and that was what mattered. By the time she neared thirty, the years of fast living had started to take their toll on Hazel. Her angles became softer, and she bleached her hair in order to remain the good-time blonde that she had always been. But now she wants to be married, and she meets a man named Herbie. Even though she had laughed the years away earlier in her life, she finds that tears come easily to her now. Herbie will have none of it, and often comes home late and drunk. Her hope is that Herbie will change.

In the meantime, she begins drinking and becomes part of Mrs. Martin's circle of friends, which includes a man named Ed. When Herbie decides to leave Hazel, she becomes Ed's woman, and he takes care of her financially. When Ed leaves, there are always other men to take his place. In a fog of alcohol, Hazel cannot remember exactly how many or who they were; she begins to lose track of dates and the days of the week, and death becomes a constant thought for her. She unsuccessfully attempts suicide and thinks as she takes her first drink upon waking that she only wants to get drunk and stay drunk.

Much of Parker's short fiction is lighthearted; underlying moments of levity in this story, though, is the inexorable decline of the protagonist. The story of Hazel Morse is nothing short of tragic and points up the danger of living a life always in the present and never cultivating a life of one's own or considering the future. She is trapped in a double standard by which the men in her life, who live much the same dissipative lifestyle as Hazel, do so with impunity, the custom of a society that views women like her as expendable.

Parker, Dorothy. "The Standard of Living" (1941). *Clifton Fadiman's Fireside Reader* (Ed. Clifton Fadiman, 1961). AMERICAN DREAM; CLASS CONFLICTS; DREAMS (of the FUTURE); FRIENDSHIP; ILLUSION v. REALITY; LABOR/JOB; SOCIETY.

Midge and her friend, Annabel, stenographers who have become inseparable, play an age-old game: What if we had a million dollars? The two walk the city streets with confidence and class. They date many men, but the men are interchangeable, simply bit actors in the fantasy lives that the women have created for themselves as they work and live at home with their families.

As the game takes on new dimensions—for instance, closely defining the process through which the fortune is gained or insisting that all the money be spent on oneself—it also acquires a dimension that belies the humor in Parker's story. When Midge and Annabel dare each other to price a string of pearls they see in a store window, they find out that the jewelry costs $250,000. Undaunted, the women decide to imagine that they have inherited ten million dollars instead of the original paltry sum.

The story exhibits Parker's typically sly humor and her keen eye for the details of a middle-class that increasingly aspires to high society, which will always be out of reach for people like Midge and Annabel. Though the women easily change the rules of their game, Parker suggests—through both their experience in the jewelry store and the title of the piece—that maintaining a "standard of living" in reality and in fantasy are two entirely different notions, depending on whether one views the story cynically or with a certain nostalgia for post-depression America.

Parker, Dorothy. "The Telephone Call" (1930). *50 Best American Short Stories, 1915–1939* (Ed. Edward J. O'Brien, 1939). DEPRESSION; ILLUSION v. REALITY; INTERIOR LIVES; JEALOUSY; MEN and WOMEN; SOCIETY; WOMEN'S ISSUES.

A nameless woman sits by the phone waiting for the object of her attention to call. Though the call is late, she convinces herself that she has done nothing wrong, that the man who said he would call has been delayed or cannot get through. As she rationalizes her situation, she slowly realizes that he will not be calling. Anticipation turns to anxiety, which becomes anger. Despite wanting to be reasonable about the relationship, which is still in its early stages, she finally wishes offhandedly that the man were dead. In the next instant, though, she convinces herself that she will count to five hundred by fives before she tries to call him.

The woman's anonymity and the abrupt beginning of the story *in medias res* emphasize the story's slice-of-life quality. With Parker's characteristic double-edged humor, the reader is given entrance into a world that exists only in the woman's mind. Her confusion and anger are touching reminders of the individual's plight in a society that often has little time for such commonplace situations as a broken promise, a call not made. Parker explores universal feelings that would be maudlin or melodramatic if they were to be presented in any other way than as an interior monologue that heightens the reader's sense of the woman's conflicting emotions.

Parker, Dorothy. "The Waltz" (1936). *The Portable Dorothy Parker* (Intro. Brendan Gill, 1973). INTERIOR LIVES; MEN and WOMEN; SOCIETY.

When the narrator is asked to dance, her reply is, "*Why, thank you so much, I'd adore to.*" Immediately after she agrees to dance with the unnamed man, however, she thinks, "I don't want to dance with him. I don't want to dance with anybody." When the two reach the dance floor, the man apparently has much difficulty not stepping on his partner, who tells him, "*It didn't hurt the least little bit. And anyway it was my fault,*" at the same time that she thinks, "I don't want to be of the over-sensitive type, but you can't tell me that kick was unpremeditated. Freud says there are no accidents." The ill-fated meeting ends with the narrator's thought that "I'm past all feeling now. The only way I can tell when he steps on me is that I can hear the splintering of bones." Her words to her partner, however, are "*I'd simply adore to go on waltzing.*"

In one of Parker's most humorous and sly vignettes, the reality is much different from the narrator's words. By combining both spoken dialogue and an interior monologue that describes the narrator's true feelings, the author is able to define the situation without using any substantive plot or descriptions outside the narrator's own thoughts. The rhythm of the woman's thoughts interspersed with her contradictory words forms a tantalizing story of want and need. While she apparently despises the thought of going on, she nonetheless acquiesces. Parker's sense of the reality of such situations is sharp.

Parker, Dorothy. "You Were Perfectly Fine" (1929). From *The Harper Anthology of Fiction* (Ed. Sylvan Barnet, 1991). HUMOR/SATIRE/IRONY; INTERIOR LIVES; MEN and WOMEN; SOCIETY.

A pale young man with a dreadful hangover drops into a chair and moans about the previous night's reveries that are causing him so much misery. The bright girl beside him reassures the man, telling him that he was "perfectly fine," and she goes on to detail the actions about which the man has no recollection, including a flirtation with another man's wife, a bout of singing, and a nasty fall on the ice. Even as the details get progressively more embarrassing for the man, his companion continues to tell him that he did nothing to be ashamed of.

In fact, the young man and the lady took a lengthy cab ride during which he revealed his feelings for her—apparently, he has given her his undying devotion, though he has no recollection of the conversation. The ride, she says, was the most important thing that had ever happened to either of them. The man, who tells her that he should join a monastery in Tibet in recompense for having made a fool of himself, is in the woman's clutches now. She kisses him on the forehead and runs out of the room. The man sits back in his chair and continues his moaning.

Parker's brief story is another of her snapshot images that detail the humorous side of the relationships between men and women. Though the man is mortified by his own actions, he has no idea how deeply he has ingratiated himself to the woman until she divulges it to him in excruciating detail. Still, to her, he was "perfectly fine."

Peck, Richard. "I Go Along" (1989). From *Connections: Short Stories by Outstanding Writers for Young Adults* (Ed. Donald R. Gallo, 1989). ART and the ARTIST; COMMUNICATION/LANGUAGE; EPIPHANY; INTERIOR LIVES.

When Mrs. Tibbetts, the narrator's English teacher, invites her students to attend a poetry reading at a nearby community college, the narrator decides to "go along." Even though every student in the class (one level below the advanced section) raises his hand, he is the only one who follows through. When he takes his seat on the bus with the advanced students, the narrator is surprised that Sharon Willis, the school's "major goddess girl," asks to sit beside him.

Although the featured poet seems to be in his early twenties, he has a command of the audience that the narrator admires. All the girls push forward in their seats to listen to the man in Levi's, a heavy belt buckle, and boots. For his last poem of the evening, he reads "High School," which humorously details the trials and tribulations of being young and in love. The narrator discusses the reading with Sharon and claims, "You can't write poems about zits and your locker combination." Sharon challenges him to try. On the bus ride home, the narrator realizes that the reading has changed his attitude toward life, "And I get this quick flash of tomorrow, in second period with Marty and Pink and Darla, and frankly it doesn't look that good."

Although the title implies that the narrator joins the group because he has nothing better to do, the poetry reading is a profound experience for the young man; his response to Sharon implies that he will challenge himself from now on in order to reach his potential. The world of the poet, he realizes, is not one of pretense and posing (the casualness of the poet's dress and his understated delivery impresses him) but rather one of passion, language, and insight—all aspects of life to which the narrator now aspires.

Peck, Richard. "Shadows" (1987). From *Visions* (Ed. Donald R. Gallo, 1987). COMING-OF-AGE; FRIENDSHIP; ILLUSION v. REALITY; LITERACY/WRITING.

The protagonist is a young girl who grows into womanhood in Louisiana under the care of Aunts Sudie and Margaret, neither of whom are her true relations. Her mother has left her without a word except infrequent letters home, and her father is dead. Like many children, the girl sees shadows in the house where she grows up; unlike most, though, she is able to communicate with one specific boy, who grows up with her as the years progress. The boy, whom she knows as "Seth," wears ragged and torn clothing and seems to be as lonely as she. Until she brings her lessons home from school so that he may learn to read, write, and do math, he is illiterate, knowing only the swamps and bayous that he inhabits.

After a time, though, "real boys" take the place of Seth in the girl's affections, and she grows to womanhood. On the night before she leaves for college, the protagonist, now a young woman, sees Seth one more time. She has not thought of him for years, it seems, and now she is afraid of the man who was once the only friend she had as a little girl. When she asks him why he has come back, Seth replies that he needed to see her one more time before she left for college. Stupefied that he should know that she is leaving the next day, the girl realizes a truth that has eluded her all along: Seth is the son of either Aunt Sudie or Aunt Margaret. The girl watches, stunned, as "a light glowing down the hall caught the profile of the living man." She has inspired the young man to follow his own dream of a career as a soldier.

The story is about the important friendships that develop between children who have been alienated from their real families and the profound changes that occur in us all as we grow from childhood into adulthood. The ambiguity of Seth's existence—Peck implies at the story's conclusion that Seth is, in fact, the son of one of the "aunts" with whom she has been staying, and not just a figment of her imagination—strengthens the spiritual bond between the two friends.

Perelman, S.J. "The Pipe" (1943). From *Half-a-Hundred: Stories for Men* (Ed. Charles Grayson, 1946). CLASS CONFLICTS; HUMOR/SATIRE/IRONY; SOCIETY.

As the narrator stands before a pipe shop debating whether or not he should make a purchase, many ideas go through his mind: he is looking at a Buntwell, the world's most impressive name in pipe making, and "it suddenly struck me that a Buntwell pipe was the key to my future." After much hemming and hawing and observing the shop's animated clientele, the narrator works up the courage to approach the salesman. Like a man trying on an expensive suit, the narrator has several different models of pipes jammed into his mouth by the condescending clerk. He finally chooses a pipe and the requisite accessories, then goes home, settles into his favorite easy chair, and lights up. When he comes to, his apartment is redolent with the smell of strong tobacco, and a stranger is taking his pulse. It seems that the tobacco has rendered him unconscious. He vows to go back to the shop and throw a brick through the window when he finally regains his bearings.

The story is typical of the author's style, which relies on observation of the minutest details and exaggeration for its comic effect. Perelman, whose travel writing made him famous in the middle of the twentieth century, has a keen eye for situations that lend themselves to satire and a rapier wit that can find the humor in any event. His commentaries often take issue with the pretense inherent in the materialistic societies that he describes.

Peretz, I.L. "If Not Higher" (1900). From *The Heath Introduction to Fiction*, 4th ed. (Ed. John J. Clayton, 1992). GIFTS/GENEROSITY; INTERIOR LIVES; POVERTY; RELIGION/SPIRITUALITY.
The fact that the Rabbi Nemirov disappears every Friday morning at the time of the Penitential Prayers is enough to raise the eyebrows of some of his more conservative followers, who wonder who will help them in the rabbi's absence. A Litvak—Lithuanian Jew—determined to get to the bottom of the mystery, enters the rabbi's rooms and hides under his bed. He follows the rabbi into the woods and watches him chop a tree into sticks and carry the wood to a poor old woman who lives in a hovel. The Litvak, seeing the rabbi's example and his passion for the dignity of human life, becomes the rabbi's disciple, telling people that the rabbi ascends to heaven, "if not higher," during the Penitential Prayers.

Peretz wrote the story in Yiddish, an abrupt and surprising break from the Hebrew. Though the tale has been passed in various forms through the generations, the author's version is remarkable for having been written by a progressive intellectual at home in the world. The story is underpinned by a conflict that arose late in the nineteenth century between intellectual thinking on Judaism and the traditional faith. Clearly, Peretz values the rabbi's action over the intellectualism that accomplishes little.

Petry, Ann. "In Darkness and Confusion" (1947). From *Miss Muriel and Other Stories* (Petry, 1971). CRIME/LAW; DEATH; FATHERS and CHILDREN; MOTHERS and CHILDREN; RACE RELATIONS; SOCIETY; VIOLENCE.
William Jones, a black drugstore janitor, is concerned for the safety of his son, Sam, who is stationed in Georgia. The family has not heard from Sam for some time, and as Jones checks the mail one Saturday morning to find no news, his concern increases. Through happenstance, Jones hears from an old friend that Sam has been put in prison for twenty years for shooting an MP (military policeman) who had demanded that Sam move to the back of the bus.

Jones does not tell his wife, Pink, what has happened. Rather, he goes to a bar the next day and witnesses a black soldier being shot by a white policeman who was harassing a black woman. In his anger, he runs into the street, where a riot has begun over the incident. Meeting his wife on her way home from church, Jones imprudently tells her about their son. She goes on a rampage of anger that ends when she collapses dead in the street.

There is little hope for redemption in Petry's dark narrative. Rather, she concentrates on exploring the circumstances that affect so many lives in a setting whose squalor and degradation are described in great detail. Jones, who has pledged to move his family but cannot because of his financial dilemma, is caught in a sea of anger and hatred whose eruption may, for a time, placate the rioters. Finally, though, the scene ends only in more tragedy and few answers, Jones's dream for his son and his family as dead as the grieving mother.

Pfeffer, Susan Beth. "As It Is with Strangers" (1989). From *Connections: Short Stories by Outstanding Writers for Young Adults* (Ed. Donald R. Gallo, 1989). COMING-OF-AGE; COMMUNICATION/LANGUAGE; DECEPTION; FAMILY; MOTHERS and CHILDREN; SIBLINGS.

Just before she goes to bed, the narrator, Tiffany, is given an unexpected bit of news. Twenty years before, her mother gave birth to a son with her sixteen-year-old boyfriend, and the young man, Jack, is visiting them in two days. Although she is ambivalent about the revelation, Tiffany meets her half-brother with an open mind. When Jack arrives, the conversation quickly turns to his adoptive family, whose patriarch owns a car dealership and is sending Jack to Bucknell. Tiffany, whose own mother is less affluent, "wanted to tell him that maybe someday I'd be jealous that he'd been given away to a family that could afford to send him to college, but that it was too soon for me to feel much of anything about him."

When Jack asks what his biological mother is like, Tiffany first tells him sardonically that she is a monster, then tells him the truth—that she is a kind, loving person. Jack leaves after dinner, and Tiffany thinks only that he is well mannered. In an uncharacteristically serious moment, Tiffany's mother tells her that she must be sure never to make such a mistake. Later that night, Tiffany hears her mother crying in her room, though she knows that she "did the right thing, not going in there. That's how it is with strangers. You can never really comfort them."

Although Tiffany seems to take the news well, she equates Jack with her own mother, about whom she knows less than she had once supposed. By not telling Tiffany about her own mistakes until she must, her mother has taken the one important relationship in her life for granted. The story is written with a lighthearted edge, though the message at its conclusion could not be more serious for a girl whose coming-of-age only complicates an already confusing life and forces her to explore her relationship with her mother.

Pfeffer, Susan Beth. "A Hundred Bucks of Happy" (1987). From *Visions* (Ed. Donald R. Gallo, 1987). COMING-OF-AGE; FAMILY; MORALITY (MORAL DILEMMA; MOTHERS and CHILDREN; POVERTY; SIBLINGS.

When the narrator finds a hundred-dollar bill lying on the street, she can only think of what she will be able to buy with the money. Since her father left the family, the girl's mother has not been able to buy her daughter and her son much beyond the necessities. The narrator tells her mother about the find, who suggests that she give it to the family to help them make ends meet. The idea does not sit well with the girl, and she goes to the mall the next day to spend the money on a leather coat. Instead of buying the coat (which, with tax, was slightly more than a hundred dollars), the girl walks back to the scene of her discovery, not "to see if there was any more money there but to leave the hundred-dollar bill smack where I'd found it." The girl's ambivalence about the money leads her to the bank, where she receives one hundred one-dollar bills, which she splits evenly between herself, her mother, and her brother. In an ironic gesture, she sends the remaining dollar to her father's post office box six hundred miles away so that he can buy the family a Hallmark card.

Themes of poverty and family are important in this story. Pfeffer also suggests a coming-of-age, the narrator's conflicting emotions about her father's leaving intertwined with her mother's predicament and a growing sense that she, too, is responsible for her family's well-being.

Pinkney, Andrea Davis. "Building Bridges" (1998). From *Stay True: Short Stories for Strong Girls* (Ed. Marilyn Singer, 1998). AFRICAN-AMERICAN EXPERIENCE; COMING-OF-AGE; COMMUNICATION/LANGUAGE; DREAMS (of the FUTURE); RACE RELATIONS; TRADITION/CONVENTION; WOMEN'S ISSUES.

Bebe has lived with her grandmother, Mama Lil, since she was six, when her parents were killed in an apartment fire. The relationship is loving, but often contentious. Mama Lil is at a loss to see how Bebe could find a man with "them chunky arms and those hoochie cut T-shirts." Bebe thinks that her grandmother smokes too much and wears too many fake gold chains.

Now, as she contemplates her future, Bebe has an opportunity to work on a renovation project on the Brooklyn Bridge. She is an aspiring engineer who sees the work as a way of transcending her situation. Mama Lil, who subscribes to convention, tells her, " 'If God had meant you to do a man's work, he would have made you a man. It's that simple.' " Though Bebe respects Mama Lil, she decides that she will forge the old woman's name on the permission slip if need be so that she can follow her dream. When, as a substitute for the job, Mama Lil brings home an application from a local beauty parlor, Bebe is incensed.

After much soul-searching, in which "she admitted what we'd both known all along. 'Your dreams are the kind that'll take you away from here . . . away from your Mama Lil. You got big hopes, child, but they gonna leave me alone, by myself,' " Mama Lil signs the paper. She knows that the Brooklyn Bridge is lucky to have Bebe.

The give and take between a young black girl and her grandmother, who cannot see beyond the narrow confines of the society that she has known for so long, is at the heart of Pinkney's story. The world that Mama Lil sees is black and white, and in her experience the white always wins out. Still, Bebe's perseverance and the strength of her dreams will carry her through. Mama Lil's selfless satisfaction when she signs the paper is a springboard to Bebe's future success.

Pirandello, Luigi. "The Horse in the Moon" (1932). From *Great Short Stories from the World's Literature* (Ed. Charles Neider, 1950). ANIMALS and HUMANS; DEATH; INSANITY; MARRIAGE; MEN and WOMEN.

Though the couple should be enjoying their honeymoon, neither the wedding party nor their guests are encouraged by the sight of the bridegroom, Nino, whose countenance reminds them of a madman. Nino's love for his bride-to-be is so intense, in fact, "that he had done perfectly mad things on her account, even to the point of attempting to kill himself." When the two are sent on their way, the bride, Ida, looks longingly after her departing parents, while her new husband seems oblivious to his surroundings.

The couple takes to the hills in an effort to catch one last glimpse of the departing carriages, and Nino struggles to keep up with his new wife. When they come upon a nearly dead horse in danger of being eaten alive by a flock of ravens, Ida has compassion for the creature, while Nino insists that they turn back. Nino becomes incensed that she should feel sympathy for the animal and none for him; slowly losing touch with reality, he sits on a rock and watches as the rising moon frames the head of the agonized horse. He falls to the ground "with a death-rattle in his throat." Ida wants to be anywhere but on that hill.

The theme of man/woman relationships is offered in the context of Ida's seeming preference for the well-being of the horse over that of her new husband; the marriage itself is in question from the outset, and Nino's actions only serve to guide Ida's own. The obsession that Nino feels for his new wife and his inability to allow her to feel—except for him, if, in fact, she does—comes crashing down upon him. Ida, through little fault of her own, is left to bear the brunt of Nino's insanity. Pirandello, as Neider points out, "was a prolific writer of short stories marked by a subtle and rather grim humor." In this case, that "grim humor" takes the form of absurd irony as Nino is immolated by his unhealthy passion.

Pirandello, Luigi. "The Soft Touch of Grass" (1959). From *Short Shorts: An Anthology of the Shortest Stories* (Ed. Irving Howe and Ilana Weiner Howe, 1982). AGING; ALIENATION/ISOLATION; DEATH; FATHERS and CHILDREN; INTERIOR LIVES; LOSS.

Signor Pardi wakes up to the gloomy morning of his wife's funeral and is faced with the emptiness of despair. As his relatives force him to look upon her body one last time, he becomes angered with their sympathy because he does not believe that they knew her well enough to understand his anguish, and therefore have no right to cry. His son, cautioning him to "be reasonable," leads him back to his chair, where he thinks about a time when his son will be married.

Pardi feels a chill when the mourners refer to his son also as "Pardi," and he realizes that in the months to come, his life will change drastically as his son becomes the man of the house and he, the old man, the dependent. Pardi is curious and frightened about his future, uncertain of everything except that all will be different. He supposes that he will be given his son's bed while the son sleeps with his new wife; instead, the young man places his father in a servants' lodge while he erases all remnants of their old life. Though Signor Pardi pretends to be content with the decision, he is confused and lost. Unable to find a place among the old or the adults, he spends his time in a garden with children who run barefoot in the grass. When he removes his shoes to do the same, a small girl calls him a "pig," and he is deeply insulted that she does not understand his situation. Pardi returns to his quarters, demeaned and despairing.

Pirandello writes of the alienation and loneliness one feels after the loss of a loved one, and the inevitable change that disrupts life. Pardi, who deals simultaneously with the death of his wife and the marriage of his son, is no longer the provider, but must be provided for. He is between adulthood and old age and does not know how to cope with his alienation from society. The title of the story alludes ironically to his lack of connection to society.

Plato. "The Death of Socrates" (4th century B.C.). *Clifton Fadiman's Fireside Reader* (Ed. Clifton Fadiman, 1961). COMMUNICATION/ LANGUAGE; COURAGE; DEATH; GRIEF; LOSS; SOCIETY.

This short piece relates the stoicism with which Socrates meets his death by hemlock. Even the servant of the governing council who delivers the poison to Socrates humbles himself before the man and makes it clear that he is only acting as he has been bidden. Socrates, who calms the small group of supporters around him, takes the poison immediately, not wanting to postpone the inevitable. He takes the cup readily, even cheerfully, and dies with a dignity that ensures the immortality of the soul about which he has spoken so often during his life. His last words—conspicuously understated even in a narrative that eschews any attempts at sensationalism—are to Crito, to whom Socrates relates that he owes a cock to Asclepius.

Plato's account of the death of Socrates is justly recognized for its eloquent simplicity and the understated strength of its message. The charges against Socrates of irreligion and "corrupting the young" are entirely ignored by Plato. Rather, the narrative focuses on Socrates' final moments, a monument to the way that he has lived his life of the mind.

Poe, Edgar Allan. "The Black Cat" (1843). From *Classic American Short Stories* (Sel. and Intro. Douglas Grant, 1989). ANIMALS and HUMANS; CRIME/LAW; DEATH; INSANITY; INTERIOR LIVES; MEN and WOMEN; SUPERNATURAL/HORROR.

The narrator describes how he blinds and then hangs a cat with which he has become obsessed. The outline of the hanged cat remains on the wall even after the man's house burns down. When another similar cat arrives at the man's new house, his wife prevents him from killing it; in return for her kindness, the woman is murdered with an ax and buried behind one of the house's walls. The narrator, as in "The Tell-Tale Heart" (which was written during the same period), is apprehended for the deed only when he brags to police about the sturdiness of the walls and, tapping one of them to prove his point, hears the yowling of a cat behind it.

Poe illustrates his ability to explore the depths of human psychology and degradation through a narrator who is clearly insane, but who manages to relate the events as if they are normal. The author's sense of irony is sharp here, as the narrator—again, as in "The Tell-Tale Heart" (in fact, the slight differences between the two stories would make a good topic of discussion in class)—trips himself up through his own overweening pride. If not for his desire to flaunt his actions, perhaps no one would have suspected what they would find behind the wall. Still, the most terrible scenes that one can find hidden in a house, Poe implies, are no more diabolical than what one may find in the darkest recesses of the human mind.

Poe, Edgar Allan. "The Cask of Amontillado" (1846). From *The Harper Anthology of Fiction* (Ed. Sylvan Barnet, 1991). ALLEGORY/LEGEND/FABLE; CRIME/LAW; DEATH; REVENGE.

Montresor obsesses about righting his unspoken grievances against Fortunato, and the wronged man puts his well-considered plan into action one night during a drunken reverie. Fortunato, a man of some power and connections, fancies himself a connoisseur of fine wine. By playing upon his sense of the finer things in life, Montresor lures his unwitting victim into a catacomb by claiming to have secured a keg of the rare Amontillado. Once in the subterranean vault, Montresor leads Fortunato into a narrow opening, chains him to the wall, and bricks up the hole so that no one will ever know what he has done. Montresor neatly fulfills his two criteria for successful revenge: that the victim should be fully conscious of the perpetrator's intention; and that he should get away unscathed. Fifty years after the fact, no one is the wiser to Montresor's scheme. The last words of his story ironically echo the single-minded hatred that he felt for his victim: Rest in peace.

The plot is diabolical and simple, an earmark of Poe's short fiction. The story is an example of the author's attention to the "single effect" in the short prose tale (of which he writes in an essay from 1842). In this case, every action that Montresor takes in order to redress the wrongs he has suffered at the hand of Fortunato strengthens the tale's tone of impending doom. The story uses foreshadowing to great effect and makes the reader implicit in Montresor's actions through subtle ironies and asides to which Fortunato, himself ironically named, is not privy.

Poe, Edgar Allan. "The Fall of the House of Usher" (1839). From *The Oxford Book of Gothic Tales* (Ed. Chris Baldick, 1992). DECADENCE/ DEGENERATION; THE DOUBLE (DOPPELGANGER); FAMILY; HEALTH; SIBLINGS; SUPERNATURAL/HORROR.
A man arrives at the House of Usher, having been summoned by his old friend, Roderick Usher. The house, like its occupants (Usher lives there with his twin sister, Madeline), is decrepit and seems to be on the verge of collapsing into the tarn (lake) that borders it. Usher's friend, in an attempt to make the man's life as comfortable as possible, engages him in discussion and storytelling, but Usher sinks still further into depression and madness. When Usher announces that Madeline has died, his subsequent actions force his friend to wonder whether he is hiding something. While Usher reads "The Mad Trist" to his friend, the action of the book mirrors the actions taking place in the house. Madeline, having been buried alive, escapes her coffin and returns to kill her brother. As Usher's friend runs from the house, it slides into the tarn, as Poe had foreshadowed in the story's opening.
    One of Poe's most famous tales (and the subject of a movie starring Martin Landau as Usher), "The Fall of the House of Usher" is an intricate exploration of the human psyche and madness—Poe's favorite subjects. The author suggests that many aspects of the relationship between Roderick and Madeline Usher, including incest, murder, and revenge, are intertwined with the life of the house itself, which cannot outlive the last of the Usher line.

Poe, Edgar Allan. "The Masque of the Red Death" (1842). From *Representative American Short Stories* (Ed. Alexander Jessup, 1923). ALLEGORY/LEGEND/FABLE; DEATH; HEALTH (SICKNESS/ MEDICINE); PRIDE; SOCIETY.
As the plague ravages his land, Prince Prospero attempts to forestall death by gathering his courtiers and walling them inside his castle. In order to celebrate their new lives free of the dread disease, which comes agonizingly quickly and is characterized by bleeding from the pores, the group gives a masquerade ball. Among the participants is a ghastly figure, a man whose face is covered in blood, which reminds the revelers of the reality of their situation. Indignant that he should be witness to such a sight in his own castle, Prospero demands that the man be caught and murdered, but no one is willing to approach the figure. Prospero, who chases the man throughout the rooms and finally confronts him face to face, dies immediately. His courtiers suffer similar fates.

The story is, like "The Cask of Amontillado," an ironic allegory. The *memento mori* (reminder of death) of the death-figure suggests the mortality even of those who believe that their station in life will protect them from the inevitable. In a sense, the overweening pride of the revelers exacerbates the situation by inviting the grim reality of the outside world to their "safe" world. The clock that figures prominently in the story also hints at the inexorable passage of time and the finiteness of human lives.

Poe, Edgar Allan. "The Purloined Letter" (1845). From *The 50 Greatest Mysteries of All Time* (Ed. Otto Penzler, 1998). CRIME/LAW; DECEPTION; INTERIOR LIVES; MYSTERY/ADVENTURE.

As they relax in a back library in Paris in the autumn of 18—, the narrator and his friend, C. Auguste Dupin, discuss criminal cases with which they are familiar (specifically, the murder of Marie Roget, which is detailed in Poe's "Murder in the Rue Morgue"). Monsieur G—,the prefect of police, appears at the door. Though neither man has seen the prefect in several years, the conversation quickly turns to the case at hand: a letter that could blackmail a prominent member of Parisian society has been "purloined," or stolen.

The case is deceptively simple. The police know the identity of the thief and his residence; still, they are powerless to do anything to arrest him without destroying the letter first, as the blackmailer has the upper hand as long the letter is in his possession. Despite the best efforts of the prefect and his men, they are unable to find the letter, though they know, given the nature of the blackmail, that it has likely remained in the thief's home all the while. Dupin, undaunted by the prefect's inability to crack the case, deduces that the letter has been hidden in plain sight, and he chastises the prefect to his friend for not being able to alter his thinking to match that of the criminal. True to his word, Dupin visits the thief, a minister in the government, and discerns the letter's whereabouts through his own analysis of the minister's habits and personality. After his discovery of the letter, Dupin embarks on a lengthy dissertation to his friend on art, algebra, and the value of knowing one's opponent intimately when such a case arises.

Clearly, Poe's tale is a precursor to the later deductive efforts of Conan Doyle's Sherlock Holmes and his sidekick, Watson. In this often-anthologized example of the detective story, the author takes his sharp eye for detail and his understanding of the human psyche to a level that has been emulated since in both American and world literature.

Poe, Edgar Allan. "The Tell-Tale Heart" (1843). From *The Story and Its Writer*, 5th ed. (Ed. Ann Charters, 1999). CRIME/LAW; DEATH; INSANITY; SUPERNATURAL/HORROR; VIOLENCE.

Though the narrator vehemently proclaims his sanity throughout (a foreshadowing of the truth of the matter), attributing to an unnamed disease only a heightened sense of hearing, he tells a tale of unremitting horror. An old man who rooms with him—the perfect boarder in every other way—watches the madman, he believes, with an "Evil Eye." In order to avoid falling victim to the eye, the narrator nightly sneaks into the old man's room and casts a single beam from his lantern on the sleeping man. One night, he wakes the old man; when the beam falls directly on the man's open eye, the narrator smothers him under his mattress. He calmly dismembers the body—all the while maintaining his sanity and congratulating himself for, to his mind, the wholly rational steps he takes to hide the man's various parts under his living room floor—and assumes that he can rest in peace.

When policemen arrive at his door, alerted by neighbors to the earlier ruckus, the narrator confidently leads them through the house, explaining away any notion that harm has come to his housemate. When they sit with him in his living room, however, the narrator believes he hears the old man's heart beating from beneath the floorboards. Finally, he cannot control his response to the noises in his head, and he willingly leads the policemen to the man's body.

The tale is one of Poe's most widely known for its exploration of the nature of human madness and the process through which a man can be driven to murder. The narrator's continued insistence that he is sane allows the author to examine society's definitions of "normalcy" and to limn the depths of man's depravity.

Porter, Katherine Anne. "Flowering Judas" (1930). From *Studies in the Short Story* (Ed. Virgil Scott and David Madden, 1976). CULTURE CONFLICTS; DEATH; DREAMS (SLEEPING); INTERIOR LIVES; MEN and WOMEN; MORALITY (MORAL DILEMMA); POLITICS; SEXUALITY; SOCIETY; WAR; WOMEN'S ISSUES.

Laura is a twenty-two-year-old American teacher in Mexico who is tangentially related to the revolutionary activities going on at the time. She visits Eugenio, a political prisoner, and returns home to find that Braggioni, the revolution's leader, is waiting for her. The beautiful woman, whose virginity is legendary in the town, cares little for Braggioni's singing and philosophizing and only wishes that he would leave her alone. Still, she is afraid of the man, whose temper is infamous.

Braggioni's wife, from whom the leader estranges himself when it is convenient for him, constantly weeps for her husband; when he finally returns to her, she offers to wash his feet for him. He finds her weeping gratifying, as it validates his power over others. In fact, the revolution's leader is nothing of the sort, as he is more concerned about his own well-being than that of his people. Laura, who delivers the drugs that Eugenio uses to commit suicide, dreams that the man has come back to take her with him. She awakes in the night, confused as to her reason for staying in Mexico.

Porter's story is both an indictment of men like Braggioni who wield their power selfishly, with no consideration for the harm that their hypocritical attitudes bring to others, and a study in the difference between perception and reality. Laura does more to help the people of Mexico than Braggioni, though she is an outcast, a "murderer" who is unable to reconcile her place—as both a woman and a compassionate individual—in a world as brutal and as capricious as the one in which she finds herself.

Porter, Katherine Anne. "He" (1927). From *The Story and Its Writer*, 4th ed. (Ed. Ann Charters, 1995). ALIENATION/ISOLATION; FAMILY; HEALTH (SICKNESS/MEDICINE); MOTHERS and CHILDREN.

"He" is about a mother's love for her second son, whom she admits to loving more than her two daughters. The boy's name, however, is never mentioned in the text; the family instead always uses the pronoun to refer to him. He is a sickly child who never speaks, and his mother often makes excuses for him, telling people that He is just too shy. The boy becomes ill during the winter and does not improve by spring. When the condition continues, a doctor tells the family that he will never get well. His parents decide to send him to the County Home for treatment. They do not tell him directly, but the boy knows what they are planning. He is placed in the back seat of a neighbor's car with a blanket; before He leaves, his mother thinks of all the love she has for him and what a pity it is that he was ever born.

Porter's use of the pronoun in place of the boy's name suggests both the Christlike qualities of the child—persecuted by life and by the people around him who little understand his predicament—and the lack of identity that He is bound to suffer throughout his life. Though He has some understanding of what will happen to him, the child has little recourse except to acquiesce to his parents' plan. The situation is tragic for everyone involved, but no more so than for the boy himself.

Porter, Katherine Anne. "The Jilting of Granny Weatherall" (1930). From *The Heath Introduction to Fiction*, 4th ed. (Ed. John J. Clayton, 1992). DEATH; HEALTH (SICKNESS/MEDICINE); LOVE; MEN and WOMEN; PRIDE.

Granny Weatherall resents the fact that her attending doctor is young enough to be her grandson. At eighty years old, she wants more than anything to maintain the control that has characterized her life. As she lies in bed, she scans the impeccably clean room. She knows that she will not live much longer—a fact that she is at first unwilling to admit to herself—and she thinks that she should destroy some old love letters that may embarrass her family if they were to find them. Her condition deteriorates, and her mind wanders back to a time sixty years before when she was jilted at the altar by a man named George. Now, on her deathbed, Granny Weatherall imagines what she will tell George when she sees him again: she has done well without him, and her children and grandchildren are strong and healthy. She recalls all the things she has done that have made her strong. Still, she cannot get the thought of George out of her mind, a kind of hell that she had hoped she would not have to face again. When George left her, she was forced to throw out the wedding cake. Her world fell apart for a time, but she survived. As she dies, she dreams that she is sitting with George in a cart. She is momentarily guilty for the image. Her last thought is one of sorrow, the memory that she would not let herself consider while she was alive.

Porter's story is one of unrequited love and a woman's rage for strength and order. Perhaps because she has not allowed herself the luxury of suffering while she is alive, Granny Weatherall (the name itself is ironic, as she can "weather all" but her last moments and the memories that have lain just below the surface of her consciousness all these years) is destined to take the memory to her grave.

Porter, Katherine Anne. "Noon Wine" (1936). From *The Collected Stories of Katherine Anne Porter* (Porter, 1965). ALIENATION/ISOLATION; DEATH; FATE; HISTORY; MUSIC; SIBLINGS.

When Olaf Helton seeks work on a dairy farm in Texas, his employer, Thompson, finds the man standoffish; still, he is an efficient worker, and despite his personal shortcomings (including an obsession with his harmonicas), he becomes a valued employee of the family. Several years after Helton's arrival, he is confronted by Homer Hatch, a bounty hunter, who accuses him of murdering his own brother in North Dakota. In the ensuing struggle, Thompson, whose main concern has always been with appearances, kills Hatch. Helton, whom Thompson thought dead, escapes, only to be caught by a posse; during his subsequent ill-treatment and imprisonment, Helton dies. Even though Thompson is acquitted of Hatch's murder, his family turns against him. Unable to reconcile Hatch's death with his own notion of what occurred during the struggle, Thompson takes his own life.

The story's title refers to the song that Helton played on his harmonicas, a connection between the past and the present (we discover that Helton killed his own brother over an argument concerning the harmonicas; later, the man would have escaped the posse if it hadn't been for his stopping to retrieve two harmonicas that had fallen from his pocket). Through the pervasive image of the harmonicas, Porter implies the inexorable chain of events that leads to tragedy.

Porter, Katherine Anne. "Old Mortality" (1938). From *The Norton Anthology of Short Fiction* (Ed. R.V. Cassill, 1978). COMING-OF-AGE; DEATH; FAMILY; HISTORY; IDENTITY; INTERIOR LIVES;

MARRIAGE; MEN and WOMEN; PRIDE; TIME (and ITS EF-FECTS); WOMEN'S ISSUES.

Miranda Gay wishes nothing more than to be like her dead aunt, Amy, when she grows up. As a girl of eight, she first saw her aunt's wedding pictures, and the family makes references to Amy that imply she was a vivacious young woman who died before her time. Marriage was nothing more than a confining institution for Amy, and some letters found in a trunk suggest that she had affairs before she settled down with Gabriel, a horse trainer.

Miranda is sent to a Catholic school when she is ten, and she meets Gabriel, who has since been remarried to a woman named Miss Honey, who offers diatribes on her husband's gambling. Some eight years later, when Miranda meets her cousin, Eva, on a train, she is returning from Gabriel's funeral. It seems he was never the same after Amy's death; Amy, for her part, was too vital for anyone to control, and the implication is that the deaths of both Gabriel and Miss Honey can be attributed to Amy's living memory. When Miranda tells Eva that she has left school, the young woman undergoes a transformation of her own that sets her apart from the legacy of her family and places her squarely in the present, where she must make her own life.

Porter's story, while focusing on Miranda and her coming-of-age, is much more complex than it first appears. As in Faulkner's stories, the past impacts the present in ways that are not superficially apparent. In fact, the information that comes to Miranda does not come from one source, but rather from a number of different family members who perceive only what is relevant to their own lives. Miranda, the one character in the story who is able to complete the picture, is more capable of making life decisions that will allow her to move outside her family's history into a world of possibility. By wrestling with the contradictions of family and the individual, she has begun to understand herself.

Powers, J.F. "The Forks" (1947). From *Studies in the Short Story* (Ed. Adrian H. Jaffe and Virgil Scott, 1964). BETRAYAL; GIFTS/GENEROSITY; ILLUSION v. REALITY; RELIGION/SPIRITUALITY; SOCIETY.

Father Eudex and the monsignor have much different views when it comes to the workers' strikes protesting wages and working conditions. The monsignor, who waves at passersby—many of whom are parishioners in the church—from his spotless sedan, cares little for the plight of the workers. When Father Eudex and the monsignor both receive checks from the Rival Tractor Company, Father Eudex, who sees the checks as hush money given to the clergy, decides that he will give his share to the workers' relief fund.

The monsignor sees the gesture as a weakness on the part of Father Eudex, and he gives as an illustration of the priest's lack of polish his use of the utensils—the "forks" of the title, on one level—when they eat together. When the priest attempts, unsuccessfully, to council a member of the church who seeks his approval, not his advice, the differences in the views of the two men become even more apparent. Father Eudex tears up the check and wonders what others would think of him.

Powers's scathing commentary on the attitudes of the Catholic Church and one priest's attention to the plight of the common man explores the contradictory notions of compassion for humanity and a desire to save the soul. Even as he supports the workers at the risk of the monsignor's wrath, Father Eudex questions his own actions. The title refers both to the monsignor's impression of Father Eudex's roughness and to the decisions that the priest must make, as he chooses a path that will make him unpopular with the powers that be. The monsignor, whose complacency, the author suggests, is antithetical to the tenets of the Catholic Church, would prefer not to deal with the answers to questions as difficult as the ones the priest raises. Still, Father Eudex realizes that his actions are meaningless in the much larger context of the church and the more powerful men who perpetuate the monsignor's attitudes.

Powers, J.F. "The Old Bird: A Love Story" (1944). From *The Stories of J.F. Powers* (Intro. Denis Donoghue, 2000). AGING; LABOR/JOB; LOVE; MARRIAGE; MEN and WOMEN; PRIDE.

Charles Newman is an old man looking for work during the holiday season. When he is offered a position as a mail clerk, Newman accepts, though he is unaccustomed to such menial tasks. His manager, Mr. Hurley, treats his elder much as he would a boy, explaining the process and instilling in him the importance of the task. Newman discovers that the job has its inconveniences—he gives himself a paper cut on the nose and struggles to keep up with the wrapping of the objects—but things seem to be working out for him until he overhears Hurley telling another manager about the "old bird" that he was forced to hire. At home that evening, he is reluctant to tell his wife about the job. When he realizes the depth of his wife's love, however, he entrusts her with all the troubling details of the day, and the two make light of Newman's situation and convince themselves that he will have work even after the holiday season has ended.

The title of the story is significant. Even though Newman is ill-equipped to handle the job that he is given, his attempts to gain some order in his own life are valiant, despite the comments of people like Hurley. More important, of course, is Newman's relationship with his wife, which supersedes any disappointment that he may feel. After all, "It is not a hopeless situation, but only because she loved him."

Pritchett, V.S. "Many Are Disappointed" (1937). From *Collected Stories* (Pritchett, 1956). ILLUSION v. REALITY; INTERIOR LIVES; MEN and WOMEN; MOTHERS and CHILDREN; POVERTY.

As four men reach what they believe to be a tavern on a cycling tour of the south of England, they encounter the mistress of the house, a plain woman with a child on her skirt. When they express their interest in having a drink, the woman tells them that she serves only tea, and that "many are disappointed" when they discover that she does not operate a pub. Despite the woman's disclaimer, the men stay and order tea.

One of them, Sid Blake, believes that he has seen the woman before; when she sends a note with her child to Blake as they sit at the table, he joins her in the kitchen. The little girl looks at a ring on Blake's finger, which the man takes off and allows her to play with. After some conversation, which implies that the two may have known each other before this meeting, Blake and his friends leave, intent on stopping at the first pub they find. The woman stands in the road with her daughter and waves good-bye.

The woman's loneliness, despite the apparent presence of a man of the house by the waistcoat that Blake sees on a chair, and the mean circumstances in which she finds herself contrasts to the aloofness of the men. While they are each disappointed for different reasons at what they find in the "tavern," the woman is the one who is truly disappointed by what life has offered her. Still, she perseveres.

Proust, Marcel. "Filial Sentiments of a Parricide" (1906). From *Great Short Stories from the World's Literature* (Ed. Charles Neider, 1950). COMMUNICATION/LANGUAGE; DEATH; IDENTITY; INTERIOR LIVES; MOTHERS and CHILDREN; SELF-DESTRUCTION/SUICIDE; SOCIETY.

When the narrator reads that Mr. van Blarenberghe has died, he writes a letter to the man's wife, telling her how his own parents would have felt at the loss. The woman's son responds to the letter, thanking the narrator, an old acquaintance of his, for the kindness. When the narrator reads in the newspaper shortly thereafter that the son has murdered his own mother before killing himself, the narrator is forced to reconcile the action with the man he had once known.

Recalling such names as Ajax and Oedipus, the narrator rationalizes the act by describing the man not as "a criminal brute, a being outside humanity, but a noble example of humanity, a man of enlightened soul," who recognized early in his own life the tragedy that awaits all of mankind. When one thinks logically of the alternatives and realizes that the young are the ones who kill those they love by "the anxiety we cause them, by that kind of uneasy tenderness we inspire and ceaselessly put in a state of alarm," only one conclusion can be reached: that life cannot withstand the vision of the Truth.

Proust's dark tale, told through both letters and the narrator's response to what he reads in the newspaper, explores the uneasiness of the *fin de siecle*, the turn of the century, in which society begins to sense the alienation and fragmentation that would become an integral part of life—and literature—in the twentieth century. Proust is the quintessential modernist who finds himself at odds with a vision of life as a series of events that we ponder nostalgically in our old age. In that sense, the story details the hopelessness of mankind. Only our own experiences and attitudes can shine light on such a dark vision.

Purdy, James. "Don't Call Me by My Right Name" (1956). From *Studies in Fiction* (Ed. Blaze O. Bonazza et al., 1982). DISABILITY/ PHYSICAL APPEARANCE; IDENTITY; MARRIAGE; MEN and WOMEN; VIOLENCE; WOMEN'S ISSUES.

Lois Klein has decided that it is time to take back her maiden name, which was McBane. She knows that the German word *klein* means "small," and she is anything but a small woman. Also, by giving up her maiden name in the first place, she has exchanged a large part of her identity to that point in her life for that of her husband. When Lois tells her husband of six months about her plans, he refuses to let her change her name. During a Halloween party, the two confront each other, and Lois's husband strikes her, knocking her to the ground. Later that evening, in a similar encounter, he repeats the violence. Passersby who are concerned about her appearance ask her if she is Mrs. Klein. She tells them that she is not. Lois strikes back at her husband and tells him to hail a cab.

Although the themes that arise in Purdy's story are common enough, the story's real effect comes from the violence that ensues when a couple is unable to communicate by any other means. All the men in the story mercilessly hound Lois Klein about her married name, and she realizes that in giving up her maiden name she has given up much more than her previous identity. Purdy suggests that the couple will continue to live as they have, though the snapshot images of the evening's various confrontations are unsettling, offering little hope for reconciliation and suggesting the perpetuation of the lack of identity that characterizes "Mrs. Klein's" life.

Pushkin, Alexander. "The Coffin-Maker" (1834). From *Great Stories of All Nations* (Ed. Maxim Lieber and Blanche Colton Williams, 1945). ALIENATION/ISOLATION; CLASS CONFLICTS; DEATH; DREAMS (SLEEPING); INTERIOR LIVES; JEALOUSY; PRIDE.

Adrian Prokhoroff, a coffin maker, moves from his home in Basmannaia to Nikitskaia, where he is invited to a neighbor's silver anniversary. During the evening, much drink is consumed, and Prokhoroff is angered by the way in which the other men at the party, businessmen in the town, disparage his profession. When he returns home drunk and ill-humored, he falls asleep and dreams that the ghosts of those he has buried in the past have come back to haunt him. The dream is so vivid that Prokhoroff is surprised when he is awakened the next morning and told that several of the neighbors have stopped by to invite him to further reveries. In his confusion, he wonders if anyone else has seen the ghoulish company that haunted him the previous night. The servant brushes aside Prokhoroff's suggestion and readies the tea.

Pushkin invokes the gravediggers of Shakespeare and Walter Scott who, he explains, have wrongly portrayed such men as "merry and facetious individuals." Instead, Prokhoroff is a man with many weighty issues on his mind. The author explores his character's relationship with death and man's essential inability—even though, in this case, death is an everyday part of the protagonist's life—to cope with death's finality. Though the coffin maker experiences what should be a life-altering dream, his actions at the end of the story suggest that life instead will go on as usual. Themes of class structure and man's desire to be accepted by society are the root cause of Prokhoroff's vision. Those themes are prevalent in much Russian literature of the time.

Pushkin, Alexander. "The Station-Master" (1831). From *Complete Prose Fiction* (Trans. and Intro. Paul Debreczeny, 1983). ALIENATION/ISOLATION; CLASS CONFLICTS; DEATH; FATHERS and CHILDREN; LOVE; MEN and WOMEN; RELIGION/SPIRITUALITY; SOCIETY.

Samson Vyrin is the stationmaster for a small train stop in the countryside outside St. Petersburg. The narrator, who stops at the station, is struck by the beauty of Vyrin's fourteen-year-old daughter, Dunya. When the narrator returns several years later, he finds that both Vyrin and the station have not withstood time well. Vyrin relates a story of how Dunya was seduced by a young officer, Minsky, and taken to St. Petersburg. Assuming that she would be discarded by the man and forced to live as a prostitute, Vyrin goes looking for her in the city. When he finds his daughter, the officer claims that the two are in love and dismisses him. Vyrin returns to the station and takes to drinking. Years later, the narrator discovers that Vyrin, who has killed himself with drink, is buried nearby. His daughter, who is obviously wealthy, visits the grave with her three children.

Though there is a religious overtone to the story—Pushkin comments more than once on a mural in the station that depicts the biblical story of the prodigal son—those remarks simply act as a backdrop for the story's focus on the love of a father for his daughter and the daughter's return after the father's death. Vyrin's belief in the evil of humanity (he was sure that she would be discarded by the officer) is exacerbated by his inability to reconcile his own position in society with his daughter's aspirations. The old man's ignorance constructs a barrier between him and his daughter, who in reality lives no such life.

Pynchon, Thomas. "Entropy" (1960). From *Nelson Algren's Own Book of Lonesome Monsters* (Ed. Nelson Algren, 1962). DEATH; DECADENCE/DEGENERATION; HUMOR/SATIRE/IRONY; INTERIOR LIVES; SOCIETY; TIME (and its EFFECTS).

Meatball Mulligan's party, which has gone on for two consecutive days, wakes Callisto, a man who lives upstairs. Callisto, who keeps his apartment as warm as a tropical jungle, nurses a sick bird with the warmth from his own body, and the relationship between the two defines the concept of entropy—the notion that the universe is expanding into chaos and will eventually die. Callisto's ill-fated attempts (the bird itself dies, perhaps signaling the onset of entropy in the lives of the characters) prompt his girlfriend, Aubade, to smash a window in order to allow entropy to enter the room. Simultaneous with Callisto's actions are Mulligan's attempts to maintain order at his own party.

Pynchon's story, much like Ursula K. Leguin's "Schrödinger's Cat," which examines Werner Heisenberg's "Uncertainty Principle," takes a difficult physical theory and puts it into practice. Much of the story is based on the philosophy of entropy and eschews the action of a typical narrative, though Mulligan's party is a humorous and ironic backdrop against which the principle is played out. While Callisto's care of the bird is a matter of life and death, Mulligan's predicament is hardly as serious.

R

Radowsky, Colby. "Amanda and the Wounded Birds" (1987). From *Visions* (Ed. Donald R. Gallo, 1987). LABOR/JOB; MOTHERS and CHILDREN.

Amanda Hart's mother has made the big time with her own syndicated radio show that helps people deal with their problems. At first, the job was something that psychotherapist Dr. Emma Hart did as a lark, when a local radio producer was looking to fill time during the dinner hour. In the several years since, the show has been aired across the country, and Dr. Hart spends much of her time helping her "wounded birds," the name that Amanda and her mother have given to the people who call the show. Dr. Hart is very serious about helping everyone who calls the show, and she is incessantly called away on lecture tours and to do special broadcasts.

The problems that face Amanda aren't unlike the problems that face any teenager—unpopular teachers and strained relationships with friends— though she finds that her mother has less and less time to help her deal with them. She has little success with the guidance counselors at school, who believe that she should know exactly what she wants to do with her life; in short, she has no one to turn to. On a whim, Amanda calls her mother's show and passes herself off as "Claire," a girl with the same problems as Amanda. Speaking hypothetically, she details the problem she has connecting with her mother. Dr. Hart suggests that she meet the problem head-on and call back with the results. On a follow-up call, Amanda slips and uses the phrase "wounded birds" to describe the people whom her mother helps. Dr. Hart knows immediately that her daughter is the caller. She tells Amanda to meet her at their favorite restaurant for lunch, and the two sit and talk into the evening.

Radowsky's story makes sense of difficult mother/daughter relationships and poses a viable solution to the lack of communication that can exist, even between a professional therapist and her own daughter.

Reymont, Wladyslaw S. "Twilight" (1916). From *Great Short Stories from the World's Literature* (Ed. Charles Neider, 1950). ALIENA-TION/ISOLATION; ALLEGORY/LEGEND/FABLE; ANIMALS and HUMANS; DEATH; DREAMS (of the FUTURE); FRIEND-SHIP; GRIEF; SOCIETY.

Sokol the horse lay dying, but not quickly enough. Even though the people let him die a natural death without killing him outright for his hide, they "rewarded him occasionally with a kick to remind him that he was dying too slowly." Though his days are fulfilling, the nights of June frighten him; he thinks he is going to die then. When he hallucinates that he sees "vast grain-fields, as limitless as the sea, stretching away to a distant, endlessly distant, horizon," his faculties begin to leave him. He imagines galloping at top speed, and then he dies. The sun goes down on the day, and the dog, Lappa, runs to greet his friend. Despite the dog's licking and pawing, his friend does not respond. When the realization of Sokol's death strikes him, he begins moaning and howling for the horse.

Reymont, who won the Nobel Prize for literature in 1924, is best known for his astute studies of peasant life in Poland. Though this brief story has a simple plot, the author's eye for detail and the dying desires of the horse are clearly symbolic of the peasant's plight in Eastern Europe at the time Reymont was writing. The tale's animal characters understate the seriousness of the situation. The story's tone is set by its title, by the opening line— "Sokol lay dying"—and by Lappa's response when he realizes his friend has died (the last line has him "howling weirdly").

Rilke, Rainer Maria. "The Stranger" (1932). From *Great Short Stories from the World's Literature* (Ed. Charles Neider, 1950). BETRAYAL; CHILDHOOD; DEATH; GRIEF; RELIGION/SPIRITUALITY; SOCIETY; TIME (and ITS EFFECTS).

The narrator has received a letter from a stranger, and the two meet face to face to discuss some weighty philosophical issues. The narrator's question to the stranger is disarmingly direct: "Do you still remember God?" He proceeds to tell the man a story about God's hands, in which the right hand has been sent to earth to tell a young woman that it wants to live. "At first there will be a little darkness about you and then a great darkness, which is called childhood," God tells the hand, "and then you will be a man, and climb the mountain as I have commanded you. All this will last but a moment. Farewell." But St. Paul cuts off God's right hand before it can be on its way. The left hand, seeing what has happened, bemoans the fate of the right hand. God's blood covers the earth, and the hand comes back to him, sickly and trembling, and cannot recover from its memories of its time on earth. The narrator tells the stranger that he thinks the hand may be on its way again.

Rilke's story, published posthumously, questions in prose many of the same issues that the author takes on in his poetry, which forms the great majority of his body of work. The hand symbolizes the small piece of God that is present in each child as he begins his life, which is supported by the narrator's assertion that when children have heard the abstract tale, "apparently it was told them in such a way that they could understand everything; for they love this story." The same is not true for the adults who hear it.

Rilke seems purposely to obfuscate the meaning of the story in order to privilege children with the knowledge and ambition that is born of innocence. In that sense, the story parallels Proust's "Filial Sentiment of a Parricide," in which the narrator cannot reconcile the brevity of life with the grand ambitions we have for it.

Rivera, Tomás. ". . . and the earth did not devour him" (1971). From _Tomás Rivera: The Complete Works_ (Rivera, 1991). COMING-OF-AGE; DUTY; FAMILY; HEALTH (SICKNESS/MEDICINE); POVERTY; RELIGION/SPIRITUALITY; SIBLINGS; SOCIETY.

The unnamed protagonist is a Chicano boy whose aunt and uncle have contracted tuberculosis. The aunt dies, and the uncle is sent home spitting blood. The boy's parents, devout Catholics, ask God to see them through their misery. The boy is enraged by their blind faith, and he feels an anger for which he has no outlet. When he must carry home his younger brother, who becomes ill from working in the fields, he curses God in a moment of unabated anger. But when his brother recovers from his illness, the boy understands that God has little to do with his day-to-day survival. Emboldened by his own actions, he becomes a man.

On the surface, Rivera's story, which is one in a series of short stories that depicts the life of migrant workers and their children, is a coming-of-age vignette. Unlike the epiphanies of Joyce, for instance, much more is at stake than first love or the realization of a wider world. Instead, Rivera writes social commentary infused with the anger of social protest, resulting in his protagonist's understanding of how one survives in the world. The story's title suggests that the boy's actions are appropriate. Far from being swallowed by the parted earth, he is able to care for his family.

Rivera, Tomás. "First Communion" (1971). From _Tomás Rivera: The Complete Works_ (Rivera, 1991). COMING-OF-AGE; GUILT; INTERIOR LIVES; RELIGION/SPIRITUALITY; SEXUALITY; SOCIETY.

As the narrator readies himself for his first Holy Communion, he must decide how many sins to confess to the priest. His mother has told him stories of hell, and the boy is sure that he does not want to go there. When he arrives early at church on the morning of his Communion, he notices a couple having sex in a shop next to the church. He watches with interest, until the couple sees him. He believes that he has committed another sin, that of the flesh, simply by having watched the act, though he does not relate this to the priest. After the morning's events, the Communion leaves him unfulfilled, and he imagines people (including his parents and his priest and a nun) having sex. He escapes the celebration and hides from his family. He recalls how much he enjoyed having watched the couple.

Rivera often combines scenes of everyday life—here illustrated by the man and the woman in their own "communion"—with religious themes. The narrator's feelings of guilt and shame are overwhelmed by the reality of life. He does not fully understand the implications of the day's events, recognizing the coupling only as an image that thrills him in an unfamiliar way. He has taken a large step toward a coming-of-age, during which he will be repeatedly called upon to reconcile those two much different views—the abstractions of religion and visceral, everyday, human events—into a life that accepts both the foibles of humanity and the possibility of eternal life. The story parallels Frank O'Connor's "First Confession," though Rivera's protagonist is more aware of the contradictory implications of the event.

Robison, Mary. "Coach" (1981). From *The Best American Short Stories 1982* (Ed. John Gardner and Shannon Ravenel, 1982). ASSIMILATION; COMING-OF-AGE; FAMILY; FATHERS and CHILDREN; LABOR/JOB; MARRIAGE; MEN and WOMEN; SPORTS.

When Coach and his wife, Sherry, move with their daughter, Daphne, to a small college town, where he will assume his duties with the junior varsity football team in the fall, the settling-in process proves to be more difficult than they had anticipated: Sherry wants to rent an art studio of her own, where she can pursue her painting, a move that is perceived by Daphne as a trial separation; a reporter from the student newspaper comes to the house hung over and gets Coach's story all wrong in the article; Daphne finds herself the object of much interest from the young men on campus; and Coach already hears rumors about how he may be the next head coach of the varsity when the current coach retires.

After a particularly hectic day, Coach sits down at the kitchen table and drinks beer while he makes out a roster for his dream team. Daphne comes home and gives her father a shirt that has the college's nickname on it, and her mother bustles into the kitchen late, having come to the conclusion that she will never be a painter.

Robison's story is a straightforward examination of a family who attempts to assimilate to a new community. Unlike the stories of Gish Jen, however, the ways in which the Noonan family adapts are more subtle. Coach must come to terms with the fact that his daughter is growing up at the same time he worries about the success that seems to be well within his reach. Sherry, too, understands that she has given painting a shot, and she is willing to be flexible as they create their new lives.

Robison, Mary. "Pretty Ice" (1977). From *The Granta Book of the American Short Story* (Ed. Richard Ford, 1992). EPIPHANY; IDENTITY; INTERIOR LIVES; MARRIAGE; MEN and WOMEN; MOTHERS and CHILDREN; SELF-DESTRUCTION/SUICIDE.

Belle, who met her fiancé, Will, at college in Boston, is expecting his arrival in her small Ohio hometown. She has never learned to drive, and her mother is taking her to the train station to meet the man. In the car on the way, Belle tells her mother that Will has been turned down for a grant because his botany research has been deemed largely irrelevant. She suggests that perhaps she will postpone the wedding because of his financial status. At the station, her reception of Will is cold, and Belle thinks that her fiancé has put on weight. After a series of decisions that implies Belle's turning away from Will, her mother comments on the beauty of their surroundings, the ice that has accumulated from a recent storm. Belle smiles at Will, perhaps for the last time.

Even though Belle and Will are to be married, Belle's actions do not suggest that she intends to go through with the wedding. She is more financially secure than Will, she finds herself less physically attracted to him than when she had last seen him, and she refuses to allow him to stay with her for the length of his visit. The story's title hinges upon the banality of her mother's observation about the "pretty ice" that remains from a winter storm. Underlying that harmless platitude is the chill of Belle's own reception of her fiancé and the knowledge that, despite the suicide of her own father and a strained relationship with her mother, she is beginning, even in her mid-thirties, to make sense of her own life.

Romero, Danny. "The Alley" (1993). From *Join In: Multiethnic Short Stories* (Ed. Donald R. Gallo, 1993). CRIME/LAW; ENTROPY/ CHAOS; FAMILY; HISPANIC EXPERIENCE; JUSTICE; LITER-ACY/WRITING.

When Cesar hears a woman scream for help after her purse has been snatched, he follows the culprit. During the chase, Cesar, who carries with him a copy of George Orwell's *1984*, a novel that one of his mentors had suggested to him, recalls his many visits to the alleys through which the two boys are now running. Because he had been forced to go to school in a new *barrio*, he "walked a thin line between drugs, gangs, and the law." Now, though, he was doing the right thing, trying to protect society from the scenes of chaos and disintegration that he was reading about in Orwell's book.

When he catches the thief and bloodies his face, he recognizes the boy as his own cousin. Because of a family dispute, he had never met the boy, though the two had acknowledged each other at a family funeral several years before. The look in the boy's eyes is like that of many junkies that Cesar has seen in the streets. As he grabs the purse from the boy's hand and watches him run away, he hopes that the incident will protect his cousin from the fate that, Cesar is sure from his own experience, awaits the boy.

Romero's story is both hopeful and tragic as he shows the two alternatives that boys like Cesar and his cousin have in the *barrio*. Though Cesar was involved with a gang several years before, he has committed himself, with the help of his English teacher, to finding a way out. Romero writes from personal experience and delivers his message through vivid detail, digression, and a limited omniscient narrator that tracks Cesar's thoughts as he runs through the alleys of his boyhood with a fresh outlook on life.

Rosenblatt, Benjamin. "Zelig" (1915). From *Modern American Short Stories* (Ed. Edward J. O'Brien, 1932). ASSIMILATION; DEATH; EXILE/EMIGRATION; FAMILY; GIFTS/GENEROSITY.

Zelig is a bitter old man shunned by his neighbors. Though his only son, a widower, has immigrated to America with his own son in tow, Zelig and his wife remain in Russia. When a note arrives informing Zelig that his son is ill, he travels to America to be with him—but only until he is able to save enough money to travel back to the Old World. Every waking moment is spent figuring out how long he will have to work in order to leave America.

Even in his new country, the old man has a reputation for caring little about what people think. In the shop where he works, the men mock him. When he is called home one day because his son has had a seizure, Zelig begrudges him the money for medical help and that night, he dies. When Zelig's wife suggests that their grandson will soon need money for college, Zelig is incensed. He thinks long and hard about what he should do, and he goes into his grandson's bedroom to render the decision. Though he knows that the boy sees him as an enemy, Zelig decides to give him the money for college.

Rosenblatt's story explores the many different themes that arise when people are removed from their native lands and forced into situations with which they are unfamiliar. In this case, despite his longing for the Old World, Zelig sacrifices the one dream that has meaning for him for the good of his only grandson. Family, in this case, is stronger than tradition.

Roth, Philip. "The Conversion of the Jews" (1959). From *The Norton Anthology of Short Fiction*, 6th ed. (Ed. R.V. Cassill and Richard Bausch, 2000). COMING-OF-AGE; HUMOR/SATIRE/IRONY; IDEN-TITY; RELIGION/SPIRITUALITY; SOCIETY.

Ozzie Freedman and his best friend, Itzie, argue with each other because Ozzie mentions Jesus Christ during their Hebrew class. Ozzie mimics Rabbi Binder's comments on Jesus's role as a historical figure who "lived like you and me." On three previous occasions, Mrs. Freedman has been called into conference with the rabbi, who teaches that Mary could only have gotten pregnant through intercourse. The rabbi, who has no satisfactory answers for the boy, threatens to stop Ozzie's bar mitzvah if he can help it, and Ozzie's mother, who is raising the boy by herself after the death of her husband, slaps Ozzie for the first time in his life when he tells her about his confrontation with the rabbi.

During a discussion in school the next week, Ozzie is forced to speak his mind. In doing so, the rabbi chases the boy onto the roof of the building.

Firemen wait on the ground below, thinking he is going to jump. All Ozzie wants is to be assured that he will never be hit again and that he is right in saying that God can make anything he wants.

The strength of this story relies on Roth's giving a young boy the power of perception. Ozzie's innocent questions are heresy, though no one he knows can give him the answers he seeks. The author maintains his sense of humor throughout the story—as in the scene where the firemen with a safety net follow the boy's movement back and forth across the top of the building—which contrasts neatly with the seriousness of the questions involved.

Roth, Philip. "Defender of the Faith" (1960). From *The Best American Short Stories of the Century* (Ed. John Updike and Katrina Kenison, 1999). BETRAYAL; DECEPTION; DUTY; FRIENDSHIP; GUILT; HUMOR/SATIRE/IRONY; RELIGION/SPIRITUALITY; WAR.

Nathan Marx has been promoted to sergeant and discovers that three of his trainees are also Jewish. Not long after Marx's commission, Private Grossbart comes to Marx seeking the first of several favors—he wishes that an announcement be made so that he and the other two Jewish soldiers can attend Friday night *Shul* (church) instead of the GI barracks cleaning party. After Marx makes the announcement, Grossbart thinks that he has the sergeant eating out of his hand and requests similar treatment when it comes to food and a weekend pass, ostensibly to go to his aunt's house for a Passover dinner. Grossbart begs a pass for his two buddies, as well, and when the three bring Marx a Chinese egg roll, he is livid at the deception.

When Grossbart has his orders to go to the Pacific switched to New Jersey, Marx pulls some strings of his own and has the orders changed back to the Pacific. After a confrontation between Grossbart and Marx, the sergeant decides that he will not feel guilty over the decisions he has made; he is sure Grossbart will find someone in the Pacific to swindle and the three friends will be just fine.

Roth's study of duty, guilt, and deception has a darkly humorous edge that is evident in much of his fiction. Though Grossbart is a character who deserves little sympathy, it seems, the author reserves that judgment for the reader. The question of faith—prevalent in Roth's stories—manifests itself in Marx's defending the faith of three fellow Jews at the same time Grossbart questions that faith with his actions. Dialogue is key to the story.

Runyon, Damon. "Butch Minds the Baby" (1930). From *Great Short Stories of the World* (Sel. by the Editors of *Reader's Digest*, 1972). CRIME/LAW; DECEPTION; HUMOR/SATIRE/IRONY; ILLUSION v. REALITY.

The narrator sits in a restaurant eating gefilte fish when he gets a visit from three people from Brooklyn—Harry the Horse, Little Isadore, and

Spanish John. Harry has an order for the narrator: take them to Big Butch, the best safecracker in the area. When the men get to Butch's place, he is on the front porch with a baby next to him. Because of his duties with the baby, Butch turns down the men's offer; finally, they convince him to take the baby with him on the job.

When they arrive at the coal company that is their target, the baby begins to cry. Butch quiets the child and discovers that he cannot open the safe; he blows the lock off, and the explosion is louder than he had thought it would be. When they leave the building, the police have been dispatched. The three men who hired Butch get into a gunfight and eventually escape. Butch, who is stopped by the police, claims to be a doctor treating the child. He tells the policeman that the baby has colic, and the cop suggests that maybe the baby is teething. Butch tells the cop that he is right, that the baby is just cutting its first tooth.

Runyon uses what could potentially be a serious situation to point up the comic possibilities of taking a baby to a heist. The payoff—an exchange between police and the man who was brash and foolish enough to take a baby on a job—is the punch line to the joke that Runyon makes on the types of people he knew so well.

S

Saki (H.H. Munro). "The Background" (1911). From *Modern American and British Short Stories* (Ed. Leonard Brown, 1929). ART and the ARTIST; HUMOR/SATIRE/IRONY; SOCIETY.

Henri Deplis is born in Luxembourg and becomes a "commercial traveler." After obtaining a small legacy, he is tattooed by Signor Andreas Pincini, one of the great tattoo artists of all time, with a portrayal of the Fall of Icarus. When Deplis is unable to fully pay the bill for the artwork on his body, the artist's widow presents the work to the municipality of Bergamo. Deplis undergoes a series of indignations, including being barred from leaving Italy because he is carrying on his person an Italian work of art.

Distraught at his circumstances, Deplis drifts into undesirable circles and has acid poured on him by an Italian anarchist. The man is reprimanded for the attack on Deplis's person and given seven years in prison for the defacement of a national art treasure. Deplis is deported from Italy following his release from the hospital, and he wanders the streets of Paris believing he is one of the lost arms of the Venus de Milo.

This frame story, told about Deplis by a narrator who previously had mentioned his dissatisfaction with the pretense of the art world and its jargon, points up the absurdity of notions of art. Saki, like O. Henry, uses ironic plot twists to great effect.

Saki (H.H. Munro). "The Open Window" (1914). From *A World of Great Stories* (Ed. Hiram Haydn and John Cournos, 1947). COMMUNICATION/LANGUAGE; DECEPTION; HEALTH (SICKNESS/MEDICINE); HUMOR/SATIRE/IRONY; ILLUSION v. REALITY; MEN and WOMEN; TRUTH v. LYING.

Framton Nuttel is a young man in the country on a rest cure. He has been given letters of introduction by his sister, and as he waits in the sitting room of a country estate for the woman of the house to see him, he is entertained by the woman's niece, who explains to Nuttel why the large French window that looks out onto the lawn is open even in October. It seems that Mrs. Sappleton's husband and her two brothers were lost in a bog during a hunt three years to the day before Nuttel's arrival. The woman cannot bear to imagine them dead, so she leaves the window open in the hope that they will return.

When Mrs. Sappleton joins the two, she cannot talk of anything else but the imminent return of the men. Nuttel is at first touched by the pathetic scene, thinking the woman mad for believing that the men are not dead, and then horrified when the three hunters wander out of the mist and into the house. In his haste to leave the house, Nuttel is nearly hit by a cyclist.

The story is full of caustic wit—as it turns out, the tale that Mrs. Sappleton's niece tells Nuttel is entirely fabricated and intended solely to alarm the frail young man—and evokes the Victorian society in which such fantastic lies are met with the great good humor intended by the author and his ingénue, for whom "Romance at short notice was her specialty."

Saki (H.H. Munro). "The Storyteller" (1930). From *Great Short Stories* (Ed. Wilbur Schramm, 1950). COMMUNICATION/LANGUAGE; HUMOR/SATIRE/IRONY; ILLUSION v. REALITY; MEN and WOMEN.

On a railway carriage coming up on Templecombe, a bachelor watches an aunt who tries to control the three children at her side by telling them the most boring of stories. At the same time, the aunt keeps an eye on the bachelor, who she decides is not an amiable type. As the aunt comes to the end of her story with little success—the children ask questions that she is either unable or unwilling to answer—the bachelor muses aloud that the aunt is a failure at storytelling. She takes offense at the man's remark and challenges him to tell a story of his own. He obliges the woman with a story about a little girl who was so extraordinarily good that her goodness eventually got her killed. The children are enthralled by the story; the aunt thinks it wholly inappropriate. The bachelor responds that at any rate, he was able to keep the children quiet for a few minutes, which is more than he can say for her.

As Schramm points out, Saki is, above all, himself a storyteller who makes "no attempt to be philosophic or weighty." This short tale is a case in point. Still, he explores and explodes the pretenses of society with a razor-sharp wit that stays with the reader long after the story is over.

Saki (H.H. Munro). "The Toys of Peace" (1919). From *The Oxford Book of English Short Stories* (Ed. A.S. Byatt, 1998). CHILDHOOD; HUMOR/SATIRE/IRONY; ILLUSION v. REALITY; SOCIETY; WAR.

Eleanor Bope shows her brother, Harvey, a newspaper piece acceding that, though "'boys love fighting and all the panoply of war . . . that is no reason for encouraging, and perhaps giving permanent form to, their primitive instincts." Harvey wants to show his nephews that they can have fun playing with toys representing John Stuart Mill and Robert Raikes, two civil-minded individuals who have little to do with the war. When he suggests that the two young boys hold an election for Parliament and count the votes, they instead tell him that they had better study. Shunned, Harvey leaves the boys alone. When he hears them playing a while later, he realizes that they have turned the peaceful town into a battlefield. Harvey tells his sister that they have "begun too late" to indoctrinate the boys in the ways of peace.

The story's historical context, the horror and annihilation of World War I, sets the tone for Harvey's unexpected awakening. The boys' unwillingness to play with the "toys of peace" in the spirit that their uncle had intended suggests the essential warlike nature of man and, more importantly perhaps, the far-reaching influence of current events on the boys' lives. If they know only war, the author asks implicitly, how can they grow up to act otherwise? The lighthearted tone of the story—after all, boys will be boys—belies the serious theme that Saki explores here.

Salinger, J.D. "A Perfect Day for Bananafish" (1948). From *Franny and Zooey* (Salinger, 1948). ALIENATION/ISOLATION; COMMUNICATION/LANGUAGE; DEATH; ILLUSION v. REALITY; MEN and WOMEN; SELF-DESTRUCTION/SUICIDE; SOCIETY; WAR.
Seymour Glass has returned from the war, and his wife, Muriel, discusses his condition with her mother, as he has become alienated and withdrawn since his return. Seymour is unstable enough, apparently, that Muriel's mother expresses concern that he has been allowed to drive the car to Florida, where the two are staying on vacation; he has also asked Muriel to learn German, so that she can read the poems from a book that he sent her from Germany during his time there.

While Muriel and her mother are conversing, Seymour walks the beach. There he meets a young girl, Sybil, who allows him to push her out into the ocean on a raft. Seymour tells her the story of the bananafish, which is so greedy that it gorges itself on bananas that it finds in holes; the fish, he tells the girl, dies when it cannot get back out because of its size. When Seymour goes back to the hotel, he makes a scene in an elevator and returns to the hotel room, where he shoots himself as Muriel sleeps.

The story, on one level, clearly illustrates Seymour's alienation from society after his return from the war. Though he seems to connect with the child—and in many ways, Seymour is childlike—he cannot connect with the adults in his world, even the wife who has waited patiently for him to find himself. It is his search for the old identity, Salinger suggests, that prompts Seymour to commit suicide, the one act through which he can transcend the torpor of his life. The story contains overtones of Virginia Woolf's *Mrs. Dalloway*.

Salinger, J.D. "Pretty Mouth and Green My Eyes" (1951). From *An Anthology of Famous American Stories* (Ed. Angus Burrell and Bennett Cerf, 1963). COMMUNICATION/LANGUAGE; ILLUSION v. RE-

ALITY; LOVE; MARRIAGE; MEN and WOMEN; MORALITY (MO-
RAL DILEMMA); TRUTH v. LYING.

A gray-haired lawyer named Lee receives a phone call from a fellow lawyer, Arthur. It is late at night, and Arthur wonders if Lee knows the
whereabouts of his wife, Joanie. Lee's girlfriend, who is with him when he
receives the call, is curious to know what the conversation is about and stares
at him as he talks on the telephone. Arthur, who is drunk, suspects that his
wife is cheating on him. Lee tries to persuade Arthur that he should go to
bed and stop worrying about Joanie. As the conversation continues, Lee
motions to the girl to light a cigarette for him.

Arthur continues about a case he has recently lost and his fear that he will
lose his job and be conscripted in the army. His babbling deteriorates into
comments about how Joanie does not love him and that they have suffered
through a mismatched marriage, and he thinks of a poem he sent to his wife
that does not remind him of her anymore. When the two finally hang up,
Lee and his girlfriend talk the situation over. The phone rings again, and
Arthur tells Lee that Joanie has come home and that she was just out with
friends. When they hang up again, Lee drops his cigarette; when the girl
moves to pick it up, he tells her not to.

Salinger's story is a commentary on human nature, the imperfection of
relationships, and our essential inability to make clear to others what is obvious to us. Communication—or the lack of it—is at the heart of the story,
and the absence of concrete action only serves to remind us the extent to
which our relationships rely not on action, but on the spoken (or, in the
case of the poem that Arthur has written to his wife, written) word.

**Saroyan, William. "The Daring Young Man on the Flying Trapeze"
(1934). From *The Treasury of American Short Stories* (Sel. Nancy Sullivan, 1981). ART and the ARTIST; COMMUNICATION/LAN-
GUAGE; DREAMS (SLEEPING); ESCAPE; INTERIOR LIVES;
LABOR/JOB; POVERTY; SOCIETY.**

The protagonist has dreams that are not unlike those of most artists:
abstract, vivid imaginings of places read about interspersed with visions of
famous authors who have influenced him. "*It is only in sleep that we may
know how to live,*" the protagonist thinks to himself, every notion somehow
tied in to the events that surround him and the writing that he loves so
dearly.

The young man is unsuccessful in his search for a job, and when he finds
a penny on the street, he wants to write about it. He wonders how many
such coins he will need to keep himself alive in the city. The only time he
can find solace in his predicament, it seems, is when he sleeps, when his
body becomes insensate, and through his mind he can become all things at
once.

The story is divided into two sections, "Sleep" and "Wakefulness."

"Sleep," the first and shorter of the two, gives entrance into the mind of the young artist. The second details the clash between his passion and the reality of the work-a-day world. The protagonist resembles the later Beats and Bohemians who deprive themselves of a certain standard of living in order to suffer for their art. The title of Saroyan's story, drawn from a song popular earlier in the century, indicates the high-wire act that the young man undertakes every day in order to fulfill his dream of becoming a writer.

Sartre, Jean Paul. "The Wall" (1948). From *Great Short Stories from the World's Literature* **(Ed. Charles Neider, 1950). ALIENATION/ ISOLATION; DEATH; HUMOR/SATIRE/IRONY; INTERIOR LIVES; WAR.**

During the Spanish Civil War, three men are taken prisoner and summarily sentenced to be executed by firing squad the following morning. Pablo Ibbieta, who narrates the story, observes how the other two men react to their similar fate. One becomes talkative, and the other, a young man with his life before him, proclaims his innocence. Ibbieta recalls certain events from his own life and realizes that, even if he were given a reprieve, he could no longer enjoy life; in the face of death, the memories mean nothing to him.

The other two men are taken away to be executed, though Ibbieta is retained while his captors attempt to get information from him on Ramon Gris, a leader of the opposition. Ibbieta finally accedes, telling the men what he believes to be an utter lie. When, through a bizarre turn of events, the story happens to be true, Ibbieta is given a reprieve from execution. He can only laugh at the absurdity of the events that have brought him to these circumstances.

Sartre is justly admired for stories and essays that question the value of man's existence, and Ibbieta's story is a profound exploration of that weighty issue. The title implies the physical wall against which the men are to be shot, though more importantly for Ibbieta, the wall is a psychological barrier that no longer allows him to enjoy his life. His response, then, is perhaps the only viable one given his situation. For him to fully contemplate and comprehend his fate—be it by firing squad or a long life without meaning—would surely drive him to madness.

Schwartz, Delmore. "In Dreams Begin Responsibilities" (1937). From *The Treasury of American Short Stories* **(Sel. Nancy Sullivan, 1981). COMING-OF-AGE/INITIATION; DREAMS (of the FUTURE); DREAMS (SLEEPING); FAMILY; TIME (and ITS EFFECTS).**

The narrator dreams that he is in a theater watching the lives of his parents and his own life unfold before him. He observes his parents' courtship, the relatively passionless way his father proposes to his mother, and their subsequent trip to the photographer's studio and finally to a fortune-teller, whom the narrator's father does not want to visit. He acquiesces to his fiancé's request and enters, though he leaves angrily after a short time. During the "film," the narrator interjects his own opinions, calling for his parents not to take the step into marriage and finally being ushered out of the theater of his dream by one of the staff. When the narrator awakes, it is his twenty-first birthday, and the snow has come.

Until the final scene, the author's message is clear on only one level: The mother and father are married, against what is apparently even their own better judgment (with the photographer, they are despondent, even as they have their engagement photo taken). The story takes on new meaning with the disclosure that the narrator is celebrating the birthday that marks his initiation into adulthood. Perhaps he is not looking forward to leaving the safe haven of childhood and entering the world of adult "responsibilities." That he awakens to this new life on a "bleak winter morning" suggests he will have much difficulty adapting to the life that he imagines has changed overnight.

Sebestyen, Ouida. "After the Wedding" (1989). From *Connections: Short Stories by Outstanding Writers for Young Adults* (Ed. Donald R. Gallo, 1989). BETRAYAL; COMING-OF-AGE; IDENTITY; LOSS; LOVE; MEN and WOMEN; WOMEN'S ISSUES.

Rusty and Jolene return to Galenburg for the wedding of Rusty's sister, which allows Jolene the opportunity to reassess her own relationship with Rusty. Jolene, who came from a broken home, lived with one family member after the next until she met Rusty one night at a Suds and Duds in Dallas. In that way, "he came into her life. Like some new wonder drug that might deaden her pain." The relationship progressed, and the two moved in together, she wholly dependent upon him until the day of his sister's wedding. After the wedding, while Jolene helps Rusty's mother clean up, he goes back to the house to sleep. Jolene, who was first drawn to Rusty by his physicality, wonders why he has left her with people she does not know. Instead of discussing the situation, he tells her that he is taking her to the Red Mill, the town's fanciest restaurant. While there, the two can discuss their relationship only in the vaguest terms; their inability to express their emotions or to make sense of the reasons why they are together results in a confrontation. Rusty stalks out, and Jolene, alone again in a sea of strangers who have been watching their fight, retains as much dignity as possible in walking out of the Red Mill.

After their confrontation in the restaurant, Rusty tells Jolene that he does not want to be with her anymore, and "She clung to his hand, knowing they were joined in the most passionate moment they had known together."

The story's title implies not only the events that occur in the present, with Jolene and Rusty awkwardly pondering their future, but the period "after the wedding," when the glimmer of infinite possibility has worn away and two people are forced to be malleable to each other's wants and needs. Rusty's most selfless act in the five months that they have been together is to free Jolene from the bleak future that awaits him, as a "Big fish in a little pond." He realizes her potential, though she is too needy for attention— any attention, it seems—to make a clean break from Rusty.

Seuss, Dr. *How the Grinch Stole Christmas* (1957). CHILDHOOD; DECEPTION; FANTASY/IMAGINATION/SCIENCE FICTION; HUMOR/SATIRE/IRONY; LOVE/HATE; MORALITY (MORAL DILEMMA).

The Whos love Christmas, but the Grinch, who lives on a mountain to the north of town, despises the holiday and everything it stands for. On Christmas Eve, he stares down at Whoville and devises a plan to stop Christmas from coming, a way to quell the happiness—and, most of all, the noise of good cheer and singing—that is palpable in the town.

He dresses as "Santy Claus," ties a horn to his dog, Max, to disguise him as a reindeer, and wreaks havoc on the Whos' plans for another glorious Christmas. When he is caught in the act by a tiny Who girl who wants to know why he is taking the tree, he tells her that the light is broken and that he is going to fix it. When he returns home secure in the notion that he has ruined Christmas for the whole town, he hears the sound of singing. At first, he is upset that his plan was foiled. When he realizes, however, that Christmas is not a material thing, his heart "grew three sizes that day." He brings back the toys and food, and as the guest of honor, he is invited to "carve the roast beast."

The most popular of Dr. Seuss's stories is a testament to the spirit of Christmas, not to the materialism that has come to be associated with the holiday. Though the author's message is a simple one, the story remains relevant even today.

Sharmat, Marjorie Weinman. "Dream Job" (1987). From *Visions* (Ed. Donald R. Gallo, 1987). DREAMS (of the FUTURE); DREAMS (SLEEPING); ILLUSION v. REALITY; LABOR/JOB.

Though she aspires to a life as a professional writer, Becky is content for a time to take a job as a $6.25-an-hour receptionist at Garth Publishing Company. Her winning smile makes her a natural for the job, but a few days later, she has a run-in with Raunchy Ezra Moore—REM—the company's irascible, eccentric best-selling author who has little creative talent.

In a panic to quit her job and leave the office, she hails a taxi, only to find that the cab driver is a woman with REM's features and the same initials. It occurs to Becky that she is in a dream—after all, everyone in the dream has the initials REM, an acronym for "rapid eye movement," the dream phase of sleep—and she hopes that her boss will wake her from the dream before people with the initials REM overwhelm her. As she waits for her boss to wake her, she muses on how difficult it is to be a sixteen-year-old girl with acne and frizzy red hair, the same characteristics that she gives to Raunchy Moore in her dream.

The story has overtones of James Thurber's "The Secret Life of Walter Mitty," which details the imaginary life of a man who is destined for greater things than the world has offered him. Becky (we find out her full name is Rebecca Eloise Montgomery—REM), though, is comfortable with her vivid imagination and looks forward to a day when she will be valued for more than her winning smile.

Shaw, Irwin. "The Eighty-Yard Run" (1941). From *The Norton Anthology of Short Fiction*, 6th ed. (Ed. R.V. Cassill and Richard Bausch, 2000). AGING; ALIENATION/ISOLATION; DREAMS (of the FUTURE); IDENTITY; INTERIOR LIVES; MEN and WOMEN; SPORTS.

During his days on the gridiron as a running back at a Midwestern university, Christian Darling broke an eighty-yard run in practice. Now, he stands on the field and thinks about the turns for the worse that his life has since taken. He married his college sweetheart, Louise Tucker, and worked for her father, the successful owner of an ink company. Louise was involved in the society life and the young couple was on the rise until the Great Depression.

Louise continues to pursue her own interests, meeting artists and intellectuals; Darling, who is out of work, begins drinking and further separating himself from her. He takes a job that requires him to travel, and Louise does not object. By the time he stands on the field and awkwardly reenacts that run from his youth, the two tolerate each other, though the relationship is essentially over. Darling thinks that he could have done things differently, but he did not stop to consider a time when two college kids would become adults with different needs and responsibilities. Now, the college kids who bemusedly watch the man in a suit running into the end zone can only imagine his reasons for doing such a thing.

As with much short fiction of the Lost Generation—Fitzgerald and Hemingway, for instance—Shaw explores the disillusionment and regret that often accompany a midlife reassessment of one's priorities. While Darling is not responsible for the Great Depression, he is culpable for not foreseeing a time in his life when he would need more than the memory of an eighty-yard run all those years before to sustain his relationship with his wife. By portraying Darling as a sweating, sheepish middle-aged man at the end of the story, Shaw illustrates the impossibility of recapturing one's youth, no matter how grand the memories.

Shaw, Irwin. "The Girls in Their Summer Dresses" (1939). From *Fiction 100: An Anthology of Short Stories*, 9th ed. (Ed. James H. Pickering,

2000). DECEPTION; JEALOUSY; MEN and WOMEN; SEXUAL-
ITY; TRUTH v. LYING; WOMEN'S ISSUES.

As Michael and Frances Loomis walk the streets of Manhattan, Frances
notices that her husband is intent on watching the pretty girls who walk by.
It is not the first time she has noticed his wandering eye, though she makes
light of the fact in a comment to him that suggests she does not condemn
him for his actions. They make plans for an eventful weekend—dinner, a
movie, the Giants game. When she catches Michael's eye wandering yet
again, however, the conversation about their relationship and Michael's happiness with his wife becomes more earnest.

When the two go for an early drink, Michael becomes effusive and admits
that he would like at times to be unfettered by his wife. Frances asks that
they end the conversation. After another round of drinks, their third, they
decide to spend the weekend with friends. As Frances walks to the pay phone
to call them, Michael thinks, "What a pretty girl, what nice legs."

As with much of Shaw's short fiction, the theme of aging with grace
comes to the fore. Frances, a contented wife with seemingly little interest
in activities outside her marriage to Michael, is distraught at the notion that
he desires to be with other women. Michael, not unlike the protagonist of
Shaw's "The Eighty-Yard Run," whose nostalgia for his college days clouds
his judgment and seems ridiculous to the couple that witnesses him recre-
ating his famous run, uses his observations to hide in a realm of fantasy
instead of admitting that he is at an age where such actions are destructive
in a relationship.

Silko, Leslie Marmon. "The Man to Send Rain Clouds" (1969). From
The Lightning Within: An Anthology of Contemporary American Indian
Fiction **(Ed. Alan R. Velie, 1991). AGING; DEATH; FAMILY; NA-**
TURE/WILDERNESS; RELIGION/SPIRITUALITY; SUPERSTI-
TION.

Leon and Ken, looking for their missing grandfather, find him dead under
a cotton tree. The two wrap him in a blanket after first painting his face and
tying a feather in his hair. As they take him home, they meet a local Christian
preacher who asks them if they were successful in locating their grandfather.
They tell him that they were, but they do not tell him that the man is dead.

When they arrive home, the grandfather is readied for burial. Though
customs such as the sprinkling of corn and medicine bags are followed,
Louise thinks that the old man should be sprinkled with holy water, so that
he "won't be thirsty." Leon asks the priest to help them. At first, the man
is hesitant; he agrees, however, and the image of the holy water recalls
August rain falling on wilted squash flowers. The priest leaves, and Teofilo's
family is glad that their grandfather received a decent burial and can now
bring them rain clouds.

Silko combines the tenets of two religions and cultures into the old man's funeral. That exploration of different points of view is prevalent in the author's work (both the short fiction and her novels) as her Native American characters assimilate to a society that, through the encroachment of European civilization into the "New World," little understands the knowledge of and respect for nature upon which that culture bases its religion. Still, Louise is able to transform a ritual as simple as the sprinkling of holy water into a spiritual event that mirrors the relationship between man and nature.

Silko, Leslie Marmon. "Yellow Woman" (1974). From *The Story and Its Writer*, 4th ed. (Ed. Ann Charters, 1995). ALLEGORY/LEGEND/FABLE; ESCAPE; FAMILY; ILLUSION v. REALITY; SEXUALITY; SUPERSTITION.

A man named Silva has a brief affair with a Pueblo woman who has left her family to follow her dream. When she tells the man that she is returning to her family, he does not allow her to go; rather, he invokes an old Indian tale about the ka'tsina spirit and Yellow Woman. She is Yellow Woman, he tells her, and he is the ka'tsina who offers her a life of passion and adventure. The woman joins Silva in his home, and they settle into the routines of domesticity.

One day, the woman discovers that Silva is a cattle rustler. On their way to sell the meat, they are confronted by a rancher who accuses Silva of the act, and Silva shoots him. Despite her desire to return to the life that she and Silva had briefly shared, she returns to her own home. She tells her family that she was kidnapped and relates to them the story of Yellow Woman.

Silko's story works on several levels. The tale of Yellow Woman and the ka'tsina is a self-contained narrative that is framed by intimations of a family life that the woman has left behind. The woman's return home at the end of the story suggests both the mythical quality of the Yellow Woman's adventure and the reality of her home life. Still, Silko suggests, the woman's quest and her infidelity with Silva will be treated as a spiritual event that will little affect her relationship with her family.

Sillitoe, Alan. "The Loneliness of the Long-Distance Runner" (1959). From *Collected Stories* (Sillitoe, 1995). COMING-OF-AGE; CONTESTS; INDIVIDUAL; INTERIOR LIVES; SOCIETY; SPORTS.

In Borstal, a reformatory school in England, Smith has been chosen to represent the institution in a long-distance race. He runs the five-mile course each morning with increasing ease, and the exercise allows him to open his mind for thought. During the runs, he outlines an individual philosophy that eschews the conformist attitudes that are preached to him at the school: He is an "Out-law" in a world of "In-laws."

Though winning the Borstal Blue Ribbon would allow him many opportunities in a society that is currently closed to him, Smith remains

254 Singer, Isaac Bashevis

adamantly against joining in. During the race, he has a comfortable lead on the second-place runner; a hundred yards from the finish line, he slows to a walk and finishes second. His impetuous behavior prompts the school's governor to punish the young man with the most menial tasks. As he does the chores, he considers what he will do when he is released in six months. He knows he will not become part of society.

Sillitoe's story presents a definition of "honesty" that is alien to many readers. Smith truly believes that if he is true to himself—that is, if he does not give in to the demands of the governor and society in general—then he has succeeded in asserting himself as in individual. Clearly, he succeeds in following through with his own agenda; whether his self-sacrifice is worth the price he pays (and will pay in the future) is in question. The story's title has become synonymous with the individual striving, alone and at odds with society, to reach a goal.

Singer, Isaac Bashevis. "Gimpel the Fool" (1953). From *The Harper Anthology of Fiction* (Ed. Sylvan Barnet, 1991). DECEPTION; GOOD/EVIL; MEN and WOMEN; RELIGION/SPIRITUALITY; SOCIETY.

For all his life, Gimpel has been known as a fool. He relates that, early in life, he decided to believe everything he heard in order to avoid being harassed for his reactions to people's jokes. Later, when he approaches the rabbi with his problem, the rabbi tells him that it is others who are the fools, not Gimpel. When he marries Elka, Gimpel becomes even more foolish. Elka will not consummate their relationship—in fact, she forces him to sleep in the bakery where he works—and she cuckolds him for each of their six children. Gimpel, in his simple goodness, decides to believe Elka when she tells him that the children are his. On her deathbed, however, she tells Gimpel the truth. When the Spirit of Evil visits him and tells him to urinate in the dough that will be eaten by the townspeople, he dreams of Elka, who tells him not to give in to the temptation to be like others. Gimpel, who takes the dream seriously, gives away his possessions and wanders the world.

Clearly, Gimpel is a good man who is abused by a society that scorns such people for the traits they lack. By not changing his attitude, Gimpel becomes a venerated man, a true believer in every sense. His "foolishness" is born not of naïveté or ignorance, but of his heart's goodness. By portraying the happiness of such a man, Singer implies the triumph of a good and simple soul over the lies and deceit that may work in this life, but are meaningless in the next.

Singer, Isaac Bashevis. "The Spinoza of Market Street" (1961). From *The Norton Anthology of Short Fiction* (Ed. R.V. Cassill, 1978). AGING; ALIENATION/ISOLATION; ENTROPY/CHAOS; LOVE; MEN and WOMEN.

Dr. Nahum Fischelson is the "Spinoza of Market Street," a man so intent on reading and living the work of seventeenth-century Dutch philosopher Benedict de Spinoza that he neglects the world around him, except to fulminate on the chaos and worldly passions that boil below him on the streets of Warsaw as he attempts to live his life according to Spinoza's dicta. Several events in his life have alienated him from society, though none more than the Revolution of 1905, and now the onset of World War I. Fischelson withdraws further into his philosophical existence, and he is convinced that he is dying.

One day, Black Dobbe, a woman who lives next door, asks Fischelson to read a letter for her. The old man is in ill health, though when Black Dobbe takes care of him, he begins to feel like living again. The woman, much like Fischelson, is alienated from society by her ugliness and her lack of prospects. Still, when the two make love on their wedding night, Fischelson revels in the passions that he had previously denied himself.

Singer's story is one of dichotomies: Fischelson's world is defined by rationality and control, Black Dobbe's by passion and a focus on day-to-day living; Black Dobbe, even in her unattractiveness to others, allows Fischelson to experience a passion that he had not known before. The author also suggests that the life of the mind is an admirable goal, though not at the expense of life's other great pleasures, especially love.

Smiley, Jane. "Long Distance" (1987). From *The Story and Its Writer*, 4th ed. (Ed. Ann Charters, 1995). ASSIMILATION; CULTURE CONFLICTS; DUTY; FAMILY; INTERIOR LIVES; MEN and WOMEN; POLITICS; SIBLINGS.

When Kirby Christianson receives a call from Meiko, his Japanese girlfriend, telling him that she will not be able to visit him over the holiday, he is relieved. He wonders whether she would have been able to assimilate to American culture (a fact that is borne out by her weeping ashamedly on the phone while Kirby listens, something that a Japanese man would never do). Instead, Kirby travels alone to his brother Harold's home in Minnesota for the family Christmas. As he drives through a snowstorm, he imagines that he is killed in an accident, and he wonders how Meiko would ever find out.

Kirby's relationship with his brothers is tenuous at best, and when Eric, a conservative who readily expresses his opinions, is baited into one of his political diatribes by Kirby, the situation only worsens. Later, when Kirby is unable to sleep, he finds Leanne, the wife of his brother Harold, alone downstairs. He tells her about his relationship with Meiko in an effort to absolve himself of the guilt that he feels. Leanne, who refuses to take sides in the sibling battle, kisses him on the cheek as he goes back to bed.

The title of the story works on several levels. Kirby is separated from Meiko by geographical distance and the differences in their two cultures, and he is estranged from his brothers, especially Eric, by the differences in their views. Perhaps most importantly, the title implies the lengths to which Kirby must go in order to reconcile his own life—and the unsatisfying relationships that characterize it—with a nebulous future. Meiko seems to be the perfect partner for Kirby, though he cannot bring himself to make the commitment that both Harold and Eric have in their own lives.

Sontag, Susan. "The Way We Live Now" (1986). From *The Story and Its Writer*, 4th ed. (Ed. Ann Charters, 1995). DEATH; FRIENDSHIP; HEALTH (SICKNESS/MEDICINE); SOCIETY.

After months of putting off the blood test that would cement his fate, Max is diagnosed with AIDS. His friends are unsure how to react to the news. One attempts to find out as much as he can about the disease in order to help his friend fight it; another comforts him by bringing him chocolates; still another wonders why Max had put himself at risk for the disease. All of them are concerned that they might catch it themselves. In a scene that now has become familiar, Max contemplates his fate, sometimes accepting what has befallen him, sometimes fighting as if he may just survive. His friends' ambivalence continues to the end of the story. Max, one friend points out, is still alive after all. That counts for something.

Sontag's story was published while the AIDS epidemic was still in its infancy, and the various reactions of Max's friends clearly illustrate the much different ways that people handled what was to become one of the most prevalent and pressing issues in our society in the fifteen years since. Sontag's view of those reactions is not didactic; instead, she presents the myriad possible responses to the situation and attempts to come to terms with a disease about which so little was understood that living itself was easily seen as little more than preparation for an untimely death. The title suggests what has become clear in the intervening years since the story's publication: We must accept the disease's presence as a fact of life, as the way we live now.

Soto, Gary. "The No-Guitar Blues" (1990). From *Help Wanted: Short Stories about Young People Working* (Sel. Anita Silvey, 1997). HISPANIC EXPERIENCE; MORALITY (MORAL DILEMMA); MUSIC; NATIONALISM/AMERICAN DREAM.

From the moment Fausto sees the rock band Los Lobos on *American Bandstand*, he wants to be a guitarist. Unfortunately, he does not have the money to buy himself a new guitar; his mother tells him that he may get one for Christmas, though she is not sure that the family will be able to afford it.

Much to his delight, Fausto finds a stray dog, which he plans to deliver to its owner six blocks away and collect a reward. He knows there will be one, especially when he lies and tells the man that he found the dog dangerously close to a heavily traveled road. The owner does, in fact, give Fausto twenty dollars for finding his beloved pet. The young man, overcome by guilt at his lie, decides not to buy the guitar after all. Instead, he places the money in the donation basket at church. When Fausto returns home, sure that he will never have a guitar, his mother tells him that she found one the last time she cleaned out her father's garage. Fausto is delighted, and his grandfather begins to teach him how to play. He's sure that one day he too will be on *American Bandstand.*

Fausto's guilt and the subsequent fulfillment of his dream to own a guitar suggest that one can do the right thing and still reach the desired goal. Soto uses Fausto's determination to live the American Dream as a backdrop against which he can explore right and wrong in a society where the answers to such questions are very often nebulous.

Stafford, Jean. "A Country Love Story" (1950). From *Great Short Stories of the World* (Sel. by the Editors of *Reader's Digest,* 1972). AGING; HEALTH (SICKNESS/MEDICINE); ILLUSION v. REALITY; MARRIAGE; MEN and WOMEN; WOMEN'S ISSUES.

When Daniel, an academician, returns to his younger wife, May, after a year spent recuperating from a lengthy illness in a sanitarium, their relationship has changed subtly but irrevocably. As the seasons change, the couple's mood changes with them. They become distant from one another, Daniel working on his research and May creating in her mind a lover who takes shape in the rusting sleigh that sits in the couple's yard. With the psychic distance between the two comes the realization for May that the relationship is not what she thought it would be. Daniel goes so far as to suggest that she could use some relaxing herself. The time away has sharpened Daniel's sense of mortality, and May begins to take refuge in her imaginary lover. Unwittingly, she has been trapped in a loveless marriage.

The primary image set forth in Stafford's title is the implication of a relationship well outside the confines of society that is allowed to flourish in the open air of the country. Instead, what awaits May upon Daniel's return is a stifling marriage that has as its backdrop the imminent mortality of the older man and the responsibility of the younger woman to care for him. By creating a lover in her mind, May has acceded to Daniel's fears that she had an affair while he was away; since that lover is imaginary, however, neither of them are satisfied, either physically or spiritually.

Steinbeck, John. "The Chrysanthemums" (1937). From *The Heath Introduction to Fiction,* 4th ed. (Ed. John J. Clayton, 1992). BETRAYAL; IDENTITY; INTERIOR LIVES; MEN and WOMEN; PLACE; SOCIETY; WOMEN'S ISSUES.

Elisa Allen, a woman who has "planting hands," a knack for growing things, gains great satisfaction from cultivating the best and biggest chrysanthemums in the Salinas Valley. One day as she tends her garden, she is visited by a man in a covered wagon who travels California year-round sharpening tools and mending pots and pans. During their meeting, the man ingratiates himself to Elisa by asking her if she will give him some seeds. Her conversation with him builds her up: they talk about the independence of the road, and the connection that they both have to the land.

When Elisa readies herself for a special dinner with her husband, she takes care to look her best. Her husband comments on his wife's appearance, and she does not know how to react. The visit with the traveling man has given her contradictory feelings about how she should view herself. As they drive toward town, Elisa sees something in the road, and she knows immediately that the man has thrown out the seeds that she gave him and kept the pot. Her husband, nonplused by her capricious responses to him, acquiesces when she asks if they will have wine for dinner. She turns away from him and cries weakly.

Steinbeck's story is one of discovery and betrayal. The man who uses Elisa's interests for his own gain has no idea of the hurt that he has caused her. For her part, Elisa, who just minutes before thought herself stronger than she could ever be, now will be satisfied simply to have wine with dinner. The flowers are a symbol of the woman's own identity and the ambivalence that she has toward fully exploring that identity when it is called into question by the journeyman's actions.

Steinbeck, John. "The Leader of the People" (1938). From *Great Short Stories* (Ed. Wilbur Schramm, 1950). AGING; COURAGE; FAMILY; FATHERS and CHILDREN; HISTORY; SOCIETY.

Jody Tiflin, the son of practical ranch owner Carl Tiflin, looks forward to his grandfather's visits because he can hear again and again how his grandfather heroically led a band of people across the country to the West Coast. Carl does not share the same enthusiasm for the old man's stories; having heard his father-in-law's tales more often than he cares to count, the farmer decides that he has better things to do with his time.

Carl's wife asks him to be patient with the old man—who considers himself a leader of the people. After all, he has very little left in life except those memories. When the old man overhears a conversation between the two, however, he understands that there is little place for him in a society that values the here-and-now over the reminiscences of an old man who wonders what the world is coming to when his grandson can spend all day hunting mice in a haystack. He bemoans the fact that there are no new places to explore, that "westering has died out of the people."

Steinbeck's strength in his short fiction is his humanity—the ability to objectively present situations in such a way as to force the reader to explore both sides of a predicament. While the grandfather is clearly a character deserving of the reader's sympathy in this story, his son-in-law is caught in a situation that finds him disregarding nostalgia with the hope of forging ahead. The end of the story suggests a reconciliation, but the questions that the author asks remain for the reader to discuss.

Stevenson, Robert Louis. "The Bottle Imp" (1893). From _The Long-man Anthology of Short Fiction: Masterpieces of Short Fiction_ (Ed. Dana Gioia and R.S. Gwynn, 2001). ALLEGORY/LEGEND/FABLE; GOOD and EVIL; LOVE; MAGIC/OCCULT; MEN and WOMEN.
Keawe purchases a bottle that contains an imp who can make the possessor's wildest dreams come true. The one stipulation attached to ownership of the bottle is that one must always sell it for less than the purchase price—and if the owner dies with the bottle in his possession, he will burn in hell. When Keawe is forced to buy the bottle back from its owner for a penny in order to cure his leprosy (and so he can marry the woman of his dreams), he believes that the love of his life has come at the price of his soul. Kokua, his wife, however, tells him that he can sell the bottle for less than a penny, if they travel to Tahiti, where the centime (one-fifth of a penny) is in circulation. Keawe, after realizing that his wife has purchased the bottle and is risking her own soul, is able to sell it to a profane man who accepts eternal damnation, as he assumes he will be going to hell anyway when he dies.

With a moral that suggests O. Henry's "Gift of the Magi," Stevenson explores the depths of sacrifice and love. Though the outcome of the story is in doubt until the boatswain's revelation at the conclusion, Stevenson uses a traditional fairy tale plot structure to present his updated story of love at all costs—and the subsequent "happy ending"—that makes the story more enjoyable for its readers, who sympathize with Keawe's predicament.

Stevenson, Robert Louis. "Markheim" (1885). From _The Short Stories of Robert Louis Stevenson_ (Stevenson, 1930). CRIME/LAW; DEATH; GOOD and EVIL; SUPERNATURAL/HORROR.
Markheim comes to a dealer of fine goods ostensibly to find a Christmas gift for a lady. The dealer, who has had transactions with Markheim before (the author later implies that Markheim has sold him stolen property), senses something odd in the man, who is angry when the dealer suggests buying a mirror for the lady. In a fit of rage that he is unable to control—"many different emotions were depicted together on his face—terror, horror, and resolve, fascination and a physical repulsion"—Markheim stabs the dealer and is left to wonder what to do with the body. His motive for killing the dealer is revealed: Markheim goes upstairs to the dealer's apartment to find the key to a safe-box.

Markheim is a man outside time after he commits the murder, and the murderer's personality is complex and contradictory; Stevenson's description of the passing of time and Markheim's essential incomprehension of what he has done sets the tone for the dialogue to follow between Markheim and the spirit who would take his soul. Despite his inclination toward evil—and the spirit's subtle insistence that Markheim could satisfy the pleasure that he seeks by allowing the spirit to help him—Markheim is able to exercise his free will when he confronts the dealer's maid and tells her that she should contact the police so that he may be held accountable for his action.

Time and masks are important to the story. Stevenson's psychological study, including Markheim's reaction immediately after he has killed the dealer and a brief flashback to a fair in a fishers' village where the young Markheim saw pictures of murderers and their victims, is reminiscent of many of Poe's analyses of the darker side of human nature.

Stockton, Frank. "The Lady or the Tiger?" (1882). From *A Book of the Short Story* (Ed. E.A. Cross, 1934). ALLEGORY/LEGEND/FABLE; DEATH; FATE; JEALOUSY; LOVE; MEN and WOMEN.

In times of old, there lived a king who was so interested in the vagaries of fate that he designed an ingenious method of testing guilt and innocence: he placed the offending party in an arena and, with the multitude looking on, that person chose one of two doors; from one would come a famished tiger, and from the other a beautiful woman, who would be wed to the man on the spot. The outcome, declared the king, was left entirely to fate and chance, and was irrevocable.

When he discovers that his daughter has fallen in love with a man of low birth, the king places him in the arena. Either way, he knows, he will rid himself of the princess's suitor. If he chooses the door that hides the tiger, the man will be devoured; if he chooses the door that conceals the maiden, he will marry her. The young man knows that his lover will be privy to the fate that awaits him; he also assumes that she will direct him to the door that will allow him to marry her. Indeed, she signals that he should choose the door on the right. He does so without hesitation.

The author asks one simple question. Knowing human nature, to which fate did the princess direct her suitor? The lady or the tiger? The story is an exploration of the nature of jealousy and fate. By leaving the ending undetermined, Stockton forces the reader to consider the two much different outcomes.

Strasser, Todd. "On the Bridge" (1987). From *Visions* (Ed. Donald R. Gallo, 1987). ALIENATION/ISOLATION; BETRAYAL; COMING-OF-AGE; EPIPHANY; FRIENDSHIP; INTERIOR LIVES; VIOLENCE.

Adam Lockwood is something of an idol for the young Seth Dawson. As the two boys stand on a bridge overlooking the highway, Adam tells his young protégé of his exploits the day before in the mall, in which Adam beat up an older, bigger boy. Seth, who is smoking his first cigarette, draws the smoke into his mouth and holds it there; Adam looks as though he is inhaling deeply and then blowing the smoke out through his nose. Seth is put off, however, by Adam's actions on the bridge, when he feigns throwing a rock down on an old woman's car, and the woman nearly swerves off the road.

Adam flicks a cigarette onto the windshield of a passing Camaro, and the three occupants, much bigger than either of the boys, stop the car. Adam accuses Seth of the deed, and Seth is thrown against the car's windshield. Though nothing is broken, his denim jacket—a sure sign of coolness when he hangs out with Adam—has blood on it. Instead of wearing the jacket with his friends and claiming that the blood was spilled by his enemies, Seth throws it into the garbage. He sees Adam's pose for what it is, and he is disgusted.

Strasser's story is a coming-of-age in which Seth, who is wholly innocent of the actions of which he is accused, is nonetheless indoctrinated into the world that Adam claims to inhabit. When Seth realizes the reality, though, Adam's stance is no longer fashionable. By throwing away the coat, Seth is turning away from Adam and everything that he stands for.

Strindberg, August. "A Funeral" (1915). From *Great Stories of All Nations* (Ed. Maxim Lieber and Blanche Colton Williams, 1945). ALIENATION/ISOLATION; BETRAYAL; DEATH; MEN and WOMEN; MOTHERS and CHILDREN; SOCIETY.

On a snowy November afternoon, the men sit in a tavern and curse the bell that begins tolling for one of the town's newly deceased, a clerk. Outside, the dead man's mother and two sisters follow the coffin to the graveyard; none of his coworkers have joined the procession. The taverners become garrulous and talk about the relative worth of the clerk in society. As the conversation deepens, the clerk's story comes out in full: When he apprised his mother and sisters of the fact that he was considering marriage, they turned bitter toward him; likewise, his fiancé had little time for the man's family.

The man "'was torn in two, piece by piece; he never married. But now he lies at rest, if the coffin nails hold; but it was a sad business for him, poor devil, even if he was a fool." Still, when his mother and his lover, who both vied for the clerk's attention—and money—meet at the funeral, they at first seem ready for another confrontation, and then they embrace. The men in the tavern who witness the sight through the window break down in sobs at the sight. The consensus is that the young clerk was stupid but sincere.

Strindberg's story is a straightforward tale of jealousy and greed that is reconciled by the prospect of death. Even though his mother and his fiancé fight for the man while he is alive, they realize the pettiness of their animosity after his death; of course, by then, it is too late to make recompense.

The introduction of a pewterer at the end of the story—the man leaves the tavern intent upon helping the clerk's family—adds a hopeful tone to the proceedings, even though the men agree that it will not help the clerk, who lies buried.

T

Tan, Amy. "Two Kinds" (1989). From *The Story and Its Writer*, 4th ed. (Ed. Ann Charters, 1995). ASSIMILATION; COMMUNICATION/LANGUAGE; CULTURE CONFLICTS; GUILT; MOTHERS and CHILDREN; MUSIC; NATIONALISM/AMERICAN DREAM; SOCIETY.

Suyuan Woo, a Chinese immigrant, has always wanted her daughter Jing-Mei ("June") to be successful in her adopted culture, a notion strengthened by her belief that she had left twin baby girls in China before her emigration in 1949 (June discovers that the girls, her half-sisters, are, in fact, still alive). The ideal of American culture for Suyuan Woo is Shirley Temple, and she prepares June for the American Dream by reading *Good Housekeeping* and *Reader's Digest*—the quintessential "American" publications—for examples of how children become successful in America.

When her mother buys her a piano and sends her to Mr. Chong for lessons, June discovers that the man is deaf. In a recital to which her mother has invited her friends and family, June performs poorly. Still, Suyuan Woo does not give up the dream, and her insistence that June can become a child prodigy results in a confrontation in which she states plainly that there are two kinds of daughters, those who are obedient to their parents and those who treat them with disdain and are too independent for their own good. Despite their different views, Suyuan Woo offers the piano to her daughter on her thirtieth birthday, a symbol of reconciliation for the two women.

The death of June's mother brings about memories of childhood and the painful process of coming to terms with a new culture and one's place in that culture. Suyuan Woo believes in the American Dream, though her notions of that loaded phrase stifle her daughter's independence and, ironically, alienate the two. Underlying the theme of assimilation is a mother's love for her daughter, fueled by her having left family behind in an attempt to create a new life.

Taylor, Peter. "Venus, Cupid, Folly and Time" (1959). From *The Granta Book of the American Short Story* (Ed. Richard Ford, 1992). BETRAYAL; CLASS CONFLICTS; DECEPTION; HUMOR/SATIRE/IRONY; SIBLINGS.

Brother and sister Alfred and Louisa Dorset can get away with their eccentricities in Chatham because they are members of one of the town's original families. Included in their rather odd acts (Louisa cleans house in the nude and both wear pajamas on their shopping trips) is an annual party that celebrates the town's upper-crust youth in a ball that has become famous as a springboard into the society. During this particular year, two of the town's siblings, Ned and Emily Meriwether, decide to play a joke on the Dorsets: They invite one of the town's paperboys to join the party, thereby undermining the party's purpose. In addition, the paperboy passes himself off as Ned Meriwether and begins to act affectionately toward Emily in front of the Dorsets. What is intended to be a joke that plays on the quasi-incestuous relationship of the Dorsets backfires: ashamed that they could not tell the difference between the town's elite and the paperboy, the Dorsets refuse to hold future parties. Even the close relationship between Ned and Emily, who had initiated the plan, cools as a result of their prank.

The title of the story refers to a work by Il Bronzio that the Dorsets have torn out of a magazine and placed on the wall. The implication is clear in the relationship between Alfred and Louisa, though the story suggests that such devotion—both of a brother and sister and of a town to its elitist conventions—must inevitably change. With that passing, the narrator implies, go the characters that make the town an interesting place.

Thurber, James. "The Catbird Seat" (1945). From *The 50 Greatest Mysteries of All Time* (Ed. Otto Penzler, 1998). HUMOR/SATIRE/ IRONY; LABOR/JOB; MEN and WOMEN; REVENGE.

Mr. Martin, who never smokes and never drinks, has been an exemplary employee in the filing department of F & S for many years. He does, however, have a vendetta against Mrs. Ulgine Barrows, a woman who was hired by the company two years before to ferret out inefficiency. Martin's intense dislike for the woman, especially her folksy sayings—including "Are you sitting in the catbird seat?"—prompt him to plot her demise before she can have him fired.

At first, Martin plans to kill her outright. When he arrives at the woman's apartment, though, a much different and diabolically clever plan occurs to him: he will use his temperance to his advantage. Mrs. Barrows realizes when Martin walks in the door that he has been drinking (he also claims to be a heroin addict), and when he begins to speak disparagingly of his boss, Mr. Fitzweiler, she plans to use Martin's words against him in order to have him fired. The next morning, however, Fitzweiler is little inclined to believe the woman when she accuses Martin of inappropriate behavior, and instead he fires her. Too late, she realizes the ingenious scheme that Martin has devised. In addition to the firing of Mrs. Barrows, Martin also has the pleasure of an apology from his boss, Mr. Fitzweiler.

Thurber's story, like most of his fiction, is a humorous portrait of average men and women in the workaday world who long to distinguish themselves in a society that has become homogenous. In this case, Mr. Martin is able to live out a fantasy that Walter Mitty would have appreciated when he exacts revenge on the woman who threatens to disrupt Martin's safe, predictable life.

Thurber, James. "The Secret Life of Walter Mitty" (1942). From *The Norton Anthology of Short Fiction*, 6th ed. (Ed. R.V. Cassill and Richard Bausch, 2000). HUMOR/SATIRE/IRONY; ILLUSION v. REALITY; INDIVIDUAL; INTERIOR LIVES; MEN and WOMEN; SOCIETY.

In the most popular of Thurber's humorous, insightful stories, Walter Mitty is the quintessential suburbanite who longs for action. While he goes along with his wife on a trip to the city, he imagines scenarios—military missions too dangerous for anyone but the intrepid Mitty, a medical operation that only he can successfully complete, a courtroom drama that concludes with a deftly delivered punch to a lawyer's jaw—in which he is the hero. His flights of fancy concern his wife, who thinks that he should see a doctor.

The irony of the story is clear. Though Mitty imagines himself in precarious life-and-death situations, the reality of his life is that he does little more exciting than search the city for overshoes and puppy biscuits, parking his car, and waiting for his wife to meet him at the hotel after her hair appointment. Despite his visions to the contrary, Mitty is utterly controlled by his wife, who chides him for driving too fast, hiding from her in the hotel lobby, and forgetting the simple instructions that she gives him when they get to the city.

Thurber's story prefigures the work of such social commentators as John Updike and John Cheever in its evocation of a country that no longer truly appreciates the individual. The author also suggests that in the battle of the sexes, men like Mitty have capitulated to the women in their lives.

Tolstoy, Leo. "The Death of Ivan Ilyich" (1886). From *The Harper Anthology of Fiction* (Ed. Sylvan Barnet, 1991). CLASS CONFLICTS; DEATH; FRIENDSHIP; HEALTH (SICKNESS/MEDICINE); INDIVIDUAL; INTERIOR LIVES; MARRIAGE; MEN and WOMEN; POLITICS.

When Ivan Ilyich, a middle-class bureaucrat, dies from an injury that occurs when he is hanging a curtain, his legacy is revealed: News of the death reaches his coworkers, and their first reaction is to wonder how it will affect their own promotions. His wife is concerned that she will not receive enough money from the government to maintain her lifestyle. Ilyich himself suffers the pangs of remorse for a life not fully lived before he finally acquiesces to death and leaves the world to its devices.

Tolstoy's most celebrated short fiction focuses on one man's death rather than his insignificant life because, the author implies, many more lives will be touched by his absence than by his presence—in both the promotions that will be given to fill his position and in the way his wife will have to live her life. The selfishness of the living is nearly comical, were it not for the agonizing manner in which Ilyich dies, alone and disillusioned until his final hours with unsatisfying memories of the life he has lived. Indeed, it is ironic given the response of his colleagues upon his death that Ilyich himself had risen two ranks through the bureaucracy because of a friend's help. The bureaucracy that has defined his life has proven to be a chimera that perpetuates itself in the words and actions of those he leaves behind. Finally, perhaps that is the most important symbol of one man's ineffectual life in a society whose institutions superseded the individual.

Tolstoy, Leo. "The Three Hermits: An Old Legend Current in the Volga District" (1906). From _Great Short Stories from the World's Literature_ (Ed. Charles Neider, 1950). ALLEGORY/LEGEND/FABLE; RELIGION/SPIRITUALITY; VANITY.
After a group of seamen pass a small island on their way from Archangel to a monastery, one of them tells the bishop a story about the island's inhabitants—three rather nondescript hermits—that intrigues him. The bishop expresses his desire to land on the island and, after a statement from the captain suggesting that the old men are not worth their time, he sets off to meet them, hoping to be able to teach them a bit about his true religion.

As the bishop had suspected, the hermits know little about the rituals of the church. They pray in an awkward way, and he will not leave until he has taught them the Lord's Prayer. When he leaves the island glad for the opportunity to have shown them the error of their ways, the three hermits follow, running on the water, "all gleaming white, their grey beards shining, and approaching the ship as quickly as though it were not moving." They have come after the ship to tell the bishop that they have forgotten the words to the Lord's Prayer. Realizing the righteousness of the three hermits and his own humble place in the spiritual world, the bishop begs them instead to pray for him.

Tolstoy's tale examines the pretense of religion and explodes the notion that righteousness is gained through the rituals of the church. The story's subtitle suggests the need for the people of the Volga District to perpetuate the tale, perhaps in order to reconcile their religious needs with the constricting views of the church. The author's epigraph, verses 7 and 8 from the book of Matthew, also implies that the mode of prayer hardly determines its efficacy, as "_your Father knoweth what things ye have need of, before you ask Him._"

Toomer, Jean. "Blood-Burning Moon" (1923). From _The Oxford Book of American Short Stories_ (Ed. Joyce Carol Oates, 1992). AFRICAN-

AMERICAN EXPERIENCE; DEATH; MEN and WOMEN; RACE RELATIONS; SEXUALITY; WOMEN'S ISSUES.

Louisa, a young black woman, works in the home of the Stone family, one of the town's leading figures. She is admired by both Bob Stone, a son of the family, and Tom Burwell, a cane-field worker who has a reputation as a fighter. When Burwell approaches Louisa to express his love for her, she accepts, and the two go to the cane field to make love. Stone, who overhears some men talking about the relationship, searches the pair out. When he finds Burwell, they fight; Stone pulls a knife on the more experienced man and is killed. In retribution for Stone's murder, the white men of the community lynch Burwell. Louisa, who knows nothing of the scene, senses that something is wrong because of the full moon that rises and foreshadows the spilling of blood.

The story is part of Toomer's short-story cycle, *Cane*, which explores the experiences of black women in the South in the first decades of the twentieth century. Race relations are key to all of the stories, and the author defines a society in which violence, sexuality, and class conflicts are intertwined with the racial attitudes of the time. Through the deaths of both of Louisa's suitors, Toomer suggests that the answer is not forthcoming.

Toomer, Jean. "Esther" (1923). From *Calling the Wind: Twentieth-Century African-American Short Stories* (Ed. Clarence Major, 1993). AFRICAN-AMERICAN EXPERIENCE; ALIENATION/ISOLATION; DREAMS (of the FUTURE); DREAMS (SLEEPING); IDENTITY; ILLUSION v. REALITY; MEN and WOMEN; RELIGION/ SPIRITUALITY; SEXUALITY; WOMEN'S ISSUES.

The story is a sequence of four snapshot glimpses into the life of Esther. As a girl of nine, Esther walks down the road, too serious to be pretty, with cheeks that look "flat" and "dead." Though she is black, she looks like a white child. As she walks, a man named King Barlo falls to his knees in a trance. People gather around him as he claims to have seen a vision from God.

At sixteen, Esther has dreams that one of the townsmen's shops is burning and that a child is saved and she keeps the child. She scorns herself for sinning and then dreams that the townsmen are spitting tobacco juice on the flames. The baby in her arms is ugly, but she loves it and her happiness makes everyone around her jealous.

When Esther is twenty-two, she works in her father's grocery store. Though she is thought of as sweet, Esther wonders why no one finds her attractive. She recalls a boy who left her because she was too nice, and a man whom she refused when he expressed an interest in her. She remembers King Barlo and decides that she loves him and she will tell him when he returns to town.

At twenty-seven, though, Esther is pale and gray and her hair is thinning.

When King Barlo returns, she suddenly comes to life. Esther explains to him that she has awaited his return, but the man does not understand, and the people in the bar mock her. The reality of her situation comes to a head, and she finds Barlo's appearance revolting. She runs into the street to find that her surroundings have disappeared and that she is alone.

Toomer examines the late coming-of-age of Esther and the disillusionment that arises when a dream (both the child's dream, which reflects her own lack of self-esteem, and her dream of the future) is not fulfilled. By not living her life in the present, Esther has alienated herself from society. In the process of establishing self-identity, she has ironically placed all her hopes on a man whom she remembers from the distant past, but who does not recognize the need that she has for him in the present.

Turgenev, Ivan. "The Country Doctor" (1852). From *Fiction 100: An Anthology of Short Stories,* **9th ed. (Ed. James H. Pickering, 2000). DEATH; GIFTS/GENEROSITY; HEALTH (SICKNESS/MEDICINE); LABOR/JOB; LOVE/HATE; MEN and WOMEN; SEXUALITY.**

A doctor, Trifon, has established a good rapport with one of his patients, and he tells the man about a house call that he once made. It seems he received a message from a worried mother saying that her daughter was dying. When he reached the sickly young woman, the doctor quickly became infatuated with his beautiful patient and tried everything he could to save her.

Trifon stayed with the family until the last day, neglecting his other patients. Indeed, the two had fallen in love. When the girl asked the doctor if she would survive her illness, Trifon told her that she probably would not. She took the initiative to make love to the doctor, not wanting to die without knowing the touch of a man. She died the next morning, but not before giving the doctor a ring as a symbol of their relationship. Now, Trifon is married to a woman who "luckily" sleeps all day.

Turgenev's doctor uses the relationship that he has with a patient to describe an extraordinary experience in an otherwise banal and depressing career as a district doctor. Trifon's story is an attempt to make sense of a life that is only intermittently—and unpredictably—enriched by chance meetings. The doctor's tone is ambivalent, though Turgenev, like many of his Russian contemporaries, reins in real emotion with the knowledge that both the good and the bad in life are fleeting.

Twain, Mark. "The Celebrated Jumping Frog of Calaveras County" (1867). From *Fiction 100: An Anthology of Short Stories,* **9th ed. (Ed. James H. Pickering, 2000). ANIMALS and HUMANS; COMMUNICATION/LANGUAGE; CONTESTS; DECEPTION; HUMOR/SATIRE/IRONY; REGIONALISM (LOCAL COLOR).**

At the request of a friend from the East, the narrator has been compelled to call on Simon Wheeler, an old man who is an incorrigible teller of tales, and to inquire as to the whereabouts of a man whom the narrator's friend claims to have known. The old man, taking the inquiry as his cue, tells the story of Jim Smiley, an incredibly lucky man whom Wheeler met in the mining camps. Smiley would bet on anything that involved animals—horse races, dog fights, cat fights, chicken fights—and in this particular instance, he brings a frog named Daniel Webster to the men in the camp and claims that it can outjump any frog in Calaveras County.

As evidence of his goodwill, Smiley offers to go to the swamp to catch a frog for his mark. In his absence, the man fills Smiley's frog with quail-shot, and Smiley is surprised when Daniel Webster doesn't even leave the starting line before the other frog has finished. The man takes Smiley's money and walks away. Too late, Smiley discovers the ruse. Even though the old man wants to tell his new friend more stories about Smiley and his animals, the narrator takes his leave, not wanting to hear about Smiley's cow with a tail like a banana.

The story is typical Twain, full of folksy, good-natured humor in the tall-tale tradition. The frame story, related by the narrator as he heard it from the old man, gives the tale a told-about quality that pays homage to the oral tradition so important in Twain's works and that enriches the reading experience.

Twain, Mark. "The £1,000,000 Banknote" (1893). From *The Treasury of American Short Stories* (Sel. Nancy Sullivan, 1981). CONTESTS; DREAMS (of the FUTURE); GIFTS/GENEROSITY; MEN and WOMEN; NATIONALISM/AMERICAN DREAM; POVERTY.

Henry Adams has all the attributes to make a success of himself in America, but when he finds himself in England after a sailing mishap, things seem to have taken a turn for the worse. When he becomes involved in a bet between two brothers who wonder how well he might survive with no money in his pocket other than a £1,000,000 bank note, he learns that he must live by his wits.

After a series of events in which Adams realizes that the appearance of money is what helps him to move up in society, he takes advantage of his intelligence and his discipline to begin life anew. He falls in love with the stepdaughter of the man who bet against his succeeding in London; by the time the bet ends a month later, he has amassed a fortune of more than a million, and he has won the heart of the girl, Portia. The two are married, and the bank note that indirectly began the affair is framed on their wall.

Twain often uses clever, resourceful protagonists in his stories to point out a way of life that, during Twain's time, was increasingly becoming known as "American." Adams has no qualms about living by his wits, and his straightforward approach to matters, including his intention to pay back the debts that he has incurred, suggests that he *should* succeed.

Tyler, Anne. "Teenage Wasteland" (1984). From *Rites of Passage: A Thematic Reader* (Ed. Judie Rae and Catherine Fraga, 2001). ALIENATION/ISOLATION; COMING-OF-AGE; IDENTITY; INTERIOR LIVES; MOTHERS and CHILDREN; SELF-DESTRUCTION/SUICIDE; SOCIETY.

Though fifteen-year-old Donny Coble's case is not unique—he has gotten in trouble again at school—his mother is concerned that she and her husband have not done what they could to assure their son's proper behavior. Despite their concerns, Donny's attitude toward school changes for the worse: he is truant, smokes in school, and has come to school with alcohol on his breath. Donny is assigned a tutor, Calvin Beadle, who is clearly not what the boy needs to turn his life around. Beadle finds the school's sanctions unnecessarily harsh, and he quickly ingratiates himself to the teenager. After Donny exhibits some semblance of "playing by the rules" for a short time, he is expelled from school.

The boy spends a great deal of time at Beadle's house—the man sympathizes with his condition and does not force him to abide by the strictures of society—but his parents take Donny away from Beadle's influence. That summer, Donny disappears. The police chalk it up as one of a number of similar situations that they have encountered. Donny's mother tortures herself by replaying what she might have done differently in order to save her son.

Tyler uses the title of a song by the rock group The Who to suggest that the society in which Donny has grown up is hardly conducive to the actions that his parents and his teachers expect from him. His mother's reaction to her son's disappearance is common enough, though in this individual case, the boy's fate is given a poignancy that would have been lacking had the reader not been privy to a grieving and questioning mother's thoughts.

U

Updike, John. "A & P" (1961). *The Story and Its Writer*, 5th ed. (Ed. Ann Charters, 1999). COMING-OF-AGE; COURAGE; EPIPHANY; ESCAPE; LABOR/JOB; MEN and WOMEN; SOCIETY.

Sammy takes a summer job as a grocery store clerk. He openly expresses his discontent with the job and with his manager, Lengel, who watches him closely for any breach of the store's many rules. When three young girls enter the store dressed in bathing suits, heads turn. Sammy and his buddy, Stoksie, watch them as they wander through the store, seemingly unaware of the stir they are causing. When Lengel embarrasses the girls as they check out, insisting that when they come into the store from now on that they be "decently dressed," Sammy impulsively quits his job. His attempt to impress the girls—especially "Queenie," the most beautiful and sensuous of the three—falls flat. Lengel, a longtime friend of Sammy's parents, tells Sammy that they will be disappointed in him. Still, he folds his personalized apron on the counter and walks out into the summer heat. When he realizes that the girls are gone for good, he focuses on a young couple screaming at their children. He knows in that instant how hard the world can be.

The story, one of the prolific author's most popular in a long career of writing for America's most prestigious magazines, offers a clear reminder of the foibles of growing up. Sammy's quitting is both a protest against the banality of the workaday world—the "sheep" who wander through the store and the rules that he must follow—and a foreshadowing of his hard-won entrance into adulthood.

V

Viramontes, H.M. "The Moths" (1985). From *Growing Up Ethnic in America: Contemporary Fiction About Learning to Be American* (Ed. Maria Mazziotti and Jennifer Gillan, 1999). AGING; COMING-OF-AGE; DEATH; EPIPHANY; HEALTH; HISPANIC EXPERIENCE; RELIGION/SPIRITUALITY; WOMEN'S ISSUES.

The narrator is enlisted to help with the care of her dying grandmother. The teenage girl knows that she is not her Abuelita's favorite grandchild, nor is she pretty like her sisters; sometimes, in the past, she has been disrespectful of the old woman, who had cured her fever with a mixture of dried moth wings and Vicks. But when the girl knows that Abuelita is dying, everything changes.

When the narrator's mother, Abuelita's daughter, asks how her mother is doing, the narrator tells her that the old woman fell out of bed twice the day before; she realizes immediately that it is the wrong thing to have said. In an epiphany of life and death, the narrator understands that a moment comes when life is extinguished, "that hour or minute or second when the sun is finally defeated, finally sinks into the realization that it cannot with all its power to heal or burn, exist forever." Her grandmother dies, and in a description that evokes the best of Gabriel García Márquez or Toni Morrison, the narrator watches the moths "that came from her soul and out through her mouth fluttering to light, circling the single dull light bulb of the bathroom" as the girl bathes the old woman one last time.

The opening line of the story—"I was fourteen years old when Abuelita requested my help"—implies the coming-of-age narrative that follows. Though she is reluctant at first to help, the girl comes to understand death and is able to express herself in "sobbing until finally the sobs rippled into circles and circles of sadness and relief."

Voltaire. "Jeannot and Colin" (1764). From *Great Stories of All Nations* (Ed. Maxim Lieber and Blanche Colton Williams, 1945). ALLEGORY/LEGEND/FABLE; CLASS CONFLICTS; FATE; FRIENDSHIP; GIFTS/GENEROSITY; POVERTY; SOCIETY.

As children, Jeannot and Colin are inseparable, sharing the secrets of boyhood with each other and believing that they will always be together. When Jeannot is presented with a velvet coat and whisked away to his fortune—the boy's father has met with great success in his business ventures—Colin feels his own insignificance. Though he writes to his newly wealthy friend, he receives no reply.

Jeannot is supplied with a tutor, but the man insists that the boy need know only how to be "agreeable," since all else will be given him in his new life. The wealthy, after all, " 'know everything without learning anything, because, in point of fact and in the long run, they are masters of all the knowledge which they can command and pay for.' " Indeed, despite his lack of knowledge about anything, Jeannot becomes popular in the fashionable society. When his father falls on hard times, however, the young marquis is helpless to lift his family out of debt. By happenstance, he sees his old friend, Colin, who readily takes him under his wing. Jeannot returns to his former life and marries Colin's sister. The family "came to see that vanity is not the true source of happiness."

Voltaire, the most famous figure of eighteenth-century enlightened thinking, offers a cautionary tale that implies the ease with which man can fall from the highest of offices. His commentary on education and wealth in this story is tempered by the inherent goodness of Colin and the "germ of that good disposition which the world had not yet choked" in the friend who forsakes him, only to accept his kindness later.

Vonnegut, Kurt. "Harrison Bergeron" (1968). From *The Story and Its Writer*, 5th ed. (Ed. Ann Charters, 1999). CRIME/LAW; DISABILITY/PHYSICAL APPEARANCE; FAMILY; FANTASY/IMAGINATION/SCIENCE FICTION; IDENTITY; MEN and WOMEN; MORALITY (MORAL DILEMMA); SOCIETY.

The year is 2081, and society has finally constructed a truly egalitarian state. Everyone who deviates the slightest bit above average is given physical and mental handicaps to bring them down to everyone else's level. When George and Hazel Bergeron's fourteen-year-old son, Harrison, is taken from them because he is so superior to everyone else as to pose a threat to society, they hardly notice. George, whose intelligence makes him a candidate for a device that assaults his brain with loud noises to disrupt his thinking, cannot find the time to think the situation through; Hazel is too dull-witted to do such a thing even without the state-imposed handicaps.

One night, as they watch ballet on television (the ballerinas themselves, so as not to make the viewers or each other feel inferior, are wearing handicaps), Harrison appears in the studio in all his splendor—seven feet tall, a beautiful young man without the trappings that would make him average. He chooses one of the ballerinas, an equally beautiful young woman, for his partner; when she removes her own handicaps, they dance together. Unfortunately, the Handicapper General, whose job it is to see that everyone is equal, arrives at the studio and shoots them both dead with a ten-gauge shotgun. George and Hazel know that something extraordinarily sad has just taken place on television, though they cannot for the life of them remember what it was.

The story is vintage Vonnegut, whose scathing social commentary is tempered by an understanding of and sympathy for human nature. By taking the notion of equality to its absurd extreme, Vonnegut explores the notion of a society whose desire for homogeneity is as dangerous as it is ludicrous.

Vonnegut, Kurt. "Who Am I This Time?" (1961). From *Studies in Fiction* (Ed. Blaze O. Bonazza et al., 1982). ART and the ARTIST; IDENTITY; ILLUSION v. REALITY; INTERIOR LIVES; LOVE; MEN and WOMEN.

The protagonist, who belongs to the North Crawford Mask and Wig Club, an amateur theatrical society, is named director of an upcoming production. He takes the assignment with one stipulation—that Henry Nash, a shy, reserved man who happens to be a phenomenal actor, play Marlon Brando's character in *A Streetcar Named Desire*. When the director approaches him about the part, Nash wonders, "Who am I this time?" The director unwittingly finds an actress in an attractive young receptionist who works at a telephone company. Though she has a bad audition, she fills the role of Stella. Henry Nash and the woman, Helene, are perfect together in the roles, and they fall in love when she gives him a copy of *Romeo and Juliet* on closing night. A week later, they are married.

In the story's last sequence, the director has been chosen to direct the outfit's next play. He contacts Helene, who tells him that they act out a different play each night, and she has been married to Othello, Romeo—the great characters of all time. When the director asks if they will take on the next play, Helene wonders, "Who are we this time?"

Though Vonnegut has a reputation as a black humorist, this is an unusual love story between the most timid of men and a lonely receptionist. When the two are onstage together—be it in front of an audience or in their own home—they are different people, drawn to each other by the identities they create through theatre, the courses of two human lives changed by illusion. Vonnegut's ability to relate complex emotions in the simplest of terms comes to the fore here.

W

Walker, Alice. "Everyday Use" (1973). From *Rites of Passage: A Thematic Reader*, 1st ed. (Ed. Judie Rae and Catherine Fraga, 2001). AFRICAN-AMERICAN EXPERIENCE; FAMILY; MOTHERS and CHILDREN; PRIDE; TRADITION/CONVENTION; WOMEN'S ISSUES.

As Dee's mother awaits her arrival, she imagines joining her successful young daughter on a talk show, one that brings together a star and the mother who has made her what she is. At the same time, she realizes the reality of her situation: she is a poorly educated, overweight, strong black woman who has tried to make a hard life a bit easier for her family. She watches her younger daughter, Maggie, who was burned in a house fire, and understands the difficulty that the girl will have in the coming years.

Dee arrives with her boyfriend in a flurry of activity. In the fashion of the time, she has taken to calling herself "Wangero." Her mother is willing to use the name, but she finds the whole thing silly. Dee insists that her mother is disregarding her heritage. She wants to take the butter churn, the dasher, and some handmade quilts back to the city with her, to hang them on the walls or use them as centerpieces, since they are *objets d'art*, not made for everyday use. The mother finds the whole discussion absurd and takes the quilts away from Dee. She gives them to Maggie, who will be able to use them when she is married to John Thomas, a local boy with few prospects of his own. Dee puts on the sunglasses that hide every bit of her face but the tip of her nose and her chin, and she leaves. Maggie, heartened by her mother's gesture, smiles a real smile as she watches them disappear.

Significantly, Walker's story is dedicated to "your grandmamma," a gesture toward the family that Dee ceases to understand when she leaves for school. The author calls into question the notion of finding one's heritage in Africa when all around us is the opportunity to cherish family and to make "everyday use" of the objects that are passed down from generation to generation.

Walker, Alice. "Roselily" (1973). From *Calling the Wind: Twentieth-Century African-American Short Stories* (Ed. Clarence Major, 1992). CLASS CONFLICTS; FAMILY; IDENTITY; MARRIAGE; MEN and WOMEN; MOTHERS and CHILDREN; WOMEN'S ISSUES.

Roselily's story takes place on the day of her wedding, and the narrative unfolds in a stream-of-consciousness that describes her emotions. The "plot" of the story, Roselily's own thoughts, is interwoven with the words from the traditional marriage ceremony: "*Dearly beloved we are gathered here today in the sight of God.*" The effect of combining those two different narrative lines is to emphasize the importance of what Roselily is doing—after all, the man she is marrying is not of her religion, and she already has three children by other men—and to give the notion of suspended time, much as Ambrose Bierce does in "Occurrence at Owl Creek Bridge."

Though she wants to marry this man for many reasons, Roselily has just as many reasons not to marry him. When she thinks of the man who will be a father to her children, she thinks of his stiff, black suits and how her own life will change when she is forced to take on his Islamic religion. When she sees her young sisters standing in the yard, she thinks that they are giggling "at the absurdity of the wedding. . . . She thinks the man beside her should marry one of them. She feels old. Yoked." The man has promised her rest—he tells her that her place will be in the home—but she wonders what she will do once she is rested. Perhaps give birth to more babies that she will have to take care of. Finally, she is not sure that she loves him, though she is seduced by his pride and "his understanding of her *condition.*" As they climb into the car that will take them to their new life, he does not look back.

Walker's story is a bittersweet rendering of a woman's journey toward a new life. Though the bride's attitude toward her new husband is hardly what the reader would expect from someone who is marrying (the match seems not to have much to do with love, but rather with the convenience, for both parties, of the merger), the author implies that perhaps the life Roselily faces will be better than the one she is leaving. Still, that nagging doubt is enough to give Roselily second thoughts even as she stands at the altar and gives herself over to the man.

Warren, Robert Penn. "The Patented Gate and the Mean Hamburger" (1947). From *Studies in the Short Story* (Ed. Virgil Scott and David Madden, 1976). FAMILY; LABOR/JOB; NATIONALISM/AMERICAN DREAM; SELF-DESTRUCTION/SUICIDE.

Jeff York is the kind of man who stands silently on the side of the street with his friends and "dispassionately estimat[es] you from the ambush of [his] thorny brows." He is also one of the few men on the street who owns property. In fact, he is especially proud of the white patented gate that surrounds his house. York is fond of taking his family to town on Saturdays, and one particular weekend, Mrs. York asks how much it would cost to buy her favorite hamburger place. In order to purchase the restaurant, the Yorks sell their house to the bank teller and buy a small place outside of town. A few days after he has completed renovations on the restaurant, Mr. York goes for a walk in the direction of his old house. He is found the next morning hanging from the white patented gate of which he was so proud. Despite her loss, Mrs. York continues to run the store and ends up flipping a "mean hamburger."

The irony of the story's ambiguous title, which at first is not apparent, suggests the fragmentation of life and the perseverance of the human spirit. Mrs. York continues even after her husband's death; her husband, however, unable to give up, quite literally, the notion of the "white picket fence," can never realize the American Dream.

Wells, H.G. "The Magic Shop" (1903). From *Fantasy: Shapes of Things Unknown* (Ed. Edmund J. Farrell et al., 1974). CHILDHOOD; FATHERS and CHILDREN; MAGIC/OCCULT.

The narrator had seen the magic shop before, though he had never taken his young son, Gip, into the store. On this particular occasion, he acquiesces to the boy's pleas and takes him inside, only to find that the magic in the shop, performed by an extraordinary counterman, is too real for comfort. The man does the usual tricks, making balls and cards and animals appear and disappear to the boy's astonishment. He also takes the illusion one step further, showing the boy and his father a room full of magic that the boy seems to understand, even though the father feels uneasy in the shop.

When the magician makes the little boy disappear under the pretense of playing a game of hide-and-seek, the father loses his temper and ineffectually attacks the man. Finally, he finds himself outside with his son, both of them unharmed. Six months later, the father finds that everything is normal, though Gip insists that the toy soldiers he got in the shop come to life with a single word.

This fanciful story is entertaining both for its content and descriptions of the shop and for the way in which Wells portrays the loving relationship between a father and his young son. Known primarily for his visionary science fiction novels, here the author delves into the world of magic. Through the young boy's understanding of the shopkeeper's tricks, Wells implies that magic is for the young, and bemoans the fact that we as adults have a difficult time giving ourselves over to possibilities that we cannot imagine.

Wells, H.G. "The Pearl of Love" (1924). From *Clifton Fadiman's Fireside Reader* (Ed. Clifton Fadiman, 1961). ALLEGORY/LEGEND/FABLE; LABOR/JOB; LOVE; MEN and WOMEN; PLACE; TIME (and ITS EFFECTS).

The narrator tells a story that takes place in North India, "the most fruitful soil for sublime love stories of all the lands in the world." In this case, a prince falls in love with and marries an incredibly beautiful woman, who dies from a venomous sting. In his grief, the prince has the young woman's body entombed and begins building a shrine to her that he calls the Pearl of Love. Like the pearl in nature, which is accreted through the pain of the host, the shrine begins as a series of screens and pillars that envelope the princess's sarcophagus. As it grows, the prince realizes new possibilities for the structure, combining different materials and colors to create the desired effect. The Pearl gains stature, until people stand in awe of the memorial's size and complexity. One day, though, the prince begins disassembling the whole structure, leaving only the sarcophagus and the body of the princess, which lay exposed like "a small valise upon the crystal sea of heaven." After much thought, the prince orders the workmen to take the sarcophagus away.

The story is unlike much of Wells's fiction, though the theme of fantasy and magic that is apparent in "The Magic Shop" prevails in the story's final lines. Even death and man's best attempts to memorialize the loss of a loved one, it seems, cannot eradicate the beauty of nature; time, too, has dulled the grief that the prince feels for his loss, and he has reconciled himself to living his life. Still, in the story's opening lines, the narrator eschews passing judgment on the story's "meaning," instead establishing himself as the objective observer who merely relates the tale as he has heard it.

Welty, Eudora. "Petrified Man" (1939). From *Major American Short Stories*, 3rd ed. (Ed. A. Walton Litz, 1994). CRIME/LAW; FRIENDSHIP; HUMOR/SATIRE/IRONY; ILLUSION v. REALITY; MEN and WOMEN; REGIONALISM (LOCAL COLOR).

Leota, a hair stylist and inveterate storyteller, has taken on boarders: Mrs. Pike, her husband, and their three-year-old son. During one of Mrs. Fletcher's visits to the salon, Leota tells her that her hair is falling out and suggests that it could be an indication she is pregnant. Indignant, Mrs. Fletcher wonders how anyone knew. Leota tells her that she and Mrs. Pike just guessed it one day when they saw her coming out of the drugstore. When Mrs. Fletcher's anger subsides, they discuss a freak show that Leota and Mrs. Pike have recently visited. At the show, the two came across a "petrified man" who has been slowly turning to stone since the age of nine. Throughout her telling of the story, Leota repeats, "How'd you like to be married to a man like that?" Apparently, Leota is unhappy in her home life and transfers her feelings toward her husband onto the petrified man. During a subsequent visit to the salon, Mrs. Fletcher is regaled with the story of how Mrs. Pike saw a picture of a man wanted for rape in a magazine and recognized him as the man in the freak show. She turned him in for a $500 reward.

Welty's ability to combine the events of everyday life with a distinct Southern Gothic storyline make this one of her most-read tales. Life-altering decisions, she implies, are made in some of our most common places, and the characters that inhabit her stories are both odd and unbearably human. Welty's dialogue rings true-to-life, the idiosyncrasies of human nature coming alive under the author's keen eye for detail.

Welty, Eudora. "Why I Live at the P.O." (1941). *The Story and Its Writer*, **5th ed. (Ed. Ann Charters, 1999). FAMILY; HUMOR/SAT-IRE/IRONY; JEALOUSY; MEN and WOMEN; MOTHERS and CHILDREN; REGIONALISM (LOCAL COLOR).**

The narrator is getting along just fine with her mother, her grandfather, and her uncle, until her sister, Stella-Rondo, returns home with a child in tow. She has separated from her husband, and she tells the family that the baby, whom they call Shirley-T., is adopted. The narrator does not believe her for a second, though the rest of the family seems not to notice a family likeness between Stella-Rondo and the girl.

On the Fourth of July, Uncle Rondo drinks a bottle of "prescription" and dresses in a pink kimono. At 6:30 the next morning, he throws a string of firecrackers into the narrator's bedroom. It seems that the whole family is against her, even her grandfather, who takes an innocent comment as a slight against the beard that he has worn all his life. The narrator is the postmistress of the local post office, and she vows to move into the small quarters in order to get away from her family. After several more confrontations, she makes good on her promise. When she has been in the post office for five days, she proclaims her happiness; if Stella-Rondo ever tries to apologize to her, she will "simply put my fingers in both my ears and refuse to listen."

Welty, who can be poignant as well as humorous, relies almost exclusively on her intimate knowledge of Southern family life for the details of this story. The mother's willingness to believe her prodigal daughter at the exclusion of the more responsible (but only by degrees, it seems) narrator is the basis for one of the author's most enjoyable short pieces.

Welty, Eudora. "A Worn Path" (1941). From *The Norton Anthology of Short Fiction* **(Ed. R.V. Cassill, 1978). CLASS CONFLICTS; COUR-AGE; HEALTH (SICKNESS/MEDICINE); LOVE; POVERTY; RACE RELATIONS.**

One December morning, Phoenix Jackson, an old black woman, embarks on a mission to Natchez. In a dress that she is determined not to tear, she walks through thorns and a barbed-wire fence and is accosted by a black dog that she ineffectually swings at with her cane before she winds up prone in a ditch. While there, she thinks that the dog has been put in her way only to forestall her from her quest. A hunter who happens upon the old woman tells her that she should be getting home, though Phoenix will not be diverted from her task. When she sees a nickel fall out of the man's pocket, she conspires to pick it up and continues toward town.

When she arrives at a clinic, the nurses take her for a charity case. Though she has forgotten her mission after the long trip, her memory is jogged when one of the nurses mentions her grandson, who swallowed lye several years before. Now, the boy is the only family that Phoenix has, and she loves him despite the infirmity that has left him speechless and often struggling for breath. She takes the boy's medicine from the nurse, who offers Phoenix a nickel as a token of Christmas generosity. The old woman decides to buy her grandson a paper windmill, something that he could never imagine existed.

The story's title suggests the old woman's dedication to her grandson: the path that she travels has been, like the woman, trod beyond its usefulness. In its depiction of Phoenix's own quiet dignity, the story is a testament to the necessity of human dignity and an implicit protest against the conditions in which she lives with her grandson. The story's ambiguity—whether her grandson is really alive or not is left for the reader to decide—also adds a poignant dimension to the lonely woman's quest, seemingly her only joy in life.

West, Jessamyn. "Lead Her Like a Pigeon" (1944). From *Great Short Stories of the World* (Sel. by the Editors of *Reader's Digest*, 1972). COMING-OF-AGE; FAMILY; MEN and WOMEN; MOTHERS and CHILDREN.

On a journey through the woods to deliver cookies to the Bents, her neighbors, Mattie stumbles upon a vacant house. The young woman is disconsolate at the sight of the empty house. While speaking to the house to eliminate the unnatural silence, she meets Gard Bent, who escorts her back to his house. There, Mattie encounters Gard's family, whom she finds rather odd. The father, like his son, reads constantly. Mrs. Bent continues to chop fish, Gard's two siblings wrestle in the dirt, and his brother plays over and over again the opening line from "Lead Her Like a Pigeon" on his homemade flute.

Upon returning home with a basket of fish from the Bents, Mattie skips dinner and speaks to her mother about Gard Bent, telling her how impressed she is with his learning and the pleasantness of his face. When her mother hints that Mattie is old enough to begin thinking about marriage, she cries out of fright at the thought of growing up and moving out into the world. Her father walks into the room, and Mattie sees that, like she and Gard, her parents have their own song.

Mattie's response to the house is clearly a reference to the young woman's desire to begin her life as an adult. Though the story is simply told and echoes many coming-of-age tales, West's details—particularly the sharing of the song that implies that the budding relationship between Gard and Mattie may turn out to be more than infatuation—bring the transition to adulthood to life.

Wharton, Edith. "The Rembrandt" (1901). From *Great American Short Stories* (Sel. by the Editors of *Reader's Digest*, 1990). CLASS

CONFLICTS; GIFTS/GENEROSITY; ILLUSION v. REALITY; POVERTY; SOCIETY.

During a trip to the Continent some fifty years before, Mrs. Fontage procured a painting that she supposes to be a true Rembrandt. Though she presents herself in a manner befitting her apparent station, the narrator, through his cousin Eleanor, who makes it her business to help out people such as Mrs. Fontage when they fall on hard times, knows that Mrs. Fontage is in need of money. Still, "It was not that she was of forbidding, or even majestic, demeanor; but that one guessed, under her aquiline prettiness, a dignity nervously on guard against the petty betrayal of her surroundings." The narrator, a museum director, notices in his perusal of the woman's house that she is attempting to fit in to a society that has become far too extravagant for her means, and he is loath to tell her that the painting is essentially worthless.

As a result of the collusion of the narrator and his philanthropic cousin, Mrs. Fontage is given a thousand dollars for the painting. Later, it becomes apparent that the entire closed society in which the narrator and Eleanor move—including the museum committee that congratulates the narrator on his act of kindness toward the old woman—has come together in order to help an old lady in need. For the first time in a year, Mrs. Fontage will be able to live without the fear of being evicted or starving. In an ironic twist, the narrator is given the painting, which he earlier describes as "'a damned bad picture.'"

Though Wharton and Henry James, especially (or Hortense Calisher, in her sharp descriptions of class life in America), are known for writing the story of manners and exploring the pretentious side of expatriate culture, this story presents a side of that culture which is seldom seen. Wharton is at the peak of her descriptive powers here, taking issue with both the art and the culture to which she was privy and writing a story that is pointed and humorous.

Wharton, Edith. "Roman Fever" (1936). From *Short Fiction: Classic and Contemporary*, 4th ed. (Ed. Charles H. Bohner and Dean Dougherty, 1999). BETRAYAL; DECEPTION; FAMILY; FRIENDSHIP; REVENGE; SOCIETY; VANITY; WOMEN'S ISSUES.

Mrs. Slade and Mrs. Ansley are two older women enjoying the sunset over Rome from a restaurant balcony. The two have known each other for most of their lives, which have paralleled one another in many ways: their youths as expatriate Americans in Europe, their choice of husbands, their nearly perfect families. Still, their personalities are different enough that there is an animosity even their intimacy cannot bridge. Mrs. Slade is jealous of Mrs. Ansley's daughter, Babs, who is being courted by the most eligible bachelor in Rome.

During the course of conversation, while their two daughters are away with their beaus, Mrs. Slade recalls an incident many years before in which Mrs. Ansley went to the Coliseum for a clandestine lovers' meeting with Mrs. Slade's future husband. Mrs. Ansley is horrified to realize that her friend knew of the affair. As it turns out, Mrs. Slade is the one who wrote the letter inviting her friend to the tryst. Mrs. Ansley has the last word, however, when she tells Mrs. Slade that she did, in fact, meet Delphin Slade at the Coliseum. He had known to come because she answered what she thought was his letter to her. Mrs. Slade is outraged and coldly reminds her friend that she—not Mrs. Ansley—was the one who got to spend her life with Delphin. Mrs. Ansley replies in kind that that may have been the case, but she—not Mrs. Slade—has the more popular daughter.

Wharton, with a sensibility that echoes that of her friend and contemporary Henry James, is aware of both the competitive spirit of the two mothers and the complexities of the expatriate culture that fuels such jealousies and ill will. She expresses them through scenes that describe the unique situations in which the inhabitants of the culture find themselves.

Wilde, Oscar. "The Sphinx without a Secret" (1887). From *Great Stories of All Nations* (Ed. Maxim Lieber and Blanche Colton Williams, 1945). DEATH; DECEPTION; ILLUSION v. REALITY; INDIVIDUAL; LOVE; MEN and WOMEN; MYSTERY/ADVENTURE; WOMEN'S ISSUES.

Lord Murchison, a man who is known for speaking the truth, arrives at a café to meet with his friend and has a fascinating story to tell: since their last meeting, Murchison has fallen in love with a beautiful, mysterious woman who has captivated the man beyond all reason. After their first encounters, which are always conducted in an odd way by the woman, who seems to have much on her mind, Murchison decides that he will ask her to marry him. On his way to her apartment, however, he watches her entering an apartment that is not hers. He picks up the handkerchief that she has dropped on the doorstep and assumes that she has been seeing another man. When he confronts the woman with his suspicions, she denies the accusation. When Murchison leaves the country for a month, he comes back to find that she has died. The woman's secret, it seems, is that she had no secret at all. She had gone to the apartment where Murchison saw her only to read books and drink tea.

Wilde's story is, in a sense, a mystery, though one that is underpinned by a common theme in short literature—the treatment of women at the hands of men. Lord Murchison is unable to grasp the fact that the woman he loves would act as she does without harboring a secret that could threaten their relationship. His inability to understand her spiritual side and her desire for nothing more than solitude costs him his love, and, more importantly, the life of the mysterious woman. Wilde's understated style and his subtle sense of humor and irony belies the tragedy of the story's conclusion.

Wilder, Thornton. "The Warship" (1936). From *Half-a-Hundred: Stories for Men* **(Ed. Charles Grayson, 1946). ALIENATION/ISO-LATION; CULTURE CONFLICTS; EXILE/EMIGRATION; RELIGION/SPIRITUALITY.**

In the early eighteenth century, the *Trumpeter*, a ship loaded with a hundred convicts and their families bound for Australia, is wrecked. Not all the ship's passengers perish, and the survivors establish a colony on the west coast of Australia. The society that they build—known to the inhabitants as "Inglan," a variation on the long-forgotten "England"—has never seen a visitor, save for a Finnish sailor who made land only to perish six years later.

The island's inhabitants crave news of the outside world, especially religion. All literate people are asked to write down Bible verses and other bits of information that may be relevant to their quest for knowledge. As the society struggles under the weight of its own isolation, Captain Roja, the son of Jonh Weever, the captain of all Inglan, sees a ship that is close enough to the island to rescue them, should they desire it. At once, the vision is seductive and ominous. Roja knows that none of his party could live in the modern world. He and the people who have come to marvel at the site move quietly back to their homes.

Wilder's story is one of isolation and fear of the unknown. Though the people of Inglan desire knowledge of the outside world, they shy away from it when presented with an opportunity to reenter that world. Far from being a utopia, however, Inglan is subject to the same problems as the society that the people forsake when they turn their backs on their potential rescuers.

Wilkinson, Brenda. "My Sweet Sixteenth" (1993). From *Join In: Multiethnic Short Stories* **(Ed. Donald R. Gallo, 1993). COMING-OF-AGE; DECEPTION; MINORITY EXPERIENCE; MOTHERS and CHILDREN; WOMEN'S ISSUES.**

Carla and Monique meet at church camp and discuss a photograph that Monique has placed on her side of the room. At first, Monique explains that the girl is her niece; later, she admits that the child is her daughter, born on Monique's sixteenth birthday. The young woman confides in her roommate that she had wanted to abort the baby and thought that she could get enough money for the procedure at her "Sweet Sixteenth" party. Though she did get enough money, she began to feel ill during the party and went into labor in her bedroom, her parents unaware of what was happening.

With help from her friend Verna, Monique gave birth and fed the baby. The girls' plan to drop the baby off at the hospital the next day failed, and Monique's parents learned the truth about their daughter. Monique is determined to finish high school, and she hasn't ruled out the possibility of making a life with her daughter's father. Still, the implications of her actions and her decision are made clear to her every day in the profound ways that her life has changed.

The story establishes plot and the relationship between the two new friends primarily through dialogue, Monique recalling with both poignancy and humor the events surrounding her daughter's birth. Though the ending of the story is essentially a positive one, Wilkinson suggests the very real changes that Monique's life has undergone, and the tragic consequences that might arise from the situation she describes.

Williams, Joy. "Escapes" (1990). From *The American Story: Short Stories from the Rea Award* (Ed. Michael M. Rea, 1993). ADDICTION; COMING-OF-AGE; ESCAPE; ILLUSION v. REALITY; MAGIC/ OCCULT; MOTHERS and CHILDREN.

The narrator, Lizzie, recalls her experiences as a young girl living with her alcoholic mother, and she especially remembers a time when she and her parents had driven to the mountains and the young girl had watched her father "pretending to be lame." Her father ultimately left the family because of her mother's condition. Lizzie and her mother now spend much time together, and they often talk about the magician Houdini.

While looking through the newspaper, they run across an ad for a magic act and buy tickets to it. At the show's intermission, Lizzie's mother disappears and then appears drunk on stage; ushers escort them both out. The usher talks to her mother about pulling herself together, and the two go to a coffee shop to chat. As they drive home, Lizzie hears her mother call out her name, but Lizzie's mind is somewhere far away.

The theme of "escape" runs through the story, from the title, to the disappearance of Lizzie's father, to the repeated discussions of Houdini, to Lizzie's own escape from her mother's alcoholism. Suffering and the difficulty of breaking away from undesirable situations are at the heart of the story; Williams implies that, while such escapes are possible, the breaks are never as clean as we would want them to be. Certainly, they are not as easy as those orchestrated by the magician onstage.

Williams, Joy. "Train" (1972). From *The Granta Book of the American Short Story* (Ed. Richard Ford, 1992). COMING-OF-AGE; DREAMS (of the FUTURE); FRIENDSHIP; ILLUSION v. REALITY; SOCIETY.

A young girl, Dan, rides the train with the family of a friend, Jane. As she observes the characters—an unhappy marriage, a raging feminist, a self-absorbed little girl—whose lives are played out in her enclosed environment, she realizes that things are not as they seem. Dan is a sweet girl who is still naïve and impressionable. She and Jane walk through the train and meet people along the way. Jane, a blunt, cynical girl, is outgoing and does much of the talking; Dan is content to watch.

As the trip progresses, Dan understands that Jane's qualities make her an unfit friend. She is snobbish toward Dan, who begins to feel lonely and thinks of the things in her life that make her happy. She realizes that she does not fit in with the people around her, and she begins to cry. The experience is a coming-of-age for Dan, who understands that life is not always the happy proposition that she had hoped it would be.

Williams is keenly aware in her short fiction of the stark contrast between the outer lives through which people communicate with one another and the rich interior lives that allow people to gauge their reactions to the world around them, in that way becoming part of the world. Clearly, the author privileges Dan's interior life over the superficial words and actions of the girl's friend, Jane.

Williams, William Carlos. "The Use of Force" (1933). From *Fiction 100: An Anthology of Short Stories*, 9th ed. (Ed. James H. Pickering, 2000). CHILDHOOD; HEALTH (SICKNESS/MEDICINE); VIO-LENCE.

Mathilda Olson's parents call the doctor (the story's narrator), suspecting the worst for their daughter, who is running a fever. The doctor, who arrives and examines the bright, attractive child, quickly realizes that although he loves the child's spunk, he will have a difficult time getting her to cooperate with him so that he can diagnose her condition. The girl breaks the wooden tongue depressor that the doctor and her father manage to get down her throat; a spoon, however, is too much for the girl, and the doctor gets a glimpse of her tonsils. He knows immediately by the membrane coating her throat that she has diphtheria.

As the title implies, the story is a study of the doctor's response to the girl. Though he has undoubtedly been in such situations before, the doctor loses his professional calm when he realizes that the child will not give him what he wants; perhaps that desire to conquer the girl is also a result of her beauty, which he recognizes immediately. Still, his goal is a reasonable one—after all, he wants to save the girl—and his methods are justified by his desire to discover the truth.

Williams-Garcia, Rita. "Into the Game" (1993). From *Join In: Multi-ethnic Short Stories* (Ed. Donald R. Gallo, 1993). COMING-OF-AGE/INITIATION; IDENTITY; MEN and WOMEN; MINORITY EXPERIENCE; SEXUALITY.

The narrator and his friends, DuPree and Manny, are headed into the city on the subway to find some action. Unlike the previous year—before they were old enough to drive, before any of them had jobs, before they had filled out just a bit physically—the three are ready to "get into the game," their phrase for stepping into life.

The narrator does not have any illusions about their chances with the girls they meet. He knows that they are "three of the weakest dudes to shoot out of the Bronx," and none of them, especially DuPree, who embarrassed them at a party with his dancing, knows what to do when they meet girls. Still, when three high school girls, whom the boys nickname Shades, My Girl, and Troll Baby, get on the subway with shopping bags, the boys' interest is piqued. They follow the girls off the train at 116th Street, which is not the boys' stop, and watch them move down the street, "Not because we were punks but because they could walk that walk and control us, even at a distance."

Williams-Garcia's take on the relationships between young men and women explores aspects of those first encounters that are as true-to-life in Middle America as they are on a subway train in New York City. The boys' indecision is contrasted to the control that the girls have over their suitors. The story is presented with good humor and understanding, especially in the descriptions of the boys' barely controlled enthusiasm at the prospect of experiencing the events of their first steps "into the game."

Wilson, Budge. "Be-ers and Doers" (1990). From *Help Wanted: Short Stories about Young People Working* (Sel. Anita Silvey, 1997). COMING-OF-AGE; COURAGE; IDENTITY; INTERIOR LIVES; MOTHERS and CHILDREN; SIBLINGS.

Adelaide's mother has always been a "doer," someone who is constantly in motion and who chastises anyone who is not. Adelaide has two siblings, Maudie and Albert. Maudie is just like her mother, but Albert, the youngest of the three, is like his father, a "be-er," someone who revels in the everyday beauty of life and the value of contemplation. Despite his disinclination for his studies, Albert is pressured by his mother to make something of himself—perhaps becoming a lawyer or a doctor.

He successfully resists his mother's attempts at changing him until one Christmas Day when the house catches fire. Albert, to the surprise of his entire family, takes charge of the fire and puts it out, saving the house, the family, and their possessions. His mother tells him how proud she is of him and that his action is just the first in many that will put him on the road to being a "doer." Uncharacteristically, Albert snaps at his mother, telling her that he will not allow her to mold him in her image. After the tirade, he collapses and spends three weeks in the hospital nursing his burns. Now, he spends his days on a secluded farm, wifeless and childless, and writes to his heart's content.

Wilson's story details the tenuous relationship of parent and child and suggests that those who live the unexamined life—the "do-ers" of the world—could learn to enjoy life from those who simply "be."

Windsor, Patricia. "Teeth" (1992). From *Short Circuits: Thirteen Shocking Stories by Outstanding Writers for Young Adults* (Ed. Donald R.

Gallo, 1992). BETRAYAL; COMING-OF-AGE; FRIENDSHIP; LOVE; SUPERNATURAL/HORROR.

For every tooth that Troy finds lying on the ground, he grows an extra in his own mouth. Still, he is not particularly concerned, as the discoveries are linked positively to the response of Lida, a girl with whom Troy is infatuated. The more teeth he finds (and each successive find is more rotten than the previous), the more willing Lida is to be with Troy. Despite being shunned in favor of Lida, Troy's female friend, Willie, supports him in his attempts to impress the girl. When Troy will not speak to Willie, however, the consequences for him are tragic. Having found yet another tooth that he keeps in his pocket for good luck, Troy invites Lida to the river walk with him. Just as he is about to kiss her, however, Lida pushes him away and screams at his mouth full of rotten teeth. Troy tries to call to Willie, but "from his mouth came only the growling moan of suffocating decay."

Windsor's story, on one level a traditional horror tale, is also an exploration of friendship and first love. While Troy uses the found teeth as a talisman to seduce Lida, his relationship with Willie—the one relationship that is truly meaningful to him—decays like the teeth in his own mouth. His calling to Willie at the end of the story signals his realization of the extent to which such an innocuous charm has gone awry.

Wolfe, Thomas. "Only the Dead Know Brooklyn" (1935). From *50 Best American Short Stories, 1915–1939* (Ed. Edward J. O'Brien, 1939). PLACE; PRIDE; REGIONALISM (LOCAL COLOR); SOCIETY.

The narrator of Wolfe's story is a lifelong Brooklynite who claims that one can live in the borough for all his life and not know the area "t'roo and t'roo." As he waits for a train, he sees a man who has obviously been drinking. Within earshot of the narrator, the man approaches another rider and asks for directions to a particular place in "Bensonhoist." When that man is unable to help, the narrator steps in and gives directions.

The traveler's attitude upsets the Brooklynite, who sees the man as an intruder on his turf and someone who should not be as wise about the area as he is. The man carries a map with him and details the places he has seen. The narrator warns the man to stay away from certain places, but the man with the map seems content to find those places, with confidence that he will be safe there. After all, those places are only spots on maps, not the city's mean streets.

Wolfe's story is a slice of urban life that makes a statement on the increasing size and complexity of society. That the man with the map thinks he can find out more about Brooklyn than someone who has lived there all his life is a testament to American curiosity; at the same time, the narrator is firm in his belief that even people who live in that area all their lives cannot find out all there is to know about Brooklyn, hence the story's title.

Wolff, Tobias. "In the Gardens of the North American Martyrs" **(1980). From** *The Norton Anthology of Short Fiction,* **6th ed. (Ed. R.V. Cassill and Richard Bausch, 2000). DECEPTION; FRIENDSHIP; IDENTITY; INTERIOR LIVES; LABOR/JOB; WOMEN'S ISSUES.**

Mary, an eminently safe academic at Brandon College, has recently been appointed to a position at a college in Oregon. After three years at the school, she receives a letter from an old colleague who had gained success and fame in academic circles by publishing a well-known book and getting a position at "a famous college in upstate New York." She tells Mary that there is an opening on the faculty, and she invites her to apply. Deciding she has nothing to lose, Mary casts her lot with the other applicants.

When she receives a call inviting her to campus to interview for the position, Mary is pleased. When she gets there, though, she finds that Louise had invited her as a perfunctory gesture; the committee has no intention of hiring her. In the lecture portion of her interview, Mary rails against her treatment at the hands of the committee (read: white men), speaking metaphorically of her torment in terms of the Iroquois and two Jesuit martyrs who were tortured by them. Mary ignores their pleas for her to stop.

In the manner of Richard Russo's *Straight Man* or Francine Prose's *Blue Angel*, Wolff's story is a satirical condemnation of academia. No one on the faculty is safe from the author's sharp eye, though only Mary, it seems, benefits from her ill-treatment at the hands of the group when she turns the tables and implicates them in her own senseless torture. She realizes for the first time, perhaps, the reality of the academic life and the little ground that she will ever gain by playing it safe.

Wolff, Virginia Euwer. "Brownian Motion" (1995). From *Ultimate Sports* **(Ed. Donald R. Gallo, 1995). COMING-OF-AGE; ENTROPY/ CHAOS; FAMILY; IDENTITY; LOVE; NATURE/WILDERNESS; POVERTY; SPORTS.**

This story is divided into the four voices of a family: Patrice, the older daughter; Jim, the father; Susannah, the mother; and Sandy, the younger daughter. Patrice begins by recounting how her father had suggested that the two of them take scuba-diving lessons to ward off the boredom of winter. When Jim nonchalantly enters a contest for a vacation to the Caribbean and wins, the family is excited to make the trip, especially with Jim and Patrice's newly developed diving skills.

Jim is astounded by what he sees in the ocean, though he can't help but think about his childhood, which he spent in relative poverty and which forced him to recognize that there are rules to be followed and, like the fish he sees on his dives, "the big guys eat the little guys." Patrice, on the other hand, has never experienced anything quite like it, and her views are not biased because she is young enough never to have seen the seedier side of the world. The trip is the closest the young woman, who is going to university on scholarship the following fall, has come to "pure, uncomplicated happiness." What does complicate matters, though, is the relationship that Patrice strikes up with Sydney, their handsome, young diving guide. When Patrice suggests that she would like to return to the island and volunteer to teach at the local school that Sydney's little sister attends, Jim and Susannah are faced with a decision they would rather not have to make.

The title of the story comes from Patrice's knowledge of Brownian Motion, a premise which dictates that even though things look serene on the surface (like Patrice's life), the molecules that make up water are colliding at an incredible rate, like the chaos of the events that swirl around Patrice and cause her to reassess the direction her life will take.

Woolf, Virginia. "Kew Gardens" (1919). From *Short Fiction: Classic and Contemporary*, 4th ed. (Ed. Charles H. Bohner and Dean Dougherty, 1999). ILLUSION v. REALITY; INTERIOR LIVES; MARRIAGE; MEN and WOMEN; PLACE.

The story takes place exclusively in Kew Gardens, just outside London, where the lives, passions, losses, and hopes of those visiting the garden are described within the context of their interactions. The characters—from a married couple to a pair of old friends to a young couple just falling in love—are developed only inasmuch as one would see them in a snapshot image or in the memory of a long-distant love affair. For instance, a man approaching middle age remembers a scene in this very spot fifteen years before when he asked his fiancé to marry him; he knew by the way a dragonfly hovered over her shoe that she was going to say no. When he broaches the subject with his current wife, she is surprised that he would hesitate to bring it up. After all, she asks him, "Doesn't one always think of the past, in a garden with men and women lying under the trees?"

This is perhaps Woolf's best-known short story—and certainly one of the most innovative to be published in the years immediately after World War I, the time of the "Lost Generation." The character that gets the most attention is, curiously, a snail, which Woolf describes in great detail as it struggles to finds its way around a leaf. That seemingly random detail and the impressionistic images that the author presents, in the manner of a Monet painting, make this story noteworthy—not for its plot, but for its ability to evoke in the reader emotions and memories that may otherwise have remained hidden, much as the garden itself evokes those memories and experiences in the story's characters.

Wright, Richard. "Big Boy Leaves Home" (1936). From *Fiction as Experience: An Anthology* (Ed. Irving Howe, 1978). AFRICAN-AMERICAN EXPERIENCE; DEATH; ESCAPE; EXILE/EMIGRATION; FAMILY; GRIEF; RACE RELATIONS; SEXUALITY; SOCIETY; VIOLENCE.

When four black boys decide to swim naked in a posted area despite warning signs, they can hardly imagine the consequences. As they sun themselves on the bank, talking and playing pranks on one another, a white woman appears. Her screams alert her husband, who mistakenly believes two of the boys are moving toward his wife and shoots them. Big Boy, who struggles with the man, accidentally shoots him. Big Boy and his friend, Bobo, head for the shelter of home, though their lives have irrevocably changed. Big Boy knows that they will be lynched when they are found.

Big Boy's family understands the implications of his actions; though his mother comforts him, Elder Peters suggests that the boy run away in order to protect himself. He hides in a nearby kiln and fantasizes about being able to defend himself from his attackers. Big Boy watches as the lynch mob tracks down Bobo and burns him, tarred and feathered. On the morning of the following day, Will Sanders approaches in a truck and hides Big Boy behind a trapdoor; he is headed north, away from the nightmare, though his life will clearly never be the same.

The implication of the title is clear: Not only is Big Boy forced physically to leave home, he is also driven inexorably away from the comfort and familial bonds that the word implies. His traveling north suggests that he has left boyhood behind; in the space of a day, the innocent boy who talked and laughed with his friends on the bank of a swimming hole understands too well the hatred and violence that he will be subjected to for the rest of his life.

Wright, Richard. "The Man Who Was Almost a Man" (1961). From *Fiction 100: An Anthology of Short Stories*, 9th ed. (Ed. James H. Pickering, 2000). AFRICAN-AMERICAN EXPERIENCE; ANIMALS and HUMANS; COMING-OF-AGE/INITIATION; FATHERS and CHILDREN; MOTHERS and CHILDREN; PRIDE; RACE RELATIONS.

Seeking respect from the men who still think of him as a boy, Dave asks the shopkeeper if he can look at the guns in a catalog. The man, who also sees him as a boy, greets him dubiously, and questions what use he has for a gun. Seeing that Dave is serious, he offers to sell him a gun for two dollars. When his mother discovers that he wants to buy a gun, she is adamantly against it. Still, he convinces her that he will be responsible; she gives him the money, with the stipulation that she will keep the gun for the family.

When he accidentally shoots a mule owned by Mister Hawkins, the landowner for whom he works, Dave is terrified. He tries to lie his way out of the situation, but ends up having to buy the dead mule for fifty dollars, much to the amusement of the crowd of both white and black men. That night, he digs up the gun from its hiding place and empties it into the air. He sees a train coming and crawls onto one of the cars, gun in pocket, and watches the rails "glinting in the moonlight, stretching away, away to some-where, somewhere where he could be a man. . . ."

Ann Charters writes that Wright's story "weaves the black farm boy's speech so skillfully with standard English narration that most readers are unaware of the effect of the deliberate juxtaposition, but this technique brings us closer to the boy's world while making an implicit social comment about his exclusion from the exploitative white society engulfing him." Wright himself has said that he was influenced by the direct style of Ernest Hemingway, though he wanted to infuse that style with commentary on African Americans in a white society. The story is a classic coming-of-age narrative; like so many similar stories, the fate of the protagonist as he enters adulthood is left very much in doubt.

Y

Yamamoto, Hisaye. "Seventeen Syllables" (1949). From *Seventeen Syllables and Other Stories*, (Intro. King-Kok Cheung, 2001). ASSIMILATION; COMING-OF-AGE; COMMUNICATION/LANGUAGE; CULTURE CONFLICTS; LITERACY/WRITING; MARRIAGE; MEN and WOMEN; MISOGYNY; WOMEN'S ISSUES.

Rosie Hayashi, the daughter of Japanese immigrants, appreciates the haiku that her mother writes, though she has little knowledge of Japanese. Similarly, Rosie's mother cannot speak English. The dynamic between Rosie's parents is evident when they visit another Japanese family in the area and Mr. Hayashi wants to leave immediately. Rosie is confused and angered by her father's actions, which have deprived her mother of carrying on a fulfilling conversation about Japanese poetry with a neighbor.

Rosie discovers the truth about her parents' relationship. Her father ruins a prize that her mother had won in a poetry-writing contest, and her mother tells the daughter that she is the product of an arranged and loveless marriage. Mrs. Hayashi, not wanting her daughter to live the life that was foisted upon her, asks Rosie to promise that she will never marry. The girl agrees, though she is confused and distraught at the implications of that promise for her own life. Rosie herself is caught up in a relationship with Jesus, a young Hispanic, who has given her a first kiss.

The title of the story—haiku are three-line poems that contain seventeen syllables—implies the difficulty that Rosie, an American by birth, has in communicating with her parents, especially her mother, who has important knowledge (much of it dealing with hardship) to impart to her young daughter. Rosie's relationship with Jesus is called into question because of the way in which Mrs. Hayashi was given over to a man who cares little for her poetry and cannot understand (in much the way that Rosie's Japanese is lacking) the fascination with language. The compressed language of the poet, in this case, is suppressed in favor of the traditions of a culture (here, Mr. Hayashi) that does not value the strength of poetic expression.

Yeats, William Butler. "The Crucifixion of the Outcast" (1894). From *The Arbor House Treasury of Nobel Prize Winners* (Ed. Martin H. Greenberg and Charles G. Waugh, 1983). CLASS CONFLICT; DEATH; EXILE/EMIGRATION; VIOLENCE.

As Cumhal, a traveling gleeman, makes his way into Sligo, he spots the crosses where local crucifixions take place. Unlike similar crosses he has seen, these make him shudder with a strange feeling of foreboding. Upon entering Sligo, Cumhal looks for a place to sleep. A lay brother gives him a guest-house for lodging, with food, water, a tub, and a blanket. The tired gleeman simply wants to eat, wash, and rest, but he finds that will be impossible. The bread is mildewed, the water is sour, the washtub is dirty, and the covers of the bed are full of fleas. Cumhal is angered and will not stand for such shoddy treatment.

When he can get no recompense from the lay brother, he curses the abbot continuously, so much so that he is taken to the river to be tortured throughout the night; when he will not cease his protest, he is crucified on a cross that he himself must cut. Though he gives his last meal to the beggars milling about, they are insulted when he asks the "outcasts" to stay with him, as wolves and birds have come to prey upon him. They leave him to die alone.

The story is clearly one of class conflict and an indictment of the treatment of outsiders, and an ironic rendering of the crucifixion of Christ, himself an outcast. This death, however, has little redeeming value; Cumhal has never fit in anywhere, even among the outcasts, and he surely will not rise again.

Yolen, Jane. "Blood Sister" (1994). From *Am I Blue? Coming Out from the Silence* (Ed. Marion Dane Bauer, 1994). COMING-OF-AGE; FAM-ILY; FRIENDSHIP; HOMOSEXUALITY; IDENTITY; NATURE/ WILDERNESS; SEXUALITY.

Selna is distraught over the loss of her childhood friend and blood sister, Marda, who has gone on a mission from the Hame for a year. Though her mother tells her that she will understand the feelings and reconcile herself to the loss, Selna seeks solace in nature. It is there that she becomes a woman and discovers her own "dark sister," the part of her that appears when she begins menstruation. Selna is wary of the figure at first; soon after the spirit is invoked, however, she is saved by her other half from an attacking cat. Though she has a new companion, she will never forget Marda.

Yolen's story is a complex exploration of a girl's journey into womanhood through the delineation of an entire culture of women, beginning with cre-ation and ending with Selna's union with her "dark sister." The disjointed narrative, offered as vignettes on "The Myth," "The Story," "The Parable," "The Song," "The Ballad," "The Legend," and "The History," coalesces into the whole that is Selna's experience. Yolen writes that "I am looking at the many ways we tell history: through narrative, parable, balladry, folk-tale, and academic explanations. None is totally correct. Like the blind men with the elephant, we cobble together the truth."

Yolen, Jane. "Words of Power" (1987). From *Visions* (Ed. Donald R. Gallo, 1987). COMING-OF-AGE/INITIATION; COMMUNICA-

TION/LANGUAGE; COURAGE; MAGIC/OCCULT; MOTHERS and CHILDREN; RELIGION/SPIRITUALITY; WOMEN'S ISSUES.

Late Blossoming Flower is a fifteen-year-old girl who is waiting to become a woman so that she can receive the Word That Changes. Though her mother and the other women in the village are somber, silent, and contemplative, the girl has learned laughter and noisemaking from Sand Walker, an outcast and the only man in the village. When the protagonist begins to menstruate, her mother sends her on her way into the unknown, and "Talking to anyone on the road this day would spell doom to them both, to her quest for her power, to the questioner's very life."

During her journey, Late Blossoming Flower unwittingly turns Sand Walker into a butterfly with the power of her Shaping Hands. When she attempts to capture the butterfly and falls over a cliff, she realizes that the Word That Changes is *Aki-la*, "eagle." She is transformed into the bird and swoops safely to the ground. Her mother, who as a mouse tempts her in her bird-form, tells her that she may turn Sand Walker back into his human form when she has the power to do so. It seems that he had allowed the girl's mother to do the same to him when she became a woman.

Yolen's story, steeped in Native American folklore, is a tale of a girl's journey into womanhood. Though Late Blossoming Flower has become a woman long after others her age, she has the power of a woman to find and use the Word That Changes. Her journey is a metaphor for the difficulties in life and the triumph of the feminine spirit.

Bibliography

Aleichem, Sholom. *Tevye the Dairyman and the Railroad Stories*. Trans. Hillel Halkin. New York: Schocken Books, 1987.

Alfred Hitchcock Presents: Stories to Be Read with the Lights On. New York: Random House, 1973.

Algren, Nelson, ed. *Nelson Algren's Own Book of Lonesome Monsters*. New York: Bernard Geis Associates, 1963.

Antler, Joyce, ed. *America and I: Short Stories by Jewish American Women Writers*. Boston: Beacon Press, 1990.

Asimov, Isaac. *The Best Science Fiction of Isaac Asimov*. Garden City, NJ: Doubleday, 1986.

Baldick, Chris, ed. *The Oxford Book of Gothic Tales*. United Kingdom: Oxford University Press, 1992.

Barbato, Joseph, and Lisa Weinerman Horak, eds. *Off the Beaten Path: Stories of Place*. New York: North Point Press, 1998.

Barnet, Sylvan, ed. *The Harper Anthology of Fiction*. New York: Longman, 1991.

Bauer, Marion Dane, ed. *Am I Blue? Coming Out from the Silence*. New York: HarperCollins, 1994.

Beattie, Ann. *Park City: New and Selected Stories*. New York: Alfred A. Knopf, 1998.

Bender, Aimee. *The Girl in the Flammable Skirt*. New York: Doubleday, 1998.

Betts, Doris. *Beasts of the Southern Wild & Other Stories*. New York: Harper & Row Publishers, 1973.

Blume, Judy, ed. *Places I Never Meant to Be: Original Stories by Censored Writers*. New York: Simon & Schuster, 1999.

Bohner, Charles H., and Dean Dougherty, eds. *Short Fiction: Classic and Contemporary*, 4th ed. Upper Saddle River, NJ: Prentice Hall, 1999.

Bonazza, Blaze O., Emil Roy, and Sandra Roy, eds. *Studies in Fiction*, 3rd ed. New York: Harper & Row, Publishers, 1982.

Brown, Leonard, ed. *Modern American and British Short Stories*. New York: Harcourt, Brace and Company, 1929.

Burrell, Angus, and Bennett Cerf, eds. *An Anthology of Famous American Stories*. New York: The Modern Library, 1963.

Byatt, A.S. *The Oxford Book of English Short Stories*. United Kingdom: Oxford University Press, 1998.

Canby, Henry Seidel, and Robeson Bailey, eds. *The Book of the Short Story*. New York: Appleton-Century-Crofts, Inc., 1948.

Cassill, R.V., ed. *The Norton Anthology of Contemporary Fiction*. New York: W.W. Norton & Company, 1988.

———. *The Norton Anthology of Short Fiction*. New York: W.W. Norton & Company, 1978.

Cassill, R.V., and Richard Bausch. *Norton Anthology of Short Fiction*, 6th ed. New York: W.W. Norton & Company, 2000.

Castillo, Ana. *Loverboys: Stories*. New York: W.W. Norton & Company, 1996.

Charters, Ann, ed. *The Story and Its Writer*, 4th ed. Boston: Bedford/St. Martin's, 1995.

———. *The Story and Its Writer*, 5th ed. Boston: Bedford/St. Martin's, 1999.

Charyn, Jerome, ed. *The New Mystery*. New York: Dutton, 1993.

Clark, Barrett H., and Maxim Lieber, eds. *Great Short Stories of the World*. Cleveland: The World Publishing Company, 1925.

Clayton, John J. *The Heath Introduction to Fiction*, 4th ed. Lexington, MA: D.C. Heath and Company, 1992.

Colette. *The Collected Stories of Colette*. Ed. Robert Phelps. Trans. Matthew Ward et al. New York: Farrar, Straus, Giroux, 1983.

Coppard, A.E. *The Collected Tales of A. E. Coppard*. New York: A.A. Knopf, 1948.

Craig, Patricia, ed. *The Oxford Book of Modern Women's Stories*. United Kingdom: Oxford University Press, 1994.

Cross, E.A. *A Book of the Short Story*. New York: American Book Company, 1934.

Day, Bradford M., ed. *Olden Tales*. Hillsville, VA: DayStar Press, 1996.

———. *The World of the Short Story*. Boston: Houghton Mifflin, 1986.

Far, Sui Sin. *Mrs. Spring Fragrance and Other Writings*. Ed. Amy Ling and Annette White-Parks. Urbana: University of Illinois Press, 1995.

Farrell, Edmund J., Thomas E. Gage, John Pfordresher, and Raymond J. Rodrigues, eds. *Fantasy: Shapes of Things Unknown*. New York: Scott, Foresman, 1974.

Foley, Martha, ed. *The Best American Short Stories, 1915–1950*. Boston: Houghton Mifflin Company, 1952.

———. *Fifty Best American Short Stories, 1915–1965*. Boston: Houghton Mifflin, 1965.

Ford, Richard, ed. *The Granta Book of the American Short Story*. London: Granta Books, 1992.

Gallo, Donald R., ed. *Connections: Short Stories by Outstanding Writers for Young Adults*. New York: Delacorte Press, 1989.

———. *Join In: Multiethnic Short Stories by Outstanding Writers for Young Adults*. New York: Delacorte Press, 1993.

————. *No Easy Answers: Short Stories about Teenagers Making Tough Choices.* New York: Delacorte Press, 1997.

————. *Short Circuits: Thirteen Shocking Stories by Outstanding Writers for Young Adults.* New York: Delacorte Press, 1992.

————. *Ultimate Sports: Short Stories by Outstanding Writers for Young Adults.* New York: Delacorte Press, 1995.

————. *Visions: 19 Short Stories by Outstanding Writers for Young Adults.* New York: Delacorte Press, 1987.

Gardner, John, and Shannon Ravenel, eds. *The Best American Short Stories 1982.* Boston: Houghton Mifflin, 1982.

Gioia, Dana, and R.S. Gwynn. *The Longman Anthology of Short Fiction: Masterpieces of Short Fiction.* New York: Longman, 2001.

Glasgow, Ellen. *Collected Stories.* Ed. Richard K. Meeker. Baton Rouge: Louisiana State University Press, 1963.

Grant, Douglas, sel. and intro. *Classic American Short Stories.* United Kingdom: Oxford University Press, 1989.

Grayson, Charles, ed. *Half-a-Hundred: Stories for Men.* Garden City, NY: Garden City Publishing Co., Inc., 1946.

Great American Short Stories. New York: Gallery Books, 1990.

Great Short Stories of the World. Pleasantville, NY: Reader's Digest Association, 1972.

Greenberg, Martin H., and Charles G. Waugh, eds. *The Arbor House Treasury of Nobel Prize Winners.* New York: Arbor House, 1983.

Halpern, Daniel, ed. *The Art of the Story: An International Anthology of Contemporary Short Stories.* New York: Viking, 1999.

Hawthorne, Nathaniel. *Selected Tales and Sketches.* Intro. Michael J. Colacurcio. New York: Penguin Books, 1987.

Haydn, Hiram, and John Cournos, eds. *A World of Great Stories.* New York: Crown Publishers, 1947.

Howe, Irving, ed. *Fiction as Experience: An Anthology.* New York: Harcourt Brace Jovanovich, Inc., 1978.

Howe, Irving, and Ilana Weiner Howe, eds. *Short Shorts: An Anthology of the Shortest Stories.* Boston: David R. Godine, Publisher, 1982.

Jaffe, Adrian H., and Virgil Scott, eds. *Studies in the Short Story.* New York: Holt, Rinehart and Winston, 1964.

Jessup, Alexander, ed. *Representative American Short Stories.* Boston: Allyn and Bacon, 1923.

Jin, Ha. *Under the Red Flag.* Athens, GA: University of Georgia Press, 1997.

Keyes, Daniel. *Flowers for Algernon.* New York: Harcourt, Brace and World, 1966.

Kincaid, Jamaica. *Annie John.* New York: Farrar, Straus, Giroux, 1985.

King, Stephen. *Night Shift.* Garden City, NY: Doubleday, 1978.

Leavitt, David. *Family Dancing.* New York: Knopf, 1984.

Lee, Hermione, ed. *The Secret Self 1: Short Stories by Women.* London: Phoenix Giants, 1995.

Lieber, Maxim, and Blanche Colton Williams, eds. *Great Short Stories of All Nations.* New York: Tudor Publishing, 1945.

Litz, A. Walton, ed. *Major American Short Stories.* United Kingdom: Oxford University Press, 1994.

Lovecraft, H.P. *Beyond the Wall of Sleep*. Coll. August Derleth and Donald Wandrei. Sauk City, WI: Arkham House, 1943.

Lovecraft, H.P. *The Dunwich Horror and Other Stories: The Best Supernatural Stories of H.P. Lovecraft*. Sel. and Intro. August Derleth. Sauk City, WI: Arkham House, 1963.

Mack, Maynard, ed. *The Continental Edition of World Masterpieces*. New York: W. W. Norton & Company, 1966.

Major, Clarence, ed. *Calling the Wind: Twentieth-Century African-American Short Stories*. New York: HarperPerennial, 1993.

Manguel, Alberto, ed. *The Gates of Paradise: The Anthology of Erotic Short Fiction*. New York: C. Potter, 1993.

Maugham, W. Somerset. *Complete Short Stories*. London: W. Heinemann, 1951.

Mazziotti, Maria, and Jennifer Gillan, ed. *Growing Up Ethnic in America: Contemporary Fiction about Learning to Be American*. New York: Penguin USA, 1999.

McCullers, Carson. *Collected Stories*. Boston: Houghton Mifflin, 1998.

Miller, James E., Jr., and Bernice Slote, eds. *The Dimensions of the Short Story: A Critical Anthology*. New York: Dodd, Mead & Company, 1965.

Milligan, Bryce, Mary Guerrero Milligan, and Angela de Hoyos, eds. *Daughters of the Fifth Sun: A Collection of Latina Fiction and Poetry*. New York: Riverhead Books, 1995.

Moffett, James, and Kenneth R. McElheny, eds. *Points of View: An Anthology of Short Stories*. New York: Mentor Books, 1995.

Nagel, James, and Tom Quirk, eds. *The Portable American Realism Reader*. New York: Penguin Books, 1997.

Neider, Charles, ed. *Great Short Stories from the World's Literature*. New York: Rinehart & Company, Inc., 1950.

Oates, Joyce Carol, ed. *The Oxford Book of American Short Stories*. United Kingdom: Oxford University Press, 1992.

———. *Telling Stories: An Anthology for Writers*. New York: W.W. Norton & Company, 1998.

O'Brien, Edward J., ed. *Modern American Short Stories*. New York: Dodd, Mead & Company, 1932.

———. *50 Best American Short Stories, 1915–1939*. New York: The Literary Guild of America, Inc., 1939.

O'Hara, John. *Collected Stories of John O'Hara*. Sel. and Intro. Frank MacShane. New York: Vintage, 1984.

Parker, Dorothy. *The Portable Dorothy Parker*. Intro. Brendan Gill. New York: Viking Penguin, 1973.

Parker, Dorothy, and Frederick B. Shroyer, eds. *Short Story: A Thematic Anthology*. New York: Charles Scribner's Sons, 1965.

Peden, William, ed. *Twenty-Nine Stories*. Boston: Houghton Mifflin, 1960.

Penzler, Otto, ed. *The 50 Greatest Mysteries of All Time*. Los Angeles: Dove Books, 1998.

Perkins, George, ed. *Realistic American Short Fiction*. Glenview, IL: Scott, Forsman, and Company, 1972.

Petry, Ann. *Miss Muriel and Other Stories*. Boston: Houghton Mifflin, 1971.

Pickering, James H., ed. *Fiction 100: An Anthology of Short Stories*, 9th ed. Upper Saddle River, NJ: Prentice Hall College Division, 2000.

Porter, Katherine Anne. *The Collected Stories of Katherine Anne Porter*. New York: Harcourt Brace Jovanovich, 1965.

Powers, J.F. *The Stories of J.F. Powers*. Intro. Denis Donoghue. New York: New York Review Books, 2000.

Pritchett, V.S. *Collected Stories*. London: Chatto and Windus, 1956.

Pugh, Cynthia Ann, ed. *A Book of Short Stories*. New York: The Macmillan Company, 1936.

Pushkin, Alexander. *Alexander Pushkin: Complete Prose Fiction*. Trans. and Intro. Paul Debreczeny. Stanford, CA: Stanford University Press, 1983.

Queen, Ellery, ed. *The Literature of Crime: Stories by World-Famous Authors*. Boston: Little, Brown and Company, 1950.

Rae, Judie, and Catherine Fraga, eds. *Rites of Passage: A Thematic Reader*. Fort Worth, TX: Heinle & Heinle, 2001.

Rea, Michael, ed. *The American Story: Short Stories from the Rea Award*. Intro. Charles McGrath. Hopewell, NJ: The Ecco Press, 1993.

Rivera, Tomás. *Tomás Rivera: The Complete Works*. Houston, TX: Arte Publico Press, 1991.

Rubenstein, Roberta, and Charles R. Larson, eds. *Worlds of Fiction*. New York: MacMillan College Division, 1993.

Salinger, J. D. *Franny and Zooey*. Boston: Little, Brown and Company, 1948.

Schramm, Wilbur, ed. *Great Short Stories*. New York: Harcourt, Brace and Company, 1950.

Scott, Virgil, and David Madden, eds. *Studies in the Short Story*, 4th ed. New York: Holt, Rinehart and Winston, 1976.

Seuss, Dr. *How the Grinch Stole Christmas*. New York: Random House, 1957.

Sillitoe, Alan. *Collected Stories*. London: Flamingo, 1995.

Silvey, Anita, sel. *Help Wanted: Short Stories about Young People Working*. Boston: Little, Brown and Company, 1997.

Singer, Marilyn, ed. *Stay True: Short Stories for Strong Girls*. New York: Scholastic Press, 1998.

Stevenson, Robert Louis. *The Short Stories of Robert Louis Stevenson*. New York: Charles Scribner's Sons, 1930.

Suarez, Virgil, and Delia Poey, eds. *Iguana Dreams: New Latino Fiction*. New York: HarperCollins, 1992.

Sullivan, Nancy. *The Treasury of American Short Stories*. New York: Dorset Press, 1981.

Tyler, Anne, and Shannon Ravenel, eds. *Best of the South*. Chapel Hill, NC: Algonquin Books of Chapel Hill, 1996.

Updike, John, and Katrina Kenison, eds. *The Best American Short Stories of the Century*. Boston: Houghton Mifflin Company, 1999.

Velie, Alan R., ed. *The Lightning Within: An Anthology of Contemporary American Indian Fiction*. Lincoln: University of Nebraska Press, 1991.

Yamamoto, Hisaye. *Seventeen Syllables and Other Stories*. Intro. King-Kok Cheung. New Brunswick, NJ: Rutgers University Press, 2001.

Index of Authors

Index of Short Stories

Index of Themes

A page number with a parenthetical notation beside it denotes more than one occurrence of a particular theme on that page.

About the Author

PATRICK A. SMITH is on faculty in the Department of English at Bainbridge College in Bainbridge, Georgia. His most recent work is *"The True Bones of My Life": Essays on the the Fiction of Jim Harrison* (2002).